A History of Shrewsbury [By H. Owen and J.B. Blakeway].

Hugh Owen, John Brickdale Blakeway

Nabu Public Domain Reprints:

You are holding a reproduction of an original work published before 1923 that is in the public domain in the United States of America, and possibly other countries. You may freely copy and distribute this work as no entity (individual or corporate) has a copyright on the body of the work. This book may contain prior copyright references, and library stamps (as most of these works were scanned from library copies). These have been scanned and retained as part of the historical artifact.

This book may have occasional imperfections such as missing or blurred pages, poor pictures, errant marks, etc. that were either part of the original artifact, or were introduced by the scanning process. We believe this work is culturally important, and despite the imperfections, have elected to bring it back into print as part of our continuing commitment to the preservation of printed works worldwide. We appreciate your understanding of the imperfections in the preservation process, and hope you enjoy this valuable book.

A History of Shrewsbury.

VOLUME I.

LONDON:
PRINTED BY S. AND R. BENTLEY, DORSET-STREET.

A HISTORY OF SHREWSBURY.

VOL. I.

EDITA PENGWERNI LATE FASTIGIA SPLENDENT,
IMPERIO CUJUS SUBJECTA POÏSIA QUONDAM
TERRA, ALTRIX ET BELLATORUM MATER EQUORUM.
URBS SITA LUNATO VELUTI MEDIAMNIS IN ORBE,
COLLE TUMET MODICO; DUPLICI QUOQUE PONTE SUPERBIT:
ACCIPIENS PATRIA SIBI LINGUA NOMEN AB ALNIS.

LELAND. *Genethliacon Eadverdi principis Cambriæ*, ver. 445.

LONDON:
PUBLISHED BY
HARDING, LEPARD, AND CO.
FINSBURY SQUARE.
1825.

Nowe Shrewsbrie shal be honourd (as it ought:)
　The seate deserves a right great honour heere:
That walled towne is sure so finely wrought,
　It glads itselfe, and beautifies the sheere.
Her beautie stands on bounty many waies,
That never dyes, but gaines immortall praise.
Her honor growes on wished well-won fame:
That people sounds of Shrewsbrie's noble name.

　　　　　CHURCHYARD'S "*Pleasant Conceite,*" 1593.

PREFACE.

The Reader is here presented with a History of Shrewsbury, Civil and Ecclesiastical, founded upon authentick documents, and cleared, we hope, from some of the errors which had previously obscured it. We cannot, however, flatter ourselves, that none remain for the elucidation of future enquirers. "It is not imaginable," says an accomplished writer, "to those who have not tried, what labours an historian, that would be exact, is condemned to: he must read all, good and bad, and remove a world of rubbish, before he can lay the foundation." It has been our uniform endeavour to consult the original authorities; and if we have thence deduced any views of the national history differing from those of preceding writers, we trust it has in no case arisen from the love of paradox or party, but from what appeared to us the interests of historick truth.

The whole value of a book like this depends upon the authenticity of the materials out of which it is constructed; and we shall therefore succinctly recount the principal ones on which we have built.

Among these, the first place, after the brief notices of LELAND, CAMDEN, and CHURCHYARD, is undoubtedly due to the anonymous CHRONICLE OF SHREWSBURY, still remaining in MS. in our School Library, and extending from 1372 to July 25, 1603. It was probably compiled by several successive individuals of the old Shrewsbury family of Lyster: at least it was certainly in the possession of their descendant, Richard Lyster, Esq. of Rowton, so many years knight of the shire, and thence generally known in Shropshire by the name of *The Senator*. Having been given by him to our learned townsman John Taylor, LL.D. when a fellow of St. John's, Cambridge, it acquired the name of TAYLOR's MANUSCRIPT; and the indefatigable Thomas Baker made large extracts from it, which are extant in the thirteenth volume of his Collections in the publick library of that university.¹ It is unnecessary to describe this chronicle, as the nature of it will be easily understood by our numerous quotations from it.

We have nothing to add to our description of OLIVER MATHEWS's Account of Shrewsbury, 1616, vol. i. p. 2. Of the author, we have only discovered, besides the information there communicated, that he was a Mercer of this town in 1576; and that on the 22d of June, 1580, he obtained a lease from the Crown for twenty-one years, of six acres of land and all tithes of grain in the town and fields of Cleobury Mortimer, parcel of the possessions of the dissolved priory of Wigmore, employed for the maintenance of a sexton in the said parish church.

EDWARD LLOYD, Esq. Barrister at Law, during his residence in the Metropolis in the early part of his life, employed his leisure in transcribing from the publick records whatever might illustrate the history of this his native county; and when he retired to his paternal seat of Trenewydd, in the parish of Whittington, he digested a part of his extensive collections into a valuable MS. volume in folio, which he entitled The Antiquities of Shropshire, and seems to have brought to a conclusion about the close of Queen Anne's reign. In this he gives a pretty full account of Shrewsbury, of which we have availed ourselves. In the absence of a complete history of the county, it is to be desired that this volume were committed to the press. It is the same which Mr. Pennant erroneously attributes to Mr. WILLIAM MYTTON.²

We are not aware, however, that Mr. Mytton ever reduced any part of his collections into a narrative form. He was a long time accumulating materials, and when these were got together, severe ill health clouded his latter years, and prevented him from arranging them for the press. Perhaps, too, like Dodsworth and others, he had devoted himself so exclusively to the labour of transcription, as to have lost all inclination for

---

¹ See Biographia Britannica, art. Baker, Note F. Some charters of Shrewsbury, and a list of its bailiffs from 1372 to 1614, are among Bishop More's MSS. in that library: and the Appendix to the first Report of the Committee on Publick Records (P. 1.) speaks of a MS. in that repository entitled "Laws and Customs of the Town of Shrewsbury," which may probably be the same book; but we did not deem it worth while to enquire after it.

² Mr. Gough has done justice to Mr. Lloyd, and quotes this MS. in his edition of Camden, as the work of its real author.

composition. It is, at least, certain, that amidst all his manuscripts relating to the History of Shropshire, we have not found a line of his own compiling. We have been indulged by John Mitton, Esq. of Halston, with the entire use of those vast collections, conducted upon the most comprehensive scale, and have introduced into the ensuing work, the whole of them which had reference to such parts of the History of Shrewsbury as are included in these volumes.

For it is obvious to remark, that in those now laid before the reader, several particulars are omitted, usually comprised in publications of this nature. But our History already exceeds, in point of extent, the limits which we originally proposed: and we feel that it is only fair and respectful to our subscribers, to release them at the conclusion of two volumes, which " may properly be deemed an entire work; and, it is presumed, may be placed, as such, in the library of an Antiquary." If a further appeal should be made to the patronage of the Publick, it will not be until we are able to ascertain the precise extent to which we should have to tax their patience.

Besides all these sources, we have made full use of The History and Antiquities of Shrewsbury by THOMAS PHILLIPS, which was announced in The Shrewsbury Chronicle, Sept. 19, 1778, and appeared in 1779. The work is creditable to the researches of Mr. Phillips,[1] and we have never wantonly deviated from his statements, when we have had to travel over the same ground.

INGENUI EST FATERI PER QUOS PROFECERIS: and in conformity with this sentiment we have uniformly expressed our obligations to the correspondents from whom we have received important communications, at the several places where their information is introduced. But we have had no opportunity besides the present, to return our thanks to the Hon. Cecil Jenkinson, of Pitchford, for his obliging communication of the Ottley papers, which have contributed largely to our account of the civil wars of Charles I.;—to the Rev. Archdeacon Corbett of Longnor, for the use of many antiquarian fragments, chiefly extracts from our municipal archives, of the late Edward Elisha, Esq., formerly steward of the corporation;—and to his successor in that office, Joseph Loxdale, Esq. for

---

[1] He died at Shrewsbury, in March 1815.

very obliging access to many other documents in that repository:—also to the Rev. John Newling, for much valuable information. And one of us would ill satisfy his feelings towards the Rev. Edward Williams, if he failed in this place to express his sense of the unvaried liberality with which that gentleman's extensive collections for a History of Shropshire have been at all times open to his use.

Our grateful acknowledgements are also due to Mr. Jenkinson for the plate of the Ottley family, drawn and engraved at his expence. The name of the artist, Peter Trauil, or Travil, should be added to our lists of painters, for we have not found it in any of those to which we have been able to refer.—Nor must we conclude without again expressing our obligations to our kind friend Dr. Prattinton, of Bewdley, for his liberal contribution of the plate of Saxon coins.

H. OWEN.
J. B. BLAKEWAY.

Shrewsbury, Nov. 26, 1825.

To diminish the disproportion between the two volumes, we have placed the List of Subscribers, with which we have just reason to be deeply gratified, at the end of the work.

A LIST

OF THE

DECORATIONS OF THIS WORK,

WITH DIRECTIONS FOR PLACING THE LOOSE PLATES, HERE PRINTED IN ITALICKS.

VOL. I.

1. South-east View of Shrewsbury, to front the Title page
2. Arms of the Earl of Powis
3. View of the British Fortress at the Berth, described at p. 8 1
4. Remains of Eliseg's Pillar 15
5. *Inscription thereon*, to front 17
6. *Coins minted at Shrewsbury in the Saxon times*, to front . . . 24
7. *Facsimile of Domesday* 29
8. *Shrewsbury Castle* 39
9. *Castle Gates* . . . . ib.
10. Sepulchral Effigy supposed of Roger de Montgomery . . . 45
11. Remaining Norman Gate of the Castle 58
12. Seal supposed of the Historian Ordericus 71
13. *Charter of Richard I.* 82
14. Seal appendant to a Charter of David ap Llewelin, Prince of Wales . 118
15. *Coins minted at Shrewsbury between* 1066 *and* 1272 . . . 134
16. *Richard II. from the initial of the Inspeximus of his 22d year* . . 172
17. *Plan of the Battle of Shrewsbury* 192
18. Monument of Simon de Leybourne at St. Mary's . . . 196
19. Glendower's Oak at Shelton 198
20. Vignette of the Battle of Shrewsbury 200
21. *Welsh Gate* 225
22. *Architectural elevation of ditto* . . . . . . ib.
23. Statue of Richard Duke of York 226
24. Armorial Bearings in the house where Henry VII. resided . . 248
25. Autograph of Henry VI. 249
26. ————— John Lord Le Strange 250
27. ————— Richard Duke of York 252

DECORATIONS.

28. *Old Stone Bridge*
29. *High Street*
30. Painted Glass at Shotton
31. *House under the Wile*
32. Facsimile of a singular Note in the School Library
33. *Internal View of Jones's Mansion under the Wile*
34. *Rowley's Mansion*
35. Jones's Mansion in Dogpole, the residence of Prince Rupert
36. *Medals of Charles I. struck at Shrewsbury*
37. *Sir Francis Ottley and Family, from the original at Pitchford Hall*
38. Plan of the Surprize of Shrewsbury, 1645
39. *Tradesmen's Tokens*
40. Corporation Insignia
41. Seal of the Shrewsbury Statute Merchant
42. *Mardol*
43. Seal of the Corporation

VOL. II.

44. *Remains of the Monastery of St. Peter and St. Paul*, to front the Title-page.
45. Abbey Seals, described at p. 133
46. Seal of Earl Hugh de Montgomery
47. Facsimiles of the Legends of St. Wenefrede
48. *Sandford's Prospect of the Abbey Church*
49. *North West View of the Abbey Church*
50. Inscriptions on St. Wenefrede's Bell
51. *The Abbey Porch*
52. Screen of St. Wenefrede's Chapel
53. *Architectural Elevation of the Abbey Window*
54. *Sandford's Drawing of the Abbey Window*
55. Ground Plan of the Abbey
56. *Architectural Elevation of the Stone Pulpit*
57. Seal of St. Wenefrede's Gild
58. Seal of the Franchise of Abbey Foregate
59. *Monument supposed of a Judge*
60. *Sepulchral Effigy in the Abbey Church*
61. *Statue of Edward III.*
62. *Monument formerly at St. Alkmund's*
63. Seal of the Hospital of St. Giles
64. Seal of Abbot Mynde
65. Do. of the Office of Celarer of the Abbey
66. Autographs of Abbots
67. *Monument of Edward Burton, Esq.*

DECORATIONS.   xiii

68. Seal of St. Chad's College	260
69. *Ancient house in the Double Butcher-row*	267
70. *Brass at St. Alkmund's*	286
71. *Monument of Thomas Corbet, Esq. of Morton*	287
72. ———— *Simon Walsh*	288
73. ———— *supposed of a Barker*	
74. ———— *of the Pontesburies*	289
75. Seal of St. Mary's College	302
76. *St. Mary's Font*	315
77. *Triple Lancet Window, in the Chancel of St. Mary*	316
78. *Stalls in the Trinity Chapel*	
79. Inscription on the Painted Glass at St. Mary's	317
80. *Effigy of Sir John de Charleton of Powis*	317
81. ———— *Sir Owen de Charleton, of Lidham*	318
82. Seals of the Gild of Drapers	340
83. *Admiral Benbow*	390
84. *Monument of Nicholas Stafford, Esq.*	397
85. *Churches of St. Julian and St. Alkmund*	415
86. Inscription on Edmond Tromwyn	434
87. *Gateway at the Council House*	451
88. *Remains of the Austin Friary*	
89. Autograph of Edward IV.	457
90. *Gray Friars*	460
91. *St. Nicholas Chapel*	473
92. Seal of the Austin Friars	488
93. Edward III. receiving the supplication of the Austin Friars	521

⁂ The first title to the two volumes represents the South Door-way of St. Mary's Church, and the border is taken from that of the South Transept.

For a reason intimated in the Preface, one or two of the above Plates have no very appropriate place in these volumes; and we have no better motive for the place which we have assigned to No. 29, than that an account will there be found of the family of Ireland, whose ancient mansion appears on the right side of that etching; and no reason at all for the place we have given to No. 42. For these, and those numbered 9, 20, 49, 51, 76, and 90, our thanks are due to the Rev. Edward Pryce Owen. We are indebted for the drawings of Nos. 55 and 56, to Mr. J. Carline; and for 10, 28, 60, 61, and material assistance in 52, to Mr. T. Carline. A young amateur artist, Mr. Instan, has obligingly contributed No. 16.

DECORATIONS.

The graphic powers of Mr. Buckler are far too well known by his various works, to receive any addition from our praise; but we must not omit our ingenious native artist Mr. Philip Browne; nor our townsman Mr. David Evans, perhaps the most successful imitator of real old glass who now practises that beautiful art, and whose accurate delineations of ancient seals, the reader will find in various parts of this work.

Various corrections occurred during the progress of the work, and are collected at the end of the second volume. The reader is requested to add the following:—

Vol. i. p. 545, l. 17, after *ib.* add Geoffrey Randolf, William Randolf.

Vol. ii. p. 198, l. 17. Mocking resigned this Deanery in 1392, in exchange for his successor's Rectory of Orpynton, in the immediate jurisdiction of the Archbishop of Canterbury; and the King ratified the exchange, 23d July.

P. 422. l. antepenult. In 3 Edw. III. 5 Nov. (1309) Master THOMAS DE CHARLETON was presented to this free chapel, and the constable of the castle commanded to deliver to him seisin thereof. Pat. ist. ann. m. 29.

Ib. l. ult. In 7 Edw. II. 21 July (1313) GALFRID DE HAKENESSE was presented to this chapel. Pat. ist. anni, p. 1. m. 23.

The Authors of the History of Canterbury are indebted to the Hon.ble Mrs. CHARLES CXCIL COPE JENKINSON M.P. for this Plate drawn and engraved at her expence from the original in Addisford Hall.

CONTENTS OF VOLUME I.

CIVIL HISTORY.

CHAPTER I.

OF PENGWERN POWIS, OR SHREWSBURY UNDER THE KINGS OF POWIS.

Various opinions of the foundation of Pengwern Powis—Probably founded by Cynddylan, in the sixth century—His history, and sepulture at Baschurch—Pengwern the metropolis of Powis—Cadelh Deyrnllug—Brochwell Ysgithrog—Eliseg—his pillar—Pengwern wrested from the Welsh by Offa, in the eighth century. . . . . . . p. 1

CHAPTER II.

OF SCROBBES-BYRIG, OR SHREWSBURY IN THE TIME OF THE SAXONS.

Ethelfleda—Athelstan—Saxon Mint at Shrewsbury—Edgar—Ethelred—Edric Streon—Duke Alfhelm murdered near Shrewsbury—Coins—Saxon customs of Shrewsbury—State of the town in the Saxon period. 19

CHAPTER III.

OF SHREWSBURY UNDER THE NORMAN EARLS.

Earl Edwin—his death—Shrewsbury burned by the Welsh—Roger de Montgomery made earl of Shrewsbury—His ancestors—estates—character—state of Shrewsbury in his time—Memoirs of the Norman earls of Shrewsbury—Earl Roger—Legend of his miraculous cure—his first Countess—her tragical end—his children—Earl Hugh de Montgomery—his death—Earl Robert de Belesme—his history —revolts from Henry I.—surrenders Shrewsbury—Earl Robert's subsequent history—and end—Ordericus the historian—vindicated—his seal. 32

CHAPTER IV.

OF SHREWSBURY, FROM ITS RESUMPTION BY THE CROWN, TO ITS RE-CAPTURE BY THE WELSH.

Henry I.—Richard de Belmeis—Jorwerth ap Bleddyn imprisoned at Shrewsbury—Origin of boroughs —Henry I.'s grant to Shrewsbury—William Fitz-Alan—Shrewsbury surrendered to Stephen—Henry II. visits Shrewsbury—Anecdote of Owen Cevelioc—Giraldus Cambrensis at Shrewsbury—First extant charter by Richard I.—King John's charters—Corporate body—King John at Shrewsbury —Llewelin the Great—takes Shrewsbury. 72

VOL. I.   *d*

CHAPTER V.

FROM THE RE-CAPTURE OF SHREWSBURY BY THE ENGLISH, TO THE FINAL CONQUEST OF WALES BY EDWARD I.

Henry III. at Shrewsbury—his first charter to the town—Merchant-gild here, the origin of the Corporation—Henry III. at Montgomery—Treaty of peace in St. Mary's church—The Welsh lay waste Shropshire—Negotiations with prince David—Two other charters of Henry III.—Civil war of the Earl of Leicester—Defence of Shrewsbury—Loyalty of Shropshire—Gratitude of Henry III. to Shrewsbury—Dispute between the Abbot and Burgesses—the town paved—Sir Walter de Hopton—Coins minted at Shrewsbury after the Conquest—Edward I.—his character—Great personages at Shrewsbury—The King removes his courts hither—visits the town—death of Llewelin—Edward vindicated from the massacre of Welsh bards—Prince David executed here—Parliament at Shrewsbury—Acton Burnell. 94

CHAPTER VI.

OF SHREWSBURY, FROM THE CONQUEST OF WALES, TO THE BATTLE OF SHREWSBURY.

State of Shrewsbury in the reign of Edward II.—He visits the town—Request of the Burgesses to him—Arrest of the Earl of Arundel—Charters of Edward III.—The great pestilence—its effects upon the language—upon this town—Castle Isabel—Richard II. visits Shrewsbury—Composition—St. Chad's church burned—Parliament adjourned hither—Henry IV. visits Shrewsbury—Civil war—Battle of Shrewsbury—Leybourne monument—Glendower's oak. . . . 152

CHAPTER VII.

OF SHREWSBURY, FROM THE REIGN OF HENRY IV. TO THE ACCESSION OF HENRY VII.

The Welsh burn the suburbs of Shrewsbury—Wiclif's reformation preached here—Petition of the burgesses to Henry IV.—State of the town under Henry VI.—Talbot Earls of Shrewsbury—their pedigree—First Aldermen of Shrewsbury—Common Council—Richard duke of York—his letter to the Corporation—visits the town—his statue—Edward IV. at Shrewsbury—incorporates the drapers—his son the Prince of Wales here—the Duke of Buckingham apprehended near Shrewsbury—the treachery of Banastre considered—escape of the young duke—Dispute between the Abbey and Town—Reception of the Earl of Richmond at Shrewsbury—Services of Sir Richard Corbet—Letters to the Corporation from Henry VI.—Lord Strange of Knockin—Edward IV. and V. . 201

CHAPTER VIII.

OF SHREWSBURY, FROM THE ACCESSION OF HENRY VII. TO THE DISSOLUTION OF MONASTERIES.

Sweating sickness said to break out at Shrewsbury—controverted—Charter of Henry VII.—Collection of the *Benevolence*—Resistance of the Burgesses—their letter to the Earl of Shrewsbury—Arthur prince of Wales visits Shrewsbury—accompanied by various noblemen—Henry VII. visits the town—his Charter—Letter of the Bishop of Lichfield—Council of the Marches of Wales—Sir Peter

CONTENTS. xvii

Newton—Journey to London—Extracts from the Bailiffs' Accounts—Archery—encrease of Paupers—Miscellaneous Occurrences—Attaint of Juries—The Fee-farm—Rice Griffith, esq.—Rowland Lee, Bishop of Lichfield—Shrewsbury, the seat of a Suffragan Bishop—its decayed state under Henry VIII.—his Letter about an Election to Parliament—The Dissolution—A plague—Leland's description of Shrewsbury. 253
Of Minstrels, Players, Sports and Pastimes 325

CHAPTER IX.

FROM THE DISSOLUTION TO THE COMMENCEMENT OF THE CIVIL WARS.

Extracts from Bailiffs' Accounts—Relique Sunday—Shere Thursday—Charter of 1542—Progress of the Reformation—Foundation of the Free Schools—Sweating Sickness—Dr. Caius—Coals—Maintenance of the Poor—Lord Thomas Gray—Sir Henry Sidney—Establishment of the Reformation—Puritans—Prophesyings and Exercises—Sir Philip Sidney—Browne's accusation of Gerard—The Plague—Letters of Mr. Prynce and Sir Andrew Corbet on that subject—Feast of St. George kept by Sir Henry Sidney—Queen Elizabeth's children—The Earl of Leicester visits Shrewsbury—Charter of 1584—First contested Election—The Earl of Essex—Camden's account of Shrewsbury—Churchyard's—Armada—Puritanical opposition to Maypoles—Sir Edward Leighton—Judge Owen—The Plague—Dearth—Ship-money under Queen Elizabeth—Watch instituted—Fall of Essex—Plague—Ship-money under Charles I.—Charter of 1638—Etymology of MAYOR—Archbishop Laud. . 335

CHAPTER X.

FROM THE COMMENCEMENT OF THE CIVIL WARS, TO THE RESTORATION.

SECTION I. Shrewsbury garrisoned for the King.

Long Parliament—Approach of Civil war—Shrewsbury put into a posture of defence—Loyalty of Shropshire—Charles I. comes to Shrewsbury—Prince Rupert's residence—Royal Mint established there—Mr. Bushell—Sir Francis Ottley made governor—Importance of Shrewsbury—new wall built—Exactions of the Military—uneasiness of the Governor—the town straitened—and exhausted—Sir F. Ottley displaced—Richard Baxter—Sir Fulke Hunckes—Sir Michael Ernley made Governor—Shrewsbury taken by the forces of the Parliament 413

SECTION II. Shrewsbury during the Usurpation.

Colonel Mytton—the Parliament jealous of and ungrateful to him—Humphrey Mackworth, Esq. made Governor—Independents gain the ascendancy—The Plague—Letter from Charles II. to Governor Mackworth—Captain Benbow shot—Mistakes concerning him—Abortive attempt of the Royalists to seize Shrewsbury—Cromwell's Major-Generals—Major Edward Waringe made Governor—Proclamation of Richard Cromwell—Restoration. . . . 457

CHAPTER XI.

FROM THE RESTORATION TO THE REVOLUTION.

The Corporation regulated—Sir Thomas Jones—Rising of 1663—Charter of 1664—Last Plague—Description of Shrewsbury by a French traveller—Costly funerals—Tradesmen's tokens—Description of Shrewsbury by Blome, 1673—Design to seize it—Quo Warranto—Charter surrendered—Charter of 1685—James II. visits Shrewsbury. 479

CHAPTER XII.

FROM THE REVOLUTION TO THE PRESENT TIME.

Association at Shrewsbury in defence of King William—Farquhar's *Recruiting Officer*—Dr. Sacheverel at Shrewsbury—Riotous demolition of the Presbyterian Meeting-house—Association against the Pretender, 1715—Salop Infirmary—Alarm at the advance of the Pretender, 1745—Execution of Lieutenant Anderson—Shropshire Militia, 1763—Decline of Shrewsbury as a market of Welsh cloth—Encrease of it as a passage to Ireland—Royal visits of 1803, &c.—New Street-act, and consequent improvement of the town—Defects still remaining. 500

CORPORATE OFFICERS.

Provosts	521
Bailiffs	524
Mayors	534
Recorders	537
Deputy Recorders	539
Town-clerks	540
Members of Parliament	544
CORPORATION INSIGNIA	554
MINOR OCCURRENCES, AND MISCELLANEOUS TRANSACTIONS	557

TO
THE RIGHT HONOURABLE

EDWARD EARL OF POWIS,

VISCOUNT CLIVE OF LUDLOW,

BARON CLIVE OF WALCOT, POWIS OF POWIS, AND HERBERT OF CHIRBURY,

In Great Britain,

AND

CLIVE OF PLASSEY,

In the Kingdom of Ireland,

LORD LIEUTENANT AND CUSTOS ROTULORUM IN THE COUNTY OF SALOP,

ONE OF HIS MAJESTY'S MOST HONOURABLE PRIVY COUNCIL,

AND

Recorder of Shrewsbury,

THIS HISTORY,

WITH EVERY SENTIMENT OF RESPECT AND GRATITUDE
FOR NUMEROUS INSTANCES OF LIBERALITY AND MUNIFICENCE TO THE BOROUGH
IN WHICH HE HAS SO LONG BORNE A DISTINGUISHED OFFICE,

IS INSCRIBED,

BY HIS MOST OBEDIENT AND OBLIGED SERVANTS,

THE AUTHORS.

CHAPTER I.

OF PENGWERN POWIS, OR SHREWSBURY UNDER THE KINGS OF POWIS.

THE Town of Shrewsbury is situated on an eminence which rises over the eastern bank of the river Severn; being surrounded by that stream on three sides. The line of Leland

Urbs sita lunato veluti mediamnis in orbe,

expresses very precisely the position of the town; which is a peninsula, having its isthmus not more than three hundred yards across, and strongly resembling the situation of Durham upon the windings of the Weare, and that of Bristol at the junction of the Avon and the Frome.

Who was the individual, or what the people, that made this happy choice, (for such it eminently is, for the purposes both of defence and of beauty,) are points respecting which great diversity of sentiment has prevailed.

VOL. I.   B

BRITISH PERIOD.

The aboriginal Britons, the same people after the departure of their Roman masters, the Saxons, and even the Normans[1], have had their respective patrons: and amid these conflicting notions, and in the absence of all positive contemporary testimony, it must be our endeavour, after briefly noticing the opinions of others, to state the few certain facts, and thence deduce that conclusion which seems the most agreeable to truth: and, if the deduction prove somewhat prolix, it must be remembered, that it involves the history, not merely of the town, but of the county at large.

Oliver Mathews, who in the reign of James I. amused his age with penning "An Account[2] of the scituation, foundation, and aunctient names of the famous Towne of Sallop, not inferiour to manie Citties in this Realme for antiquitie, godlie government, good orders and wealth," delivers himself in the following terms. "This most aunctient and famous towne was first founded by the noble and victorious kinge of Brutaines, Dyffenwall Moell-myd, whom the Romans, Saxons, Normanes, and Danes, called Mulmutius Dunwallo. The which fowndation was first begonne about 669 yeres after Brutus' first entraunce in Brutaine, which before was called Albion, anno mundi 3525, before the incarnation of our Savioure Christe 438. This most noble king, Dyffenwall Moell-myd, made the Castle there, and the North Gate, and a wall from the Castle to Seaverne, and also from the Castle to Seaverne on the north side; leavinge Seaverne to be a wall and a defence to the towne round abouts, saving the wall before mentioned: and called the town by her first name, *Caer Odder yn Hafren*, which is by entrepretation, *The Cittie or the Towne of fallinge or slydinge grounde within the wombe of Seaverne.*"

We dare not dispute the existence of such a prince as Dyffenwal. He is mentioned as a legislator in the Welsh code, entitled *The Laws of Hywel Dda*[3], and in the *Triads*: and though we know not the age, nor consequently the authority of these last; and though the passage in the Welsh Laws referring to his history, is a later addition, (not older, in the opinion of

---

[1] Dr. Nash (Hist. of Worcestersh. ii. 274) writes, "About the Conquest were built diverse towns to guard the frontiers of Wales; Bristol, Gloucester, Worcester, *Shrewsbury*, and Chester; these were garrison towns of the Marches of Wales." It is scarcely necessary to observe, that every one of the places here named is known to have existed many centuries antecedent to the date thus assigned to them.

[2] It is printed by Hearne at the end of his edition of the History of Glastonbury, from a MS. of Mr. Stafford Price, of Pertheirin, in Montgomeryshire. All that I have been able to learn concerning this earliest historian of our town, is from some other papers of his printed by Hearne in the same book. From these it appears that he was a Welshman by nation; since he terms Mr. *Philip Jenkins*, of Bristol, his "natural countryman," and subscribes himself "your old friend and *Brittaine*." He is styled of *Bishop's Castle*, in the Heralds visitation of *Shropshire*, and writes from *Snead* near that town. His wife, daughter of Edward Broughton, of Broughton, was buried at Bishop's Castle, 9th Jan. 1611, by the name of Jane, wife of Oliver Mathews, gent. How long he survived we have not seen; but in a paper dated the 18th day of March, 1615, he mentions his being "aged 95 yeres:" and his History of Salop bears date July 1616: an observation which disarms all criticism on his strange and unauthorized assertions.

[3] Lib. ii. cap. 19.

Dr. Wotton, than the reign of Henry II. and borrowed from the fabulous narrative of Geoffrey of Monmouth,) yet it may possibly represent some ancient tradition respecting this ruler of the Britons. But that his sceptre extended over the whole island, that he measured its length and breadth[1], that, in the words of Spenser[2],

> He made sacred laws,
> By which he freed the traveller's heighway,
> The churches part, and ploughman's portion,
> Restraining stealth and strong extortion—

in particular, that he had any concern in the foundation of Shrewsbury, are points for which not a trace of authentic support can be found. If we choose to credit Holinshed, Shrewsbury was a place of importance A. D. 28, and then called Coriminium[3], when "the greatest lordes and estates of the Brytaynes" held an assembly here to oppose the Romans, and Arviragus, who had allied himself with the emperor Claudius, and "went about to bring them wholy under servile subjection and thraldome of the same Romaines."[4] For all this, we believe, Holinshed had no other authority than the noted fabulist Hector Boece: and it is just as authentic as the portraits of Pictish and Caledonian sovereigns with which he adorns his pages; or as the *Earl* of *Amwythig*, a guest of king Arthur, according to Geoffrey of Monmouth, at his grand festival in Caerleon.

If the Welsh chronicle called Tysilio's were authentic, and there were any proof that Digoll mentioned by him was this town, as his editor affirms[5], there could be no doubt that it owed its foundation to Maelgwn Gwynnedd; and herewith would agree the testimony of Ross, the Warwick antiquary, who asserts that Mailgo, king of Britain, as he chooses to call him, built or repaired Shrewsbury. That there was such a personage as Maelgwn, and that he was king of a part of North Wales, we have no doubt. He founded the see of Bangor about the middle of the sixth century[6], and died in 565. Gildas, who calls him Maglocunus, severely arraigns his vicious conduct: and the celebrated Taliessin dissuades one of his friends from residing any longer in the court of so profligate a prince. But there is

---

[1] So say the Welsh Laws (loco citato). He found its length 800 miles from Blathon in Scotland to Penwaed in Cornwall; its breadth from Crugill in Anglesey to Shoreham, 500 miles.

[2] Faery Queene, b. ii. canto 10. st. 39.

[3] Probably meant for Cornavium, Shropshire belonging to the Cornavii in the Geography of Ptolemy.

[4] Hist. of Scotland, p. 33.

[5] See the Chronicle of the Kings of Britain, translated by the Rev. Peter Roberts, p. 173.

[6] Rowlands's Mona Antiqua, p. 147. 2d edition. Dr. Humphrey Foulkes, the learned rector of Marshwiel, in his dissertations on Welsh literature, a MS. among the collections of Mr. William Mytton, writes "out of an antient copy of Cradoc of Lancarvan, on vellom, now (1727) in the hands of Mr. John Griffiths of Penynant, in the parish of Ruabon, that Daniel, the son of abbot Dinoth, called great Dinoth ap Pabo, built Bangor vawr yngwynedd, when Bangor Monachorum, or that in Iscoed, was destroyed." Bangor Iscoed was not ruined till forty years after the death of Maelgwn.

no reason for believing that this court was held at Shrewsbury. On the contrary, his dominions seem to have been entirely confined to the upper part of North Wales, the modern counties of Caernarvon and perhaps Merioneth. Tysilio, in other words Geoffrey of Monmouth, is a writer much too fabulous; and Ross, who lived in the fifteenth century, an authority much too recent, to sustain Maelgwn's claim to be considered the founder of Shrewsbury. These periods of its origin are placed too high.

The learned Humphrey Lhuyd, in one passage of his excellent little essay on the history of Britain[1], brings the foundation of it too low, and seems to make the Saxons its builders; for he remarks, that "all the more considerable towns on the banks of the rivers Severn and Dee are seated on the *eastern* side of those streams, for the greater security against the invasions of the Welsh:" which he likens to the policy of the Romans, who built, says he, "their fairest cities on the western bank of the Rhine, for the purpose of repressing the predatory irruptions of the Germans into Gaul." As Lhuyd could not have forgotten that Shrewsbury is situated in the manner which he describes, we may infer, that when he wrote this passage, he was inclined to attribute its foundation to the Saxon invaders at a late period of their history; when they, in their turn, became exposed to the inroads of their Cambrian neighbours.

We conceive the truth to lie between these two last periods; and that our town was built *after the Saxon invasion;* but that it owed its foundation *to the Britons.* We cannot claim for it any pretensions to the dignity of a Roman station. No vestige of that imperial people has ever been discovered within its circuit. But a few miles lower down the river, at the present village of Wroxeter, was the flourishing town of Uriconium: and here doubtless, after the Romans had finally withdrawn their forces from the island, the Britons continued to occupy the seats deserted by their ancient masters, until they were driven from them by superior force; to the time of which we may approximate within no very wide range of years. We are in possession of the valuable poems of Llywarc Hen: valuable, notwithstanding their great obscurity, for the few rays of light which they scatter over the darkest period of our history. He was a prince of the Cumbrian Britons; who, pressed by the Northumbrian Saxons, retired, towards the end of the sixth century, to his countrymen in Powis, among whom he is said to have protracted his life to the unusual extent of 145 years, deriving thence the epithet of *hen,* or *the old.* His writings contain several proofs of his acquaintance with the district now called Shropshire. Its streams, Severn, and Morlas, and Tern; its mountains, Digoll, Ness Cliff or Clegyr,

---

[1] Fragmentum commentarioli Britannicæ description. ed. 1572, p. 24. It was translated into English in the following year, by Thomas Twyne, gent. under the title of The Breviary of Britayne. Lhuyd was a physician, and lived in Denbigh Castle. Foulkes ut supra.

BRITISH PERIOD.

and Digon[1]; its towns, Baschurch, Ercall, Hodnet, all appear in his poems: and when he speaks also of Pengwern, and when it is known that this was the Welsh name of Shrewsbury[2], we need not doubt that he designed by that appellation to mark our town, and consequently that it had then arisen.

Llywarc sought an asylum at Pengwern with a prince named Cynddylan; but he did not find much repose there. He only exchanged a northern scene of conflict for one more to the south. The Mercian Saxons, or more properly Angles, had by this time fought their way into the plain of Shropshire; and Cyndrwyn, the father of Cynddylan, had been several years before the arrival of Llywarc, expelled from Tren (probably a town on the Tern) by a Saxon chieftain; to whom our Cumbrian bard, with the pride of superior civilization, can afford no better name than the contemptuous epithet of *Twrch*, or *the Hog*. When Llywarc came into Powis, Uriconium was still standing, and in possession of the Britons; for he speaks of it by the name of Ddinlle Vrecon[3], (i. e. the city of Vrecon,) the very name which the Saxons translated into Wrekenceastre, by contraction Wroxeter, the city of the Wreken. But Pengwern, as we have observed, was also in existence. Llywarc calls it Llys Pengwern[4], or *the palace of Pengwern*; for it was the residence of his friend and protector Cynddylan: and hence the conclusion follows, that it was just in the poet's time, and when he was already an aged man, perhaps about the year 570 (for he was born in 502), that the Britons of Wroxeter, finding their station there no longer tenable, retired before the flames of the Saxon army, (for it has manifestly been destroyed

---

[1] The Dygon was a hill near Havren (the Severn), and is thought to have been the Breiddin. Cefn Digoll is still the name of the Long Mountain.

[2] The learned William Baxter (Glossar. Antiq. Brit. p. 244, 2d edit.) chooses to transfer Pengwern to Berriu in Montgomeryshire; but he loved to be singular. His sole argument is, that Pengwern was upon the river Tren, for which he quotes Llywarc; but Llywarc says no such thing: and if he did, there is no proof that the Tren and the Riu, or Rhiew, were the same stream. Mr. Barrington, in his Observations on the Welsh Castles, (Archæologia, vol. i. p. 302.) evidently considers Pengwern as not being at Shrewsbury: but he does not tell us where it was. Every other writer whom we have seen, concurs with the assertion of the text. But a very eminent Welsh scholar, to whom we are under great obligations for much valuable information, says, that the chronicles never mention Shrewsbury by the name of Pengwern, but always by that of Amwythig: and hence he seems inclined to doubt, though he does not absolutely deny, the identity of the two places. We confess, there does not appear to us much force in the objection. Reasons may have existed, unknown to us, for giving two names to the same place. The case is not without a parallel. Idsall, alias Shifnal, in this county, is one in point: Ludlow, alias Dinant, is another. Pengwern may have been the language of poetry; the other that of common speech: or, to adopt the notion of my learned friend, the former may have been the title of Cynddylan's palace, the latter that of the town in which it was situated. It is at least sufficient for us, that we express the opinion of Giraldus Cambrensis, who lived in the reign of Henry II., ("Locus ubi nunc castrum Slopesburiæ situm est, olim Pengwern, i. e. caput alneti, vocabatur." Cambriæ Descriptio, cap. 4.) and of the legendist of St. Monacella, perhaps an earlier writer ("urbe tunc temporis Pengwern Powys, nunc vero Salopia). What they found the current opinion of their age, must surely be the truth; at least, it is too late for us now to controvert it: and if we err, which we cannot believe, we do so with as great masters of this learning as Humphrey Lhuyd and Dr. David Powell.

[3] P. 95.

[4] P. 70.

by fire[1]) and sought a place of refuge[2] higher upon the Severn; where, protected by its deep bed, its sinuous windings, and the morasses of its banks, they might shroud themselves among the alders[3] and willows which hid the foot, and the thickets which crowned the summit, of the lofty and peninsular knoll, now covered by the capital of Shropshire.

In estimating the degree of protection imparted to Pengwern by the Severn, we must not take our notions from the condition of the river in our present advanced state of cultivation. Whenever any country is thinly inhabited, trees and shrubs spring up in the uncultivated fields, and spreading by degrees, form large forests, which confining the exhalations of the soil, and obstructing the course of streams, cause the rivers to overflow and stagnate into lakes and marshes.[4] An approved geographer[5] even supposes that all the channels of rivers have been formed by art; and in the country

---

[1] Gildas describes with all his powers of language, the ravages of this destructive element in the Saxon invasions: the flames that were spread from sea to sea by the sacrilegious Easterlings (orientali sacrilegorum manu), the cities and fields laid waste, the crackling of fire, &c. Gale's XV Scriptores, p. 8. Taliessin calls a Saxon commander, Flamddwyn, the flame-bearer. This propensity of the Welsh bards to designate their enemies by epithets is a loss to history.

[2] "De tantæ urbis ruderibus," says Baxter, speaking of Uriconium, " caput suum extulit Verconium novum ... ut vulgo fertur, dictum Pengüern." Glossar. p. 244.—"The destruction of Roxcestr was by all likelyhood the caus of the erection of Shrewsbury." Leland, Itm. iv. pt. 2. p. 96. Many similar instances are to be found in the kingdom: as at Penrith, Richmond, Derby, Atherston, Brecon, Chepstow, all of which have sprung from Roman stations in their vicinity.

[3] Gwern is an alder in Welsh; Pengwern, the hill or head of alders. Whence Leland, in his lines on our town,

"Accipiens patria sibi lingua nomen ab alnis."

This has been admitted to be the etymology of the name, at least as long since as the days of Giraldus. See Leland, Coll. iii. 93. Mr. Owen, the editor of Llywarch Hen, interprets it the head of the meadow; which is, indeed, another sense of gwern, derived from the fact, that such fields abound in alders. The other allusions in the text will be explained hereafter. I will add, since we are upon the British names of Shrewsbury, that Baxter derives its modern Welsh appellation, Amwithic, as he writes it, from Amwyth, fruticeta, shrubberies. Mr. Lloyd, of Trenewydd, in his Antiquities of Shropshire, MS. following Sir John Price, writes the name Y Mwythig, "which," he proceeds, " is as much as to say Placentia; and in several respects it resembles the city of that name in Italy, seated upon the Po, and so denominated from the pleasantness of its situation." Mr. W. Davies says, that Amwyddig is a place surrounded with wood, or conspicuous all around. As I am no Welsh scholar, I cannot pretend to decide between these conflicting derivations; to which Mathews adds another, " we have forgon anger," allusive to the quiet which " the fiftie brethren of Sallop" enjoyed in their new habitation. The bard of Owen Glyndwr eulogizes the profusion with which Cwrw Amuithig, Shrewsbury ale, then a beverage of high renown, was dispensed in the mansion of his hero. We have yet another etymology to propose. Mwythau are dainties: and hence an ingenious Welsh scholar suggests, that his countrymen, coming from the hard fare of their mountains, to the delicious viands, the cakes, the ale, the simnels and brawn of Shrewsbury, may have entitled it the town of dainties. It is certain that the metropolis of England derived its ludicrous appellation, which made the stout Earl of Norfolk call our Henry III. the King of Cokeney, from an analogous etymon, Coquina.

[4] An Italian antiquary, describing the desolation brought upon Calabria by the Saracens in the tenth century, says, " Frattanto, mentre i campi incolti si riempiono di bronche e di spine, ed i fonti inondano la campagna," &c. Paoli, Rovina di Pesto, p. 62. The historian of Norfolk (ix. 456, 8vo.) speaks of certain commons in that county, which he supposes to have been in early ages covered with water; as well as the low grounds adjoining to the rivulets which rise from them. " Such," he adds, " we know is usually the state of countries little cultivated." It is no unwarrantable stretch of the imagination to suppose, that the same cause would operate the same effect on the borders of the Severn.

[5] Varenius.

BRITISH PERIOD.

of which he was a native (Holland) this is perhaps not far from the truth. The Rhine, which in the days of Tacitus never reached the sea in the form of a river, but was lost in marshes, now empties itself by innumerable mouths, formed by the industry of the inhabitants, who have thus rescued for themselves large tracts of useful soil. The Severn, on the eastern side of Shrewsbury, ran at least in five channels, forming, within these last hundred years, four islands, and spreading, most probably, in the days of Cynddylan, into a marshy lake from the foot of the Wyle, at least as far as the site of the Abbey. On the north-west, ancient tradition attests, and the face of the ground confirms the idea, that Coton hill was connected with Frankwell by a bank [1], which caused the river to spread over the rich meadows called the Pur-ditches in a broad lake, and forced its waters under Hencot and Crosshill, (in a channel still strongly marked by its banks, and discernible at all times, particularly during floods,) till they found their way into the present channel, at Bagley bridge. Thus at the time when the Britons abandoned Wroxeter, the situation of Pengwern was one of eminent natural strength.

How long the fugitives remained unmolested in their new seats, it is vain to inquire; for our authorities present us with no notes of time at this period. But they were followed hither by the Saxons; who, as at Uriconium before, reduced the place to ashes: and the elegy of Llywarc calls upon the maidens of Pengwern " to quit their dwellings, and behold the habitation of Cynddylan, the royal palace of Pengwern, wrapped in flames." The British chief hereupon retired farther to the west. E. Lhuyd [2] quotes an ancient poem, intimating that he fell in battle at Drev Wen, or the *White Town;* and as the Saxons were much in the habit of translating into their own language the Welsh names of places which they found established, of which it would be easy to adduce abundant proof, this may have been Whittington, near Oswestry, as Lhuyd thought it was. But since Megaint's elegy quoted below speaks of Cynddylan as having led an armed force across the Tren, it is much more probable (and herein we express the opinion of a learned Welsh scholar) that the *White Town* near which our chieftain lost his life, was *Withington* beyond Haghmond Hill, near which village we may suppose he passed the Tern to face the Saxon spoiler.

---

[1] When this bank was eaten through, and before the channel under Hencot was choked up, Coton would be an island; and accordingly Richard Colfox, parson of Hanmer, by a deed dated at Salop, March 30th, 7th Hen. V. (1419) grants to William Toure of that town, all his lands, arable and not arable, woods, waters, and pastures, lying between Shardewallemore and Longemore infra insulam de Coton, *within the island of Coton,* (inter cartas Joh. Mytton ar.) From another part of the same deed it appears that Shardewallemore lay at the back of the castle (retro castrum), and near the street leading towards Hennecote; so that the ancient insularity of Coton is fully established.

[2] E. Lhuyd, Archæol. p. 260. There is another elegy on the death of Cynddylan, by a bard named Megaint. The language is so antiquated, as to be scarcely intelligible: but it speaks of the general estimation in which he was held, the universal grief felt for his loss; and it mentions his having led an armed force beyond the Tren.

It is certain that he was interred at Baschurch. " The churches of Bassa," says Llywarc (and this is another instance in which the Saxon name is a translation of the Welsh,)—" the churches of Bassa are enriched this night, containing the departed remains of the pillar of battle."

About a mile from this last named village, is a very remarkable British fastness, of which a more particular account will be given in the note[1]. It was in this spot, as I conceive, that Cynddylan, imitating his aboriginal forefathers, who, as we know from Cæsar, fortified themselves in woods and marshes, sought an asylum after his expulsion from Pengwern. Whether he was slain at Withington or Whittington, no reason can be assigned why he should be buried at Baschurch, but that his residence was in its immediate vicinity. And it lends some force to this opinion, that Baschurch was in the reign of the Confessor part of the royal demesne of the Crown of England. It is natural to suppose that such demesne was, in Mercia, derived from the Mercian kings; and it is likely that Offa, in his conquest of western Shropshire, would retain in his own hands all the possessions of the native sovereigns of Powis. Thus the place is connected by no improbable links with the time of Cynddylan. Baschurch preserved some traces of its ancient importance as late as the Conqueror's days. It gave name to an hundred; and its church is one of the very few (only eighteen in all) recorded by Domesday as existing in the whole extent of Shropshire.

---

[1] This strong-hold consists of two positions: one, a natural eminence about forty-five feet high, surrounded at the bottom by a circular vallum; the other an elliptical entrenchment, on which more pains have been bestowed, very much lower than the other, and perfect on three sides; the fourth being open, and apparently extended into a wider and more irregular form, the traces of which are rather indistinct and uncertain. The vallum of this elliptical entrenchment, where it faces the eminence described above, is thrice the height of any other part of it. The back parts were probably defended by water or bog.

The whole of these two positions, with the exception of a kind of causeway to be mentioned presently, is surrounded on one side by a deep pool called the Berth, on all other sides by an extensive morass of black peaty soil; which, though much hardened by draining, is still very soft and wet in the winter, and was, in all probability, a thousand years ago, covered by water. The works are connected by a low road, made, by incredible labour, of small stones heaped together, and edged by large ones; and both are connected with the main land by a similar road, leading across the morass in a curve. If this road was covered with water, as probably it was, to the depth of a few inches, strangers would not know where it was: and the loftier fortress had a farther defence in an interruption of the roads, which do not reach all the way to it, but cease within a few feet of the point of junction, and thus act as a kind of rude drawbridge: where the inhabitants might lay down a plank for their friends to come over. At the point where this interruption of the road exists, was evidently the entrance into the fort, which is there defended by two outworks, one on each side, of stones heaped up, in the manner employed by the British Caractacus, of whom Tacitus tells us, in modum valli saxa præstruit. The works of the lower fort are also, as has been observed, much more laboured at the point where the road connects it with the higher one. The pool is called Berth, which in Welsh is *beautiful*, an epithet which the spot in some sort deserves, being an eminence in the midst of a country quite flat; and here the Britons, availing themselves of a natural knoll, and a natural bed of gravel, of which the lower eminence consists, enjoyed in security, pasturage for their cattle, the fish of the neighbouring piece of water, and, at intervals, the pleasure of the chase: in a word, every thing which the late learned editor of Homer demands for his urbs primaria, or first settlement—mons, planities, et scaturigo aquæ; an eminence, a plain, and a supply of water. Vide R. P. Knight Prolegomena in Homerum, § 55.

BRITISH PERIOD. 9

But the situation of Pengwern, once descried and appreciated, could not long remain without an occupant; and a few years after its destruction under Cynddylan we find it inhabited by a king of Powis, the capital of his kingdom, and even ranking among the twenty-eight cities of Britain.[1] The kingdom of Powis at this time comprised [2] the south-western parts of the counties of Cheshire, Flint, and Denbigh, the whole of Montgomeryshire, portions of the counties of Radnor and Brecon, and as much of Shropshire as was unoccupied by the Saxons: i. e. at least as far as the river Severn. It is a mistake to suppose that it first originated as a territorial division, in the partition of Wales between the three sons of Roderick the Great in 876. Powis existed long before. Nennius, who finished his work in the year 858, describes the arrival in Britain of Saint Germain of Auxerre, about 430; his inhospitable reception by a king of Jal (Yale in Denbighshire), the miraculous destruction of that prince, and the consequent elevation of *Ketel Durnluc*, a poor man[3] who had slain his only calf to supply the wants of the holy bishop; " and from Ketel's seed," concludes Nennius, " is the region of Powis governed to this day." If the historian

---

[1] Geoffrey of Monmouth would have us believe, that there were in Britain, during its days of Paganism, three arch-flamens, and twenty-four flamens, established in twenty-seven cities; and that king Lucius, on becoming a Christian, substituted as many archbishops and bishops in their room. Lib. iv. cap. 19. Nennius has none of Geoffrey's fables, which were the invention of a later age; but he has a catalogue of twenty-eight cities of Britain, (Gale's Scriptores XV. p. 115) which was probably handed down by ancient tradition. Usher has bestowed much pains upon this catalogue (Britann. Eccles. Antiq. cap. 5) and finds three of the number within the limits of Shropshire: viz. Cair Caratauc (the Gaer ditches near Clun) Cair Urnach (Wroxeter) and Cair Darithou (Drayton). Thomas Rudborne, in his Historia Major, (cap. 2. ap. Wharton, Anglia Sacra, v. i. p. 181) gives a different catalogue of cities. In this there is no mention of Wroxeter, but instead of it, Cair Pengren, id est, Salopia, says Rudborne. It should seem as if the former town had fallen, and the latter arisen in the interval between the formation of the two lists. Unfortunately Rudborne, who lived in the fifteenth century, does not cite the author of that which he produces, so that we cannot estimate its date or value.

[2] For the limits of Powis, see Sir John Price's Description of Wales, prefixed to Dr. Powell's History, and Pennant's Tour in Wales, 1773, vol. i. p. 274, ed. 1810. I conceive that Chester belonged to the kingdom of Powis at the period referred to in the text.

[3] Certain Welsh genealogies derive his pedigree from Vortigern, and in the fifth degree from that prince. Nennius, it is plain, knew nothing of this royal descent. He only calls Ketel " unus de servis Regis:" yet I suspect that this pedigree was invented as early as the ninth century. We read on Eliseg's pillar, of which more will be said presently, of some one whom Germanus blessed, (QUE BENED .. GERMANUS,) which can be no other than Cadell; and mention occurs, though from the mutilated state of the inscription we know not to what effect, of GUARTHI ... in all probability Gwrtheirn or Vortigern; and of PASCEN ..... most likely Pasgen or Pascentius, called the father of Cadell. At the time when this pillar was erected, the posterity of Cadell had filled the throne of Powis for four centuries, a space of time quite long enough for the fabrication of a pedigree in honour of the reigning monarch. It stands thus in a MS. volume of Welsh pedigrees possessed by Mr. Vaughan, of Shrewsbury, and apparently about 300 years old.

GWRTHEIRN, or VORTIGERN.
  KYNDEIRN VENDIGARD, 2d son.
    RYDD FEDDWL FRYCH.
      RYDWF.
        PASKEN.
          KADELL DEYRNLLYG, King of Powis.

Britons soon after gained over the Northumbrian, on the banks of the Humber, to our Salopian chieftain, assisted by Cadfan, the father of Cadwallader, and other leaders. Brochwell must have died soon after; and in extreme old age, if the genealogies are correct, which represent his grandsire, Kadell Deyrnllyg, to have attained mature age nearly two centuries before the battle of Chester; and we should now set down some account of his descendants, who wielded the sceptre of Powis within the palace of Pengwern till their expulsion by the Saxons, if any materials could be found worth recording. But all history is silent concerning the kings of Old Powis, and even their names are obscured by uncertainty.

The legend of Monacella relates, that Brochwell was succeeded in the kingdom by his son Tissilian. This prince embraced a religious life, ranks among the British saints, and has given name to several churches in Wales. On his resignation, his brother Cynan succeeded. "Afterwards," continues the legend, " Tambryd, and then Curmylle, and Durras Gam, held the principality." But these three names, we are assured by a most competent authority[1], have no affinity to the Welsh, and bear every mark of monkish fiction.

Mr. Vaughan's MS. quoted above, gives several descents of a very different pedigree; which has all the evidence in its favour of which such a series is capable, being indeed a part of the genealogy of the very ancient family of Blayney, of Gregynog, in the county of Montgomery.

KYNAN GARRWYNN, son of BROCHWEL YSGYTHROG.
   SELYF SARFF KADAV.
      MAEL MYNAN.
         GWENOC.
           ELISSAV.

Gwenoc is the same denominated Guoillauc on Eliseg's pillar, which furnishes the following descents:

GUOILLAUC.
   ELISEG.
      BROHCMAIL.
         CATTELL.
           CONCENN.

Nest, sister and heiress of Concenn, was mother of Merfyn, father of Roderic the Great, whose third son Merfyn became the patriarch of the princes of

[1] Rev. Walter Davies, of Manafon, to whom we are indebted for many valuable remarks in this chapter.

New Powis; and this is nearly all that we have to relate concerning the kings of Old Powis, several of whom, no doubt, resided in Pengwern, and all of whom were assuredly engaged in perpetual hostilities with the English.

For, notwithstanding what the Saxon Chronicle says of the "nahtnesse" (cowardice) of the Britons, we are not to suppose, as has been too hastily done, that the natives yielded at once to the power of their northern invaders; or that the Angles and their companions acquired an immediate and easy settlement in their new conquests. So far is this from the truth, that the Britons maintained a glorious conflict of three centuries; and had it not been for their vicious form of government, broken into almost innumerable states, and hence convulsed by continual dissensions; and had not the Saxons of the continent, with the Jutes and the Angles, poured in successive reinforcements, they must have retired to their native seats on the banks of the Elbe and the Weser, and left the British isles in possession of their aboriginal princes. The heroic actions of Aurelius Ambrosius, his brother Uther, and nephew Arthur, in the south of England, evince the persevering valour of the Britons; and our Salopian chieftains displayed, no doubt, the like prowess, though time has deprived them of the renown of their achievements. One, almost the only legible line of the inscription on the pillar of Eliseg, (sixth descendant of Brockwell Yscithrog,) near the abbey of Valle Crucis, informs us that "this is that Eliseg who recovered his inheritance of Powis by his sword from the power of the Angles." Some one of his ancestors, then, had lost it, and he had regained it. But this is all we know. As to the extent of the acquisition, or its date, we are alike destitute of positive testimony. It is only certain that it was not till the victorious reign of the Mercian king Offa, which continued from 755 to 794, that the finest part of Powis became a confirmed part of the Mercian territory; and that Shropshire was permanently annexed to England by that stupendous dyke which still bears his name. As this will synchronize tolerably well with the probable time of Eliseg's reign[1], Pengwern may have been the portion of his "inheritance of Powis" which he recovered from that powerful Saxon; but which, finding it untenable without a greater force than he could maintain, he relinquished by treaty; and retiring into the more mountainous parts of his Powisian territory, found sepulture in the Vale of the Cross, and in the parish named after his sainted kinsman Tissilio, and

---

[1] If we suppose Brochwell to have been born in 510, his son Cynan in 555, and Cynan's five descendants, to Eliseg, to have been thirty-three years of age, when their eldest sons were born— which is a probable calculation,—Eliseg will have been born in 720, and consequently of an age to cope with the Mercian sovereign, and to have commanded those armies which are said to have ravaged Mercia during the early part of Offa's reign.

bequeathed his name to the rocks which shade his sepulchral column[1]. There are not wanting reasons to countenance the view here taken of this whole transaction; and with these we shall conclude this most difficult and unsatisfactory period of our history.

Though there can be no doubt that the cession of Shropshire was obtained from the British prince only by the military preponderance of the Saxon, yet it seems equally certain that it must have been finally the subject of a pacific negociation. A work of so much labour as Offa's dyke, evidently designed, according to his practice in other places[2], as the line of demarcation between two kingdoms, could never have been carried into execution without the concurrence of the sovereigns on each side of that boundary[3]. In like manner, the surrender of Pengwern by the Britons seems to have been ultimately the result of positive treaty; and the whole native population appears to have accompanied their prince into Montgomeryshire. Had the Saxons obtained it by a siege or by assault, they would doubtless, as elsewhere, have retained a portion of the inhabitants in a state of servitude; but we shall find reason hereafter to infer that this was not the case. The British prince, thus despoiled of the fairest portion of his dominions, retired to Mathrafal, on the Vyrnwy, five miles beyond Welsh Pool; while Pengwern, degraded from the dignity of a metropolis, passed under the yoke of an English conqueror, and is henceforth to be known by the denomination of SHREWSBURY, a name of Saxon origin.

Of the state of our town under its native princes, its extent, and its buildings, we possess no means of information. The arts of civil life, which the Britons had cultivated not without success under their Roman masters, disappeared in the course of three centuries of uninterrupted warfare. A ditch, or a rude rampart of unhewn logs, inclosing a few hovels, in dignity far inferior to a modern barn, for the residence of the prince[4], and the offices of religion; some wattled huts, with a

---

[1] Edward Lhuyd derives the Glwysig rocks in the Valley of Llangollen from the Powisian prince here spoken of. See his letter in Rowlands's Mona Ant. p. 302.

[2] He had a similar boundary against Wessex, which still retains traces of his name, being called Avesditch. Kennet, Par. Ant. p. 40. The Devil's ditch on Newmarket-heath had the same object.

[3] This is also the opinion of a very competent judge, Mr. Lewis Morris. See Cambr. Reg. ii. 498.

[4] Two centuries later than the period when the Cymry evacuated Pengwern Powis, their domestic architecture was in the lowest state of rudeness. One of Hywel Dda's regal mansions was constructed of peeled rods, and derived its name, Ty Gwyn, *the white house*, from this circumstance. (Leges Wallicæ, p. 6.) His laws have no other criterion for estimating the value of houses, even the king's hall, than by counting the number of posts. (Ib. 3, cap. 6.) A gentleman (mab uchelwr) had usually six posts to his hall. (ib.) These were filled up, we presume, with wattled twigs and clay. The doors, we know, were so constructed. (§ 8.) "Indeed, the word *adeiladu* to *build*, is composed of the particle *ad* and *eilio*, alternare, to wattle together." MS. Essay on the literature of Britain. It was an ancient tradition at Glastonbury, that the first religious edifice there was constructed in the same manner; inferius per circuitum

BRITISH PERIOD. 15

fold or two for the sheep and cattle, composed, it is probable, the whole of Pengwern Powis; an authentic sketch of which, if it could now be recovered, would be as interesting to the modern inhabitants of Shrewsbury, as the picture which Virgil presented to his readers, of the future mistress of the world, when first visited by Æneas and his companions.

. . . . . . tecta subibant
Pauperis Evandri, passimque armenta videbant
Romanoque foro, et lautis mugire Carinis.

virgis torquatis. Wm. of Malmesbury, in Gale's XV Scriptores, p. 293; and the same thing is related of St. Columba's original college, or monastery in the island of Iona. Many years have not elapsed since all the cottages, and most of the small farm-houses in the higher parts of Montgomeryshire, were wattled only, without even an outer coat of plaster.

As the inscription on the Pillar of Eliseg is almost the only authentic memorial of the kings of Old Powis who reigned in Shrewsbury, a copy of it is inserted below from the mutilated transcript which we now possess. Archbishop Usher is the first person that occurs to us as having noticed it: and he probably had it in a condition more perfect than can now be recovered. Usher transmitted it to his learned correspondent Dr. Gerard Langbaine[1], but it is not now to be found among his papers in the Bodleian. As the column was called a cross, it was thrown down during the civil wars, and broken into two pieces; indeed from two indentations on one side of the socket, or base, fitted to receive the knees of a man, (and which may be observed in the vignette,) I suspect that it had been for ages considered as an object of worship, and consequently adapted to excite the pious horror of the fanatical inhabitant of the neighbouring Abbey at that time[2]. In this state Mr. Robert Vaughan of Hengwrt, the great antiquary, saw it on the 22d of April, 1662, and took a copy, which Edward Lhuyd transcribed and sent Sept. 14, 1696, to the learned Dr. Mill[3], principal of Edmund Hall, and also inserted in his Welsh Itinerary, of which a transcript is among the collections of Mr. William Mytton. It then consisted of thirty-one lines. In 1779, Mr. Lloyd of Trevor hall, erected the upper part of the column, containing sixteen lines of the inscription, on its ancient base, which he placed upon a ruder one of rough stones, and set it on a rising ground close to the turnpike road leading by Valle Crucis Abbey from Llangollen to Ruthin. The remaining part of the stone has long disappeared. The whole that can be made out of Mr. Vaughan's copy runs thus[4]; what we consider doubtful is in Italics.

---

[1] Langbaine says, " I have received both your inscriptions; and shall send my thoughts of that at Vale Crucis; *but the other I give over as desperate.*" The Doctor therefore did not despair of the inscription now before us; and in another place he says, " I may possibly hereafter give some better account than as yet I can, of that of Vale Crucis." Usher's Letters, p. 551. Langbaine's papers are in the Bodleian, which has been ineffectually searched for this farther explanation; from the pen of a person so deeply learned, it would have been most valuable.

[2] See Mr. Pennant's account of Davies, " the blue shaver," who plundered the royalists, or, for a proper consideration, would protect them. Welsh Tours, ii. 11.

[3] Mr. Gough says (Camden, ii. 582) *to Wanley:* but he was not a clergyman, and Lhuyd's letter begins *Reverend* Sir. The proper superscription appears in a late publication, " The Cambro-Briton," No. ii. p. 55. Wanley was keeper of the Harleian MSS.; among which this letter of Lhuyd's was preserved, and hence, perhaps, Mr. Gough's mistake. It is not the only one which he has made. He says of our inscription, " it commemorates Concenn, or Congen, grandson of Brochmail Yscithrog, who was slain at the battle of Chester, A.D. 607." But, though it mentions Concenn, it was designed to *commemorate* Eliseg: and the Concenn mentioned in it was not *grandson*, but *ninth* descendant of Brochmail *Yscythrog:*—nor was Brochmail Yscithrog slain at Chester. Mr. Pennant makes the same confusion of the two Brochwells: and even Mr. Vaughan (Brit. Antiq. Revived, 4to. 1662, p. 6) seems not to have known the last.

[4] The copy inserted below is taken from Gough's plate, with a few corrections from Lhuyd's MS Itinerary. Lhuyd has printed a part of the inscription in his Archæologia, p. 229.

BRITISH PERIOD.

       Concenn filius Cattell, Cattell
filius Brohcmail, Brohmail filius
Eliseg, Eliseg filius Guoillauc.
Concenn itaque pronepos Eliseg
edificavit hunc lapidem proavo
suo Eliseg + Ipse est Eliseg qui recuperavit
hereditatem Povosie post mortem
Cattelli per vim e potestate Anglo
rum gladio suo parta in igne
    que *restituerit* manuscriptum
       benedictionem super
       Eliseg + Ipse est Concenn
  . . . . . manu
     regnum suum Povosea
          quod

        mortem

       monarchiam
Maximus Britanniæ
Pascen
     filius Guarthi
que bened. Germanus que
peperit ei S. eeira filia Maximi
Regis qui occidit regem Romano
rum + Conmarch pinxit hoc
Chirografu rege suo poscente
Concenn + Benedictio Dnī in Con-
cenn et sā ī totā familiā ejus
Et in totā ragionē Povois
Usque in . . . . .

To this effect in English:

    Concenn was the son of Cattell, Cattell
the son of Brohcmail, Brohmail the son
of Eliseg, Eliseg the son of Guoillauc.[1]
Concenn therefore the great-grandson of Eliseg
built this stone to his great-grandfather
Eliseg + This is the Eliseg who recovered his inheritance of Povosia after the death
of Cattell[2] by force out of the power of the Angles by his sword . . . . . fire
. . restored the inscription . .
     blessing upon
. . Eliseg + This is Concenn
   . . . .
   his kingdom of Povosea
  . . . . . which

  . . . . . death

---

[1] We find a Guallawc among the British kings who in the north of England maintained the struggle against the sons of Ida in the sixth century. Turner's Hist. of Anglo-Sax. i. 301.

[2] The Cattell here mentioned (if he is mentioned, for I suspect this part of Mr. Lhuyd's reading,) must be distinguished from him of the same name mentioned before.

BRITISH PERIOD.

. . . . .
. . . . the monarchy
. . Maximus of Britain
. . Pascentius
. . . son of Guarthi [1]
whom Germanus blessed, whom
. . bore to him S. eeira daughter of Maximus
the king who slew the king of the Romans [2] + Conmarch engraved [3] this
inscription, at the request of his king
Concenn + May the blessing of the Lord be upon Concenn and . . on his whole family
and on the whole region of Povois
for . . . .

---

[1] Guarthi is probably the beginning of Gwartheyrn, or Vortigern. Some writers give him a son Pasgen, or Pascentius. An elaborate pedigree in lib. Salusbury (inter coll. W. Mytton) makes Pasken fourth descendant of Vortigern, father of Cadell Deyrnllwg: who was evidently the person mentioned in the inscription as having been "blessed by St. Germanus."

[2] About the year 409, Count Gerontius slew the Emperor Constans, (whom Dr. Milner would have us believe King Arthur's uncle, Hist. Winchest. i. 61.) and set up one Maximus, who seems to be here mentioned. The Welsh call him Macsen Wledig. It is impossible sufficiently to lament the mutilated state of an inscription in this most interesting and embroiled period.

[3] *Pingo* was sometimes used for any kind of marking. Bellarmine, speaking of the cross in baptism, calls it, signum crucis, in fronte *pingendum*. l. iv. c. 2. de verbo non scripto.

CHAPTER II.

OF SCROBBES-BYRIG, OR SHREWSBURY, IN THE TIME OF THE SAXONS.

Our town did not, it appears, receive much improvement from the Britons, who had subjects of more immediate necessity to occupy their attention. If they found it *a Hill of Alders*, they left it in nearly the same condition; for we may fairly infer the state in which the Saxons received it from them, by the appellation which it obtained from its new masters, *Scrobbes-byrig*, importing that it was a *bury*, or fenced eminence, but overgrown with *scrubs*, or *shrubs*.[1] What Shrewsbury lost, therefore, in nominal consequence, as metropolis of a kingdom, by this great revolution, it ultimately gained in external splendour and real importance. This is evinced, among other proofs, by the erection of five ecclesiastical foundations of considerable opulence, which we know to have existed here anterior to the Norman conquest, and all of which assuredly owed their origin to Saxon piety.

From the time that Shrewsbury became a part of the Mercian kingdom, nothing memorable is related of it for many years. It experienced, undoubtedly, the successive revolutions of that kingdom, on which it is unnecessary to dwell; till, with the remainder of the Heptarchy, Mercia

---

[1] Our modern *shrub*, was anciently *skrub*. Thus Holland, in his translation of Pliny: "But such will never prove fair trees, but *skrubs* only." So in the survey of Glastonbury: "Also there is a wood—the moste parte whereof standeth by *scrubbed* and lopped trees." Langtoft's Chronicle, v. ii. p. 373. The word has not lost its hard sound in some counties; witness Wormwood Skrubs, near Hammersmith.

That this is no etymology of modern fabrication, take the words of Higden: "Salopia urbs est in confinio Cambriæ et Angliæ, super Sabrinam, in vertice collis, posita,—quæ Anglice dicitur Schrobbesburia, de dumis et fructibus (l. *fruticibus*) in illo colle aliquando crescentibus sic dicta."

It is observed to me by a very learned and intelligent traveller, that the etymology of Frascati is similar to that of Shrewsbury. "The Romans," says he, "destroyed Tusculum, which stood upon the hill above the modern town, in A.D. 1191: after this the inhabitants moved below, and from the number of *bushes* (frasche) the new town derived its name."

After these etymologies, it may be not unentertaining to read the following account of the name of this town, given by Oliver Mathews. "And nowe to retorne to the fiftie brethren of Sallop. After they had escaped the cruell Pagan motheringe enemies, the Saxon and Irishe men, set on by the Romanes, and had bin in the towne a tyme, and there had kepte and *shrowded* themselves from there mortall enemies, they tourned the name of the towne from Penne gwerne Powis to *Shrewsbury*, because they there kepte and *shrowded* themselves, as aforesaid, from theire enemies; and scithence, to this daie, the towne hath bin and is called *Shrewsbury*."

VOL. I.   E

was united under the dominion of Egbert[1], king of Wessex, about the year 823. During the whole of this period, Shrewsbury was, it is reasonable to suppose, a place of slender consequence. Mercia, though the largest of the Anglo-Saxon kingdoms, was still not sufficiently important to give dignity to more than one city; London was its capital: and if our town was the seat of some subordinate governor, yet that officer could hardly be of such a rank as to confer much elevation upon the place of his residence.

Mercia thenceforward ceased to exist as an independent sovereignty; but it retained somewhat of its separate form for more than a century. Alfred granted it, about the year 884, to his son-in-law Ethered, with the title of Ealderman[2]. On the death of this nobleman in 912, his widow, Ethelfleda, Alfred's daughter, succeeded to the government of Mercia; but with a territory considerably diminished, as her brother king Edward deprived her of London and Oxford, and, no doubt, of the counties intervening. The *Lady of the Mercians*, thus restricted to the western district of the kingdom once ruled by her husband, devoted much of her attention to Shropshire, whither she was frequently called by her hostilities against the Welsh. She built castles at Chirbury and Brugge, (i. e. Quatford near Bridgenorth), and must frequently have visited Shrewsbury; in which she founded the collegiate church of St. Alcmund, in honour of a Northumbrian prince who died more than a century before, and had, we presume, been recently canonized. During the period of which we are now treating, it is principally to transactions of an ecclesiastical nature that we are indebted for the few slight notices which respect those minute details of local history connected with our present subject.

The reign of Athelstan, however, affords us one authentic, though slight, memorial of the town. That great king, for such he truly was, first

---

[1] Though under Egbert the different kingdoms of the Heptarchy are generally thought to have been consolidated into one dominion, yet this did not take place all at once. It appears, for instance, from the Saxon Chronicle, that there were kings of Mercia after the conquest of that kingdom by Egbert. Some of these, doubtless, reigned as vassals to that monarch and his successors: but others assumed an independent authority, as rebels from his allegiance, or as protected by the Danes. We do not find that Egbert ever assumed the title of King of England. His son, Ethelwolf, in his great charter of tithes, only calls himself King of Wessex, " Rex occidentalium Saxonum," (Fuller's Ch. Hist. p. 110.) and the accession of *his* son Alfred, 871, is recorded in the Saxon Chronicle in no other terms. It is not till the subsequent part of his reign that he is called simply THE KING, without any qualification. John de Wallingford, ap. Gale, p. 535, calls him Primus Monarcha.

[2] In the year 894, the 23d of Alfred's reign, the Danes, having landed in Essex, followed the course of the rivers Thames and Severn, and overran the whole country, till they were most signally defeated at Buttington. Thus the Saxon Chronicle. Henry of Huntingdon adds, that the invaders built a castle at Scrobrih, which Camden conceives to be Shobury, in Essex. Mr. Morant, however, in his history of that county, will have it to be our town; and if he were right, it would be an acceptable incident to add to our local history, in so barren a period. But I think it is incontrovertibly evident, from the words of Huntingdon, that Camden's is the true interpretation. Hasting, the Dane, says the Monkish historian: invasit Essexe, et castrum fecit apud Scrobrih, indeque permeantes venerunt usque Budingtune juxta Severnam, et ibi castrum fecerunt: unde tamen bello repulsi, fugerunt ad castrum in Essexe. De Gestis Ælfredi, p. 351.

of all our English monarchs paid any attention to the state of his coins: at least he is the first whose regulations on that head are recorded. He ordained that only one sort of money should be current *throughout his empire*[1]; and farther, with the view, no doubt, of securing such uniformity, directed that no person should presume to coin except within towns; and then, after specifying eight cities[2] or towns which he considered as sufficiently important to have a plurality of moneyers, he concludes, that there shall be one in other boroughs. Hence arose the practice of impressing upon the current money, in addition to the name of the workman who coined it, as had been the previous practice, that of the place in which it was struck: and as we have several pennies of this monarch bearing the name of Shrewsbury, it is plain that in his time it was a borough important enough to have the privilege of a Mint, though not sufficiently so to be specifically enumerated. As the English sovereign is designated on those coins REX. TO. BRIT., I infer that they were not minted till after the time when, having conquered Cornwall, expelled the Danes, repressed Wales, and overrun Scotland, (which last event is placed by Simeon of Durham in 934,) he had established his right to the lofty title of KING OF ALL BRITAIN.

When England began to repose for a short interval from the dreadful devastation of the Danes, and Edgar the Peaceable, who reigned from 959 to 975, undertook, by the direction of Archbishop Dunstan, to restore the Monks to those foundations from which they had been ejected; we read that he reformed his great-aunt's foundation at St. Alcmund's, and instituted a new one at St. Mary's. These acts, and the motives which led to them, belong more properly to another part of our work; but it was necessary briefly to touch upon them in this place, as they afford some insight into the relative importance of this town, at the period of which we are treating.

The system of the great Alfred, who delegated, as we have seen, the government of this part of his dominions to one of his subjects, with a title referring to the kingdom of Mercia, was continued by his successors. In the year 1006, Ethelred, known to posterity by the significant epithet of the *Unready*, having been pursued from place to place by the Danes, and wandering over his dominions, "*passed over Thames into Scrobbes-byrigscire*," says the Saxon Chronicle, and spent his Christmas[3] in this town.

---

[1] In toto regni imperio. Bromton, p. 843, in Twysden's Scriptores.

[2] They are all in the South. Canterbury, Rochester, London, Winchester, Lewes, Hastings, Shaftsbury, and Exeter.

[3] The words of Henry of Huntingdon denote that our Saxon kings had a settled residence here. "Rex autem Adelred, cum mœstitia et confusione erat ad firmam suam in Salopscire, sæpe rumorum sauciatus aculeis." Lib. vi. p. 206, b. It was the practice of the Saxon monarchs, borrowed from the French court (Menagiana, vol. ii. p. 110, edit. 1695.) and continued by the early princes of the Norman race, to feast in public with great state, and wearing their crowns, at the three great festivals of the year: and the places where they

Conscious, it may be, of his own inability to hold the reins of government with a steady hand, he was desirous of easing himself of a part of its toil; and accordingly in the next year, 1007, committed the government of the whole kingdom of Mercia to his son-in-law Ædric.

Ædric, Streona[1], or Sueona[2], for he is called by both names, occurs as *earl, duke,* or *alderman* of Mercia, and made this town the place of his occasional residence, since it was in its neighbourhood that he was guilty of an atrocious assassination. Having determined to effect the destruction of Alfhelm, a duke, or earl (for the titles were then synonymous) of the royal blood, he invited him to Scrobbesbyrig, one of the seats of his government. Here, after having entertained him sumptuously for four days, he took him out a hunting, and employed a butcher[3] of the town, Godwin Porthund, or Porkhund, by name, whom he had placed in a wood, to murder him. This flagitious action made a deep impression, we may suppose, upon the kingdom at large, and upon the inhabitants of this town in particular; and was probably the origin of the custom recorded in Domesday, that twelve of the chief burgesses should guard the king, when engaged in the chase, during his residence here. Milton chooses to assert that the king was privy to this assassination; but there are no grounds for the imputation. Ethelred's character seems rather to have been weak than wicked. On the contrary, as soon as he heard of this murder, he caused the eyes of two of Ædric's sons to be put out[4], as was the barbarous usage of the time, in testimony of his

---

kept these feasts are generally recorded by our historians. So Robert of Glocester says of William the Conqueror, " Thre sythe he ber croune a yer: to Mydewynter at Gloucester," &c. Kings, even in their greatest depression, do not willingly part with their accustomed ceremonial: and Ethelred seems to have kept up, even at this crisis, the stated recurrence of feasts.

[1] Ordericus calls him Streona; that is, says he, *acquisitor.*

[2] The Saxon Chronicle speaks of him by this last title, where it relates the accusation preferred by his brother Brihtric against Wolfnoth Cilt, thane of Sussex. Mr. Nichols, in his History of Leicestershire, has styled him "Edric de Stretton, of Stretton, in that county, by some called Streona, or treacherous." How this word can have two meanings so opposite, or in what language it has either of them, we are unable to say: and the attentive peruser of that History, p. 1024, n. 5. 1025, 1027, n. 2., will find reason to infer that there is no good ground to suppose our duke was ever seated at Stretton. For this last remark we are indebted to the late eminent and regretted antiquary, Mr. Wolferstan.

[3] So says Florence of Worcester; quidam Scrobbesbyrigensis carnifex: and Matthew of Westminster; quidam carnifex nomine Godwinus. But I suspect here an undue imputation upon that ancient fraternity. Walter of Coventry, in his Annals, quoted by Leland, (Collectan. v. i. p. 284.) calls the murderer the Porthund of earl Edric: à Godwino *Porthund Edrici comitis.* Porthund is the *town dog,* and so it is rendered by Florence: which gives no intelligible sense, as the servant of a nobleman. But if we read *Porc hunt,* all will be clear. *Chace porc,* the hunter of hogs, occurs as a surname in Dugdale's Chronic. Jurid. A. D. 1253. *Porc hunt* is the same in English, and Godwin may have been *master of the boar-hounds* to the alderman of Mercia. The wild boar ranged, no doubt, at that time, in the neighbouring forests; his existence is recorded in that remarkable hollow, the Boar's Den, near Betton: and it was, probably, while engaged in the chase of that animal, that the Saxon earl fell a victim to the malice of his enemy.

[4] Milton has misunderstood this part of the story. He makes the two unfortunate youths thus barbarously deprived of their sight, to have been sons of Alfhelm. But the words of Matthew of Westminster are express to the contrary. " Quidam carnifex nomine Godwinus quem Eadricus ante donariis corruperat, ex insidiis subito prosiliens Ducem Athelstanum [so Matthew writes the

abhorrence of their father's guilt: and it is probable that this shocking outrage drove Ædric into those measures of revolt and perfidy by which his memory is stained, and for which our historians have been unable to account.

The Saxon annalist, who seldom interposes his own opinion on the characters of the personages whose actions he records, steps, however, out of the accustomed dryness of his narrative, to attribute to Ædric the general misconduct of the reign of Ethelred. Yet the Mercian alderman seems to have had at least the merit of protecting his own part of England from the Danish ravages. Nor were the people of this town and county deficient in gratitude for the exemption which, through his means, they enjoyed from those evils so sensibly experienced by the remainder of the kingdom: since we find, that, though they had so lately afforded an asylum to the English monarch, yet, when the alderman of Mercia thought proper, for reasons which are not detailed, but which we have perhaps assigned above, to desert the cause of his father-in-law, and to join the standard of his adversary Canute, the people of Shropshire followed his example. For this desertion of the royal standard our countrymen were, however, severely punished in the following year, 1016, when the gallant prince Edmund, having in vain endeavoured to excite his fickle and irresolute father to a vigorous prosecution of the war, joined earl Uhtred in a predatory incursion to Shrewsbury, and into the neighbouring counties of Stafford and Chester [1].

From the monies coined in this town under our Saxon monarchs we derive, as has been already observed, some notion of its importance during that period. Before the reign of Athelstan, the place of minting seldom, if ever, appears on coins; but from his time, the productions of the Salopian Mint are numerous. The various names of the minters, seven of whom have been discovered in the reign of Canute, and ten in that of Edward the Confessor, (and many more probably exist of which we have no knowledge,) prove that the regulation of Athelstan, who permitted only one minter in ordinary boroughs, was gradually relaxed; and we shall see from Domesday that three were recognized by the sovereign in the Confessor's reign.

name] nefarie nimis peremit.—In cujus rei *ultionem* duo filii ejus jussu regis Æthelredi excæcati sunt. sub anno 1006." And this decides the meaning of the phrase of Florence, which might otherwise be somewhat ambiguous. " Quidam Scrobbesbyrigensis carnifex, Godwinus Porthund, i. e. Oppidi Canis, quem multo ante donis magnis multisque promissionibus pro patrando facinore excæcaverat Edricus, ex insidiis subito prosiluit, et Ducem Alfhelmum nefarie peremit. Parvo interjecto tempore filii ejus Wulfeagus et Wegeatus jussu Regis Æthelredi apud Cocham [Walter Coventre says Cocerham; Cockerham, near Lancaster] ubi tunc degebat cæcati sunt." The blindness of our great poet, under which he composed his history, sufficiently apologizes for this inadvertence.

[1] Clito Edmundus et Uthredus Northymbrorum comes .... prius Staffordensem, deinde Scrobesbyriensem et Legacestrensem provincias devastavere, quia adversus Danorum exercitum ad pugnam exire noluerunt. Simeon Dunelm. p. 172.

A list of such Salopian coins of the Saxon æra as are now known is subjoined.[1]

AETHELSTAN.
924—940.

[2] 1. EÐELSTAN REX TO BRIT.   A cross.   Mr. Haycock.
      BERHTEL M SCROB

2. EÐELSTAN REX TO BRIT.   A rose of dots.   Mr. Combe's plates,
   FROTGER MO- SCROB   pl. 18. n° 26.

   ETHELSTAN REX TO BRIT   Mr. Southgate's
   EDRED MO SCROB   MS.

EADGAR.
959—975.

3. EADGAR REX ANGLOX   Gough's Camden,
   ÆÐELSIGE MŌ SCRO   ed. 2. pl. 2. n° 14.

AETHELRED the Unready.
979—1016.

ÆTHELRED REX ANGLO   Mr. Southgate's
ÆVIC MO SFROBBES   MS.

ÆTHELRED REX ANGO   Ditto.
ÆLFHEM MO SCRO

ÆTHELRED REX ANGLO   Ditto.
ÆLFSTAN MO CROBE

CANUTE.
1017—1036.

4. CNVT RECX   Brit. Mus.
   ETSIGE ON SCRO

5. CNVT RECX   Ditto.[3]
   PVLFMER ONN SCR

6. CN RECX A   Mr. Haycock.
   BRVNGAR ON SRO

7. NVT REX ANGLORV   Brit. Mus.
   ETSIG ON SRO

   CNVT REX ANGLORVM   Mr. Ruding, from
   GEFFEL MON SR   Brit. Mus.

---

[1] It is chiefly derived from the private communications of the late Rev. Rogers Ruding, whose profound knowledge of the subject is appreciated by every reader of his "Annals of the Coinage:" but the great national repository in the British Museum, and the private collections of Mr. Sharp of Coventry, and Mr. J. Haycock of Shrewsbury, have furnished other additions. The numerals refer to the Plate, which contains all of which we have been able to procure a sight, and for which we are indebted to our worthy friend Dr. Prattinton of Bewdley, who has kindly interested himself on this subject, and most liberally contributed the engraving.

[2] The numerals refer to the Plate.

[3] Vertue is said to have derived his head of Canute from this coin.

SAXON PERIOD.

8. CNVT REX ANCLO
   CRINNA SCROBR — Brit. Mus.

9. CNVT REX ANCLORVM
   BRVICAR ON SC — Mr. Sharpe.

10. CNVT REX ANCLOR
    ÆLFELM ON SCoB — Ditto.

11. CNVT REX ANCLO ⊹
    CRIMAN ON SROB — Ditto.

EDWARD the Confessor.
1042—1066.

EDVERD REX
LEOFWINE ON SROB — Mr. Southgate's MS.

EDVERD REX
ILMER ON SCRoBE — Sir A. Fountaine, pl. 7. n° 22.

12. EDVE D REX
    CODESBRAND ON SC — Brit. Mus.

13. EADVARD RE
    VVLMÆR ON SCOBE — Ditto.

EADVEARD RE
CODSBRAND ON SCR — Mr. Southgate's MS.

14. DVAR°RD RE
    VVDEMAN O COB — Brit. Mus.

Obverse as the last.
VILMÆR ON SCOBE — Mr. Ruding, from Brit. Mus.

EADWARD REX
LOELRIE ON SCR — Mr. Southgate's MS.

EADWARD RE
CODWINE ON SCRO — Ditto.

15. EADVARRD RE
    CODVINE ON SCRO — Brit. Mus.

16. EADVARD REX
    CODVINE ON SROBB — Mr. Sharpe.

17. EADVARD REX
    VVLMIER ON SROI — Ditto.

18. EDVARD REX AI
    EARNVI ON SROP — Ditto.

19. EADVARD REX
    CODE?BRAND ON ? — Brit. Mus.

20. EDVERD REX
    GODESBRoND ON SCR — Mr. Sharpe.

21. EADVARD REX ANCL
    LEOFSTAN ON SCRO — Ditto.

22. ⊹EDVERD RE
    LMER ON SCRoBE — Hickes's Thesaurus.

23. EDVE D RE
    ⊹ÆLMER ON SCROBE — J. B. B.

SAXON PERIOD.

HAROLD II.
1066.

HAROLD REX ANG
PAX.GODESBRANT ON SR

Mr. Southgate's MS.

The inscriptions of these coins, it will be seen, varied under different monarchs: under the three first, after the name of the minter, his title, M. or MŌ for *Monetarius*, is subjoined: afterwards that title is omitted, and the minter is merely stated to reside ON, i. e. *in* the town: and on the whole we learn that in the reign of Athelstan, persons named Edred, Frotger, and Berhtel, exercised their art within our walls; in the reign of Edgar, one Æthelsige; under Ethelred, Ælfhem, Ælfstan, and Ævic; under Canute, Ælfclm, Brungar or Bruicar, Crinna or Criman, Etsige, Geffel, and Wulfmer; under Edward the Confessor, Ælmer, Earnwi, Godesbrand, Godwin, Loelric, Leofwine, Leofstan, Wudeman, Wigmær, and Wulmer; and under Harold, the same Godesbrand who appears as a minter in the reign of his predecessor. The word PAX on the reverse of Harold's coin has not been satisfactorily explained.

Of the state of our town in the reign of Edward the Confessor, son of Ethelred, and brother, and at length successor, to Edmund Ironside, we gain some information from Domesday.

"In the town of Shrewsbury," says that record, "there were 252 houses in the time of king Edward, with a burgess residing in each house; these altogether paid an annual rent of 7*l.* 16*s.* 8*d.* King Edward enjoyed the following branches of revenue in this town.

"If any person wilfully infringed a protection given under the king's own hand, he was outlawed. He who violated the royal protection[1] given by the sheriff, forfeited 100*s.*; and the same sum was exacted for an assault committed on the highway[2], and for a burglary[3]. These three forfeitures were paid to king Edward in all his demesne lands throughout England, over and above the reserved rents.

"When the king resided in this town, twelve of the better sort of

---

[1] Pacem regis manu propria datam. So in Chester, "Pax data manu regis, vel suo brevi, vel per suum legatum." *Peace*, in our old language, seems to have had the signification of *protection*. Thus we say, "against the king's *peace*, his crown, and dignity:" i. e. the trespass or assault complained of is in violation of that protection which the sovereign owes to all his subjects, and consequently tends to the diminution of the dignity of his crown. The Saxon Chronicle, sub ann. 1048, relating the temporary banishment of earl Godwin and his sons, says (we prefer the modern type, as shewing the affinity of the language) that he and Swegen gewerdon begeondan sae, *went beyond sea*, and gesohton Boldewines grid, *and sought Baldwin's peace*, i. e. the protection of Baldwin, earl of Flanders; while Harold went to Ireland, and was in that king's *peace*. See also sub ann. 1086.

[2] Forestel.

[3] *Heinfare;* Higden reads it *Hamfare*, and interprets it, *insultus factus in domo;* from ham, hame, home, p. 202, edit. Gale. Du Cange interprets it, a forfeiture paid by a servant who ran away from his master; which does not seem very probable.

citizens kept watch over him; and when he went out a hunting, such of them as had horses guarded him. The sheriff used to send thirty-six footmen to the stand [1], when the king was present; and at Marsetelie park [2] that officer was bound by custom to find the same number of men for eight days. When he made a progress into Wales, every person who did not obey his summons to accompany him forfeited 40s.

"A widow paid the king 20s. for license to marry; a maiden 10s. for the same permission. If a house was burnt by accident without negligence, the burgess who inhabited it paid a fine of 40s. to the king, and 2s. each to his two next neighbours. The king had 10s. for a relief [3], upon the death of every burgess dwelling within the royal demesne; and if it was not paid by the time which the sheriff appointed, a fine of 10s. more was exacted. If a man wounded another so as to draw blood, he paid 40s. for this offence. When the king departed from the town, if he went southwards, the sheriff sent twenty-four horses with him as far as Leintwardine [4]; and he furnished the sovereign with the same number also to the first stage in Staffordshire, when he travelled that way.

"The king had three [5] moneyers in this town, who, after they had purchased their money dies in the same manner as the other moneyers of the

---

[1] Stabilitionem. The hunting of the Saxons seems to have been similar to that practised in Germany to this day. The wood is surrounded on all sides, and the beasts of chase driven to a spot where the company is assembled, who take aim at them as they pass by.

[2] We are ignorant of the situation of this park. It was doubtless kept for the royal diversions. There is a place called Marsley, in the parish of Habberley, and another called Marlow, near Leintwardine. One of the Domesday hundreds was Mersete: it corresponds to part of the present hundreds of Oswestry and Pimhill.

[3] Relevamento. Fiefs were originally for life only. In process of time they gradually became hereditary. But the heir, when admitted to the feud which his ancestor had possessed, used to pay a fine or acknowledgement to the lord, in horses, arms, money, or the like, for such renewal of the feud. This was called a *relief*, because it re-established, or, as it were, *lifted up again*, the inheritance. In the language of the feudal writers, incertam et caducam hereditatem relevabat.

[4] Hence it appears that Leintwardine was at this time the road southwards out of Shropshire: that is, the old Watling-street way was then still used; and it may be traced from the Strettons through by-lanes to that village in the present day.

[5] Athelstan, as we have seen, directed that there should be only one minter in all boroughs, except eight cities or towns which he specifies. But it is probable that as early as the time of Canute, and it is certain that in the time of the Confessor, this restriction was relaxed. Shrewsbury, we see, had three minters. The cause of this relaxation may be found in the fact, that our Saxon monarchs derived no inconsiderable revenue from the coinage; and in the manner in which they derived it. In order to prevent the confusion which such a multiplicity of minters would have produced in the currency, if they had all executed their own stamps, the king kept the dies in his own hands, and furnished the country minters with them as they were wanted. He did not, of course, do this gratuitously; and, besides the price which he exacted for his dies, (probably an arbitrary one,) had a farther demand upon the minters, within a few days after their being issued: and this laid the sovereign under irresistible temptation, frequently to *renew his money*, that is, to call it in and recoin it. Hence the multiplicity of minters in the provincial towns, and the great variety of our Saxon types. It was, probably, only the *obverse* of the coin, representing the effigy of the sovereign, that was furnished by the king's engraver; it would have been impossible for him to supply the great variety of *reverses* which are found, though it is possible that every part of the reverse also might be sent down from London, except the name of the minter. The mode of coinage at the time of which we are treating, was simply to fix the die for one

country, were bound, within fifteen days after, to pay the king 20s. each, whilst the new coinage was in progress. Upon the whole, the town paid an annual rent of 30l., two thirds of which went to the king, and the remainder to the sheriff.

"In the reign of king Edward, this town[1] was assessed to the Danegeld at the rate of an hundred hides; of which

"The Church of St. Alcmund held two hides.
"St. Julian half a hide.
"St. Milburg one hide.[2]
"St. Chad one hide and a half.
"St. Mary one fourth of a hide.
"The Bishop of Chester one hide.
"Ediet three hides."

[The individual thus unceremoniously noticed, was no less a person than Edith, the daughter of earl Godwin, sister of king Harold and wife of king Edward. She held also the neighbouring manor of Meole, and those of Cleobury Mortimer, Kinlet, and Farlow, in the south-east corner of the county; was undisturbed by the Norman invasion, and survived it eight years, but died before the completion of Domesday.]

"The Bishop of Chester possessed in Shrewsbury sixteen masures, each inhabited by a burgess; he also possessed other burgesses. He had also sixteen canons in the town, who were all exempt from the payment of Danegeld."

As engravings in fac-simile of this venerable record (the most ancient public monument in its kind of which any European nation can boast) are not very common, it has been judged that a copy of so much of it as relates to the customs of Shrewsbury, might be acceptable to the reader. To assist those to whom the character and abbreviations of the original are not familiar, the following transcript is subjoined: in which the Italics denote the letters omitted.

---

side of the coin on an anvil or block of wood, to place on it the silver blank, and over that a puncheon with the die for the other side of the coin, when a smart stroke with a hammer produced the desired effect. This explanation, the whole of which that contains positive assertion, is derived from the excellent work of Mr. Ruding, vol. i. pp. 82, 130, 179, &c. will, it is hoped, make intelligible the passage of Domesday relative to our Shrewsbury mint. We have adopted his translation, though we are not clear that the words *hoc fiebat moneta vertente* signify more than that the same payment of 20s. was due *every time the coinage was changed.*

[1] *Civitas.* Through the whole of the present extract, we have translated this word by *town.* Our native antiquaries, with a natural patriotism, represent Shrewsbury as being then a city. But the distinction between the two was never in the contemplation of the rude period before us. (Madox, Firma Burgi, p. 2.) Thus Leicester is called both *civitas* and *burgus* in the same passage of Domesday. Our lawyers seem to know no other definition of a city than that it either is, or has been, the seat of a bishop; but this is a doctrine more recent than that ancient record; for neither Shrewsbury nor Leicester have ever been episcopal sees. Dr. Brady says the great distinction grew after cities were made counties by charter. (On Boroughs, Pref. p. 3.)

[2] The Abbey of Wenlock.

In Civitate Sciropisberie Tempore Regis *Edwardi*
erant cc^{tæ} L II domus et totidem burgenses in ipsis domibus
reddentes per annum VII libras et XVI solidos et VIII denarios de gablo
Ibi habebat rex *Edwardus* has subterscriptas consuetudines
          scienter
Siquis pacem regis manu propria datam infringebat utlagatus
fiebat Qui vero pacem regis a vicecomite datam infringebat
c solidis emendabat & tantundem dabat qui forestel vel heinfare
faciebat. Has III forisfacturas habebat in dominio rex *Edwardus* in omni
Anglia extra firmas
Quando rex jacebat in hac civitate servabant eum vigilantes
XII homines de melioribus civitatis. Et cum ibi venationem
exerceret. Similiter custodiebant eum cum armis meliores
burgenses caballos habentes. Ad stabilitionem vero mittebat
vicecomes XXXVI homines pedites. quamdiu rex ibi esset.
Ad parcum autem de Marsetelie inveniebant XXXVI homines
per consuetudinem VIII diebus
Cum in Walis pergere vellet vicecomes qui ab eo edictus non
pergebat XL solidos de forisfactura dabat
Mulier accipiens quocunque modo maritum. Si vidua erat. dabat regi
XX solidos. Si puella X solidos quolibet modo acciperet virum.
Cujuscunque burgensis domus combureretur aliquo casu vel eventu
sine negligentia XL solidos regi dabat pro forisfactura et duobus
propinquioribus vicinis suis II solidos unicuique [De relevamento.
Burgensis qui in dominio erat regis cum moriebatur habebat rex X solidos
Siquis burgensis frangebat terminum quem vicecomes imponebat ei
emendabat X solidis Qui sanguinem fundebat XL solidis emendabat
Cum rex abiret de civitate mittebat ei XXIIII caballos vicecomes
lenteurde et ipsos ducebat rex usque ad primam mansionem Strafordscire
Tres monetarios habebat ibi rex. qui postquam coemissent cuneos
monete ut alii monetarii patrie XV die dabant regi
XX solidos unusquisque et hoc fiebat moneta vertente.
Inter totum reddebat civitas ista per annum XXX libras Duas partes
habebat rex et vicecomes terciam.   comiti
precedenti anno hujus descriptionis reddidit XL libras Rogerio
Hec civitas Tempore Regis *Edwardi* geldabat pro c hidis
De his habebat Sanctus Almundus II hidas Sancta Juliana dimidiam hidam
Sancta Milburga I hidam Sanctus Cædd hidam et dimidiam Sancta Maria I virgatam
Episcopus de Cestre I hidam Ediet III hidas quas habet Radulfus de Mortemer
Dicunt angligene burgenses de Sciropesberie multum grave sibi esse
quod ipsi reddant totidem geldos sicuti reddebant tempore regis *Edwardi* quamvis castellum
comitis occupaverit LI masuras et alie L masure sint vaste et XLIII
francigene burgenses teneant masuras geldantes tempore regis *Edwardi* & abbatie quam facit
ibi comes dederit ipse XXXIX burgenses olim similiter cum aliis geldantes
Inter totum sunt cc masure VII minus que non geldant

Such was the state of Shrewsbury at the time of the Norman conquest, as far as it can be collected from Domesday; and in all this, except perhaps in the Bishop of Chester being said to *possess* burgesses, we discern nothing of that degraded state in which the burghers of many other towns appear in that ancient record. Freedom was of the genius of the Saxon constitution. That people brought it with them from their German forests; and maintained it among themselves in their new settlements, to the utmost extent in which it was consistent with a state of social order. But it is certain that Domesday presents us, in innumerable places, with villeins, slaves, labourers, and, in some towns, burgesses, confined to the soil, unable to quit their tenements without the permission of their superior lord, and transmitting hereditary servitude to their unfortunate descendants. Hence it has been conceived that the whole of the native inhabitants of England did not fly before the Scandinavian intruders, into Wales, Cornwall, and Armorica; but that a numerous body remained to occupy the towns, and to till the lands, under the controul of their ferocious conquerors; and it is to these that the slavish part of the Saxon polity has been thought to apply. We see nothing, however, in the customs of Scrobbesbyrig (with the exception mentioned) inconsistent with the character of a free man; and it has therefore been inferred above, in our first chapter, with what probability the reader must decide, that the abandonment of Pengwern by the British inhabitants was total, and that they were succeeded by a colony consisting entirely of Saxon settlers.

There are grounds to believe, as will be more fully stated hereafter, that the upper part of the street called the *Wyle Cop* was the first part of the town inhabited by the Saxons; and this lends some confirmation to the legend which places Brockwell's palace on the site of the collegiate church of St. Chad. It is reasonable to suppose, that the early British settlers would seat themselves as near as they could to the royal residence; and that the Saxons would occupy the huts (for they were little better) deserted by the Britons. From the spot just mentioned, the town gradually extended itself, at first chiefly towards the north; as is marked by the respective æras of our churches: St. Alkmond's at the beginning, St. Mary's at the close, of the tenth century. From the ordinances made for the reception and entertainment of the sovereign, it is plain that the town was an occasional residence of our Anglo-Saxon monarchs, who, as a great part of their revenue consisted of payments *in kind*, corn, cattle, &c. made frequent progresses through their dominions for the purpose of consuming their rents with greater advantage[1]; nor, though the first record we have of *stone* walls belongs to the reign of Henry III., is it possible that the town should con-

---

[1] The kings of France, when they travelled, took up their residence for the time they halted, at the house of a vassal, if they had not a castle of their own in the neighbourhood. This was called the *droit de gîte*. Convents were subject to it; and it was transferred from the prince to his messengers or commissioners. A similar right enjoyed by the higher ecclesiastics was the origin of the procurations now paid by the parochial clergy to the archdeacon and bishop: and the presents made to the judges by the corporations through which they pass on their circuit, seem a remnant of the same custom, which, before the establishment of inns, was very necessary. The whole was copied from the Romans: see the commentators on Horace, S. i. 5. 46. To what an excess it was carried in the reign of Henry I. we learn from Eadmer, who informs us, that the farmers deserted their houses when they heard of the king's approach. See also in Whitaker's Hist. of Manchester, b. I. ch. viii. § 3, the provision exacted for the princes of Wales from their tenants.

SAXON PERIOD.

tinue without protection to so late a period.[1]. Defensible as the situation was by nature, especially in the former state of the Severn, it would still require the assistance of art, such art as could then be obtained. It must have been at least surrounded with a rampart of earth, when Athelstan gave it the privilege of a minter, and when Edgar or Ethelred honoured it with their residence; and that rampart, in all probability, pursued nearly the same circuit which was afterwards adopted by the *masons* of Henry III. and which the form of the ground would indeed strongly point out. This is confirmed by Domesday, which proves the town to have been nearly of its present size in the reign of the Confessor; comprising the same number of parishes, and at least one of its suburbs, the Monks or Abbey Foregate.[2] But we must not suppose that the circuit surrounded by this rampart was filled, as now, with the habitations of men closely wedged together. The 252 burgesses in the reign of the Confessor, if each of them, on an average, had a wife and three children, will not give a population of more than 1260 souls. The state of society at that time was not sufficiently matured to permit the operations of husbandry to be safely conducted at any distance from fenced towns. If a precarious harvest were sometimes snatched from the adjoining country, it was all stacked and thrashed[3] within the town; and, at the time of which we are treating, much corn was probably grown on spots now occupied by streets[4] and alleys and gardens; and we may believe that each of the Saxon burgesses had, as is still the case in some states of Germany, his little acre or field of arable land, for the supply of the immediate wants of his family, contiguous to the burgage in which he dwelt.

---

[1] Here we have another of the reveries of O. Mathews. " The towne then beinge smaller builded, and the walles verie sclender, and most parte unwalled, saveinge on the north side, as before I have said, by the Castell, the said late Bangorian brethren cast trenches aboutes the towne betwixt Seavron and the towne, to keep that the water should not waste the ground above the trenches, which they made about the water side for saveguard of the ground."

[2] Erat in suburbio civitatis parva satis ecclesia, &c. In primis vicum unum eidem ecclesiæ contiguum; qui vicus Anglice dicitur Biforieta, &c. This is also a proof that, in the Saxon times, there was a gate to defend the bridge; for *Biforieta* is *before the gate*.

[3] That the interior of fenced towns comprised much of the detail of agricultural operations, at a period considerably later than that of which we are now treating, appears from the curious account which Ordericus gives of the sacking of Breteuil, lib. xiii. p. 918. " Roger de Toney," says he, " attacked it on a sudden on the 7th of September, and threw fire into it to its utter ruin. For the threshers were threshing the harvest in the streets, and great heaps of straw and chaff lay dispersedly before the houses, as is usual at that season of the year; whence the flames quickly spread, and thus this opulent town was in an instant of time reduced to ashes."

[4] Many traces of farm-yards have been found in the heart of the town on sinking for wells; and when the foundations were dug in 1783 for the new County Hall, appearances of a great deposit of something like manure were there discovered. As late as 1538 it was agreed, at a meeting of the Corporation, that all *hedges of thornes* that staund in any strete of the town shall be removed. Corporation Minutes, 8 Oct. 30 Hen. VIII.

CHAPTER III.

OF SHREWSBURY UNDER THE NORMAN EARLS.

THE Norman invasion (A. D. 1066) produced in its consequences an almost total revolution of English property, and a temporary subversion of the English constitution. It does not, however, appear to have been the desire of William the Conqueror to carry matters with so much violence and rapacity. His claim to the Crown was not conquest, but testamentary succession; a title very much in the taste of that time, and extremely reverenced by our Saxon ancestors. It was at least better than that of the usurper whom he had conquered; and he was evidently anxious at the commencement of his reign to be considered as the peaceful successor, as he was the near kinsman, of the pious Edward; and by the lenity of his measures, to disguise from the nobles and people, that the sceptre had passed from the hand of their native sovereigns into that of an alien and foreign dynasty.

At the time of this great event, the earldom of Mercia, with extensive estates in Shropshire, was possessed by Edwin, son of Algar and grandson of Leofric and the celebrated Godiva; a youth, says our countryman Ordericus, equally eminent for the comeliness and beauty of his person and for the benignity of his disposition, greatly beloved not only by the English, but also by the Normans. He opposed the invasion of his country[1]; but, after the decisive battle of Hastings, submitted to the Conqueror, with his brother earl Morcar, Edric the Wild, and the other nobles of these parts, and was confirmed in the possession of his earldom.

Things remained in this quiet posture till the following year, 1067, when William went over in March to revisit his native dominions; nay, so well cemented was his recent usurpation, that the year was far advanced before a spirit of revolt spread through the disaffected English. Among the foremost in this rebellion were the Mercian earl and his brother. But the

[1] Dugd. Monastic. vol. i. p. 305. Edwin and Morcar were among those nobles who, after the battle of Hastings, concurred in placing Edgar Atheling on the vacant throne. Carte, i. 391. Yet in the same page he represents them as aspiring themselves to the crown, and retiring from London, with the Mercian and Northumbrian forces, in discontent; but he quotes no authority for this assertion, which is inconsistent with what he has said just before.

Conqueror, hastening his return, came back in December, whereupon Morcar fled to Ely.[1] The remainder of his story I shall give in the words of Ordericus, who was perhaps the more affected by the melancholy tale, as being himself a native of Shrewsbury.[2]

"King William," says he, "seduced by wicked counsel, injured his fair fame, by fraudulently entrapping in the isle of Ely the illustrious earl Morcar, who was neither plotting, nor suspecting any evil. This he effected in the following manner. When the king knew that the earl was in that island, he sent certain perfidious emissaries, who advised him to surrender himself to the royal authority, and assured him of a gracious reception. In these false assertions the earl simply confided, and leaving his strongholds in the isle, repaired to William, who, apprehensive lest by his influence the English might be excited to revolt, threw him into chains, and kept him in prison all his life, under the ward of Roger de Beaumont.[3]

"When the comely youth earl Edwin heard this, he burned with revenge; six months did he pass in craving assistance from Scotland, Wales, and Ireland. Thus employed, he was betrayed by three brothers, his principal confidants; and while with twenty horsemen he defended himself against the Normans, he was slain on the banks of a river, from which he could not escape, on account of a high tide. His death was lamented by men of all parties: born, as he was, of religious parents, and inclined to many virtues, notwithstanding the worldly affairs in which he was engaged; his person was remarkably handsome, and he was an especial benefactor to clerks, to monks, and to the poor. The king wept when he heard of the treason by which this Mercian earl fell, and banished from his presence the traitors who brought to him their master's head."

---

[1] According to Carte, (i. 399.) the Conqueror took the earl, and his brother Edwin, in his train to Normandy; thus, under pretence of paying them a compliment, providing for the safety of England during his absence. If this were so, it was natural that they should seize the first moment of their return to withdraw from this honourable kind of captivity.

[2] See also fragment. Cadomens. ap. Camden, Scriptt. Normann. which fragment is in truth an excerpt from the 7th book of Ordericus: a fact of which Mr. Carte seems to have been ignorant. William left orders, upon his death-bed, for the liberation of Morcar, (Carte, i. 447.) which accordingly took place; but the unfortunate earl enjoyed his liberty only for a few days. Coming over from Normandy in company with the new king, Rufus no sooner got him as far as Winchester, than he again shut him up in that city, (Carte, i. 452.) after which we hear no more of him. The Norman dungeons were genuine *oubliettes*—whoever was once shut up in them was generally forgotten ever after.

[3] Ordericus, l. iv. p. 521. The scene of his imprisonment was Normandy. The authors of the new Magna Britannia (Cambridgeshire) p. 6. seem willing to fix the capture of Morcar and death of Edwin in 1074, and quote a Cottonian MS. to that effect; but this is incompatible with our best histories, and the whole stream of contemporary authorities, none of whom propose so late a date. We have followed the chronology of Ordericus, which appears most consistent with the train of events:—the Saxon Chronicle places those transactions in 1071, and Mr. Carte, in order to retain both these dates, supposes a reconciliation of the king and the Saxon earls between their first revolt and final ruin; but for this we find no authority.

Here follows the best account we are able to give of the genealogy of our Mercian earls.

DUKE LEOFWINE.

GODWIN.	EDWIN	NORMAN, executed by Canute, 1017.	LEOFRIC, Earl of Mercia, founded the abbey of Coventry, ob. 1057. Descended from Leofric, Earl of Mercia under Ethelbald.	GODEVA, daughter of Thorold, Sheriff of Lincoln.	A daughter, mother of Leofric, abbot of Burgh (i.e. Peterborough), Burton, Coventry, Crowland and Thorney.
		HENRY DE TEMPLE, *said to* be ancestor of that family. Collins.	ÆLFGAR, Earl of Mercia, to whom, in 1051, was granted Harold's earldom. Chron. Sax. sub ann. ob. 1059.	According to Ordericus, ÆLFGAR's wife must have been GODEVA.*	
		EDWIN, Earl of Mercia.	MORCAR, elected Earl of Northumberland in 1064 by the people, on the expulsion of Tostig. Sax. Chron.	EDGITHA, or ALDIT, wife of Griffith ap Llewelin, Prince of Wales, and of Harold, King of England.†	

* But in Domesday we read of ÆLVEVA comitissa mater Morcari.
† Ingulphus makes Lucy the Countess the only daughter of Earl Ælfgar. Gale's Scriptores, vol. ii. p. 66. She was wife of Ivo Taillebois, (Kelham on Domesday, p. 123.) 2dly, of Roger de Romara, and 3dly, of Ranulph, Earl of Chester. See Dugdale Warw. in Coventry.

Hereward, Lord of Brunne in Lincolnshire, who opposed the Conqueror, and left an only child, the wife of Hugh de Evermont, Lord of Deeping, is by Mr. Kelham (on Domesday, p. 230) made a son of Earl Leofric: but it is evident from Ingulphus (p. 67) that the Leofric, father of Hereward, was a different person.

The death of Edwin rather excited than checked the spirit of revolt among the Welsh. The British *kings*, as all contemporary authorities invariably style them, did not cease, from the time when they were so unjustly bereaved of the fertile plain of Shropshire, to regard it with a longing eye, and with a secret determination to seize the first favourable opportunity of regaining it. With this view, they appear to have been ready to join the Danes in the expulsion of the Saxons, and now to have entered into an alliance with these latter, to drive out the Normans. Not from any real good will for either of the contending parties, but that they hoped, in the struggle, to find some means of ridding their country of both these intruders. In the same year, a powerful Saxon thane who has been mentioned already, Edric the Forester[1], nephew of the celebrated Edric

---

[1] He is called in Latin *Sylvaticus*, and thence, by corruption, the *Savage* and the *Wild*—names, we presume, which he did not acquire till after his revolt: though he is enumerated by Ordericus (lib. iv. init.) under the name of Edric Guilda, among the principal nobles who swore allegiance to William immediately after his coronation. In the first rebellion, however, (that in Yorkshire,) "Many of the English," says the historian, "took up their abode in tents, disdaining to reside in houses, lest they should thereby be relaxed," and so, we suppose, the less able to resist the French invaders, "whence some of them received from the Normans the appellation of *men of the woods:*"—in tabernaculis morabantur; in domibus, ne mollescerent, requiescere dedignabantur: unde quidam eorum à Normannis *Sylvatici* cognominabantur. Lib. iv. p. 511. The ancient family of *Weld*, formerly seated at Willey in this county, and still remaining at Lulworth in Dorsetshire, conceive themselves to be descended from this Wild Edric.

NORMAN PERIOD.

Streon[1], and possessed of an immense estate in Shropshire, undismayed by the defeat of Edwin, rose against the Normans, and called in the assistance of the Welsh.

Griffith ap Llewellin, king of North Wales, had lately been slain (it was in 1063) by the brothers Tosti and Harold, the last of whom soon after became the husband of Griffith's widow Agatha, sister of Edwin and Morcar, the lamented earls of Mercia. When, therefore, the Welsh prince Bleddyn ap Cynfyn, uterine brother of Griffith[2], in compliance with the invitation of Edric, entered Shropshire with an hostile army, (as he did, in conjunction with Riwallon, prince of Powis,) he probably preferred advancing the claim of his nephew, the infant son of Griffith, as heir of the Mercian earls, to a revival of those pretensions of his British ancestors, which would have awakened the jealousy of his Saxon confederates. However this be, it is certain from Ordericus, that, in the general defection from the Conqueror in 1068, the natives of Wales and Cheshire laid siege to the king's castle at Scrobesbury[3], being assisted by the townsmen, the powerful and warlike Edric Wild, and "other fierce Englishmen." The king dispatched two earls, William and Brienn, to the relief of the castle; but before they could arrive, the rebels had departed, having burned the town. In revenge for this insult, the king left York, where he had been keeping his Christmas, and marched his army early in the year 1069[4] against these invaders, *et Merciorum regione*, says Ordericus, *motus hostiles vi regia compescuit*: and if he ever honoured Shrewsbury with a visit, as one old memoir of suspicious authority[5] says he did, it was probably on this occasion.

Shropshire thus settled, and its ample domains thrown into the hands of the Crown by the death of Edwin, and the rebellion of his numerous adherents, William determined to abolish the high-sounding and invidious title of earl of Mercia; but conferred the earldom of Shrewsbury upon his kinsman Roger de Montgomery, viscount of Ozyme, (now Hiesmes,)

---

[1] Carte, i. 393, calls him great nephew of Streona, and lord of Wigmore; but at p. 401, represents him as here in the text, viz. son of Alfric brother of Edric Streon; and he is described in the same terms on a monument at Lulworth, where, however, Streon is written Stretton.

[2] Yet Carte, i. 403, represents Bleddyn as nephew to Edwin: a proof that the most accurate historian may occasionally stumble in minor points.

[3] Orderic. l. iv. p. 514. The reader is desired to note this expression, *the king's castle*, as it proves Shrewsbury to have been in the hands of the Crown at this time, and shews the existence of a fortress here anterior to that erected by our first Norman earl. And this seems to be a proof that the chronology of Ordericus is correct, and that of Mr. Carte erroneous; for if the estates of Edwin earl of Mercia, were not forfeited till 1071, as, according to him, they were not, Shrewsbury could not have been a royal castle in 1068.

[4] P. 516. Carte places this expedition of the king's from York in the spring of 1070 : vol. i. p. 409.

[5] An old French Chronicle of the Fitz Warins (in Ashmole Libr. MSS. Dugdale, vol. xxxix.) has it thus: In tempore Oweyn Gwyned, Prince de Gales, vaylant et bon guerrieur qui gasta tout la Marche, de Cestre al Mont Gilbert, le roy Willin Bastard vient a Salopbury et don a Roger de Belisme la comte de Salopbur, &c. Carte (i. 398.) speaks of his making a progress into the provinces of the Mercians and West Saxons, in the interval between his coronation and his first voyage to Normandy after that ceremony.

VOL. I.   G

who, having just visited England for the first time in the train of his sovereign, had recently been gratified with the earldoms of Chichester[1] and Arundel.

Richard I. duke of Normandy, (grandson to Rollo, and great grandfather to William the Conqueror,) married Gunnora, sister of Herfastus the Dane, on whose grandson William Fitz Osberne, his kinsman the Conqueror conferred the earldom of Hereford. Wevia, another of the sisters of Herfast, became the wife of Turolf, lord of Pontaudemer, son of Torf the Rich, and brother of Turchetil, ancestor of the ancient family of Harcourt. By this lady, besides five sons, (one of whom, Humphrey de Vetulis, was progenitor of the old lords of Leicester and Mellent,) Turolf had issue a daughter, Joscelina, who married Hugh de Montgomery, lord of the Norman town of that name. Roger de Montgomery, the son of this marriage, was thus allied in blood to some of the first families in Normandy, as well as to its duke the Bastard William. According to William Gemeticensis, or de Jumieges, Roger had made himself extremely obnoxious to the regents of the duchy during the minority of that prince; and had, for his perfidy, been driven into banishment; during which time he took up his residence at Paris. He became, however, an early and an unvaried favourite of his sovereign. We are told that in the war which that duke, before he mounted the English throne, carried on with Geoffrey Martel, count of Anjou, he laid siege to Damfront; and having received information that the count was marching to the relief of the place, he sent Roger de Montgomery and William Fitz Osbern to reconnoitre. These two messengers, says Malmsbury, "with the alacrity natural to youth," speedily advanced many miles, till they came up with the count, to whom they made such a report of the forces of their master, that the count thought proper to retire[2]. These are the only material facts respecting the viscount of Ozyme, during the time that the duke of Normandy was content with his hereditary dominions. But it is plain that he was then honoured with a large share of his master's confidence, since he was one of the first to whom the resolution of invading this country was disclosed; and, though not engaged in active warfare, or in the decisive battle of Senlac[3], yet he was associated with the duchess

---

[1] Ordericus has it Cestriam; but this is certainly an error either of his own or his editor: most likely the latter.

[2] The following passage is curious and characteristic. The historian having mentioned the vainglorious boasting of the count to Montgomery and Fitz Osbern,—ostensurum mundo quàm praestet in armis Andegavensis Normanno,—adds,—Simul, eximia arrogantia colorem equi sui, et armorum insignia, quæ habiturus sit, insinuat : (Will. Malmsbur. de Gestis Regum, lib. iii. p. 54:) which appears to have been meant as a challenge to the duke:—"I shall be mounted on a horse of such a colour, and with such and such devices on my shield, if he has a mind to attack me." This has been quoted as a proof of the use of armorial bearings in the times preceding the Conquest; which, however, it is plain from the Baieux tapestry, were not then known.

[3] So Ordericus always terms the battle of Hastings. Camden (in Sussex) says the place was called Epiton. But the greatest writers are not infallible, which should teach indulgence to the readers of inferior ones. The words of Ordericus are, in

Matilda, in the more important and very anxious charge of providing for the safety of Normandy, during the absence of its prince on the English expedition. On king William's return to England in December, 1067, he was for the first time accompanied by the viscount, our future earl; *quem tutorem Normanniæ, dum ad bellum transmarinum proficisceretur, cum sua conjuge dimiserat*[1].

His remuneration was equal to the importance of his services; none of the Conqueror's followers reaped a larger share of territory. To the earldoms of Arundel and Chichester, with large possessions at Cilgarran in Pembrokeshire and elsewhere, was added a grant of the town of Shrewsbury, the entire earldom, and all the demesne of the Saxon monarchs, with certain manors thereunto appertaining[2]; producing a revenue equal in effect to at least 60,000*l.* at the present day; besides which he enjoyed the feudal supremacy of nearly the whole of Shropshire, which he parcelled out among his own dependants, and had permission to seize all the territory which he could win from the Welsh by the sword. Ordericus thus records the donation of Salop, under the year 1070: "King William gave to Roger de Montgomery, first the castle of Arundel and city of Chichester; to which he afterwards added the county[3] of Schrobesbury, which is placed on a hill above the river Severn. This earl was wise, and moderate, and a lover of justice, and delighted in the company of wise and modest persons. He long retained in his service three wise clerks, Godebald, Odelerius[4], and Herbert, by whose

epitumio Senlac, vii. 659. *Epitumium* is a field. *Senlac* is expounded *Sangue lac*, a *field of blood;* but the scene of this famous contest had borne the name long before, " antiquitus vocabatur," (id. l. iii.) so that the etymology must be sought elsewhere. William of Jumieges (vii. 35) and after him Mr. Carte (i. 388) represent our earl as the commander of one of the three columns of the Norman army in that battle, and in this erroneous statement most of our historians concur: but at p. 401, Mr. Carte, forgetting what he had written before, describes him as being then governor of Normandy, which was the fact.

[1] Ord. l. iv. p. 509.

[2] Earl Roger kept in his own hands the manors of Baschurch, *Berwick*, Bolbec, Chetton, Chirbury, Corfton, *Culmington*, Cundover, Doddington, Donnington, Eardington, Edgemond, Ercall, Ellesmere, Ford, Hodnet, *Lidham, Loppington,* Morville, Ness, Quatford, *Sireton* (perhaps Scifton), Stottesden, Stretton, Tong, Wellington, Whittington, and Wrockwardine, besides eleven others not specified; the hundreds of Comestane, Patinton, Witetre, and Mersete, the castle and territory of Montgomery, and the district of Yale. His demesne, or land kept in his own occupation, was 132 carucates, or 15,640 acres, and this was tilled without any expense to himself, as his villeins held 213 carucates, or 25,560 acres, on the tenure of cultivating his land for him. The places printed in italics were part of the forfeiture of Edric Savage, and may have descended to him from the dukes of Mercia. The shortest way of stating the rest of Roger's vast property in Shropshire, is to observe, that of 406 manors, if we have counted them rightly, into which the property of the county in lay hands was divided, all but 49 were holden under him.

[3] Comitatum Scrobesburiæ. *County* has acquired in our language a sense so peculiarly restricted to a certain local district, that we do not readily conceive of it as a title of dignity, though it is indeed exactly synonymous with *earldom.* But the earldom of *Shrewsbury* would not convey an adequate idea of the extent of the Conqueror's grant to his kinsman Roger—which was the earldom of that county of which Shrewsbury was the capital: *Shrewsbury-shire*, by contraction, *Shropshire.*

[4] Father of the historian Ordericus. Herbert was the son of Helgot, a companion of the Conqueror, from whom Castle Holgate, in Corvedale, derives its name. The memory of the third of these clerks is retained in the neighbouring village of Preston Gubbals, i. e. the *priest's town* of *Godebald.*

sage advice he directed his measures. To Warin the Bald, a man of low stature, but lofty courage, he gave Aimeria his niece, and the government (*presidatum*) of Scrobesbury: by this Warin he bravely repulsed the Welsh and his other foes, and quieted the whole province committed to him. He set over his county William surnamed Pantulf, Picold, Corbat, with his sons Roger and Rodbert, and other faithful and valiant men; by whose abilities and courage being kindly assisted, he flourished greatly among the greatest nobles."

The state affected by the great Norman lords is well known. When released from their attendance in the king's court, they retired to courts of their own, where they in their turn were surrounded by a numerous train of vassals[1], chiefly their own countrymen; the English now experiencing in their own case the oppressions which they had exercised five centuries before upon the Britons. The following passages of Domesday refer to the condition of Shrewsbury[2] at the period in question. " In the year preceding this survey, earl Roger received a rent of 40*l*. from the town." (This was 10*l*. more than the burgesses had paid to the Confessor, while their means of payment were diminished, as appears from the next extract.) " The Saxon burgesses complain that they pay the same danegeld as they did in king Edward's days, although the castle erected by the earl occupies the site of fifty-one houses, while fifty houses lie waste, and forty-three, which paid to the taxes at that time, are now holden by Normans. Besides which, the earl himself has given thirty-nine burgesses to his Abbey, who.

---

[1] A writer in Mad. de Sevigné's Letters speaks of Le goût des grands seigneurs du bon vieux temps, qui se trouvoient fort bien chez eux, et dont l'ambition se trouvoit bornée à demeurer maîtres des grandes possessions que leurs pères leur avoient laissées. Ils alloient par respect visiter leur souverain: mais leur cour faite, et ce devoir rendu, ils n'étoient pas fâches de se trouver souverains eux-mêmes, et de revenir représenter à leur tour.—vol. viii. lett. 104.

[2] Written in that record, *Sciropesberie*. Though Rollo brought with him from Scandinavia in 876 no other language than one cognate to the Saxon, yet it had in seventy years so completely yielded to the French, that his son William was obliged to send *his* son to Bayeux to learn the speech of his grandfather. At the time of Domesday, a Norman scribe was, we see, unable to pronounce the harsh Saxon *Scrob*, without the interposition of a vowel, and the change of a consonant; and thus to turn it into *Scirop*, of which traces continue in the name of the county, borrowed, as most of the shires were, from the county town: originally Scrobbes-byrigscire, and now, by contraction, Shropshire. *R.* as is well known, is a letter insurmountable by many organs, and in all languages has been occasionally exchanged for *L*. Hence arose a farther corruption of our Saxon name, which, from Sciropesberie became *Salopesberie*, of which the first instance which we have seen is on the Pipe rolls of 2 Henry I. Such seems the best opinion of the origin of the name Salop; nor is that of Mr. Baxter very dissimilar, p. 244. However, we must not omit other conjectures, among which the reader will select which he prefers. *Sel*, in Saxon, is *good*; *seal* is a *willow*; *hope*, the *side of a hill* (Camden's Britannia, p. 138): thus *sel hope*, or *seal hope*, may be the *pleasant* or the *willowed side of a hill*. Mr. Pegge has yet another etymology. *Selwig* is, according to him, an *alder*; this in Saxon characters, is Selpiȝ. The Norman scribes mistaking, he says, the *p* for p, read it *Selpig*: as from WILLEM, stamped on the early English coins, PILLEM, has been formed in his opinion our familiar appellation Bill, in Staffordshire, Pill. Such is the conjecture of the venerable rector of Whittington in a letter dated Nov. 3, 1786, and addressed to the late Rev. Charles Newling, formerly the respected head-master of our Free Grammar School. Leland (Collect. iii. 95) writes our town Salæp, perhaps to bring it nearer (as he was stored with classical literature) to the Apulian Salapia, which so bravely resisted (Livy xxvii. 28) the assaults of the Carthaginian invader.

are, therefore, freed from the tax; and there are now two hundred houses, save seven[1] which pay nothing."

The burgesses were ruled by an officer called in Latin *præpositus*. This is the word which constantly represents the Saxon *gerefa*. But the Norman præpositus had little in common with that ancient English magistrate. The latter was judge of his district, and bound to decide according to law[2]; but the Norman præpositus, which we may best render *provost*, was little more than a collector of rents; who extorted as much as he could for his patron, and cared as little as he might for the tenants: and thus the honoured name gerefa, the very same with the lofty German *grave*, sinking into *greffier*, the clerk of any petty town, and into *reve*, the steward of any little manor, the caustic remark of the satirist[3] was literally verified in a way he could never have foreseen.

One of the first works commenced at Shrewsbury by the earl, was the construction of a stately castle, or rather the enlargement of a smaller one, on that narrow isthmus which commands the only passage through which the town can be approached by land. This was a measure of immediate necessity, not only to curb the reluctant spirit of the English, but also to restrain the hostile incursions of the Welsh. As the earl was obliged to be frequently absent from Shropshire, he appointed as his vicecomes[4], or substitute, the above-mentioned Warin, who, however, had deceased without children, at least without male issue, before the compilation of Domesday, and was succeeded in that honourable office by his brother Reginald, or Rainald.

The subsequent history of Shrewsbury during this period is intimately connected with that of its earls, of whom we have the most circumstantial

---

[1] The number of void houses enumerated above amounts only to 183, which is 200 save 17: we cannot suppose that the compilers of Domesday were unable to count; so that there must have been ten houses exempt from the danegeld on some other ground not specified. The oppression exercised by the Norman earl over the English burgesses of Shrewsbury was exactly the same as that which the author of *The Estate of English Fugitives* relates of Philip II. in the Low Countries: " But which is most beyond reason, whereas, within the townes manye of the houses lye vacant and unhired, yet the owners of them are taxed according to the value in which they were wont to be rented: insomuch, that in Antwarpe and other townes, it is a matter very usual for men to disclaime and quite theyr owne houses."

Tasso says the same of the Saracen king of Jerusalem:
"Scemo i publici pesi a suoi pagani,
Ma piu gravonne i miseri Christiani."—i. 84.

[2] Wilkins, p. 48.

[3] Juvenal, to mark the slavish awe in which the citizens of Rome were kept by the tyrant Domitian, says that the præfects were become nothing more than *bailiffs*:—attonitæ positus modo *villicus* urbi. iv. 77.

[4] As this word will frequently occur during the remainder of this and the succeeding chapter, it may here be stated, that throughout the Norman period, the word *vicecomes* is rendered by *vice-count*, rather than by *sheriff*, because the latter term denotes the Saxon officer, the *shire-reeve*; whereas the vice-count was the deputy of the earl.

account in the writings of our countryman Ordericus; and as his work has only once been printed, in a large and costly folio of rare occurrence, (the Normannici Scriptores of Du Chesne,) we hope not to trespass too much on the patience of our reader, if we exhibit their eventful story in the words of that intelligent monk, occasionally interspersing a few particulars from other original documents.

And first, of the period before the Conquest: he writes that Roger de Montgomery, then viscount of Oxyma, was incited by the example of the family of Grentesmesnil[1], to turn "a religious house, which his father Hugh had erected at Troarne for twelve canons, into an abbey for monks, on account of the *gulosity*, lust, and secularity of the canons[2]." Roger married Mabil, daughter of William de Belesme[3], called also William Talvace[4]: she was, says the monk of Uticum, "very powerful and mercenary, cunning, loquacious, and excessively cruel, *multum potens et secularis, callida et loquax, nimium crudelis*. However, she much loved the man of God, Theodoric abbot of Uticum, and harsh as she was to other religions, obeyed him in many things; and caused her eldest son, Robert de Belesme, whose cruelty hath in these our days raged against the wretched people, to be baptized by him and other monks residing at Sagium[5]," (Seez.)

The violent aversion which this lady entertained towards the monks of Uticum, appears from an anecdote related by Ordericus in the following page. "Herself," he says, "and her father bore an especial hatred to the family of Geroy, patrons of the abbey; yet, because her husband Roger de Montgomery loved and protected the monks, she did not venture to attack them with open violence, but oppressed them by frequent visits, accompanied by a numerous guard. One day (it must have been in 1067) when she came with a retinue of a hundred knights, the abbot, Theodoric, rebuked her for thus devouring the substance of his brethren, and told her,

---

Selden incontrovertibly proves that the Norman earl was in effect his own shire-reeve. Tit. Hen. pt. ii. c. 5. § 12. p. 675.

[1] This family had, in 1050, restored the abbey of St. Ebrulfus of Uticum, and our historian was a monk of that abbey.

[2] Lib. iii. p. 642.

[3] Belesme is a city in the Upper Perche, on the side of Normandy and Maine. There seems to have been another family of Belesme; for Ordericus, under the year 1136, mentions Robert de Belesme, a French knight, as engaged on the side of Robert de Toeni in a petty warfare, exercised by him against Gualeran and Robert, earls of Mellent and Leicester, l. xiii. p. 905. He is also mentioned at p. 908, where he is styled Robert de Belesme who was called Poardus, and was taken prisoner by these earls, into whose service he appears afterwards to have entered; for in 1141, this Robert took Richier de l'Aigle prisoner, and confined him in Breteuil till Robert earl of Leicester released him. Robert de Belesme soon after experienced the like fate, together with Maurice his brother. l. xiii. p. 923.

[4] Ordericus, in lib. viii. p. 707, speaking of Robert de Belesme, son of this Mabil, says, that on account of his hard-heartedness he was justly called *Talvace*. Mr. Lloyd, in his MS. Hist. of Shropshire, tells us, that Talvace signifies a *large shield*; we suspect, however, that he was thinking of *Paroce*, which *has* that signification: and which Du Cange (v. Pavisarii) derives from the Welsh *Pafais, scuta grandiora*. The first syllable of Talvace one might suppose to be derived from *talliare*, to cut.

[5] Page 470.

she would sorely rue the consequences; accordingly, the same night she was seized with a severe distemper *(passio)*, and immediately fled from the estates of St. Ebrulf, in terror. In her flight she passed by the house of a burgess, one of whose children, a female infant at the breast, she seized, and put its mouth to her cheek, in which the disease was principally seated. The poor child sucked the part, and quickly died. Mabil lived near fifteen years after this, but never set her foot at Uticum more: and settled the cell of St. Martin upon it, from regard for abbot Theodoric."

In the disputes which arose in 1063 between duke William and his nobles, we are told by our monk, that Roger de Montgomery and Mabil his wife rejoiced much, and, " by flattering the duke, excited him to still greater indignation, and gained his favours to themselves." Under the next year he tells us how this lady attempted to poison Ernald de Escalfoio, by which means, without intending it[1], she caused the death of Gislebert, the only brother of her husband, a young man of much honour and knightly prowess—" *equestris probitatis.*"

We have spoken of Roger's first visit to England in 1067, and of his acquisition of Shrewsbury in 1070: and this may be the proper place to relate what little is known of his conquests in Wales. Our two first princes of the Norman race permitted their subjects, as has been intimated above, to levy war, at discretion, on the natives of that country; and to appropriate to themselves, in full regality, whatever they could thus acquire. This strange policy led to the erection of the Marcher lordships, that is, of more than an hundred petty sovereignties, and thus became the fruitful parent of innumerable disorders, till their suppression in the reign of Henry VIII. The earl of Shrewsbury was not the last to avail himself of this permission; he subdued a large portion of the territory still remaining to the princes of Powis, but subsequently from himself denominated the County of Montgomery, and he built the town of that name, which the Welsh call Tre Valdwin, from Baldwin, his lieutenant.[2]

In proceeding with the biography of earl Roger, it is necessary to interweave some memoirs of his eldest son Robert, (called after his maternal

---

[1] This may remind the reader of the honest Parisian, whom Louis XI., *without intending* it, ordered to be tied in a sack, and drowned in the Seine! Are we as thankful as we should be, for a state of society in which such enormities cannot be practised, whether by design or negligence?

[2] Of this Baldwin we can find nothing in our histories, though he was evidently a person of distinction: But the manor of Hodnet was holden by the service of being seneschal, or steward, of the honour of Montgomery; and the lord of that manor was provided at the cost of the earl, with a dwelling-house within the ballium of Montgomery castle, for himself, his esquires and pages, his lady and her female attendants. This establishes a connexion between the town of Montgomery and Hodnet. Now the Christian name of Baldwin was used by many generations of the family of Hodnet: from the combination of which facts it is, we think, perfectly clear, that the Baldwin who gave its Welsh name to Montgomery, was the progenitor of that ancient line of the Hodnets, which has descended, by heirs general, through the Ludlows and Vernons, to Richard Heber, Esq. M. P. for the University of Oxford, now lord of the manor of Hodnet, by lineal descent from the lieutenant of Roger de Montgomery.

ancestry, De Belesme) : as the turbulent and intriguing character of that young nobleman displayed itself in the life-time of his father, and indeed at a very early period. In 1079, when Robert, called Curthose[1], or Gambaron, the Conqueror's eldest son, revolted from his father, Robert de Belesme took part with the rebellious prince, and invited his brother-in-law, Hugh de Novo Castello, to follow his example[2]. In consequence of this, his lands were confiscated[3], but were restored, it may be presumed, on that reconciliation of the king and duke, to which earl Roger of Shrewsbury was so instrumental[4]. At the time of the Conqueror's death, this young nobleman was hastening to court to confer with him respecting certain matters of importance; on his arrival at the entrance of Brionne, the news reached him. " Hereupon he immediately turned his horse's head, and proceeded to Alençon, from which he expelled the king's garrison. The like he did at Belesme, and all his other castles ; and not only in his own towns, but likewise in those of his neighbours, with whom he disdained to be upon terms of equality; either subjecting them to his power by pouring in troops of his own, or dismantling them, to prevent any future resistance to his commands."[5]

On the Conqueror's death, the earl of Shrewsbury, and this his eldest son, espoused the pretensions of Robert Curthose to the vacant throne[6]; Malmsbury[7] suggests that those who adopted this party, among whom were the bishop of Baieux, uncle of the competitors, were chiefly induced by an apprehension of the fierce temper of William Rufus, which, as the historian asserts, was strongly depicted in his countenance. The bishop of Worcester, on the other hand, respected the testamentary title of Rufus, to whom the deceased sovereign had bequeathed the English sceptre. Hereupon our earl took up arms to reduce that city to the obedience of Curthose[8]. He assembled his powerful neighbours and great vassals, Bernard de Nefmarch, Roger de Laci, Ralph de Mortimer: he even called in the assistance of the Welsh; and marching from Scrobesbury, at the head of this ill-assorted army, laid waste the whole of Worcestershire, to the gates of its capital, with fire and sword. The bishop commanded in the castle: the royal forces were few in number, but they relied with confidence on the sanctity of their leader, the holy Wulstan, and the thunders of excommunication which, in his spiritual character, he launched against the impious invaders of his episcopal estates[9]. We need not therefore wonder, if, in

---

[1] Camden tells us, that this young prince received the first of these appellations " from his using *short hose*, and shewing the use of them to the English." Remains, p. 251. But he had little to do with the English, and we know from Ordericus and Malmsbury, that he was so called by his father, because he was short and fat. Gambaron is much the same: from *Gamba*, base Latin for a *leg*.

[2] Orderic. l. iv. p. 546.
[3] Carte, i. 433.
[4] Ibid. 434.
[5] Orderic. l. viii. p. 666.
[6] Idem, l. viii. p. 668.
[7] De Gestis Regum, l. iv. p. 120.
[8] Id. de Gestis Pontif. l. iv. p. 281.
[9] Florent. Wigorn. sub ann. 1088. Bromton, p. 598.

NORMAN PERIOD.

such an age, the bishop's troops routed their enemies with ease: and Malmsbury asserts, though he owns that he does not expect to be believed, that "certain" of our earl's followers were miraculously struck with blindness.

The result of this expedition was so little creditable to Roger de Montgomery, that Ordericus has omitted all mention of it; but the testimony of Malmsbury and the other authorities quoted, suffice to establish its general truth, and it is certain that our earl soon saw cause to alter his opinion concerning the title of Rufus. Matthew Paris has a story, that the king won him over by an offer which he made as they were riding out together, that he would resign his pretensions to the crown, if that measure were judged expedient by himself and the other persons under whose directions the late king, his father, had commanded him to act[1]. However this be, when the contending parties flew to arms, and Rufus actually besieged his uncle the bishop of Baieux and Robert de Belesme, in Rochester castle, in the summer of 1088, the earl of Shrewsbury adopted a measure which was calculated to secure his possessions, whatever might be the event of the struggle: he joined with the king to besiege his own son[2], though, as the historian informs us, he endeavoured clandestinely to afford the besieged all the succour in his power[3]. Ordericus mentions certain "*ancient barons*," whose temporary defection the king was content to overlook, after his victory over the revolters, through a memory of their past services; and there can be no doubt that the earl of Shrewsbury was one of that number. His son had also, before the end of the autumn of the same year, made his peace with the king; as we find him returning into Normandy at that time, in company with prince Henry, afterwards king Henry I.[4], to whose good offices this reconciliation is attributed. This return of Robert de Belesme with prince Henry excited the jealousy of the Norman duke, Robert Curthose; he conceived that they came over with intentions unfavourable to him; accordingly, as they were landing from their vessel, they were seized and thrown into prison. An act so violent brought over to Normandy the earl of Shrewsbury, and induced him to garrison all his fortresses against the duke[5].

How great was the influence of this powerful family in that duchy, may be collected from the harangue which Ordericus puts into the mouth of Odo, bishop of Baieux, upon this occasion. The earl of Shrewsbury having, as we have observed, set himself in a hostile posture to rescue his

---

[1] Sub ann. 1088.
[2] This has been a common expedient of crafty politicians in all ages. Lord Clarendon says of the earl of Northampton, "he did not, like some other men, who warily distributed their families on both sides, one son to serve the king, while this father, or another son, engaged as far for the parliament; but this earl entirely dedicated all his children to the (king's) quarrel." ii. 151.
[3] P. 667.
[4] P. 672, and Carte, i. 459.
[5] Id. p. 673.

son from captivity, the warlike prelate endeavours to rouse the duke, his indolent nephew, to attack his contumacious vassal, and to drive him and his sons out of the country. " Now is the time," says he, " to get rid of all the Talvaces, that restless and mischievous race, none of whom has died the death of other men; if you lose the present opportunity, in vain will you look for another; they possess strong castles, Belesme, Luberçon, Axey, Alençon, Damfront, St. Cenery (Cenericum), Roche de Jalgey, Mamercies, Junac, and many others, proudly erected by William de Belesme, Robert, Ivo, Warin, and others their successors, or wrested by force or fraud from the lawful owners, and which you may obtain, if you emulate the prowess of your valiant sire. That puissant monarch held these places to the day of his death; nor was it till after that event, that Robert de Belesme, whom you now keep in chains, made himself master of those important fortresses[1]."

Suggestions such as these roused, for a time, the sluggish nature of Curthose: after a successful expedition into Maine, he directed his arms against the castle of St. Cenery, the asylum of Robert's family. The place made a stout resistance, till famine compelled the governor to surrender. The enraged duke rewarded his fidelity to his trust by putting out his eyes; and many of the garrison were punished with loss of limbs for their resistance to their prince. This terrible example operated to the speedy surrender[2] of Alençon, Belesme, and several other fortresses. Fortunately for the family of Montgomery, the duke grew tired of pursuing his successes, and accepted the proposals of the earl of Shrewsbury for a pacification, and for the release of his captive son.

The first earl of Shrewsbury survived the Conqueror six years, and dying[3] on the 6th of the calends of August (17 July) 1094, was honourably interred, says Ordericus, in the new church, which he had founded at Shrewsbury, between two altars[4].

---

[1] Ordericus (l. viii. p. 691) mentions other castles erected by Robert de Belesme at Fourches and Chateau Guntier.

[2] Carte only says, they were ready to surrender at the first summons. i. 460.

[3] Doctor Powell, from the Welsh Chronicles, strangely relates that he was killed in a skirmish near Caerdiff; and Mr. Jones (Hist. Brecknock. v. i. p. 94) adopts the same tale. But the Welsh Chronicles are too often unworthy of any regard, when they treat of English affairs; and are not always safe guides in the transactions of their own principality. If the earl of Shrewsbury had been thus slain, Ordericus could not have been ignorant of it; but he died peaceably in his bed, being previously, according to the usual superstition of his age, shorn a monk of his own foundation, and thus placing himself in the number of those, who, in the words of our great poet,

"to be sure of Paradise,
Dying, put on the weeds of Dominic,
Or in Franciscan think to pass disguised."
Par. Lost, iii. 480.

[4] P. 80, n. Inter duo altaria, i. e. between *the* two altars, viz. behind the high altar and before that of our Lady: for abbot Henry, about the year 1228, orders certain lights to be burned *in the Lady chapel, before the founder's tomb*, at his anniversary. See the account of the Abbey. It need not be observed that the chapel of the Virgin was in almost all cases immediately behind the high altar.

NORMAN PERIOD. 45

In 1623, when the heralds came to Shrewsbury, in the course of their visitation, they found, among the ruins of the Abbey-church, a mutilated figure of a warrior: of which a better idea will be derived from the engraving here annexed, than from any description that could be made of it. As far as can be judged from its remains, it resembles some of the cumbent images in the ante-chapel of the Temple church, London; and the earliest date that can be assigned to it is the reign of King John. If, therefore, it was intended to represent the great earl of Shrewsbury, it must have been executed long after his decease; a case which is not without a parallel, in the monumental effigy of his contemporary Robert Curthose, still remaining in the cathedral of Gloucester. Whether, in thus appropriating the figure before us, the heralds were assisted by any consideration of the spot where it was found, cannot now be known: though it is highly probable that in 1623 the situation of the two altars might not be forgotten. Certain it is that those officers considered it to be the cumbent figure of the Norman earl, and as such ordered it to be set up within the Abbey-church, where it lay north and south under the eastern window of the south aisle, till 1807, when, with greater attention to ancient usage, it was placed at right angles to its former position, on a spot immediately contiguous.

In Ormerod's History of Cheshire, vol. i. p. 242, is a strange paper, purporting to be a charter (we presume the translation of one) from "Roger Beleme, erle of Shroesbury," granting to his minstrel (who, it seems, had been the means of curing him of his leprosy[1], by

[1] The legend is imagined in the true style of those childish compositions. The candle mentioned in the text kindled of its own accord at the birth of our Saviour, and an angel carried it through the air to "Araske," where it continued to burn ever since without wasting, "and so shall to the day of doom." A vision having revealed to the earl of Shrewsbury that some of this wax would cure his leprosy, he imparted this intelligence to his council, by whose advice he repaired to Araske with twelve attendants. There they continued in prayer forty days, and every third day had a sight of the candle, but at a great distance from them. Hence they inferred that it was withholden on account of the vicious life of some of their company: they determined therefore that each of them should pray one day by himself: and when it came to the minstrel's turn, the candle descended to him, within the length of a lance, and a drop of the wax fell on his right hand, which he put into a silver bottle, and before he could take it to the earl, it had filled the whole vessel. It is needless to add, that the cure was

procuring from heaven some wax of a candle, "which was with our Lady, Christys Moder, in Bedeleme[1], at the birthe of our blessed Lord,") that he might have a taper always burning at Shrewsbury, and that every minstrel resident in Shropshire should repair to Shrewsbury on St. Peter's day, to elect a master, who should take an oath before the earl of Shrewsbury or his assigns " treuly to rewle his brothern after the law of armes:" every such minstrel to pay 4d. to the master: and every minstrel sojourning in the county to pay the same sum, if he gained so much by his instrument: and the said earl states himself to have granted that the light should remain in the church of "St. Alkunde," and in the Abbey of Shrewsbury. This charter, which for the clumsiness of its forgery may vie with Ireland's Shakspeare, was confirmed at Shrewsbury on St. Matthew's day, 23 Hen. VI. by John, earl of Shrewsbury and Weysford, lord Talbot and Furnyvale.

———

Some account has already been given of the earl's first wife, the countess Mabil. The manner of her death strongly paints the ferocious character of the age: it happened in the year 1082. She had taken from one Hugh a castle situate on the rock of Jalgey, thus depriving him unjustly of his hereditary property. In revenge for this violent seizure, Hugh, summoning to his assistance his three brothers, stout and valiant knights, approached the countess's chamber by night, in the town of Buris, on the river Diva, cut off her head as she was taking her repose on a couch after the refreshment of the bath; and in the frenzy of their rage hacked the mangled corpse in pieces. "Thus," says Ordericus, "did that sanguinary woman, stained with the blood of so many victims, and fattening on the spoils of the nobles whom she had, by her oppressions, reduced to beggary, meet with the due recompense of her crimes. The murderers fled into Apulia[2], leaving behind

---

immediately effected: but it is to be lamented, that as soon as the wax had accomplished its purpose, the remainder vanished away.

We are ignorant of the situation of Araske; and perhaps the legendist was equally so. On a story which does not contain a syllable of truth (for the earl's faithful historian Ordericus would never have omitted his leprosy, if it had existed, or the cure, which was so much to his own taste) it is unnecessary to dwell a moment: but the fabulist having assigned this important office to a *minstrel*, is at least some proof, that that profession had not sunk in the reign of Henry VI. (when we presume the whole narrative was invented) to that very low pitch which Mr. Ritson would have us believe, in his intemperate animadversions on bishop Percy's Essay.

[1] There can be no doubt that the forger of this charter conceived the earl to derive his name of Belesme (which, however, was never *his* name) from the city of David. Belesme is actually written *Bethlehem* in the Testa de Nevill, not two hundred years after the time of his death: so uncertain was the orthography of that age.

[2] The subsequent history of Hugh is curious and interesting, and forcibly pourtrays the restlessness and dread consequent upon guilt. After the assassination of Mabil, he had fled, with his brothers Ralph, Richard, and Gosnel, first to Apulia, afterwards into Sicily, and at length took refuge in the court of the emperor Alexius, at Constantinople. "But finding he could be safe no where, through the diligent search made for him by the king of England, and the family of Belesme, who offered rewards to any one that would kill him,—in order to escape the strong hands and long arms of so great a king, he quitted Christendom (totam Latinitatem), and took refuge among the infidels, where, for twenty years, he adopted their customs and speech." When the crusaders laid siege to Jerusalem, June 6th, 1099, anxious, no doubt, once more to revisit his native soil, he came and made a tender of his services to the duke of Normandy, Robert Curthose, as his natural lord. His knowledge of the language and manners of the East made him extremely useful to the Christians in their attack upon the holy city, by the insight which he gave them into the practices of

them a country exulting in its deliverance from a ferocious mistress. Hugh de Montgomery, her son, was in the town at this time with sixteen knights; but, though the news of his mother's deplorable end quickly reached his ears, yet he could not follow the perpetrators of the deed, as they had taken the precaution to break down all the bridges after them. It was winter; the night was dark, and stormy; and the country was laid under water by the rivers which had overflowed their banks; all this impeded the pursuit. It remained only to inter her mutilated remains; which was done in the convent of Troarne, on the nones of December, by the abbot Durand; who set over her tomb an epitaph, corresponding rather to the partiality of her friends, than to her real character." Then follows the epitaph, of which the only lines worth preservation are those descriptive of her figure; and from which we learn that her person was tall and slender, her demeanour commanding; that she was elegant in her dress, and expensive in her habits of life.

EXILIS FORMA SED GRANDIS, PRORSUS HONESTA,
DAPSILIS IN SUMPTU, CULTA SATIS HABITU.

Thus Ordericus; in estimating whose character of the countess, her hatred of his abbey must, however, be taken into the account. After the murder of Mabil, continues he, " the earl took to wife Adelais, daughter to one of the greatest nobles of France, Ebrard de Pusay. She was very different from her predecessor, and by her religious example brought her husband to the love of monks and the relief of the poor."

We are unable to state earl Roger's age at the time of his decease, but he must have been far advanced in years. According to William of Jumieges[1], he had five sons old enough, during the minority of William the Conqueror, to engage in the different factions which, at that unsettled period, disturbed the peace of Normandy. But this must be a mistake. That minority commenced in 1032, when duke Robert set out for the Holy Land; and ended at the latest in 1044, when the Conqueror attained his age of twenty-one: if then we assume at a medium 1038 as the period when Roger's five sons engaged in the factions mentioned above, and suppose the youngest of these sons to be then seventeen, it is impossible to place the birth of the first earl of Shrewsbury later than 996: and this would make him very nearly one hundred years old at the time of his death; but in all probability much more: for it is very unlikely that his five sons should

the unbelievers. Lib. ix. p. 753. In this passage, Ordericus calls him Hugh Buduel, the son of Robert de Jalgey.

[1] Wilhelm. Gemiticens. de Ducibus Norman. l. vi. cap. 2.

follow each other so close, as, on this supposition, they must have done; and not much less so, that a youth of seventeen should take an active part in public affairs. Besides, if we may believe Malmsbury, as quoted above, the earl himself was but a young man at the siege of Damfront; and that did not take place till after the duke had himself assumed the reins of government. The account of Jumieges, therefore, must be rejected as inconsistent with chronology; the more so, because in the names of the sons he differs, as we shall see hereafter, materially from Ordericus. But though the date above assigned for his birth is much too early, yet he was assuredly an old man when he died: Domesday was completed in 1086, and his *third* son, Roger of Poictou, was then a tenant *in capite* in various counties of England; that is, in all probability, he was not younger than thirty years of age: and if we suppose the father to be forty when this his third son was born, it will place his own birth in 1016, and make him about seven years older than the Conqueror, and about seventy-eight years old at the time of his death, which is perhaps not far from the truth.

By his first wife the earl had, according to Ordericus, five sons and four daughters.

1. Robert de Belesme.
2. Hugh de Montgomery, of both of whom hereafter.
3. Roger of Poictou, so called from the country of his wife, had extensive possessions in Lincolnshire, Essex, Norfolk, Suffolk, Amounderness, or that part of Lancashire which lies between the Ribble and the Mersey, and elsewhere, with the title of earl, not annexed, as it seems, to any territory, but merely personal. He, with his surviving brothers, espoused the title of Robert Curthose, in opposition to that of Henry I., and thereby forfeited all his English possessions, to the number, as it is said, of 398 manors.
4. Philip the Clerk, so called because he was brought up to letters, with the intention, perhaps, of enjoying some of the higher ecclesiastical honours, and made considerable progress in his studies. But the martial spirit of his family disdained so peaceful an occupation. He accompanied his sovereign, Curthose, to the first Crusade, 1096[1]; and Malmsbury[2] celebrates his prowess in that romantic warfare; dwelling with particular satisfaction on a combat in which he fought by the side of the Norman duke, and defeated the Turks, with the loss of their leader. He made a good end, says the historian, within the walls of Jerusalem, and must therefore have been living in May 1099, when the holy city was taken by the Christian army. The noble family of Eglinton derive their pedigree from this Philip, with what truth we shall not inquire; but we know that he

[1] Ordericus, l. ix. p. 724.   [2] P. 153.

left at least one daughter, Matilda, who succeeded her aunt Emma as abbess of Almanisches[1].

5. Arnulph. He, like his elder brother, assumed the paternal name Montgomery[2], and bore a considerable share in the public affairs of his time. The oldest part of the noble castle of Carew in Pembrokeshire, one of the most interesting remains of castellated architecture which time has spared us, is believed to owe its foundation to this young nobleman; and the stile of its architecture corresponds with this supposition. Farther mention will occur of his story hereafter. He married Lafracoth, the daughter of a king of Ireland[3], and directed his ambition to the obtaining of his father-in-law's crown. But Henry had offended the whole family too much to suffer any of them to continue within the British isles. Arnulph retired to Normandy, where he enlisted in the service of the duke, who had taken up arms to chastise the insolence of Arnulph's brother, Robert, the banished earl of Shrewsbury. But as the slothful duke soon remitted his warlike preparations, Arnulph was obliged to quit the country; for in 1103 we find him in Ireland, where the king, his father-in-law, took from him his daughter, and endeavoured to put him to death. He made his escape, and led a rambling life for twenty years; at the end of which time, being now an old man, the king consented to his return home, where, marrying a young wife, he was found dead in his bed the next morning[4]. Our genealogists have given him as ancestor to the noble family of Brydges; but their descendant, Sir Egerton Brydges, rejects this notion as unsupported by any authority.

The Carews likewise derived their descent from Arnulph. According to Leland, who seems to have received this information from the family, their name was originally Montgomery; and he had either seen or heard of old evidences, in which they were stiled Montgomerick, lord of Carew (Itin. iii. 56): and if this be admitted, that ancient family were, till their extinction, the representatives in the male line of the first Norman earl of Shrewsbury.

Besides these five sons mentioned by Orderious, the earl had, according to another writer, two others by his first wife, viz. William and Gislebert; of whom, probably, as deceasing in Normandy before the Conquest, the first named historian takes no notice. William of Jumieges, describing the disordered state of Normandy during the minority of the young duke, tells us that William, son of Roger de Montgomery, slew Osbern, major domo *(procurator principalis)* to Herfast, nephew of the countess Gunnora, and his own near kinsman, as he was lying fast asleep in the bedchamber of

---

[1] Orderic. lib. xi. p. 808.
[2] Malmsbury, p. 157.
[3] Père Anselme (Histoire généalogique, iii. 289) erroneously calls her daughter of Lafracoth, king of Ireland.
[4] Orderic. xi. 812.

the duke himself: to avenge whose murder, Barno de Glotis, Osbern's bailiff *(præpositus)*, assembling a body of active champions *(pugiles)*, beset the house in which William and his accomplices were at rest, and put them all to death, as they well deserved[1]. The whole presents a frightful picture of society and manners. Neither of these sons is inserted in the subjoined pedigree, because their existence is doubtful. Some modern antiquaries[2] have given our earl another son, Urso de Abetot, sheriff of Worcestershire, but without a shadow of authority. Of the daughters, Emma was a nun and abbess of Almanisches; Maud became the wife of Robert, earl of Meritol; Mabil was married to Hugh de Neufchastel; and Sibil to Robert Fitz Hamon, whose only child carried her vast possessions to Robert, the famous earl or consul of Gloucester, natural son of king Henry I. According to Camden, this Sibil was also wife of John de Reynes. She founded a preceptory of knights hospitalers at Shengay, in Cambridgeshire, in 1140. (Dugdale Mon. ii. 546.)

By his second wife Adelais, the first earl of Shrewsbury had one son, Ebrard, who, says Ordericus, being brought up to literature among the king's chaplains, dwelt in the court of the kings William and Henry, and is still living[3].

Great as was the opulence to which the companions of the Conqueror were raised by the spoils of the plundered English, (for Ordericus owns very honestly that many of the Normans obtained here vassals richer and more powerful than their own parents were in Normandy[4],) they still regarded their continental property with a natural preference, and generally bequeathed it to their eldest sons, while they left their English estates for their younger children. This was the course adopted by earl Roger: the first-born, Robert, succeeded to all his Norman possessions, while his next brother became earl of Shrewsbury.

HUGH DE MONTGOMERY, SECOND EARL OF SHREWSBURY, for his valour surnamed *Probus* or *le Preu*[5], and by the Welsh, from his complexion, *Goch*, or the *Red*, appears to have possessed a milder and more easy temper than his brother Robert. Indeed Ordericus tells us so.

---

[1] Wilhelmus Gemiticensis de Ducibus Norman. lib. vi. cap. 2.

[2] Dr. Nash (Worcestershire, Domesday, p. 17) and Mr. Kelham (on Domesday, p. 89).

[3] He officiated in the chapel royal in a subordinate capacity. In capella Henrici regis clericali officio inter mediocres functus. Orderic. viii. 708. A deep descent for the potent stock from which he sprang. [4] iv. 522.

[5] *Prudius* is from the French *Preu*, brave, which is itself derived from the Latin *probus*. As among the Romans courage was esteemed the most excellent of qualities, and got the name of *virtus*: so for a like reason did it, in a lower period, that of *probitas*. Du Cange derives it from *prudens*, but see the words of Ordericus above. The nine *preux chevaliers* of France are well known. Chaucer endeavoured to introduce the sense into our language.

There n'as a man of gretir hardiness
Than he, ne more desired *worthiness*.
(Troilus and Cressida, i. 567) i. e. bravery.

Accordingly his name seldom occurs in the history of that period. He was, however, implicated in the conspiracy (1095) excited against William Rufus[1] by earl Mowbray; but the treatment which upon that occasion he experienced from his sovereign, proves the general estimation in which he was held: since the king was content to reprimand him privately, and to accept his apologies; though not without payment of 3000*l.*, in compliance with the practice of those days, in which the royal favour was openly bought and sold.

The short remainder of this earl's life was chiefly engaged in hostilities with his Welsh neighbours. His father, indeed, must have left him in a state of warfare: for in 1094, we read that Shropshire was laid waste by the Welsh incursions[2] under the command of Griffith ap Cynan, king of North Wales, and Cadwgaun, prince of Powis[3]; and in the following year they destroyed the castle of Montgomery[4].

The earl's reprisals are said to have been disgraced by many acts of wanton barbarity and impiety; which, if the truth of them be admitted, materially detract from the character which has been given of him. The ferocity of a rude age was inflamed by religious dissension. The clergy of Wales had not yet bowed to the yoke of Roman bondage; and hence our earl's attacks were studiously directed against the ministers and edifices of public worship. His cruelties towards an aged priest are too shocking to be related[5]; and the indecency of kennelling his hounds in the church of Llandyfrydog cannot be excused. But so much of fable is mixed with these relations, that it throws a shade of doubt over the whole. The poor animals were struck with instant madness; and a miraculous stone, highly revered by the people of Anglesey, being contemptuously thrown by the Salopian earl into the sea, returned next morning to its pristine situation[6]. We cannot wonder that to these insults his contemporaries imputed that violent end, which speedily ensued.

The circumstances attending it are thus related by Ordericus: " Mag-

---

[1] Ordericus (viii. 704) places this transaction in 1093, Mr. Carte (i. 468) in 1095; and it should seem that the latter was in this instance more correct, as Hugh could not become earl till the death of his father in 1094.

[2] Hoveden ap. Leland Coll. v. iii. p. 201.

[3] The Welsh having revolted from William Rufus, that king entered their country in 1097 with a powerful army, but was obliged to retire with great loss; the Welsh having elected several chiefs to oppose him, " Of whom," says the Saxon Chronicle, " the worthiest was Caduugaun, brother's son to king Griffin." Bleddyn, the father of Cadwyan, was uterine brother of Griffith. Are we to refer to this warrior the chapel and cross which bore his name at the end of Frankwell, of which so frequent mention is made in our ancient records?

[4] Camden.

[5] Brompton, 994. Fabyan, f. 149, ed. 1533, says " But thys preste was of such virtue, that by myracle he was restored to helthe within iii dayes ensuynge." In the edition of 1559 this passage is omitted.

[6] Gough's Camden, v. ii. p. 572. It is not improbable that this was done in contempt of the Welsh clergy, who, because they pertinaciously adhered to the simplicity of the faith preached among them by the apostles or apostolical men, were regarded as schismatics by those of the Romish communion. The miracle is quoted by William Wyrcestre from Giraldus Cambrensis, and was probably credited by both of them.

VOL. I.

nus the Barefoot, king of Norway, having set forth an expedition against Ireland, and having subdued the Orkneys, arrived at Anglesey, (1098) intending to attack Ireland; but finding the Irish prepared for defence, he directed his course to the Isle of Man. At a certain time, one of his commanders sailed for England with six ships, having set up on his mast the red shield in token of peace. But this pacific signal did not quiet the alarm excited on the British coast by the appearance of an hostile squadron. A large force was quickly collected out of Mercia; which was the more readily assembled because the English and Welsh were then at war. The two earls who then bore the chief rule in Mercia were both called Hugh. They levied an army of French and English from Cheshire and Shropshire, and mustered their forces in Dagannoth, near the sea.

"Hugh de Montgomery arrived first at the rendezvous, and waited for his allies, cautiously watching that neither Welsh nor Norwegians should invade his country. But happening one day, as his people were drawn up fronting the Norwegian fleet, to spur his horse, while he was directing his men to keep their ranks close, and being rendered conspicuous by the prancing of his charger, one of the barbarians pierced him with an arrow, and as he writhed in the agonies of death, exclaimed with ferocious exultation, *Leit loupe: let him leap*[1]. He fell from his horse into the sea, and his body was with difficulty found at low water. Magnus was much grieved at this misfortune, and sent offers of peace to the other earl, Hugh Dirgane or the Fat; 'for,' said he, 'I do not wage war against the English, but against the Irish.'

"The earl was buried at the end of seventeen days in the cloister of the monks at Shrewsbury, to the grief of all; for he was the only one of Mabil's

---

[1] This anecdote we owe to Giraldus Cambrensis, (Itin. Cambr. ii. 7) who, as he visited Anglesey only ninety years after the earl of Shrewsbury's death, might easily have collected this and other particulars from old people who must have heard the transaction in their youth; and it is a story which would be likely to impress itself upon the memory. But when he adds that it was the Norwegian king himself who shot the deadly arrow, he is at manifest variance with the circumstantial and contemporary Ordericus, and what is more, with the undoubted fact; for if the Norwegian had been victor, he would not immediately have drawn off his forces without pushing his conquest. An early Danish author agrees, however, with Giraldus. "Magnus Barefoot, king of Norway, stretched from the Hebrides towards the south into Bretland, and commenced a sharp battle in the strait of Aungulsey against two Britannic counts, Hugo the Fat and Hugo Prudi. The fight was long and severe: at length, however, Hugins Prudi fell, and the Brittons being put to flight, king Magnus obtained the victory: but he lost many brave men, and a great number were wounded." Vita Sancti Magni, cap. 7. Hafniæ, 4to. 1780. St. Magnus was present at this battle, but would take no part in it, because, as he said, none of the opponents had given him any offence. Yet to shew that his inactivity was not from fear, he sate on deck (in interscalmio ante mediam navem), and recited the book of psalms while the warriors were engaged. Mr. Hume writes with great carelessness on the subject. "In the *eleventh* year," says he, "of William Rufus, (who reigned only *ten* years,) Magnus, king of Norway, made a descent on the isle of Anglesea, but was *repulsed by Hugh earl of Shrewsbury;*" and he quotes Simeon Dunelm. p. 223, though Simeon in that page tells the story of the earl's death exactly as it is given above. Mr. Hume goes on, "This is the last attempt made by the northern nations against England:" however, in 1133, this very king Magnus was slain in another attempt upon Ireland. (Orderic. l. xi. p. 812.)

sons that was mild and amiable. His death happened about the end of July, having survived his father four years." Upon the death of earl Hugh his brother Robert begged the earldom of Shrewsbury from the king[1]. It was not the usage of that age to bestow any thing gratuitously, but he obtained it for a payment of 3000*l.* sterling.

In order to afford our readers a connected view of the active life of this enterprising and restless nobleman, ROBERT DE BELESME, THE THIRD NORMAN EARL of our town and county, it will be necessary to go back some years anterior to the period at which he succeeded to this last-mentioned dignity.

We have already seen him thrown into prison by the duke of Normandy for his connexion with that prince's brother Henry. After his release from that captivity, he never ceased to burn with revenge, and gave Curthose much disturbance and uneasiness during the fifteen years that they continued together in Normandy. "He was a great favourite," says Ordericus, "with king William, who bore an especial love of his parents. By the mediation of that king, he had to wife Agnes, daughter of Guy count of Ponthieu. He behaved with as much cruelty to his wife as he did to every one else within his reach. At one time he shut her up in his castle at Belesme like a common malefactor. Having made her escape from this state of confinement by means of a trusty chamberlain, she took refuge at the court of Adela countess of Blois and Chartres, daughter of William the Conqueror; whence she passed into Ponthieu, and never returned to her tyrant[2]. By her he had a son named William, heir and peaceful possessor of ample domains in that country as well as in his native duchy. For Robert did not scruple to usurp all the vast estates of his ancestors both in Normandy and Maine, to the disherison of his brothers." Yet it does not appear that they were in hostility to him; on the contrary, they, or at least some of them, promoted his interest; for in the war which arose between this earl and Hugh de Grentesmesnil in 1090, Ordericus expressly mentions the assistance which Roger and Arnulph afforded to their brother. (p. 692.)

The general relaxation of all discipline and order which took place under the unsteady government of the duke of Normandy, was favourable to the grasping views of a man of this stamp. Ordericus mentions several noblemen from whom he wrested their castles. His kinsman Goisfred or Geoffrey, count of Maurienne, was the only one who dared to withstand the general

---

[1] The Saxon Chronicle says, "His brother Rodbert was his heir, as he had begged it of the king." And in another place, "Earl Rotbert of Belesme, who held the earldom in Scrobbes-byrig, which his father Roger earl formerly had; and much riches both on this side the sea and beyond it."

[2] Orderic. l. viii. p. 708. The historian of Ponthieu (Abbeville, 12mo. 1767) treats the great earl of Shrewsbury with very little ceremony. "Ce même Guy," says he, "avoit marié sa fille à *un seigneur* nommé Belesme, *autre scélérat*." (vol. i. p. 93.)

plunderer; and the conduct of our earl towards this count does not seem very consistent with his reputation for valour. Goisfred laid claim to the castle of Damfront, but was unable to find his enemy in the open field; for " Robert de Belesme, who was afraid of all his neighbours, kept himself within his fortifications, permitting his lands to be ravaged by Goisfred, under an apprehension that if he ventured out beyond his own walls, he should be abandoned by his servants, and left in the hands of his enemies." Such is the wretched and suspicious condition of a tyrant.

In the civil war which ensued in Normandy (1090,) through the intrigues of William Rufus, our young nobleman took a distinguished part; and in the war carried on by the same monarch against Philip king of France for the Vexin, he was commander in chief, and conducted himself in a manner that gave great satisfaction to his master[1]; and probably procured for him the earldom of Shrewsbury on better terms than he would otherwise have obtained. In the course of this war he built the castle of Gisors.

Being made earl of Shrewsbury, he exercised great severities over the Welsh for four years. Yet he seems, in conformity to the character of a talent for business, which is given him by Ordericus, to have attended to the "affairs and amelioration of his new estates." Giraldus tells us that he " improved the breed of horses in Powis, by introducing sires out of Spain; whence," says that writer, " the horses of this country are eminent for their make[2] and speed. He removed the town of Quatfort, and built a very strong castle over the Severn at Bruges[3]. He also obtained from the king, Blida and all the land of his kinsman Roger de Buthley, for which he paid a large sum; but the more he acquired, the prouder and more cruel he became; so that the English and Welsh, who had formerly heard of his cruelties and tyrannies with indifference, as of things in which they were not concerned, now groaned under his iron fangs. On some pretext, the particulars of which are not detailed, he confiscated the estates of one of the most considerable of his Shropshire barons, William Pantulph of Wem: and we shall presently see how severely this rash measure, and his obstinate perseverance in it, were visited with exact retribution.

---

[1] Lib. x. p. 766. Carte, vol. i. 477.

[2] Itin. Wall. l. ii. c. 12. So we translate *membrosa sua majestate*, because the Welsh horses do not seem ever to have been remarkable for their size, which the words of Giraldus would otherwise seem to import. The late Arthur Blayney, esq. of Gregynog, a liberal patron of every useful institution in his native county of Montgomery, and the genuine descendant of its ancient sovereigns, the kings of Old Powis, took great pains to collect and maintain a fine breed of strong and active, but not tall, horses; which he considered as the true posterity of the stud of Robert de Belesme.

[3] Part of the earl's building at Bridgnorth continued till the summer of this year (1821). It was a Norman arch which had been long concealed by buildings, the removal of which for the purpose of opening the street, exposed it again to view. It confirmed what Ordericus says of the earl's skill in architecture, for it was an arch of fine proportions: and as the continuance of this last relic of *the founder of Bridgnorth* might have been rendered perfectly consistent with the convenience of the public, its demolition is to be lamented as unnecessary.

On the death of William Rufus, (Friday, Aug. 2, 1100,) Robert Curthose entered Normandy; and in the Sept. of the next year, (1101,) Robert de Belesme, with his brothers Roger of Poictou and Arnulph de Montgomery, William de Warenne, earl of Surrey, and other nobles, engaged in a confederacy to place the duke on the throne of England. In autumn, Curthose landed at Portsmouth: this was the signal for Belesme and the others to desert the new king, Henry I. But the duke having had a personal interview with his royal brother, and matters being accommodated between them, he returned to Normandy before the approach of winter, taking with him William de Warenne and many others who were disinherited for his sake. In 1102, we find that Henry, attacking the revolters separately by form of law, had compelled most of them to quit England. Having thus weakened the confederacy, he summoned the most powerful of them all, Robert de Belesme, to his court. The king had employed a year in forming articles of accusation against him, and these were now exhibited to the number of forty-five. The earl appeared to the charge; but finding the affair grow serious, he availed himself of the customary permission indulged to a defendant, of retiring to consult with his counsel, and made his escape, the king and his barons in vain expecting his return into court[1]. Henry caused him to be publicly proclaimed an outlaw, and after a second ineffectual summons, prepared to lay siege to his castle of Arundel. The commanders of the garrison sent for instructions to Robert, who was then in Shropshire fortifying his new town of Bruges. Finding that Arundel could not make any effectual resistance, he directed the garrison there to surrender upon the best terms they could procure. From Sussex, the king marched to Blida castle, which, having formerly belonged to Roger de Buthley, opened its gates upon the approach of the royal army[2]. In the

---

[1] We learn from an anecdote in the Menagiana, that it continued down to modern time, an usage of the French courts of justice to allow culprits the privilege of conferring with their counsel in a private apartment. "A thief having been apprehended in the Great Chamber [a hall of audience in the parliament of Paris] in the very act of cutting a purse, the court assigned him an advocate for his counsel. This learned gentleman taking his client aside, said, 'Is it true that you stole the purse in question?' 'Yes, sir,' said the thief, 'but——' 'Hold your tongue,' said the advocate, 'the best advice I can give you is, to take to your heels as fast as you can.' The thief profited by this counsel, and ran down the back stairs. On the advocate's return, M. le President asked him what he had to say in defence of his client: 'My lords,' said he, ' the poor fellow acknowledged his crime to me; and as he was not in custody, and I was named his counsel, I thought myself bound to give him the best advice in my power: accordingly I recommended him to make his escape, and he has done so.' This threw the court into a roar of laughter." (v. i. p. 8. ed. 1789.) If we rightly understand the language of Ordericus, our Norman earl acted much the same part with the Parisian pick-pocket.—The default of the common vouchee in our fictitious form of *recoveries*, shews that similar incidents were of daily occurrence in the rude æra of our early jurisprudence.

[2] This fourth castle of earl Robert is by all the other historians (except the Welsh Brut y Saeson, which styles it *Bledense*) called Tykehil or Tickenhull. The castle of that name in Yorkshire was anciently connected with Blythe (in Domesday Blide) in the county of Nottingham, and was holden at the time of that survey by Roger de Busli: so that there can be no doubt that, in the opinion of Ordericus, it was the Yorkshire Tickhill, to which Henry I. led his forces. It may be justly deemed

mean time, Curthose was compelled by his brother to submit to the disgraceful task of taking possession of the Norman estates of his confederate[1].

Henry, having given his army some repose, assembled all his forces, in the autumn of this year, (1102,) and led them into Mercia, where he laid siege to the castle of Bruges, which Robert had entrusted to Roger, son of Corbat, Robert de Neufville and Ulger the Hunter, having also garrisoned it with a body of eighty stipendiary soldiers[2]. The earl himself retired to Shrewsbury; and having effected an accommodation with Cadogan and Gervase (or Jorwerth) sons of Rees, he employed their troops to harass those of the king. He now perceived the fault he had committed in seizing on the estates of William Pantol (so Ordericus writes him); but his fierce and lofty spirit could not bend to circumstances; and when that brave soldier took the opportunity of the critical posture of the earl's affairs, to offer his services to this his feudal superior, the latter thought fit to reject them. Whereupon Pantol repaired to the king, who, knowing his activity, received him with open arms, and entrusted to him the care of Stafford castle, with two hundred soldiers. He, continues the historian, above all others, injured and molested the earl.

The speedy surrender of Bridgenorth, which submitted at the end of three weeks[3], though the earl conceived it capable of sustaining a protracted

presumptuous at this distance of time to hint a suspicion that the historian was mistaken: yet we can find no trace of any connexion between the earl of Shrewsbury and the county of York: but lower down the Severn is a place bearing the same name, and of great importance to the Norman earl, as securing to him the possession of that river, on which his other castles, at Quatford, at Bridgenorth, and at Shrewsbury, were seated. This is Tickenhill, near Bewdley, which bears unequivocal marks of having been an ancient castle, erected on a position of great strength: and if, from the recesses of his Norman abbey, Ordericus, hearing of that attack upon Tickenhill, fixed upon the wrong place, and gave to the Worcestershire Tickenhill a name (Blida) which belonged only to the Yorkshire one; or if, hearing of an attack upon Bewdley, he was deceived by the similarity of name, and transferred it to Blida, the mistake in either case was natural. Humphrey Llwyd (Britann. Descript. Comment.) seems to have been of the opinion suggested above; for he says, that Beaudley was "olim castro de Tychil notissima," "very wel knowne in old time by the castle Tychil," as Twyne renders it, which we know not to what to refer, unless to this transaction. If, however, it be true, as Simeon of Durham relates, that Henry entrusted the siege of Tychill to the bishop of Lincoln, this, it must be owned, throws a great shadow of doubt upon our conjecture.

[1] Order. lib. xi. p. 806.
[2] This was, we presume, in addition to the tenants of Corbet and the others.
[3] The incidents attending the fall of this important fortress are too characteristic of that loyalty to their sovereign, for which the gentry of Shropshire have been always remarkable, to be entirely omitted in this place; though the fuller detail belongs to the history of the town in the neighbourhood of which they occurred. We owe them to Ordericus. The great nobles of the realm, it appears, had no mind that the king should become too strong for them, by the total overthrow of the most powerful of their body. On a day, therefore, when Henry had made some progress in the siege of Bridgenorth, they held a meeting in the field where the royal army lay encamped; and, advancing to the king, proposed terms of accommodation between him and his stout vassal. This assembly was not so secret, but that the purpose of it transpired. The country gentlemen of Shropshire (so I would translate the phrase, *pagenses milites*, in an age when every gentleman was a soldier,) who had so long groaned under the tyranny of their earl, took the alarm. Pantulph, whose only hopes of restitution were founded on the defeat of that noble-

siege; and the loss of his Welsh allies, whom William Pantulph succeeded in detaching from the confederacy, drove our earl to the brink of despair. But when the victorious monarch had actually surmounted the dangerous pass of Wenlock edge, (or Hunel hege, as Ordericus writes it[1],) when he descended into the fertile plain beneath, and was advancing with hasty strides towards the walls of Shrewsbury[2], the earl's despondency was com-

man, contributed, we may conclude, to excite their fears. It is certain that they assembled, to the number, says my author, of three thousand, on one of the hills which surround the scene of the transaction; and no sooner did the earls and barons open their proposition to the king, than these valiant progenitors of our Shropshire gentry lifted up their voices, and exclaimed, " Sir king, regard not what these traitors say. Remember the repeated treasons of this your enemy, how often he has conspired against your life, and lay not aside your purpose. Storm the town. We will support you, and never leave you till your foe is brought alive or dead to your feet."

Encouraged by this representation, which was, perhaps, concerted between him and these gentlemen, the king rejected the terms offered by his nobles; and summoning Corbet and the other governors into his presence, he swore to them before all his court, that if they did not surrender in three days, he would hang up the whole garrison. The governor, terrified by these threats, but at the same time desirous to save appearances with their lord, took their kinsman Pantulph aside, and requested his advice. He was at much pains to persuade them into a compliance with the king's pleasure, and held out to them a promise on the part of that prince, that they should be remunerated by a donation of lands to the yearly value of 100l., to be levied, I presume, out of the future confiscations of the earl. Ord. xi. 807.

Mr. Hallam (View of the Middle Ages) adduces this transaction as a curious instance of the cleverness with which Henry I. converted the hatred of the English against the Normans to his own purposes. But it is no such thing. These *knights* or *soldiers of the villages* were the lords of manors, holding under their great earl; and we are sure from Domesday, that, with very few exceptions, these were all of Norman race, and not a few of them, in all probability, actual Normans, who had fought at the battle of Hastings.

[1] Ordericus gives a very particular description of Wenlock edge, which he probably remembered in his childhood. Either through an error of his own, of his transcriber, or of his learned editor Du Chesne, the name is strangely disfigured (a sight of the original MS. would, perhaps, detect the source of the error); but the situation and accompaniments identify the spot. It was after the capture of Bridgenorth, that Henry I. commanded his army to pass through Hunel-hege, and lay siege to Shrewsbury. " Hunelge-hege is the English name for a certain passage through a wood. In Latin it may be called *malus callis*, or *vicus*: for it was a hollow way of a mile in length, full of great sharp stones, and so narrow as scarcely to admit two horsemen abreast. It was overshadowed on each side by a dark wood, wherein were stationed archers in ambuscade, who greatly annoyed the army with arrows and other missile weapons. But as the king had more than 60,000 men in his army, he detached large parties to cut down the wood, and make a wide road, which should endure for the use of posterity." lib. xi. p. 808.

From this period, then, we may probably date the existence of a road over this steep ridge, which has since been rendered more commodious, and has laid aside most of its pristine horrors. Many of the passes, however, down this ridge retain all their ancient ferocity: one, in particular, termed Blakeway hollow, from the little hamlet adjoining, is nearly as impenetrable now as it could have been in the days of Henry I.

[2] " Robert de Beleeme, not thinking his father's fortifications of sufficient strength in case the town should endure a siege by the king's forces then marching against him, drew a wall from each side of the castle over across the isthmus down to the banks of the Severn." Lloyd's History of Shropshire (erroneously quoted by Pennant as Mr. W. Mytton's) MS. among the Halston collections. Mr. Pennant represents this as " the first attempt towards erecting the walls of Shrewsbury." (Tours in Wales, 8vo edit. iii. 234.) It is true that the castles of the great were, in those times, the places of defence chiefly considered; but it is surely incredible, that in a barbarous and lawless period, a town like this, comprising four parish churches, should have continued a mere open village from the reign of Offa to that of Henry I.; nor does Lloyd, Mr. Pennant's authority, say any such thing, though he does suppose, that " when the town was taken by king Stephen, and burnt in king John's time by the partizans of the barons, it was no otherwise defensible, than as it was left in Henry the First's reign." MS. ut supra.

58   NORMAN PERIOD.

plete; his haughty spirit was now subdued, and he condescended to implore the mercy of his offended sovereign. But Henry was in no disposition to consent to an accommodation: the power of the earl, and the deep measure in which he had offended, rendered his total ruin a measure of necessary policy. The king sent word, that nothing was left for him but to surrender at discretion. However odious Robert had now become; though his turbulent and vindictive character had left him but few friends, the scene which followed must have been affecting, to those who could reflect, if such there were, on the instability of all human grandeur. On the king's approach to Shrewsbury, the earl quitted his town[1], perhaps for the last time; bearing

⊢——⊣ *1 foot*

[1] The gateway of the castle, out of which the last Norman earl of Shrewsbury issued to make his submission to Henry I. still exists: it is the only part of the Norman structure which does so, and this is the place to introduce it to the notice of the reader. "Architecture," it has been well

himself[1] the keys of the gates, he threw himself at the victor's feet, acknowledging his treason, and sued for mercy.

The terms on which Henry himself stood with his nobles were too critical to permit him to exasperate them by an example of unmeasured severity: he gave the earl a safe conduct to the sea coast with his arms and horses: seizing in the mean while all his honours and lands, together with those of his brothers Roger and Arnulph; and receiving the congratulations of the country, which unanimously agreed, that now at length was Henry truly a sovereign, since he had triumphed over Robert de Belesme.

The rage and fury with which the banished earl retired to his vast possessions in Normandy, may be easily conceived; Ordericus compares him to the dragon in the Apocalypse, "Woe to the inhabiters of the earth, for the devil is come down upon you, having great wrath, because he knoweth that he hath but a short time."

He still, however, cherished hopes of restoring his fallen fortunes. The duke of Normandy, to whom any of his brother's enemies could not fail to be acceptable, received him and the other exiles with kindness. The earl had even the address to inspire Curthose with hopes of ascending the English throne by his assistance. He so far ingratiated himself with the duke, as to procure from him the restitution of all the domains of his father, earl Roger: and upon the death of his father-in-law, William count of Abbeville, the duke granted the county of Ponthieu to William Talvace[2], son of our Shropshire earl.

But a due estimate of his Norman sovereign's inactive character and inadequate resources obliged Robert to rest his hopes of restitution to Shrewsbury and his estates in our county, on the milder basis of supplication and pacific negotiation. How foreign soever such lenient measures might be to the turbulence of his own disposition, they best suited the temper and condition of the duke, who, in 1103, came over on a visit to his brother[3], the ostensible motive of which was to request the restitution of

---

said, "forms a perpetual commentary upon the pages of the historian, who can ill dispense with the aid which the imagination thus receives." If intellectual impressions are strengthened by visible objects, and if history be "philosophy teaching by examples," it is surely the reverse of wisdom wantonly to demolish the monuments of antiquity: to demolish them, we mean, when neither utility nor convenience require their destruction.

[1] According to Malmsbury, the inhabitants of Shrewsbury sent the keys of the castle to the king privately, by the abbot of Seez, in token of their readiness to surrender (156); but the people of Shrewsbury, we take it, had no voice in public affairs at that time: the keys of the castle would not be theirs to send; and Ordericus is express that our earl was the bearer of them himself.

[2] I have mislaid this reference, but the fact is certain. The counts of Ponthieu were named indiscriminately after that county, or its capital, Abbeville: but the earl's father-in-law was certainly Guy, and, according to the historian of Ponthieu, (i. 91,) he was the same who seized the person of Harold, when he landed on his mission from Edward the Confessor to the first William, and whose portrait, under the name of Wido, is introduced in the Bayeux tapestry.

[3] This visit was certainly in 1103, though in Ordericus, who too often neglects the order of time, it precedes the expulsion of the earl from Shrewsbury.

William de Warenne to the earldom of Surrey. But the king gave him a very cold reception; and though he ultimately carried that point, it was not without the surrender of a considerable pension, which he had himself been accustomed to receive from the English treasury. He became even apprehensive of his own personal freedom, and was glad to return to Normandy, there to repent at leisure his hasty, unadvised journey[1]. In 1104, king Henry, with the view of establishing an interest in that duchy, which might enable him at a future opportunity to wrest it out of the hands of his careless brother, passed over sea into Normandy. During his visit, he took occasion, in a conversation with the duke, to expostulate with him on his breach of promise, in making peace with Robert de Belesme, contrary to his express stipulation. The king returned to England before winter; but the complaints of Normandy, oppressed by the turbulence of Robert de Belesme, and the indolence of the duke, afforded him the opportunity he had long sought, of acquiring those dominions. He revisited the duchy in the spring of 1105, landing at Barfleur in the last week of Lent. Having spent Easter Sunday at Carenton, he employed the summer in reducing Bayeux and Caen; but failing in an attempt upon Falaise, he seems, after establishing garrisons in his recent conquests, to have returned to England with some precipitation; at least, the transactions of that year in the history of Ordericus, break off rather abruptly, so that we are at a loss to explain how the late earl of Shrewsbury obtained permission to visit England at the close of it[2].

If his view was to effect an amicable composition, his journey was unsuccessful; for he returned into Normandy during the feast of Christmas, "with an hostile mind," and was followed by the duke, (1106,) who had visited his brother, in hopes of obtaining restitution of those places in his duchy which the king had seized; but Curthose was as unsuccessful as Belesme. Henry found himself too firm on his throne to be any longer under the necessity of keeping measures with either of these personages. He rejected all their advances, and about July, says the Saxon annalist, " went over into Normandy; and almost all that were in that land were at his command, except Robert de Belesme, and the earl of Moretoin." Ordericus places this expedition earlier in the spring, and makes the king in Whitsunweek hold an ineffectual interview of two days with his brother. In autumn the English monarch marched against Robert de Belesme and the earl of Moretoin. The duke of Normandy advanced to their aid, and the battle of Tenerchebray ensued, September 27, whence the late earl of Shrewsbury took flight early in the engagement, and the duke was made prisoner. Historians conjecture that this flight of our earl, with all the previous steps which led to that fatal battle, had been concerted between him and the

---

[1] Carte, i. 492.   [2] Before Christmas, says the Saxon Chronicle.

king; and it cannot be denied that the crafty character of Henry, and the unprincipled one of Belesme, coupled with the fact, that he soon after made peace with his sovereign, lend but too much countenance to this supposition. He even obtained a grant of all the offices in Normandy which had been enjoyed by his father, Roger de Montgomery; the price, it is supposed, of his perfidy to the unfortunate Curthose.

The good order introduced into the affairs of Normandy by the firm administration of Henry controuled the restless spirit of the banished earl of Shrewsbury, and retained him in unwilling repose for many years, during which we hear nothing of him; nor, indeed, is his destiny any farther connected with the history of our town. But as we are generally curious to know the end of any celebrated character of whom we have read, it may be pardoned if the writer pursues the history of our earl as far as it can be traced. We have seen the rage with which he quitted his Salopian domains. He continued to cherish this passion, and an unabated hatred of the king; and it was, perhaps, more from that motive, than from attachment to the Norman duke, or compassion towards the unfortunate, that he espoused the interests of that illustrious captive's eldest son. But Henry's vigilance was not to be surprised.

In 1113, he repaired to Normandy, and finding Robert on the point of taking up arms against him, summoned him, (Nov. 4th,) to his court; a measure which placed our earl in an embarrassing dilemma. If he appeared in conformity to the summons, he trembled for his personal security: if he disobeyed the call, his Norman property became exposed to confiscation. He devised an expedient, which he hoped might save both. The kings of France and England were at war. Robert was a subject of both monarchs; and he trusted that the sacred character of ambassador, with which he procured himself to be invested by the former, would secure him a safe reception in the court of the latter. But Henry did not choose to sacrifice so favourable an opportunity of crushing this formidable enemy, to the observance of a nice punctilio: no sooner had the earl delivered the propositions with which he was charged, than the king ordered him to be arrested[1], or, as the Saxon annalist has it, connived at his being thrown into prison. Here he lay, while the king proceeded to seize his estates. On the first of May following, that prince laid siege to Belesme. These violent measures seem to have been taken in contemplation of the broils, which, now that his nephew prince William was advancing towards manhood, might be excited by the king's unjust aggression of Normandy, and his disputed title to it, that gave him full employment for many years.

[1] Mr. Carte (i. 504.) places this transaction two years earlier, viz. in 1111; but the contemporary authorities seem to support the date here assigned it.

In the following summer, the king sent our earl over to Warham castle in England[1], where he languished in captivity.

This detention of the earl in prison forms one of the articles of accusation brought by the French king against Henry at the council of Rheims, October 1119. " My ambassador, Robert de Belesme," says Lewis, " by whom I had sent a message to the king, he arrested in his court, put him in irons, and still detains in prison[2]."

The ultimate destiny, and the period of the late earl of Shrewsbury's decease, were unknown even to the Monk of Huntingdon, nearly, if not quite, a contemporary. That writer, in his epistle " Of the Contempt of the World," hath selected this nobleman as a memorable instance of the vicissitudes of fortune. He ransacks his invention for features of tyrannic cruelty with which to charge his character; till, unable to find language strong enough to express his detestation and horror, he has recourse to the fabulous beings of Pagan mythology, Pluto, Megæra, and Cerberus, as topics of comparison. If indeed, as this monk affirms, the earl preferred the bloody pleasure of murdering his prisoners, to that of satiating his avarice by their ransom; if he took delight in impaling men and women alive; if, while he was fondling his infant son under his cloak, he amused himself by plucking out his eyes, it can excite no surprise, that " The *marvels* of Robert de Belesme" should have passed into a proverb. But the writer impairs the credit of his narrative by the ardour of his invective: savage as was, no doubt, the nature of this Norman, the last of these deeds of horror is surely a fiction. " At length," says the monk, " we come to the end of this man : he who had so long tormented others in prison, perished himself in the prison of king Henry. Fame, which had so long waited as his attendant, knew not whether he was alive or dead; yea, the very day of his decease is lost in oblivion[3]." Ordericus has touched his character with nicer discrimination and greater appearance of justice and probability. " He was," says the monk, " of a lofty stature and firm habit of body; brave and powerful in arms; eloquent, expert, and indefatigable in business and in the management of his affairs; and skilled in the fashionable exercises of the age. He was conversant in architecture, and an ingenious

---

[1] Saxon Chronicle.

[2] Orderic. xi. 858. This is the last mention made by that writer, of the exiled and captive earl of Shrewsbury.

[3] Vidisti Robertum de Beleeme qui princeps Normannensis in carcerem positus erat: Pluto, Megera, Cerberus, vel si aliquid horrentius scribi potest: nec curabat captos redimere, sed interimere. Filioli sui oculos sub clamide positi quasi ludens pollicibus extraxit. Homines utriusque sexus ab ano usque ad ora palis transforabat. Erat ei cedes horribilis hominum, cibus jucundus anime. Erat igitur in ore omnium positus, ut diceretur in proverbiis Mirabilia Roberti de Beleemo. Tandem venimus ad finem, ad rem scilicet optabilem. Qui ceteros carcere vexaverat, in carcere perhenni à rege Henrico positus longo supplicio sceleratus deperiit. Quem tantopere Fama coluerat, dum viveret in carcere utrum viveret vel obiisset nescivit :—diem quoque mortis ejus obmutescens ignoravit. Epistola Henrici Huntindonensis de Contemptu Mundi: ap. Dugd. MSS. vol. x. 2. p. 150.

mechanic:—these were the favourable points of his character. On the other hand, he was deceitful and subtle, cruel, covetous, and lustful, an inexorable and bloody executioner in the infliction of tortures; lastly, he was a contemner and oppressor of our holy mother the Church[1]."

His punishment must be allowed to have at least equalled his crimes, let their magnitude have been as atrocious as imagination can paint; and if he had been read in holy writ, he might with propriety have adopted the avowal of the savage prince of Canaan[2], "as I have done, so hath God requited me." Imprisonment, imprisonment for life, is under any circumstances, one of the severest penalties which law or tyranny can inflict. But how must it be aggravated in the case of an active-minded, illiterate, profligate nobleman, with no other employment, through many a tedious year, than the melancholy task of meditating on his former crimes and guilty pleasures, and contrasting the rude merriment and cumbrous state of his early days with the abject, forlorn condition, to which he was reduced by his own vices! What evils has not the wild-beast man inflicted on his brethren, and on himself, when armed with power, and insensible to the calls of religion and conscience! HOMO HOMINI LUPUS!

> Man, proud man,
> Drest in a little brief authority,
> Plays such fantastic tricks before high heaven,
> As makes the angels weep.

A few words must be said of the earl's posterity. His only son, deprived of the great estates of his father, ultimately succeeded to those of his mother: and from him descended the counts of Ponthieu and Alençon, specified in the annexed pedigree. The last count of Ponthieu left at his death in 1225 an only child, Mary; who, by her first husband Simon de Dammartin, had two daughters, one of whom became the wife of Ferdinand king of Castile, and mother to Eleanor wife of our Edward I., who thus introduced the blood of the Montgomeries into the royal family of England; and his son Edward II. did homage for the county of Ponthieu as heir of the Talvaces. (See Ross, Hist. Regum Angliæ, p. 154.)

---

[1] P. 675. At 707 he has drawn the earl's impious and cruel character more at length.
[2] Judges, i. 7.

Genealogical table: Descendants of Roger, lord of Montgomery, in Normandy.

- Roger, lord of Montgomery, in Normandy.
  - Hugh, lord of Montgomery = Joscelina, dau. of Turolf, of Pontaudemer.
    - Roger de Montgomery, earl of Shrewsbury, Arundel, and Chichester, ob. 27 July, 1094. = Adelais, dau. of Ebrard de Pumay, 2d wife. / Mabilia, dau. of William Talvace, lord of Belesme.
      - Robert = Agnes, dau. of Guy, C. of Ponthieu.
        - Robert de Belesme, E. of Shrewsbury. m. 1. Matilda, d. of …; 2. … d. of Bernard de St. Valeri.
          - William Talvace, count of Ponthien and Alençon, ob. 1171. = Ala, dau. of Odo, duke of Burgundy.
            - Guy, C. of Ponthieu, died at Ephesus V. P. = Ina, son of Walter de Mediana.
              - John, C. of Ponthieu. m. 1. Maud, d. of …; 2. … d. of Bernard de St. Valeri. = Beatrice, d. of Anselm, C. de Saint Paul.
                - William, count of Ponthieu, born after 1178, died 1225. = Alice, dau. of Louis VII. king of France.
                  - Mary, countess of Ponthieu, mar. 1. Simon de Dammartin, 2. Matthew de Montmorency, she died 1251.
                - John, last heir male, born 1199, ob. 1214.
              - Guy, lord of Norelles, C. became a monk.
              - Agnes, abbess of St. Autreberta.
              - Adela, mar. 1178, Renald de St Valeri, and afterwards his brother Thomas.
              - Margaret, w. of Enguerand de Poquigny.
            - Ala, mar. 1. William, E. Warenne; 2. Patrick, E. of Sarum.
          - Philip, 2d son, d. young.
          - John, count of Alençon, d. 6th May, 1191. S. P.
          - William, C. of Alençon, died 1203, S. P.
          - John, count of Alençon, d. 24th Feb. 1191. 3d son. = Beatrice, dau. of Helias, C. of Maine.
            - Robert, count of Alençon, died 8th of September, 1217. = Johanna, d. of Joubert de Guerchy, 1st wife.
              - Alice, mar. 1. Robert Malet, lord of Graville; 2. Almaric visc. of Chatelherault.
              - Matilda, w. of Theobald, count of Blois.
              - John, ob. 8th Jan. 1212, S. P.
            - Emma, dau. of Guy de la Val, 2d w. remarried Matthew de Montmorency.
              - Alice, dau. of Bartholomew de Royes; remar. to Ralph de Neale.
              - Robert, a posthumous son, last count of Alençon, S. P.
          - Maud, abbess of Almeneaches.
        - Hugh, earl of Shrewsbury, 2d son 1098.
      - 4. Philip, a clerk, called Grammaticus.
        - Emma, abbess of Almeneaches.
      - 5. Arnulph de Montgomery, keeper of Pembroke castle, m. 1. Lafracoth, d. of … K. in Ireland; and 2. … d. of …
      - A daughter, mother of Ameria, wife of Waria the Bald, viscount.
      - 3. Roger, called the Poictovin, lord of the honour of Lancaster.
        - Maud, w. of Robert, earl of Moritoil.
        - Mabil, wife of Hugh de Neufchastel.
      - Almodis, d. of Audebert, count de la Marche.
        - Sibil, wife of Robert Fitz Haman, E. of Glocester.
        - Pontia, w. of Wulgrim, C. of Angoulesme.
          - Eudo.
          - Boso.
        - Audebert, C. de la Marche. = Orengardis.
          - Audebert, C. de la Marche, d. at Constantinople, 1180. = Marchisa, w. of Guy visc. de Limoges, S. P.
            - Audebert, only son, d. 1177.
          - Boso.
      - Gosfrid, (only surviving brother) poisoned by countess Mabil.
      - Everard, chaplain to Will Rufus, & Hen. I.
    - Robert.
    - William.
    - Gilbert.

As to the armorial bearings of the Norman earls of Shrewsbury, the heralds assign them Azure, a lion rampant within a border Or: and when it became the fashion for religious houses to have coats of arms, of the time of which strange perversion we confess our ignorance, the monks of Shrewsbury assumed this coat in compliment to their founder, surmounting the lion with a crosier in bend. But the truth is, that neither Roger de Montgomery nor his sons bore any coat of arms, for the best of all reasons, because there were no coats of arms then to be borne. Heraldry owes its origin to the crusades, and we believe to the second of those romantic expeditions, that of 1147; before which we see no satisfactory proof of hereditary arms. But long before that time, the descendants of earl Roger had ceased to have any connexion with England. William Talvace, however, the son of Robert de Belesme, *may* have had a coat of arms: and La Roque in his genealogical history of the house of Harcourt (tom. i. p. 295) gives him Argent, three chevrons Gules. Anselme and Fourny (in their Histoire Généalogique de France, tom. iii. p. 300) assign to his son Guy, Or, three bends Azure, which seems to be designed as one half of his father's coat, to denote, perhaps, that he succeeded only to a moiety of his estates.

This biography of the Norman earls of Shrewsbury will not be complete without some account of their biographer: who, it will thence be seen, had especial means of obtaining accurate information respecting them; and he has a just claim to notice in the present work, as being the first Salopian author of whom we have any knowledge.

He was born, as he tells us himself, February 16, 1075, nine years after the conquest of England; being son of Odelerius Constantius, of Orleans, a chief counsellor, as we have seen, to Roger de Montgomery, earl of Shrewsbury. He had two brothers, Ebrard or Everard, who succeeded to that part of the estate which was not dissipated by the religious zeal of his father; and Benedict, a monk of St. Peter's at Shrewsbury, placed there by Odelerius with an oblation of two hundred marks. Our historian, the eldest of the three, was baptized at Attingham (Atcham) on the Easter Sunday following his birth, by Ordericus, the clergyman of the place, who was also his godfather, and gave him his own name.

In 1080, when he was five years old, he was sent to school at Shrewsbury, to one Siward, "a noble priest," who appears to have been minister of the little church of St. Peter and Paul, on the site of which the stately Benedictine abbey was afterwards built. Being destined by his father, who was deeply imbued with the religion of the age, to the monastic profession, he there acquired the rudiments of those instructions which were requisite for that station: the Latin tongue, and the art of chanting:—and having made some proficiency therein, he took leave of his friends in 1086, for the abbey of Uticum. But we will transcribe his own account. In the beginning of the fifth book of his History he calls himself an Englishman, brought hither (i. e. to Uticum) at the age of ten years, from the farthest limits of Mercia. "I begin this book," says he, "from the year 1075, because on the 14th of the calends of March, in that year, I was born; and on the Easter Sunday following was baptized by the ministry of Ordric the priest, at Ettingesham, in the church of St. Eatta the Confessor, which is seated on the bank of the river Severn. At the age of five years, my father committed me to the care of that noble priest Siward, to be instructed in literature; and under his tuition I remained five years. At the age of eleven years, my father, for the love of God, parted with me; and from England I was consigned, a tender exile, into Normandy, to fight under the banners of the Eternal Father. Here, received by the venerable father Mainer, and clothed with the monastic garb, for forty-two years have I cheerfully sustained the yoke of our Lord, and walked in the way of God according to our rule. The ecclesiastical customs and service have I laboured to learn, and have applied my mind unto all things profitable to salvation."

The life of a monk consists of little more than the date of his several orders; those of Ordericus, henceforth to be called Vitalis, he has himself recorded. In October 1086 he received the tonsure, was ordained sub-deacon[1] in March 1091, deacon in March 1093, and priest in Jan. 1108.

This uniform and peaceful existence was favourable to the cultivation of letters; and our monk seems to have made a good use of all the advantages which he possessed. He appears to have been inquisitive in making, and diligent in recording, the events of his time; no mean poet; well versed in Scripture; above all, of a piety ardent and sincere.

He began his history at the instance of his abbot, Roger, who was elected to that office in July 1091; but it is dedicated to his successor Warin, who sate from 1120 to July 1137: and a few years more are added, as he brings it down to the capture of king Stephen, February 1141, when he was himself arrived at the sixty-seventh year of his age; and he probably did not live much longer, as the habit which he had adopted of recording the transactions of his own times, would endure as long as the faculty of writing was indulged to him[2]. He has thus produced a work of great merit for the age in which it was written, if the reader has candour enough to excuse the legends and miracles which are interspersed with no very sparing hand. It is entitled an Ecclesiastical History; but might in fact, with great propriety, be called a History of his Own Times, displaying very extensive and varied research; is divided into thirteen books, and occupies six hundred folio pages of Du Chesne's great collection of Norman historians.

The generous mind which can sympathize with the feelings of nature, even when most distorted by adventitious circumstances; and has risen superior enough to the prejudices of its own age, to respect and allow for those of a former one; will, we are persuaded, thank us for the following pathetic strain of devotion, and forcible, though rude eloquence, with which our Salopian historian concludes his great work.

" Lo, I, borne down by age, seek to close this my book. Whereunto diverse causes move me. For I now am passing the sixty-seventh year of my life in the service of our Lord Jesus Christ: and while I behold the great men of this world afflicted by weighty misfortunes, by the grace of my God, I rejoice in my poverty, and in the security of subjection. Lo, Stephen king of England groaneth in the walls of a prison[3]; while Lewis,

---

[1] He was ordained sub-deacon by Gislebert Maminot, bishop of Luxovium, whose negligence in his see he therefore declines to dwell on. An odd kind of forbearance, which produces the very effect it professes to deprecate.

[2] Mr. Steevens places his death in 1143. See Malone's Shakspeare, by Boswell, xi. 296. We know not where the ingenious commentator found this date. Saxius has it not.

[3] He was taken prisoner at the battle of Lincoln, which was fought on the 2d of February, 1140-1, and was released in the following November; so that the period when Ordericus finished his history is nearly ascertained.

the king of France, leading his troops against the Goths and Gascons[1], is oppressed by the burden of many cares. Lo, the episcopal throne of Lisieux[2] standeth vacant, through the decease of its bishop; and when it will have such another prelate[3], I know not. What more shall I say? Amidst all these things, O Almighty God, I turn my voice to Thee, and implore Thy mercy. To Thee do I offer my thanks, who madest me without my aid, and hast guided me according to Thy will. Thou art my King and my God: I am Thy servant, and the son of Thy hand-maid: who, from the earliest days of my youth, have served Thee to my power.

"I was baptized on the sabbath of Easter, at Attingesham, a village of England, seated upon the great river Severn. There, by the ministry of Ordric the priest, didst Thou, O my God, beget me anew, by water and the Holy Ghost, and gavest unto me the name of my godfather, the aforesaid priest. Thence, at the age of five years, was I sent to school in the city of Scrobesbury; and offered unto Thee the first services of my clergyhood in the church of St. Peter and St. Paul the apostles. There did Siguard, a famous priest, teach me, for the space of five years, the rudiments of the Latin tongue, and instructed me in psalms and hymns, and other necessary parts of education. In the mean time, Thou didst exalt the aforesaid church, which belonged to my father, and which was situate on the river Mole, and didst erect the venerable Abbey, through the pious devotion of Roger the Earl.

"It was Thy pleasure to remove me from Thy service in that spot, and to take me from my kinsfolk, lest the ties of blood, which are so often an hindrance to Thy servants, might estrange my affections from the observance of Thy laws, to the lusts of the flesh. Therefore, O God of glory, Thou, who of old didst command Abraham to remove out of his country and from his kindred, didst in like wise inspire my father, Odelerius, wholly to renounce me, for Thy love, and to resign me entirely to Thee. Many were the tears which he shed, when he delivered me, a weeping infant, to the charge of Rainald[4] the monk, banishing me for ever from my native land. Nor did he ever see me from that moment. Instead of my native land, and the caresses of a tender father, he promised unto me, on Thy part, the joys of paradise. Do Thou, O God of Sabaoth, receive his prayers, and grant those his petitions.

"Thus, at the age of ten years, did I cross the British sea; unknowing and

---

[1] Louis the Young was at this time engaged in a war with Theobald, count of Champagne.

[2] Luxovium.

[3] John, bishop of Lisieux, died June 1142. It is difficult to reconcile this date with that in note [5], page 67. Perhaps this sentence, respecting the vacancy of Lisieux, was added by our monk on transcribing his first copy, without reflecting that it did not exactly tally with what he had previously written; which is a frequent source of inconsistency.

[4] Rainald was one of the two monks who first came from Seez to Shrewsbury in 1083.

unknown, I arrived in Normandy. Like Joseph, I heard a strange language. Yet, under Thy protection, I experienced all the gentle offices of humanity at the hands of foreigners. In the eleventh year of my age, I was admitted a monk in the monastery of Uticum, by the venerable abbot Mainer, and on Sunday the 21st day of September received the tonsure, after the manner of clerks. At the same time, instead of my English name, which sounded harsh in their ears, they called me Vitalis, in allusion to one of St. Maurice's companions, whose feast fell on that day[1].

"In this abbey have I, by Thy favour, dwelt for fifty-six years, loved and respected by my brethren and companions, far beyond my deserts. I have borne the heat and cold, and the burden of the day, among Thy labourers in the vineyard of Sorech[2], securely expecting the penny, my wages; for Thou art faithful that hast promised. Six abbots, Thy vicars, as my fathers and masters have I reverenced: to wit, Mainer and Serlo, Roger and Warin, Richard and Ralph, who presided over the convent of Uticum, as men who were aware that they must render an account of the souls committed to their charge.

"At the age of sixteen, on the 15th of March, I was ordained sub-deacon by Gilbert bishop of Lisieux, at the instance of Serlo, abbot elect. Two years after, on the 26th of March, Serlo bishop of Seez invested me with the stole of deacon; in which order I cheerfully served Thee by the space of fifteen years. At length, when I had arrived at my thirty-third year, William archbishop of Rouen loaded me with the burden of priesthood, on the new year's day. At the same time he ordained two hundred and forty-four deacons and one hundred and twenty priests, with whom I approached Thy altar, in the Holy Spirit, and have now fulfilled Thy sacred ministry for thirty-four years, with readiness and fidelity.

"Thus, thus, O Lord God, Thou who didst fashion me, and didst breathe into my nostrils the breath of life, hast Thou, through these various gradations, imparted to me Thy gifts, and formed my years to Thy service. In all the places to which Thou hast led me, Thou hast caused me to be beloved, by Thy bounty, not by my own deserving. For all Thy benefits, O merciful Father, I thank Thee, I laud and bless Thee: for my numberless offences, with tears I implore Thy mercy. For the praise of Thy unwearied goodness, look upon Thy creature; and blot out all my sins. Grant me the will to persist in Thy service, and strength to withstand the attacks of Satan, till I attain, by Thy grace, the inheritance of everlasting life. And what I have prayed for myself, I pray, O God, for my friends and well-

---

[1] Hence we see the impropriety of styling our historian, as is often done, Ordericus Vitalis; which is as improper as if, speaking of the late Pope, we were to call him *Braschi Pius*. He may be denominated by either of those names separately, but not by the two combined together.

[2] See Judges, xvi. 4. *Sorek* is *hissing*:—perhaps he alluded to the contempt which the servants of God experience from a perverse and wicked generation.

doers. The same also I pray for all the faithful: and forasmuch as the efficacy of our own merits cannot suffice to obtain those eternal gifts, after which the desires of the perfect aspire,

"O Lord God, Almighty Father, Creator and Ruler of the Angels, Thou true Hope, and eternal Blessedness of the righteous, may the glorious intercession of the Holy Virgin and Mother Mary, and all Saints, aid us in Thy sight, with the merits of our Lord Jesus Christ, Redeemer of all men, who liveth and reigneth with Thee in the unity of the Holy Ghost; world without end. Amen."

Sir David Dalrymple chooses, it is difficult to say why, to call our Shropshire historian " an ignorant blundering monk ;" and adds, " his errors are so many and so gross, that I will never quote him[1]:" and, having noticed what he conceives to be an error in this writer, he observes, " yet this Vitalis has had the good fortune to be quoted as an historian of singular credit[2]." Never was censure more unjust, or determination more rash ; to which whoever conforms, will lose much information, highly useful, authentic, and interesting, respecting most important transactions of our history. It might have become Sir David to remember his own just maxim, " if we would judge with truth and candour, we must try men by the standard of their own age." Baron Maseres, a much better judge than the Scottish annalist, has not thought our Salopian historiographer unworthy of a place in his selection of ancient documents respecting the history of England; and before him, MM. de S[t]. Marthe, eminent critics in historical antiquities, style him, *virum accuratum, et rerum abstrusarum indagatorem sedulum*[3]; and we must be permitted to add, that wherever we have had the opportunity to collate his narrative with authentic records, he has been found eminently veracious and worthy of credit. Nor is it easy for us, with our well-stored libraries, our public journals, and our unrestrained intercourse, to judge of the difficulties which the inhabitant of an obscure and provincial monastery must have encountered, in the collection of such information as would enable him to complete a work like that of Ordericus. In saying this, we would not be thought insensible to his defects, some of which have been touched above: nor will we controvert the opinion of bishop Nicolson, that " he is immoderate in the praise of his friends, and

---

[1] Annals of Scotland, v. i. p. 9. All this spleen seems excited, only because poor Ordericus asserts, that Malcolm of Scotland swore faithful obedience to William the Conqueror by his messengers.

[2] Ib. p. 24; and at p. 67, he says, " Ordericus Vitalis is an historian so ill-informed, especially with respect to the affairs of Scotland, that I dare not rely upon his evidence." Yet this very fact, which Lord Hailes would not believe on the authority of our Salopian, is related by another contemporary, and allowed for genuine history by the most eminent antiquaries. See Archæologia, vol. xix. p. 249.

[3] Quoted by Chiflet, Lilium Francicum. Antwerp, 1658, p. 60.

the dispraise of his enemies[1]," though it would have been more satisfactory, if the learned prelate had supported this last assertion by some examples, which perhaps he would not have found it easy to adduce. Our monk's occasional suppression of facts derogatory from the reputation of the heroes of his tale, has been already noticed in the preceding narrative.

The late Lewis Buckeridge, Esq. of Lichfield, had a brass seal-ring, of rude workmanship, and of the size of the annexed cut. The inscription, in Longobardic characters, bears the name VITALIS, with the figure of a key subjoined: and the ring part is of small diameter, not more than sufficient for the finger of a child twelve years old. We have seen in the above account of our author Ordericus, that he was professed a monk at the age of ten years: and as his father was a personage of distinction in the court of the earl of Shrewsbury, it is probable that the religious would be glad to confer on the son some office of little account, which might please a child, and shew their respect for the parent. The porter of a Benedictine abbey, who held a post of importance, "had always a boy under him, who lay at the gate with the sub-porter, and took the key, after curfew, to the cellarer's bed[2]:" and if young Vitalis was appointed to this office[3], he might at the same time be presented with a ring containing his name, and denoting his situation in the monastery. Nothing of all this is certain, but that the characters of the inscription are such as were in use about the commencement of the twelfth century when Ordericus lived, and that the size of the ring corresponds with his age at the time of his profession.

---

[1] English Historical Library, part ii. chap. 3. One of the anecdotes related by our historian which may be deemed the least credible, is that of the countess Mabil, related above, in p. 41; yet, if modern authorities are to be believed, it may be more than paralleled in the case of Hyder Ally, to whose back, it is said, that the liver of an infant was daily applied, as a remedy for a malignant boil, which is common in India, and which occasioned his death. The physician, it is farther said, defended the practice, by remarking, that they were *only the children of his own slaves*, whom he sacrificed to this expedient. See the notes on Irwin's Ode on the death of that tyrant. The same savage temper, fostered by the same plenitude of power, may have produced the like barbarity, in countries and periods the most remote.

[2] Fosbrooke, p. 198.

[3] The University of Caen, in 1476, as a token of their gratitude to the lord of Reviers for his good offices in obtaining them a grant of their schools, appointed his son to be porter of the same, *claviger* (literally *key-bearer*) scholarum. Abbé de la Rue, Essais Historiques sur la ville de Caen, t. i. p. 168. This, it will be allowed, is at least a remarkable coincidence with the supposed act of the monks of St. Peter, in the case of young Vitalis.

The form of this very rude seal-ring is as ancient as the times of classical antiquity. See specimens in Montfaucon, Diarium Italicum, p. 140.

CHAPTER IV.

OF SHREWSBURY, FROM ITS RESUMPTION BY THE CROWN, TO ITS RE-CAPTURE BY THE WELSH.

WE now resume our history of the town from the fall of its third and last Norman earl.

"Rex Henricus I. totum honorem Rodberti et hominum ejus qui cum illo in rebellione perstiterant possedit."—King Henry took possession of the whole honour[1] of earl Robert and of his vassals who adhered to him in his rebellion, are the words of Ordericus, (lib. xi. p. 808).

Thus, in the space of thirty-six years from the Norman conquest, did the greater part of the estates in Shropshire again change hands. Besides the reasonable inference, that the dependants and vassals of Belesme would follow the fortunes of their lord and master, some proof of this fact may be drawn from existing records. We have indeed no list of Salopian proprietors for fourscore years after Domesday, viz. till the Liber Niger in 1167[2]. but this last valuable record, besides a catalogue of the proprietaries of the county in that year, contains also a list, though an imperfect one, of feoffments under Henry I., and it is certain that in that list we read scarcely a single name[3] which occurs in Domesday. Hence the conclusion arises,

---

[1] By the *honour* of earl Robert, Ordericus intends his landed estates; as in the laws of the Longobards, a count who failed to execute justice on robbers, was to lose his fief and *honour*, beneficium et honorem. (ii. 40. 3.) And (in ii. 54. 2.) bishops and counts are exhorted to live harmoniously in their dioceses *(parochiis)* and counties, for the security of those who reside within their *honours*. The word subsequently assumed a technical signification in our English law, and denotes a paramount lordship, having other manors and lordships dependant upon it: as the *honour* of Montgomery, the *honour* of Arundel, &c.

[2] It were to be wished that this record was printed by public authority, after the manner of Domesday: the transcript printed by Hearne being manifestly incorrect. Indeed any edition of a bare catalogue of names and places must be necessarily inaccurate, where the editor is not assisted by local knowledge; and the only way to attain that would be by a transmission of the part relating to each county to some competent person within it, previously to its being printed off. Even the printed Domesday, with all its vaunted accuracy, is far from being immaculate, as we have ascertained in this county, by inspecting the original: and if this be the case in Shropshire, the result of an examination would probably be the same in other counties.

[3] One of these is Pantulph, who, we know, adhered to the king. And the family of Eyton, who held under him and perhaps descended from him, have ever since continued in Shropshire.

1086—1102.   HENRY I.   73

that the far greater part of the superior class of those who held lands in Shropshire in 1086, when that record was compiled, were dispossessed by this second great revolution; and that those very few families among us who can trace their lineage up to the Conquest, (with the exception of Corbet, who, as we have seen, originally stood out against king Henry, and afterwards made his peace,) must have been among the *pagenses milites*, who espoused the cause of their sovereign in opposition to his rebellious subject.

The earldom of Shrewsbury being thus vested in the crown, one of the first acts of the king was to appoint a deputy, with the title of Sewer or Steward[1]. This was Richard de Belmeis[2], an able minister, who immediately took up his residence in the castle of Sciropesberie, and in the same year (1102) in which he was entrusted with this important charge, evinced his promptness and ability, by seizing the person of prince Jorwerth, (a younger son of Bleddyn ap Cynfyn,) who had been detached by the king from the confederacy of Robert earl of Shrewsbury. This prince having

---

[1] Ordericus calls him sheriff, (Vicecomes Scrobesbirie, xi. 833,) but it does not appear that he ever styles himself so.

[2] Leland calls him Richard de Belesmo, (Collect. v. ii. p. 354,) but the orthography of Ordericus, as just cited, Richardus de Belmesio, is doubtless more correct. We have not yet seen any authority to satisfy us that he was "Warden of the Marches:" a title, we conceive, greatly posterior in time. But that he was *steward* or *sewer* of this county, appears from the contemporary authority of a charter in the leiger book of Shrewsbury abbey. Aldred, who was son of Siward the Gross, (which Siward was lord of the spot on which Shrewsbury abbey stood,) having on his father's death kept possession of the village of Longfeld, (Cheney Longville near Wistanstow,) which Siward had bestowed on the monks, was induced to restore it by the mediation of his master, Richard de Belmesio, qui tunc *dapifer* hujus comitatus erat, et postea episcopus Londonie. (Cartulary, No. 1.) This was in the time of abbot Fulchered. A proof of the jurisdiction exercised over Shrewsbury by this bishop occurs in the suit which arose between the monks of Shrewsbury and one Hubert, son of Richard, a prebendary of Morfield, concerning his father's prebend; on which occasion Henry I. directed this prelate to hold plea of the matter, *ut inde rectum teneret*. (ibid.) And again, (in the same number,) it is said of a certain grant, that it was made " licentia et testimonio Ricardi Episcopi qui in diebus illis istum comitatum sub Rege gubernabat, et Rainarii qui tunc prefectus erat." Nor must we omit the following charter of this prelate, which, though it may seem more immediately to belong to the abbey, throws much light on the government of the county at the period to which it belongs:—

R. dei grā London. episcopus omnibus Baronibus comitatus Scropesberiensis salut. Nostis quod Paganus fil. Johannis, qui post me suscepit regimen vicecomitatus Scrop. in primo placito quod habuit apud Brugiam, quesivit a me et a nobis [l. vobis] omnibus, ipse et Walterius constabulator, utrum Abbas S. Petri, &c. ... in short, whether the abbey was to be free from furnishing military aids.... Nos vero omnes una voce respondimus quod verum erat quod abbas predicte ecclesie nunquam illud dedit, &c. (Chartul. No. 353.)

This Walter the constable was father of Milo, earl of Hereford, whose daughter carried the honour of constable into the family of Bohun, and so, through Thomas of Woodstock, to the Staffords, dukes of Buckingham.

We have rendered *dapifer* by the word *steward*, though it more properly denotes a *sewer*, because we find these words were anciently synonymous. (Willelmus *dapifer* qui et *senescallus* appellatur. Vetus Chronicon ap. Du Cange, in v.) Both are significant of offices in the household of great men. *Seneschall*, the *elder* (i. e. the most honourable) *servant*. (Wachter.) Sewer, from Suiare, Icelandic, a *butler*. The definition of Hickes corresponds exactly with the office borne by Belmeis: *Senescallus* idem ac Minister domini vicarius, vel Minister in aliquo munere domini vices gerens. Erant præterea administratores redituum totius fisci dominici.

repaired hither in the hopes of reward[1], was thrown into prison, and confined here as long as Belmeis continued in office, which was till the year 1107, when he was appointed bishop of London.

The agitations attendant upon a contested succession and a recent conquest being thus happily appeased by the dexterity and firmness of Henry, that sagacious and prudent monarch directed his attention to the arts of peace. The cities and towns of his realm experienced a happy change and amelioration in their condition, and Shrewsbury, among others, was not overlooked by its royal earl. Under the civilized empire of the Romans, their municipal towns all partook of a certain freedom of constitution: and were in some degree fashioned upon the great model of Rome itself, into the partial semblance of a republican form. They were generally governed by two magistrates[2], annual and elective, *(Duumviri,)* a deliberative body of elders, *(Decuriones,)* with an occasional appeal to the people; while the members of these incorporations enjoyed various civil rights and privileges. Such, no doubt, was the constitution of the towns and cities of Roman Britain. But the Saxon invasion swept away all these elegant fabrics of civil life, and though that people reserved to themselves a rude and precarious kind of freedom, yet the inhabitants of towns were, generally speaking, reduced to a state of servitude; deprived of those rights which, in social life, are deemed most natural and unalienable, being incapable either to bequeath their property or transfer it, or even to quit their places of residence, without the permission of their superior lord[3]. The Norman invasion depressed still lower the inhabitants of our boroughs; and we may conceive the insolence with which those foreign settlers, exulting in their connexion with the earl, and in their freedom from taxes, trampled on the wretched burgesses of Shrewsbury.

The towns of Italy were the first to throw off the yoke of servitude. Somewhat more enlightened than their northern neighbours, the memory of their former freedom had never been entirely extinct. Enabled by their situation to convey the merchandize of the east to the nations of the west,

---

[1] Dr. Powell in his History of Wales, (sub ann. 1101,) represents this somewhat differently, and the reader will do well to compare the two accounts.

[2] M. de S. Foix observes in his learned and lively Essais historiques sur Paris, (v. ii. p. 27): Les Français, après la conquête des Gaules, ne changèrent point la forme de police et d'administration qu'ils trouvèrent établie dans les villes. See on the government of the municipal towns of the Roman empire a paper by M. Bonamy, in the Mem. de l'Acad. des Inscr. xvii. 18. The government of Avignon, says lady M. W. Montague, (Works, vol. iv. p. 5,) retains a sort of imitation of the old Romans; having two consuls chosen every year: the first from the noblesse.

[3] A learned writer in a modern periodical work claims for our Saxon boroughs a much higher rank than that which is given them here. His examples are very few, and in our opinion very weak. The discussion is too long for a note, and of no importance except as a point of curious inquiry: for surely no one can suppose our liberties endangered by the decision. If antiquarian research is once to be guided by party feeling, there is an end to historical truth.

they soon acquired considerable wealth. Commerce naturally begat a spirit of independence; and either by purchase or violence, all the considerable cities in that favoured country obtained large immunities from the emperors of Franconian race, and erected themselves into free cities, some of which were in process of time to take a distinguished place among the sovereigns of Europe, and to continue till they were swallowed up by the convulsions of that eventful period which we have recently witnessed. In the mean time, the other countries of Europe were not indifferent spectators of this important change in the state of the Italian cities. Many of those in Germany trod exactly in their footsteps. In France the policy of the sovereign anticipated the struggles of the subject, and imparted that as a boon, which might otherwise have been claimed as a right.

England, from its insular situation and convulsed state, was more tardy in adopting these novelties. London indeed forms somewhat of an exception. Even in the Saxon times, that city was considered as a member of the state; and in 1036, the " shipmen of London" are mentioned in conjunction with earl Leofric and the northern thanes, as assisting at the great Witenagemote holden in Oxford upon the death of king Canute, and as uniting with them in the election of Harold [1]. But London engrossed nearly the whole national trade of that era; and even our Saxon monarchs could perceive that commerce brought money into their treasury, and that it could not consist with a state of slavery. The Conqueror's charter, however, to that metropolis of the kingdom, while it confirms " the laws that were in Edward's days the king [2]," evinces the dependent and slavish state of the citizens. The clause, " I will that each child be his father's heir after his father's days," proves that, in general, this was not the case. In short, we have seen the condition of Shrewsbury after the Norman Conquest from Domesday; and we have no reason to believe that it was in a worse condition than its neighbours. Enslaved and oppressed, it was reduced to a mere village of Russian boors: the earl's castle frowned upon it in sullen and despotic state, and its chief magistrate was a *reeve* or *prepositus*, a servant of that nobleman, charged with the office of oppressing the burgesses, and exacting the ferms, or rents due to his master.

With whatever violence Henry I. might use his power after the suppression of the rebellion of Robert de Belesme; and we are told that he assumed a very despotic authority after that event; he had yet the merit of relaxing the chain of servitude by which the burghers of his realm were oppressed. His travels had made him acquainted with the institutions of other countries; his good sense enabled him to discern their expediency; and his disputable title compelled him to court the affections of his people. To how many of the cities and towns of his realm he extended those franchises which corpo-

[1] Chron. Sax. sub ann.   [2] See the curious charter in Stow.

rate bodies on the continent then enjoyed, we cannot say: but that to him we are to look for the mitigation of Salopian thraldom, is evident from the charter of his descendant John, who confirms to the burgesses of this town, *all liberties, and free customs, and quittances,* " omnes libertates, et liberas consuetudines, et quietancias, sicut eas habuerunt tempore regis Henrici proavi nostri," *as they held them in the time of king Henry, our great-grandfather.* The nature of these grants we cannot exactly ascertain. The charter of Henry I. (if indeed his grant was ever reduced to writing[1]) is no longer extant; but we may reasonably conjecture that it restored in part those privileges which the burgesses enjoyed under the Confessor's reign, and we know that the *ferm*, or rent, which they paid to the Crown, was greatly diminished, in comparison with what had been exacted by the Norman earl.

On the promotion of Richard de Belmeis to the see of London in 1107, he was succeeded in the office of vicecount or sheriff by Payn, or Pagan Fitz John, who was probably indebted for this presidency over Shropshire to the interest of his brother Eustace, chief counsellor, and (if kings can have such) intimate friend to Henry I.[2] The new sheriff had previously filled a post immediately attendant on the royal person—that of Chamberlain: and a trifling incident, which occurred during the period in which he held that office, as recorded by a writer who lived not long after, is so characteristic of the manners of the age, and of the king's good-nature, that we shall give it in a note[3]. Fitz John, promoted to this important control over our town and county, as well as the adjoining one of Hereford, " advanced his power," says a contemporary historian[4], " to such a pitch in the reign of king Henry, that from the river of Severn even unto the sea, through all the

---

[1] Mr. Hallam thinks, in opposition to Lord Lyttelton, that there are no examples of civil incorporations in England (except London) till the reign of Henry II. (Middle Ages, i. 211.); and this is perhaps correct.

[2] Henrico I^{mo} regi summus et popularis amicus. Gesta Regis Stephani, edited by Du Chesne among the Norman Writers, p. 939.

[3] The author is Walter Mapes: we exhibit it in the translation of Camden (Remains, p. 323). " There was allowed a pottle of wine for *livery* every night to be served up to king Henry the First's chamber, but because the king did seldom or never use to drink in the night, *Paine Fitz-John, his Chamberlain*, and the pages of the chamber, did carowse the wine among them. On a time it happened the king at midnight called for wine, but none was to be found: Paine and the pages bestirred themselves in vain, seeking wine here and there. Paine was called in to the king, who asked him if there were not allowance for *livery*: he humbly answered, That there was a pottle allowed every night, but for that he never called for it (to say the truth in hope of pardon) we drunk it up amongst us. Then, (quoth the king,) have you but one pottle every night? that is too short for me and you: from henceforth there shall be a whole gallon allowed, whereof the one pottle shall be for me, the other for you and yours. This I note, not for any gravity, but that the king in that age was commended herein both for bounty and clemency." *Livery* was a slight meal generally taken between the early supper of our ancestors and their time of retiring to rest.

[4] Gesta Regis Stephani, p. 932. Paganus filius Johannis, Herefordensis et Salopesbiriæ provinciæ dominatum gerens: qui intantum in tempore Regis Henrici potentiæ suæ culmen extenderat, ut a Sabrina flumine usque ad mare per omnes fines Angliæ et Waloniæ omnes placitis involveret, et angariis oneraret.

marches of England and Wales, he involved all men in litigations, and loaded them with exactions[1]."

During the time that this great man presided over our county, his royal master appears to have honoured Shrewsbury with a visit. In the leiger book or chartulary of the abbey, is a charter of this king in favour of abbot Godefrid[2], which bears date at Conedouere. That village had been a manor, and, no doubt, an occasional residence, of the earls of Shrewsbury; and the king could scarcely have been there without visiting the neighbouring capital of the county[3].

The earldom of Shrewsbury continued in the crown for the space of twenty-four years. At the end of this period in 1126, Henry I. having convened an assembly of his prelates and barons at London during the feast of Christmas, gave the county of Salopesbury, says the historian[4], to his second wife, daughter of the duke of Lovaine. The queen appointed for her viscount or sheriff, William Fitz Alan, " a baron not inferior to earls," in the estimate of a contemporary writer[5]. To this office he had a sort of hereditary claim, if it be true, as the genealogists affirm[6], that his father Alan, son of Flaald, took to wife Ameria, the daughter and heir of Warin, the vice-count of Roger de Montgomery. This William was elder brother to Walter Fitz Alan, steward of Scotland, patriarch of the royal line of Stewart; and he was himself ancestor of the noble family of the Fitz Alans, earls of Arundel; of which the duke of Norfolk is now the representative.

On the death of Henry I., and the violent usurpation of Stephen, William Fitz Alan adhered to the cause of the rightful heir to the crown, the empress Maud; and held the castle of Shrewsbury against the arms of the usurper. Stephen laid siege to it in July 1138[7], and the account which Ordericus gives us of this siege contains some curious particulars.

---

[1] Fitz John survived to the reign of king Stephen. He is enumerated by the author of that king's "Acts," among the nobles who at first stood out against him, but afterwards (i. e. in 1136) came to his court at an early period of his reign. He died, says the same writer, in a miserable manner, " without repentance," (i. e. without the offices of the church,) as he was waiting an opportunity to revolt; being shot through the head with an arrow as he was engaged in a skirmish with the Welsh, and he was the only man in his army who fell on that occasion. Dum Walenses persequitur, solus inter suos missili capite perforato succubuit.

[2] We should have placed this visit to Cundover in 1114, when the king marched a grand expedition into Wales, and entered the principality in three places; but it appears from the names of the attesting prelates, that the charter mentioned in the text could not have been executed earlier than the following year.

[3] We have omitted all mention of the general assembly said to be holden here in 1116, at which the nobility of England did homage and swore fealty to William son of Henry I.; because the ancient writers place it at Salisbury.

[4] Will. Malmsbury Hist. Novell. lib. i. sub init.

[5] Gesta Regis Stephani, p. 356.

[6] The early part of this ancient pedigree is involved in much difficulty. It is certain from the foundation charter of Haghmond Abbey, founded by this William Fitz Alan, that his mother's name was Avelina, not Ameria. She may, however, have been daughter to Warin the first vice-count.

[7] Ordericus writes that Shrewsbury was captured in the same week in which the battle of the Standard was fought. This seems to fix, with

"William Fitz Alan, castellan and sheriff of Scrobesbury, who had married a niece of the earl of Gloucester[1], adopted his party, and held the city against the king for the space of nearly four weeks. At length, in the month of August, the royal arms prevailed, and the king took the castle by assault, William having previously effected his escape.

"Arnulf de Hesding[2], a warlike and rash soldier, uncle to the young sheriff, had frequently during the siege, with many disrespectful terms of

undoubted accuracy, the time when our town surrendered to the arms of Stephen. For Roger Hoveden places the battle of the Standard in August 1138, (p. 484); and the Mailros chronicle gives the very day, the 22d of that month; (and so are Carte, i. 531; and Chalmers, Caledonia, i. 623) though Dr. Whitaker, History of Richmondshire, p. 80, fixes it in 1137; and the Messrs. Lysons (Magna Britannia, Cumberland, p. viii.) in 1139. Dr. Whitaker's mistake arose from his eye having inadvertently glanced over the succeeding year, which commences on the 482d page of Hoveden, in Savile's edition. It is remarkable, that Leland, in his Collectanea, quoting Hoveden, has twice (i. 198, ii. 204) fallen into the same error with the historian of Richmond.

Stephen's charter to Buildwas abbey in the Monasticon, is dated, apud Salopesberiam, in obsidione, anno incarn. dominice M.C.XXX.IX. regni vero nostri tertio. This would seem, at first, to countenance the date of Lysons; but it cannot be reconciled with truth. Henry I. died Dec. 1, 1135; and it is natural to suppose that his successor would begin to compute the years of his reign from that very day. We know that he did so; because we have a charter of his, dated apud Oxeneford, anno ab incarnatione Domini M.C.XXX.VI. et regni mei primo. (See the facsimile of it in the late magnificent edition of The Statutes of the Realm.) The year 1139 would consequently be the *fourth*, and not the *third*, year of Stephen. How is this to be reconciled? There is no error in the printed date of the Buildwas charter, for it agrees with the transcript of Dodsworth, the real compiler of the Monasticon, vol. 110, (MSS. in Bibl. Bodl. for which we are indebted to the Rev. Edw. Williams); yet it is impossible to acquit the date of error, either in the year of the Lord, or the year of the king; and as it is more likely that the clerk of chancery attendant at Shrewsbury on the great seal, should, amidst the din of arms, mistake the former, then an unusual mode of computation, than the latter, we conceive that he set down 1139 when he ought to have written 1138: and herewith agrees Mr. Lloyd (Hist. of Shropshire, MS.) who places our siege in this latter year.

[1] This was Robert, commonly called the Consul of Gloucester, a natural son of Henry I. The wife of Fitz Alan is stated, upon good authority, to have been the daughter of Helias de Say, of Clun: if she was niece to the earl of Gloucester, Henry I. must have had another natural daughter, not enumerated by the genealogists, and she must have been the wife of the lord of Clun.

[2] A person of this name, possibly the same who appears in Domesday as a land-holder in Berkshire, was father of Rotroc, earl of Perch, who married Maud, a natural daughter of Henry I. It is probable that this Arnulf may have had a son of both his names, brother of Rotroc, and here called uncle to William Fitz Alan. If Maud, the widow of the earl of Perch, married also Helias de Say, the pedigree might be nearly reconciled. They would then stand thus:—

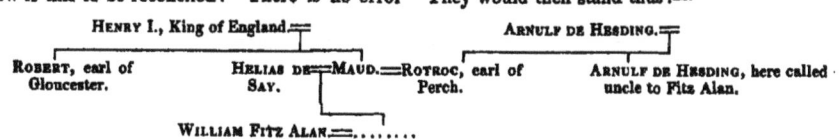

HENRY I., King of England.
├── ROBERT, earl of Gloucester.
└── HELIAS DE SAY.═MAUD.═ROTROC, earl of Perch.
         │
         WILLIAM FITZ ALAN.═........

ARNULF DE HESDING.
└── ARNULF DE HESDING, here called uncle to Fitz Alan.

Other proofs of connexion subsisting between the families of Hesding and Fitz Alan occur. Reginald de Hesding, probably a son of the second Arnulf, is a witness to the charter whereby William son of William son of Alan, at the request of Fulke Fitz Warin, grants the said Fulke's land at Alveston to Reginald de Le. It appears, from the Pipe Rolls of 2 Richard I., that, in that year, Hesding was what we should now call undersheriff to Fitz Alan:—

Salopescir.
Willus f. Alani. Regin. de Hesdin r. c. [reddit compotum] pro eo.

The same person occurs on the Pipe Rolls of 15 John. He had considerable estates in the parishes of Baschurch and Oswestry; in which last, he gave his land of Aston to the canons of Haghmon. Chartulary of that abbey; in which his name is uniformly written Hedinge.—Hesdin is a town in Picardy.

contumely, rejected the conditions offered by Stephen; and had been very instrumental in protracting the resistance made by the besieged. On the fall of the fortress, he and his companions were brought into the king's presence; who, finding," continues my authority, " that lenity had only produced the effect of rendering him contemptible, and that the nobles who had been summoned to assist him had, on that account, refused their services, judged it expedient to make a severe example. Accordingly he consigned Arnulf, and ninety-three others, to the ignominious execution of the gallows, notwithstanding all the splendid offers of a vast ransom, which they laid before him. The effect was immediate. In three days, the country flocked in with various excuses for their delay; and many brought the keys of their castles, and made a voluntary tender of their services.[1]"

The assertion of Ordericus, that Stephen conducted this memorable siege in person, is further proved by his charter of confirmation to the abbey of Buildwas, which had been founded two years before. This charter is dated at Shrewsbury during the siege, " *apud Salopesbiriam in obsidione.*"

Fitz Alan remained in exile for fifteen years; following the fortunes of the young duke of Normandy, Henry, son of the empress Maud, and rightful heir of the English throne. At the end of this period, in 1152, that prince landed in England to assert his claim; and gained considerable advantages over the usurper, taking many of his castles. Among the other conquests of the young duke, was the castle of Shrewsbury[2], which we may presume he again confided to the care of Fitz Alan. It is at least certain, that when Henry, on the death of Stephen in the following year, quietly ascended the throne of his ancestors, this loyal baron was re-instated in all his vast possessions, both in Shropshire and elsewhere; and in an interesting contemporary document[3], we see him at Bruges (Bridgenorth)

---

[1] The manuscript from which Du Chesne published the *Gesta Regis Stephani* is defective in that part which would have related the siege of Shrewsbury. This is the more to be lamented, as the author every where furnishes various particulars of the transactions which he relates, that are no where else to be found. We have taken much ineffectual pains to learn whether any more perfect copy exists in the libraries of France, and our best thanks are due to Henry Petrie, Esq. keeper of the King's Records in the Tower (from whom we expect, with eagerness, the accomplishment, under parliamentary encouragement, of that great national desideratum, a Body of our early Historians), for his very kind attention to our inquiries. He assures us that no perfect transcript of the *Gesta Stephani* has been yet discovered. A learned ecclesiastic of Normandy was less obliging.

[2] The only authority which I have seen for this fact, is Dr. Powell's History of Wales, sub ann. p. 172. Hoveden, Huntingdon, Walsingham, and Paris, do not notice it. But Caradoc of Llancarvan, the Welsh chronicler, Dr. Powell's author, was a contemporary, since he flourished in 1157, and perhaps lived in the vicinity of Shropshire. Mr. Carte, i. 550, represents the empress Maud as being in possession of all the counties of England lying on the Severn, as early as 1143, all which were in perfect tranquillity.

[3] Omnibus Sancte Dei ecclesie filiis ad quos presentes litere pervenerint Johannes Extraneus salutem. Quod vidi et audivi, ut in futurum ratum habeatur, et nulli liceat contra ire, testificari dignum esse credo. Will. fil. Alani, die, igitur, qua homagium ab hominibus suis apud Brugiam suscepit, adunata multitudine baronum et militum, coram omnibus, ecclesiam de Wroccestre, pro salute domini Regis qui terram suam sibi reddiderat,

receiving the homage of his "men" (i. e. his vassals) in an assembly of barons and knights; and granting the church of Wroccestre (Wroxeter) to the canons of Hagamon, " for the good estate of his lord the king, who had restored him to the possession of his land."

On the accession of Henry II., therefore, Shrewsbury returned into the same state in which it had been left by his grandfather: that is, enjoying, perhaps, most of the free customs which their forefathers held in the days of the Confessor; but still liable to be taxed arbitrarily, at the pleasure of the crown[1]. In his second year, (1155) the burgesses paid an aid into the king's exchequer of ten marks, or 6l. 13s. 4d.[2], a sum of money equal, perhaps, in effect to 350l. at the present day[3]. In the sixteenth of this king (1170), the burgesses of Salopesberie paid two marks of gold to have their town at farm, i. e. that they might be permitted, in lieu of the several payments and forfeitures due from the burgesses to the crown for certain transactions and offences, to pay a fixed rent: and it is certain, that this king granted to the town additional privileges. This we collect from his son's charter, hereafter to be mentioned.

In the summer of 1158, he made an iter, or progress, through his kingdom, administering justice, and holding his court wherever he went[4]. It was, perhaps, upon this occasion that he visited Shrewsbury, where he

---

et pro salute anime sue, omniumque antecessorum suorum et successorum, ecclesie S. Joh'is Ewangeliste de Hagamon et canonicis ibidem Deo et S*°. Johanni servientibus imp'petuum elemosin', me etiam presente, dedit et concessit. Et ut certius sit testimonium meum, presenti scripto et impressione sigilli mei corroboro et confirmo. Hujus donationis et concessionis testes sunt Abbas de Wighem͞, Walter' de Dunstanville, Hugo de Laci, Wido Extraneus, Hugo Pantulf, Sim̄ de Perepunt, Willm̄ fil͞ Radulfi, Will͞us fil Walteri, Robertus Dardif, Willus de Perepunt, et multi alii. E cartis hon. Cecil Jenkinson, olim Tho. Ottley, ar.—It is preceded in the Haghmond chartulary by a similar attestation of Roger de Powis, who seems to be the Rogerus Walensis of the Liber Niger.

[1] There was no time when the freeholders of England could be taxed without the consent of the great freeholders, the tenants in capite; of whom our parliaments at first consisted: but the state of the burgesses was widely different. They were liable to be tallaged at pleasure, without being represented; which the freeholders, in some sort, always were. See the excellent View of the ancient Constitution, by Baron Maseres, Archæol. v. 2, the best treatise, perhaps, which has yet been written on this beaten subject.

[2] Madox, H. Exch. v. i. p. 602.

[3] In all our inquiries into ancient times, no subject has more difficulties than the comparison of the effective value of their money with ours. About the year 1145, the tenant of a place was to pay yearly 20s. or seven oxen. Fleetwood, Chron. Pret. p. 71, from Matthew Paris. An ox, therefore, was then worth 2s. 10½d., and consequently, 6l. 13s. 4d., the aid paid by the burgesses of Shrewsbury to Henry II. in 1155, would have purchased nearly forty-six oxen. We must not suppose that the oxen of that day were equal in value to the large and well-fed cattle of the present time: they were in all probability very small and very lean; yet we can scarcely suppose that one of them could now be purchased for less than 6l.: and this will swell the ten marks of 1155 to no less than 276l., a vast sum for the few families then residing in the town, (perhaps not many more than in the days of the Confessor,) to raise among themselves: and it is rendered at all credible only by the recollection, that our forefathers of the twelfth century were ignorant of the accumulated burdens of assessed taxes, excise duties, and poor's rates. In the above calculation, we have taken no notice, as is often done, of the superior quality of metal in the coin of that age; three times as much as at present, (though *that* somewhat diminishes the wonder of the low price of an ox;) because it was in money of that period, and not in money of our time, that the composition recorded by Matthew Paris was made.

[4] Carte, i. 568.

granted to Haghmon abbey exemption from toll through his whole land of England and Wales. He was then attended by Richard de Luci, William Fitz Adeline, his sewer, and Hugh de Laci, who witness this grant. Robert Marmion was also in attendance upon him at the same time; for there is another charter of the same king dated here, and attested by the said Marmion, Luci, and Laci, granting to that abbey the church of Hanmere. Here also it was that Gilbert Fitz William, lord of Hadnall, surrendered a moiety of that village, and all Hardwicke, into the king's lands; possessions which he immediately granted to the canons of Haghmon. See the chartulary of that house.

Henry's occasional visits to this town are farther proved by the anecdote which Giraldus relates of Owen Cevelioc; who, lineally descended as he was from the Brochwels and Elisegs of ancient Pengwern, was now reduced to a rank little, if at all, superior to the proud courtiers of the English monarch. "Once," says our author, "this British prince, sitting at table with the king at Salopesbury, his majesty sent to him one of his own loaves, as a mark of distinction. Owen immediately cut it into small pieces, after the manner of an almoner, and then began to eat, first of all, those pieces which were farthest from him, and so, by degrees, all of them; and when the king asked what he meant by this, he only answered, with a smile, 'I do but follow the example of my lord the king;' hereby," adds the writer, "covertly and wittily upbraiding the avarice of Henry, in his retention and tardy distribution of ecclesiastical benefices[1]."

In the thirty-first of Henry II. (1185) our burgesses paid 20l. and two hunters, *pro firma burgi*[2], that is, they paid so much, only the half of what earl Roger exacted of them, for the rent of their town: and, through the whole of this reign, our local history is principally confined to these domestic details: though there can be little doubt, that, engaged as the king was in frequent warfares with the Welsh, it was the scene of many a negotiation and contest unnoticed by history[3].

Giraldus speaks with much complacency of the comfortable accommodations which he found here, after his tedious journey with Baldwin, archbishop of Canterbury, over the bleak and barren mountains of Wales.

[1] Itin. Wall. l. ii. c. 12. The elemosinarius, or almoner of an abbey, cut his bread into pieces for the purpose of distribution to the poor.

[2] Madox ut supra. This phrase has been explained above.

[3] According to the old chronicle of the Fitz Warins, in Leland's Collectanea, Yarward Drwyndon, prince of Wales, wasted all the lands of the marches from Chester to Worcester, in a war which lasted from 1172 to 1176, at the end of which time the king of France made peace between the king and prince at Salopesbury; upon which occasion the king (this must have been Henry II.) gave to Llewelin, the prince's son, an infant of seven years, his daughter Jonet in marriage, with Ellesmere as her portion. But this chronicle is such a strange medley of circumstantial falsehood, that no dependence whatever can be placed upon it. It was his illegitimate sister Emma whom Henry gave in marriage to David ap Owen, prince of North Wales, with the territory of Ellesmere in 1177. Carte, i. 693.

From Oswestry, says he[1], that prelate and his retinue came after Easter (1188) to Slopesbury, where they remained some days to recruit and refresh themselves; and many assumed the cross in obedience to the precepts of the archbishop, and the gracious sermons of the archdeacon of St. David's. Here also they excommunicated Oen de Cevelioc, because he alone, of all the Welsh princes, had not advanced to meet the archbishop[2].

The reign of the gallant Cœur de Lion, so glorious to his military fame, and so oppressive to his subjects, affords no incident of a general nature with which this town is concerned; but is important in our local history, as being the earliest date to which we can refer any portion of our *chartered liberties*. We are sure that a written charter of Henry II. once existed, for it is mentioned in one by his son John, and it protected the free customs of the burgesses of Salopesbury, by a penalty of 10*l*. denounced against any who should presume to violate them: but that document has long since perished (at least as long ago as the reign of Elizabeth, when the charters were copied into a quarto volume), and that of Richard I. is the earliest now preserved in the archives of the corporation.

It bears date the 11th day of November, in the first year of his reign, not three months after his arrival in England (for he was absent on the continent at his father's death): and on account of the rank which it holds in our documentary evidence, a copy of it is subjoined, for the satisfaction of the reader, engraved in fac simile.

Ricardus dei gratia Rex Angliæ Dux Normanniæ Aquitaniæ Comes Andegaviæ Archiepiscopis Episcopis Abbatibus Comitibus Baronibus Justiciariis vicecomitibus & omnibus ministris & fidelibus suis. salutem. Sciatis nos concessis se Burgensibus de Salopesberia villam de Salopesberia tenendam de nobis pro xl. marcis argenti.

Unde x marce sunt pro duobus fugatoribus quos reddere solebant. Quare volumus & precipimus quod predicti Burgenses habeant & teneant predictam villam cum Omnibus pertinentiis suis pro xl. marcis argenti reddendis per annum. cum Omnibus Libertatibus & liberis consuetudinibus suis. quas habuerunt tempore domini Regis Henrici Patris nostri. Testibus Hugone Dunelmensi Episcopo Galfrido filio Petri. Hugone Bardolf. Hugone Pantulf. Data apud Westmonasterium xi die Novembris per manum Willelmi de Longo Campo Cancellarii nostri. Regni nostri Anno primo.

It grants the town of Salopesbiri to be holden by the burgesses thereof for forty marks of silver of annual rent; by which holding of the town, they were exonerated, we apprehend, from an arbitrary enhancement of their

---

[1] Itin. Wall. ut supra.
[2] A fine at Salop, 35 H. II., before Ralph the archdeacon, Maurice de Berkele, William Fitz Alan, Thomas Noel, Hugh Pantulf, Master Robert of Salop, (who, in 1181, was co-governor of Ireland with Hugh de Lacy. Carte, i. 711,) Robert de Hasel, Nicholas Briton, justiciary. Dodsw. v. 109, from the cartulary of Littleshull.

THE REMAINS OF THE MONASTERY OF S.T PETER & S.T PAUL,
From the East.

No 2

Castle Gates.

NUMMI SAXONICI SALOPIAE CUSI AERE ROCIDI CURAVIT
PROPRIIS SUMPTIBUS AMICITIAE ERGO PETRUS PRATTINTON M.B.

In Civitate SCROPESBERIE T(em)p(o)r(e) R(egis) E(dwardi)
erant .CC.L.II. dom(us). 7 v(e)l d(i)c(itu)r burgses in ipsis domib(us)
redd(en)tes p(er) annu(m) VII. lib. 7 XVI. solid. 7 VIII. den(arios) de gablo.
Ibi habeb(at) rex .E. has subterscriptas c(on)suetudines.
S(i) q(u)i pace regis manu p(ro)pria data infringebat ut(la)g(us)
fiebat. Qui v(er)o pace regis a uicecomite data infringebat
C. solid emdab(at) 7 tantund(em) dabat qui forestel uel hemfare
faciebat. Has .III. forisfacturas habeb(at) i(n) d(omi)nio rex .E. in omi
anglia extra firmas.
Quando rex iaceb(at) in hac ciuitate sequebant cu(m) uigilantes
XII. hoes de melioribz ciuitatis. Et cu(m) ibi uenationem
exerceret. simili(te)r custodiebant eu(m) cu(m) armis meliores
burgses caballos habentes. Ad stabilitione(m) u(ero) mittebat
uicecomes .XXXVI. hoes pedites. quandiu rex ibi esset.
Ad parcu(m) aut(em) de Marsetelie inueniebant .XXXVI. hoes
p(er) c(on)suetudine(m) .VIII. dieb(us).
Cu(m) in Walis p(er)gere uellet uicecom(es) qui ab eo edictus non
p(er)gebat .XL. solid de forisfactura dab(at).
Mulier accipiens quocu(m)q(ue) m maritu(m). si uidua erat. dab(at) regi
XX. sol. Si puella .X. solid. q(ua)libet i(n) accipet uirum.
Cu(m)cu(m)q(ue) burgsis dom(us) cob(ur)eretur aliq(u)o casu uel euentu.
siue negligentia .XL. solid regi dab(at) p(ro) forisfactura. 7 duob(us)
p(ro)pinquiorib(us) uicinis suis .II. solid unicuiq(ue) de relevam(en)to.
Burgsis qui in d(omi)nio erat regis cu(m) moriebat(ur). habeb(at) rex .X. sol
Si q(u)is burgsis frangeb(at) t(er)m(inu)m que uicecom(es) imponebat ei.
emdab(at) .X. solid. Qui sanguine fundeb(at) .XL. solid emdab(at).
Cu(m) rex abiret de ciuitate. mitteb(at) ei .XXIIII. caballos uicecom(es)
Leuue(n)orde. 7 ipsos duceb(at) rex usq(ue) ad p(ri)ma(m) mansion(em) sup(er) Stafordschire.
Tres monetar(ios) habeb(at) ibi rex. qui postq(uam) c(o)emissent cuneos
monete ut alii monetarii patrie .XV. die dabant regi
XX. sol unusquisq(ue). 7 hoc fiebat moneta uertente.
Int(er) tot redd(eba)t ciuitas ista p(er) annu(m) .XXX. lib. Duas partes
habeb(at) rex. 7 uicecom(es) tertiam.
p(re)cedenti anno hui(us) descriptionis. redd(i)t .XL. lib Rogerio com(iti).

Hec ciuitas T.R.E. geldab(at) p(ro) C. hidis.
De his habet S. Almund(us) .II. hid. S. Iuliana d(o)m(inicas) hid
S(an)c(t)a Milburga .I. hid. S(an)c(t)us Cedd(a) hid 7 dim. Sanctus v(e)rii
ep(iscopu)s de Cestre .I. hid. Edr(icus) .III. hid qi b(e)t Rad(ulfus) de Mortemer.

Dicu(n)t anglici burgses de Scropesberie. multu(m) grave sibi ee
q(uo)d ipsi redd(en)t tot geld sicut redd(eba)t T.R.E. quamu(is) castelli
comit occupauerit .LI. masur(as). 7 alie .L. mature sint vaste. 7 XLIII
francig(eni) burgses teneant masuras geldantes T.R.E. 7 abbatia qua(m) facit
ibi comes dederit ipse .XXXIX. burgses oli simil(i)t(er) cu(m) alis geldantes.
Int(er) tot f(iun)t .CC. masur(as) VII. min(us) que n(on) geldant.

☩ CONCEN FILIUS CATELI CATELL
FILIUS GROHCMAIL GROHMAIL FILIUS
ELITEZ ELITEZ FILIUS SUOILLAUC
☩ CONCENN ITAQUE PRONEPOS ELITEZ
EDIFICAVIT HUNC LAPIDEM PROAVO
SUO ELITES ☩ IPSE EST ELITEZ QUI RECR
.AT HEREDITATEM POYOS .IPC MORT
OAVIEM PER UIM . . EPOTESTATE ANGLO
RUM . . . . . IN GLADIO SUO PARTA IN IGHE
— — — — IMQYE RECITUERIT MANET CR.P
— — — — IM DET BENEDICTIONEM SUPE
— — — — — ELITES ☩ IPSE EST CONC HH
— — — — — SUS . C . C MEIUNG C MAHV
— — — — — — EAQ REZ HHM SUUM POYOREA
— — — — — — E . IT IU 6AU1 . T. E QUOQ
— — — — — — T/ YEAIS . UCAUES MEC
— — — — — — — JM . EIN . MONTEM

                        ILE .. K . JMONARCHIAM
    AIL MAXIMUS BRITTANNIAE
    NN PATSEN   MAUI : ANNAN
    BRITUA.T.M FILIUS SUARTHI
    QUE BENED. SERMANUS QUE
    ≡ PEPERIT ET T EEIRA FILIA MAXIMI
    SIT . QUI OCCIDIT RESEM ROMANO
    RUM ☩ CONMARCH PINXIT HOC
    CHIROZRAFŪ REZE SUO PORCENTE
    CONCENN ☩ BENEDICTIO DNĪ IN CON
    CENN & FṪ TOTA FAMILIA SIUS
    ET IN TOTA RAZIONE POVOIS
    URQUE IN — — — — — — —

The first line is taken from the Original. A proof that Gough's copy is not very correct.
Printed by C Hullmandel.

the countrey and he agreed not; he being too much a soldier, and too civil for many of them, and they procured him to be removed; and sir Richard Ottley first, and after sir Michael Earnley, made Governors. Sir Fulke was confident when he went, that their drunkenness and carelessness would shortly lose the town." Here are various mistakes. The historical relations of Baxter are as little to be depended upon as those of Burnet. Not from any intentional falsification in either of those eminent persons; but because both of them, writing from recollection, many years after the facts occurred which they propose to record, and not distrusting their memories, took no pains to ascertain the truth of what they deliver. The mistake of sir Francis's Christian name is trivial, compared with the misstatement of the date of his government, which, it is certain, continued from February 1642-3 to November or December 1644.

But though the gentleman mentioned by Baxter never occupied the station which the biographer assigns him, he was, as we have seen, a distinguished character in Shrewsbury at the time in question[1], and, being a good officer, might very probably witness a great deal more of licence and negligence in the garrison than he could approve of. A family of his uncommon name, and therefore most likely his own, held lands at Northwich in the county of Worcester, at an early period[2]: and the same, or another family of the name, possessed the manor of Preston upon Stour in Gloucestershire, for three descents, in the 16th century[3]. Sir Fulke's father Thomas, also a knight, appears to have married a Tracy; for Baxter says that his mother-in-law (meaning his step-mother) was " cousin german to sir Robert Harley's wife:" and that lady, (Brilliana Conway,) was daughter of Dorothy, daughter of sir John Tracy, knight, of Todington in the county of Gloucester. Colonel Hercules Hunks, who commanded the guards at the trial of Charles I., and who wisely refused to sign the warrant for the execution, though he was one of the three officers to whom the warrant of the pretended high court of justice was directed[4], was in all probability his brother. Sir Fulke was himself a person of much discretion; since on his examination, Oct. 29, 1641, before the lords committees touching Percy's plot for a rising in behalf of the King, it appeared that he had discouraged that attempt[5], though we now find him ranged under the royal standard[6].

---

[1] The Perfect Occurrences of Parliament, from May 31 to June 7, 1644, speaks of col. Mitton having taken some carriages "that were going from Ossister to Col. Hunks at Shrewsbury worth 6 or £7000." Another paper, (The Scottish Dove sent out and returning, No. 34) for the same week, raises the value of this capture of Col. Hunks' " treasure" to £20,000. If a colloquial word for a *miser* be derived from the name of this officer, it adds one more to the numerous instances of the durable effect produced upon language from local and temporary circumstances.

[2] Nash, i. 98. Thomas Lyttelton, esq. of Spetchley, t. Hen. VIII., married Anne, daughter of Tho. Huncke of Northwich, co. Worc. MS. of Le Neve inter Coll. W. Mytton. [3] Atkyns in v.

[4] Trial of the Regicides, p. 183; and Kenny on Pretended Reformers, p. 290.

[5] Husbands, p. 232.

[6] There was a major Hunckes governor of Bar-

The real successor of sir Francis Ottley in the government of Shrewsbury was sir Michael Ernley, a knight of an ancient Wiltshire family[1]; a "gallant gentleman who understood the office and duty of a soldier by long experience and diligent observation," and is enumerated among the colonels taken prisoner by sir Thomas Fairfax at Acton Church near Namptwych, Jan. 25, 1643[2], but who, as he became Governor here, must have been subsequently exchanged. Being totally unconnected with Shropshire, he was restrained by no compunctious visitings from adopting any measure however harsh, which might enable him to maintain his post: and a journal of the times asserts, that, at the sessions of peace in Shrewsbury, the justices and other gentry of the county were so sensible of the wrongs they had received from the King's army, that they "consulted upon a way to right themselves; which so farre incensed the Governor, that he drew up the bridges and shut the gates, and would not suffer them to return to their homes[3]."

Though this representation is taken from a party paper, there seems good reason to believe it authentic, and that the magistrates were obliged to promise compliance before they could obtain their liberty. That they did make such promise is clear, from the following very sharp letter, addressed by sir Michael to his predecessor in his new character of high-sheriff, which lets us completely into his views and temper, as well as into the exigencies of his situation. Indeed we know from other authorities[4], that the defeat of lord Byron in his attempt upon Montgomery Castle, when he was glad to escape with all his horse to this town; together with the taking of Red (i. e. Powis) Castle, which had surrendered in October; made the Parliament masters of all Shropshire to the west of Shrewsbury, and "the town was much streightened hereby during the winter."

"Sir,

"Although you pleased to joyne with the Gentlemen of this County to promise me contributions speedily to be brought in for the subsistance of this Garrison, yet neither you nor they have performed, by meanes whereof I am in extreame hazard of a mutiny; which I can noe less then conceive to bee the ayme of those that brought mee to this distraccōn. Here is not now any moneys towards the pay of the soldiers twelve-pences: I shall desire you

---

badoes in the reign of Charles I. who quitted that office in 1641. See Edwards's Hist. of the West Indies. In all probability this was one of the two persons mentioned in the text: both of whom (if they were brothers) must have been past the middle age of life at this time. For Mrs. Baxter was born in 1575, if she was, as her step-son says, 96 at her death in 1681.

[1] Michael Ernley, esq. of Cannings in that county, married Susan, daughter of sir William Hungerford of Farley Castle, and grand-daughter of Walter lord Hungerford, beheaded in 32 Hen.

VIII. See more of the family in Kimber's Baronetage, vol. ii. p. 147. edit. 1771. art. Ernle of New Sarum. Sir Michael Earnley "captain of the Queen's troop," who was taken prisoner at Rowton heath near Chester, Sept. 24, 1645, "with a scarf which the Queen" (the beautiful Henrietta Maria) "gave him from about her neck for his colours," (Burghsh's Journal, ut supra, p. 944) must have been a son of the governor of Shrewsbury. [2] King's Vale Royal, edit. 1778, p. 622.

[3] A Diary, or an exact journal, No. 36, from 16th to 23d Jan. 1645.   [4] Carte, iv. 510.

to give them notice hereof, and to take some present course that I may be presently supplied, otherwise I must be enforced to suffer the Soldiers to live as they may. I also desire you to give mee your speedy answeare of the letter you received from Prince Maurice his highness, and what assistance of the county I may expect from you for the diverting of the enemies course from Chester. I hope you and the Gentlemen of the County will send mee not lesse then a thousand. If they shall prove backward in a business of soe great consequence to the service of his Ma^{ty}, I am confident you must conclude with mee that they want affect̃on to his Ma^{tys} service, and that other their undertakings are noe more then mere pretences. I shall desire your answeare by the Bearer.

"Extreame hastily rest,
"Salop, 23^d January, 1644. "Yo^r humble Servant,
"MIC. ERNLEY.

"For his Maties speciall service.

"To Sr Francis Ottley, high Sheriffe of the County
of Salop, theis p'sent. MIC. ERNLEY,

"Hast, hast."

Prince Maurice had now succeeded his brother Rupert in the command of these parts; and on the 19th of January had written from Worcester to his Majesty's commissioners for the county of Salop, complaining that the warrants of the Governor of Bridgenorth for the advancement of the works there had been disobeyed, and desiring to know the reason[1].

From a newspaper of the time it appears that he was in this neighbourhood soon after, retreating before sir William Brereton towards Shrewsbury; and again, having reinforced his army, offering battle to that general near Chester. From the same source of intelligence[2] we learn that sir Francis Ottley and other commissioners of the Prince had been taken prisoners somewhere in this immediate neighbourhood. The article requires insertion, and the reader will observe the studied contempt with which this vulgar writer affects to speak of so eminent and excellent a person as the late Governor of our town.

"1645. Mund, Feb^{ry} 24th. By Letters out of Shropshire it was advertis^d y^t Sr W. Brereton had endeavoured to find out P. Maurice and pursued after him near unto Shrewsbury, ye Prince still avoiding him and refusing to give battel; upon wch Sr W. perceiving he could not force him to fight, and being unwilling to tire his men out in following through difficult ways an enemy which rather wished that way to prejudice his army than to fight with him, he is retreated back towards Cheshire, and it is reported that P. Maurice is since gotten over Severn at Shrewsbury, and is bending tow^{ds} Chester, gathering all ye Welsh forces he can get, to make his army numerous: and by forcing ye Welsh couuties, he is s^d to be 6 or 7000 strong; but this I can assure you, y^t Master Glyn, Master Fowler, Master Owen (son and heire to Sir W. Owen) all men of good estates, *and one Oatley, not long since Govr of Shrewsbury*, being sitting on a Commission of Aray for raising of men for P. Maurice, with diverse other Gent^s. of quality, were taken by our forces in ye pursuit after the young Prince: for which immediate service, valiant Col. Price deserves commendation."

These operations of prince Maurice and his brother Rupert against Chester had most important results upon Shrewsbury, which, as we have

[1] Ottley Papers. [2] Weekly Account, dated as below.

seen, was now much straitened. The country towards Wales, as well as the greater part of the rest of Shropshire, was already reduced by the Parliament. The town was quite unequal to the charge of maintaining the garrison; and there was within it a party busy to foment all causes of disgust, and to convey intelligence to their friends without the walls. The Governor, who is described to have been an excellent officer, was lying at the point of death under a consumption, and thus " unable to perform all the offices of vigilance to which he had been accustomed." Of this, indeed, there soon appeared abundant proof [1].

There had been resident some time before in Shrewsbury a Mr. Huson, a native of Ireland [2]. He is called " a minister;" by which, from his residence in a royalist town, one might have inferred that he was a clergyman of the establishment, if his subsequent conduct had not pretty plainly indicated the contrary; for the regular clergy were almost universally attached to the monarchy; and Huson was, as presently appeared, a zealous parliamentarian. It can, indeed, be scarcely doubted, that he came to this town with the intention of spying out the nakedness of the land, and of concerting measures with some whom he left in it, to co-operate with his designs for its surrender to the Parliament: and about the time that sir Francis Ottley relinquished the government, Mr. Huson, apprehensive, perhaps, of the more vigilant inspection of an old soldier like Earnley, decamped, and repaired to the parliamentary committee for Shropshire, the gentlemen to whom the House of Commons had delegated the promotion of their cause in this county [3]. These he assiduously urged to make an attack upon Shrews-

[1] The relation which follows is compiled from four contemporary writers: three of them official, viz. the several dispatches of the committee, sir W. Brereton, and col. Mytton, to the House of Commons; the fourth, an anonymous article of intelligence: and we should willingly have inserted them all at the end of this section, that the reader might have judged for himself, whether the narrative in the text, which has been drawn from a consideration of the whole, is correctly stated. He would in this case not have failed to remark the characteristic phraseology of sir William, the evident wish of the committee to suppress the exertions of col. Mytton, and the natural resentment of the colonel at their conduct, in sending off their dispatch without shewing it to him, or giving him an opportunity of sending one of his own: their motives for which are very obvious, on a comparison of the two dispatches. But the length to which these historical details have extended, obliges us to omit these curious documents.

[2] It is likely that he was a kinsman of the celebrated John Hewson, who, from a cobler, rose to be a colonel, one of the Irish members of Barebone's House of Commons, and at length a lord of Cromwell's " Other House." Mr. Walker, the brave defender of Londonderry in 1689, after mentioning that the eighteen clergymen of the establishment had prayers and sermons every day, in their turns, when they were not in action, adds, " the seven non-conforming ministers were equally careful of their people, and kept them very obedient and quiet: much differing from the behaviour of their brother Mr. Osborn, who was a spy upon the whole North, employed by my lord Tyrconnel; and *Mr. Hewson*, who was very troublesome, and would admit none to fight for the Protestant religion, till they had first taken the Covenant." This gentleman, who appears, like the colonel, to have been a native of Ireland, may have been the same who has occasioned this note. If he was twenty-five years old when he led on the attack upon Shrewsbury, he would not be seventy when he stickled for the Covenant at Derry.

[3] By the *committee* of a county or place was meant the persons who were appointed by the House of Commons to carry on the designs of the Parliament within it; and who were sometimes

1644,5. CHARLES I. 449

bury; describing to them a vulnerable point which he had observed; and by which, he insisted, they might easily effect an entrance. His instances were so far regarded, that the garrison of Wem had actually advanced, during the night between the 14th and 15th of February, within a mile of the town. But the night was so dark, and the road so full of wet, that day came upon them before they could effect their enterprise; and they returned unobserved to their quarters, to wait for a more favourable occasion; which soon occurred[1].

While the princes were advancing on the Welsh side of the Dee to relieve Chester, besieged by the Parliament forces, and sir William Brereton was lying on the north of that river, to counteract their designs, intelligence arrived (Tuesday, Feb. 18) at his quarters, from the Committee of Shropshire, that they had formed a plan to surprise Shrewsbury[2], and requesting from him some assistance to co-operate with colonel Mytton. The Governor had, two or three days before, dispatched a considerable detachment of his garrison, on an expedition which is not specified; perhaps to join the princes' army mentioned above. This information quickened, no doubt, the activity of the parliamentary party in Shropshire. Brereton consented to this request of the Committee, and the next day (Wednesday the 19th) detached 400 horse of Cheshire and Staffordshire, 300 foot of the latter county, and a company of his own regiment, with petards and other ammunition necessary to storm the town, and burst open the gates. These forces, under the command of colonel Bowyer, arrived at Wem the same night. Here, on the following day (Thursday 20th), they were joined by colonel Mytton, who hastened from Oswestry, and got together as many soldiers from the garrisons of Wem, Moreton, and Stoke, as composed in the whole a body of 1200 men[3]. On Friday, instructions arrived from the committee, for

called the *committee of parliament* for that district, sometimes the *committee* alone, or the *committee for sequestrations*. See an account of them in Walker's Sufferings of the Clergy, pt. i. p. 87.—The Shropshire, or, as it was afterwards called, the Shrewsbury committee, was particularly active. " The Shrewsbury committee," says Mercurius Veridicus, No. 13. July 5 to 12, 1645. " doe commonly goe out with the souldiers in all their military designs; and are example, and the way, to keep concord and unity amongst them."

[1] If a parliamentarian news-writer deserves credit, the town had received an alarm about a week before. " Out of Shropshire it is advertised, that on the 8 of Feb. at night Pr. Maurice came into Shrewsbury with 30 horse; the rest of his army were quartered some few miles of. The next night 20 of the Parliament's souldiers, belonging to the garrison of Wem, would undertake to goe and give Shrewsbury an alarum, which accordingly they performed, and (having leave) these brave spirits, taking 20 firelocks with them, went towards Shrewsbury, and coming undiscovered to the Court of Guard neare the great wall, fired altogether upon the sentinells, killed foure, whereof one was *Kidna*, a great Malignant, and tooke foure other of the sentinells, which they carried with them to Wem without any losse. This being in the middle of the night, put the enemy into so great a feare, that they knew not what to doe, nor whence the enemy should come, but were in a great hurlyburly all the night, till they heard the next day they were Wem souldiers." Mercurius Civicus from Feb. 13 to 20, 1644, No. 91. Unless the writer mistook the situation of the Court of Guard, there must, as will be seen, have been *two*.

[2] Carte MS.

[3] The Committee's letter says 1100; Mr. Carte 1200: and this last agrees with sir W. Brereton's dispatch. Yet from this the committee materially

the execution of the enterprise; and the morning was occupied in arrangements for carrying it into effect. The command of the infantry was assigned by the direction of the committee to lieutenant-colonel Reinking; that of the horse to Mytton himself. It was evening before they left Wem: and it is obvious to remark on the superior secrecy of the parliamentarians, since not a syllable transpired in all this time, to the authorities either civil or military in Shrewsbury: a striking proof of the attachment of the general population of the country to the cause of the Parliament. The force, thus commanded, marched under the cover of night, and halted at the end of the Castle Foregate about 4 o'clock on the Saturday morning (22d), where the horse remained, till the foot should effect an entrance themselves, and obtain one for their companions. The infantry turned off on the left to the river; and for the use of the reader who may wish to understand the further operations, and is not assisted by local knowledge, the following slight sketch of the scene of action is subjoined.

Before he quitted the horse, colonel Reinking marshalled his own men. The van was led by the minister Huson, (such an union of professions so discordant was not unusual in that warfare,) and a countryman of his, captain Wyllier, who led on a party of firelocks, as lieutenant Benbow, a Shrewsbury man, and consequently well acquainted with the ground, did another of dismounted troopers. They advanced from the end of the Castle Foregate, through the fields, to the Castle Ditch, which ran down from the N. E. end of the Castle to the Severn, and was defended on the town side by a stout palisade of wood and a breast-work of earth. While this was going on, colonel Reinking, who had embarked in a boat with eight carpenters and other persons fit for that employment, had arrived on the town side of this palisade, and began to saw down the pales. Careless or treacherous as the sentinels appear to have been, for they are said[1] to have been either intoxicated or privy to the design, this could not be done without alarming others of the garrison, more sober or more trusty: and these, after some pause, began to fire upon the assailants. But a breach was by this time effected; and the Parliament soldiers eagerly helping one another over the ditch, and climbing through the palisade, got over the breast-work. Having

varies. According to sir William, he detached 700 besides his own company: according to them he detached only 600 in all. There is evident in both parties a wish to raise themselves at the expence of the other. The "Weekly Account, Wedn. March 5, 1645," has it somewhat different. "The forces which were employed in the design were about 1200; whereof 800 were sent from sir William Brereton, who, as I told you last week, was returned towards Chester, which joined with 400 of colonel Mitton's Shropshire forces." But this again is at variance with the statement of the committee, which makes the sum of the Shropshire forces 500. Other proofs will occur of an incipient jealousy between the several members of the parliamentary party.

[1] Garbet's History of Wem. All the royalist writers concur in this opinion. "Shrewsbury, a most important and strong garrison, was by some treachery, not yet brought to light, betrayed just at the conclusion of the treaty of Uxbridge." Heath, p. 72.

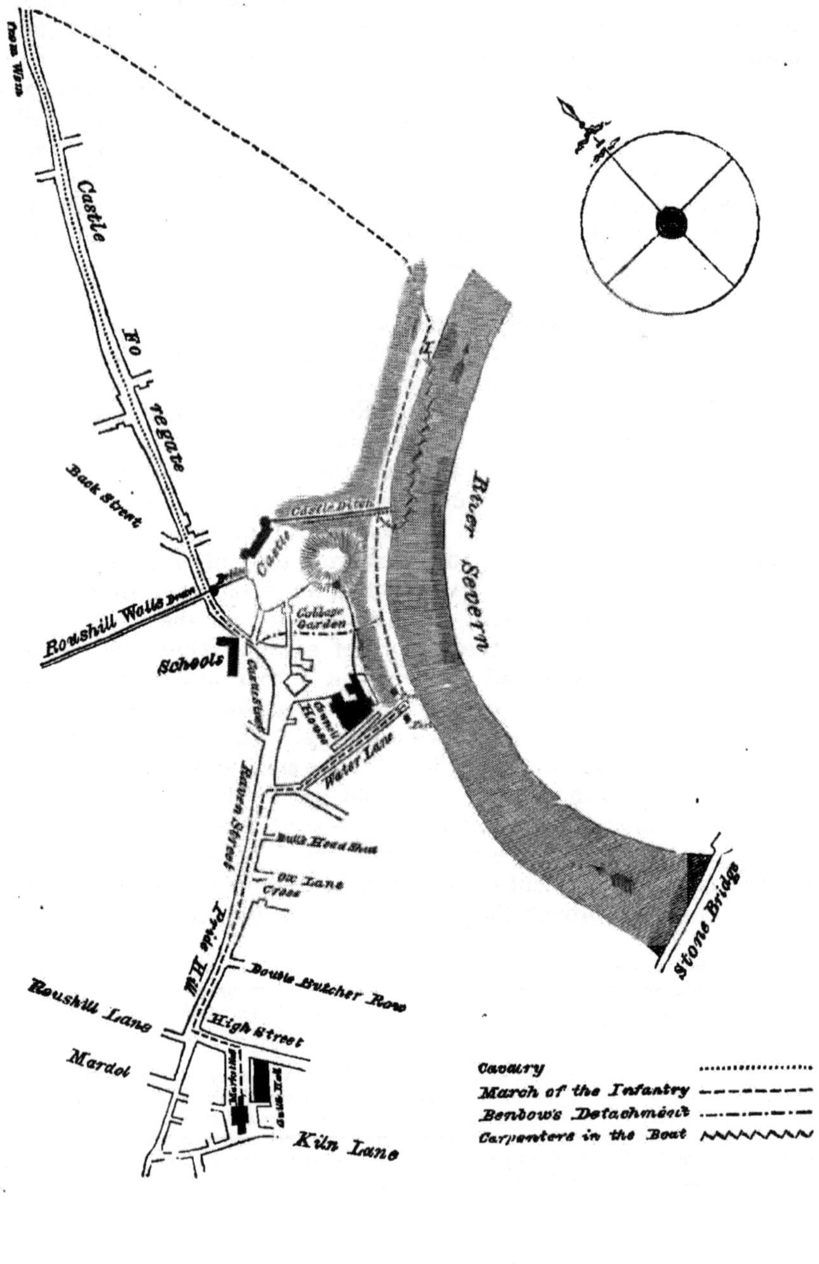
Castle
Fo
regate
Back Street
Castle
Roushill Walls
College Garden
Schools
Water Lane
River Severn
Stone Bridge
Raven Street
Bull Head Street
Ox Lane
Cross
Pride Hill
Double Butcher Row
Roushill Lane
High Street
Mardol
Kiln Lane
Cavalry
March of the Infantry
Benbow's Detachment
Carpenters in the Boat

thus far succeeded, they appear to have divided into two parties[1]. One, headed by Benbow, ran up the bank, now that part of the Council House garden, which lies nearest to the Castle, and scaling the wall which crowns its summit, by light ladders which they had brought with them, hastened to the North or Castle Gates. The other party rapidly filed along on the narrow path by the river side under the Council House, then the residence of sir William Owen, followed by the main body of 350 foot under the command of Reinking, and soon reached the bottom of the Water-lane. This bold step led them to a spot then commanded, as appears, by two forts (one at the bottom of that part of the Council House garden which lies nearest to the Water-lane, and the other on the very spot where a warehouse is now building), and where consequently they might have been cut to pieces by a far inferior force. No military commander of the least conduct would have placed his men in such a situation, had he not been assured of finding the gates (for there were two, defended, as we have said, by a tower) in St. Mary's, Water-lane, left open for his admission. This was the case; and up this lane colonel Reinking entered the town in good order, being, as is thus made plain, mainly indebted to treachery for his success.

The Court of guard[2], as the place where the guard musters was then called, was held in the Market-place. Thither the assailants marched with all expedition: and exchanging very few shot, for they encountered scarcely any resistance, hastened on to the Market-place to attack the main-guard. Here they were twice beaten back: and, as colonel Mytton seems to intimate, would probably have been mastered[3]. But the gates had by this time been burst open by the first party that mounted the Council House bank, the draw-bridge was let down, and the horse, with colonel Mytton at their head, galloped down to the court of guard, where they found their comrades engaged with the royalists. The contest there, which had till then been doubtful, was now soon decided; not however till captain John Needham, who was then on guard, with five of his men, had been killed. Together with the cavalry, the gentlemen of the committee entered the town, and immediately proceeded to the exercise of their authority. For while this skirmish was going on at the court of guard, small parties of the military, directed by such as knew the way, in all probability Huson, Ben-

---

[1] This is the only way in which we can reconcile the two accounts of the Committee and Colonel Mytton; the former of which makes no mention of the ladders. A reason will hereafter be assigned for the spot where we have placed Benbow's escalade. Thus too the parliamentary and royalist statements may be made consistent. The latter of whom uniformly impute the surprise of Shrewsbury to treachery, of which the former say nothing; wishing, naturally enough, to have it attributed either to the skill and courage of their friends, or to the negligence of their enemies.

[2] We find the word in Shakspeare. "The lieutenant to-night watches on the *court of guard*." Othello, ii. 1; where the commentators furnish other examples.

[3] Here the colonel and the Committee are completely opposed to each other. They assert that the assailants first surprised the main-guard, and then let in the horse.

bow, and some of the parliamentary townsmen, proceeded to the houses of the mayor and other leading inhabitants of the place, and secured their persons. The two sir John Welds, father and son, are particularly specified as having been surprised in their beds; and the vivid description of a city surprised in the dead of night, as depicted by the imagination of the poet, will apply in all its parts with remarkable closeness, to that of Shrewsbury on the occasion before us.

> Invadunt urbem somno vinoq; sepultam :
> Cæduntur vigiles ; portisque patentibus omnes
> Accipiunt socios, atq; agmina conscia jungunt.[1]

Lord Clarendon had heard, that the invaders, by the same treachery that had admitted them into the town, got possession of the Castle; where the Governor, " rising upon the alarm out of his bed, was killed in his shirt, while he behaved himself as well as was possible, and refused quarter, which did not shorten his life many days." But this is a mistake: the Governor could not be slain, for he was taken prisoner, and the Castle was certainly not surrendered till about noon.

It was now about break of day, and we may readily conceive the uproar and alarm which prevailed in the town; for nothing could restrain a victorious soldiery from pillage. Some threw down their arms; others cried, "*Arm, Arm;*" while colonel Mytton availed himself of the confusion, to gain possession of every post in the town. Indeed this excellent officer appears to have displayed a very eminent share of promptitude and conduct. He took care to prevent the Governor and chief officers from getting into the castle; for they appear to have slept out of it; and he did all in his power to save the " well-affected " inhabitants, as they were henceforth to be styled, from the depredations of their friends the soldiers.

Baxter, in his Life, says, " I was especially pleased with the surprise of Shrewsbury, both because it was done without loss of blood, and because my father and many of my dear friends were thereby redeemed. Upon the departure of governor Hunckes, my father was made one of the collectors of taxes for the King, which he justly performed: but he wo[d] not forcibly dis-

---

[1] Strait they invade the city, buried deep
In fumes of wine, and all dissolved in sleep :
They slay the guards, they burst the gates, and join
Their fellows, conscious to the bold design.
There is nothing to forbid the supposition that Virgil might have read Livy's description of the surprise of Chalcis by the Roman general Cento. " Provectus Chalcidem *paulo ante lucem*, quæ infrequentissima urbis sunt, paucis militibus turrim proximam murumq; circa, scalis cepit ; *alibi sopitis custodibus, alibi nullo custodiente.* Progressi inde ad frequentia ædificiis loca, *custodibus interfectis, refractaq; porta,* ceteram multitudinem armatorum acceperunt. Inde in totam urbem discursum est." Liv. lib. xxxi. c. 23.—The great Roman poet, like our English one, " served himself by reading, as much as he could :" and no one knew better, how much, in all the imitative arts, sketches copied from life exceed the suggestions either of the fancy or of the recollection.

trein of them that refused to pay, as not knowing but they might hereafter recover it all of him: for wch he was laid in prison by them that swore he sho^d lie and rot there. But he had been there but a few weeks, before the keeper in the night came to him, and begged his favour to save him and his house; for the parliament's soldiers had surprised the town. My father would not believe it, till he heard and saw that which compelled his belief: and with what joy, I need not tell[1]."

Thus did the town of Shrewsbury fall into the power of the Parliament. Its conquest was not however completed. Two posts might have given the colonel some trouble: the Castle, and the fort in Frankwell called Cadogan's. The former, however, capitulated about noon, on conditions to which no extremity should have made them consent: for though the garrison was suffered to march off to Ludlow with their arms, they abandoned the unfortunate Irish among them, whom it was the usage of that day to hang up without trial[2], to the tender mercies of the Committee; who immediately ordered them to be put to death, to the number of thirteen[3]. The fort was delivered up immediately after at discretion, i. e. on bare quarter.

This important conquest was atchieved with a very inconsiderable loss. On the side of the Parliament only two men fell; one of them, Richard Wycherley, a native of Clive, and kinsman, no doubt, of the dramatic writer once so celebrated, seated at that place. On that of the King, only a captain and five men. The number of prisoners was consequently great[4],

[1] P. 46. Baxter believed that Charles I. was kept in ignorance of the loss of Shrewsbury till after the defeat at Naseby, when he wished to fly hither for refuge. Life, p. 50.—This we may boldly pronounce impossible. We have seen when this town was taken. Naseby field was fought nearly four months after! Yet the anecdote is curious, as evincing the credulity of party, and the strange notions entertained of the royalists by their opponents at that heated period.

[2] Heath says, that under the name of Irish many Englishmen suffered. Chron. of the Civil Wars, p. 75.—This writer derives the proverbial phrase "*Abingdon Law, hang first and try afterwards,*" from the practice of the parliamentary garrison of that town.

[3] Prince Rupert retaliated, which produced the following curious article in Perfect Passages, April ye 3d, 1645. "This day the House of Commons being informed that Rupert, before he came from North Wales, had hanged 13 honest Protestants, countrey-men, that lived about Shropshire, because that there were 13 Irish rebels hanged in Shrewsbury, the House had some debate thereon, and ordered, that a letter should be sent to Rupert, the substance whereof is thus: Letting him know how much both Houses resent his crueltie, in hanging of 13 of our English Protestants, because wee hanged so many of the Irish rebels. That there is a great difference between these rebels and the English Protestants: the King and Parliament having by divers acts of Parliament proclaimed them traytors; that if he shall proceed to hang up more of our prisoners in cold-blood, wee must and shall retaliate."

How completely religious and political bigotry can extinguish the sentiments of natural equity, may be seen by this example, which is thus further descanted upon in the Perfect Diurnal of March 27th; "Letters was intercepted and brought up this day to the House from the Secretary of pr. Rupert, expressing much joy for the execution of ten Englishmen, (by sentence of pr. Rupert,) who had formerly served the King in Ireland, and since revolting to the Parliament: and indeed a lamentable consideration that such *faithfull upright men* sho^d be taken away in lew of the *cursed Irish rebells* that come over thence to fight against the Parliament."

[4] One gentleman had a very narrow escape. In

and their rank more so. For Shrewsbury had been esteemed a secure retreat, to which, as we have observed, many of the neighbouring gentry had fled for refuge from the insecurity of their country seats; and " eight knights and baronets, forty colonels, majors, and captains, and 200 private soldiers," are enumerated[1] among the captured. A list of such as have been specified by name is subjoined. The King also lost here, what he could ill spare, 14 pieces of ordnance, several barrels of gunpowder, several hundred stand of arms, and the magazine of prince Maurice; who was himself very near being seized, having been here a short time previous to the surprise. Several tradesmen were ruined by the plunder of their goods; and the plate and other property of gentlemen and strangers which had been lodged for safety in the Castle, enriched the soldiers with a plentiful booty.

The several documents upon which the preceding account of the capture of Shrewsbury has been founded, are omitted for the reasons assigned above: but we subjoin the list of prisoners contained in the last of them, to which are added, in the notes, the sums which such of them as were admitted to compound for their estates, paid respectively for their loyalty.

" Sir Michael Earnley, Kn[t], and his Brother, Sir Rich[d] Lee[2], Sir Tho. Harris[3], Sir Henry Frederick Thinn[4], Kn[ts] and Barrownets.

" Sir W[m] Owen[5], Sir John Welde, Sen[r 6], Sir John Welde, Junior, and Sir Tho. Lyster[7], Knts.

" Francies Thornes[8], Herbert Vaughan, Tho. Owen[9], Edw[d] Kynaston[10], Rob[t] Ireland[11], Rich[d] Trevis, Tho. Morris, Arthur Sandford[12], Rob[t] Sandford[13], Pelham Corbet[14], and Tho. Jones[15], Esq[rs].

---

a Letter from Namptwych, dated March 26, 1645, and printed in the Perfect Passages of April 2nd, it is said, " There were some malignants that escaped us in Shrewsbury, as we heare since, as particularly Mr. Alestrey, formerly a member of the House of Commons, but a deserter, and a treacherous one to honest Derby that chose him: he was their Recorder, and for his perfidious dealings towards them, deserves to be recorded by them; he got away before he was discovered, by a woman's means, that got a ticket for herselfe and her man, which he pretended to be, and so escaped; but he and divers more that have got away, are in great distresse, and know not what to do."—The " desertion and perfidy" here spoken of, was joining those members of Parliament who sate at Oxford in opposition to those at Westminster. William Allestrey, esq. of Alvaston, co. Derby, the person intended, was the descendant of a very ancient family of that county; one of whom, William Allestry, a gallant English esquire, bore the banner of Sir John Chandos [of Radbourne in the same county] at the battle of Najara, 1367. Barnes's Hist. of Edward III. p. 707. Robert Allestree of Uppington in Shropshire, so he wrote the name, steward to the Newport family, was son of William Allestrey of Alveston, and father of Richard Allestree, or Allestry, D.D. a very distinguished loyalist during the civil wars, and after the Restoration, Provost of Eton, Canon of Christ Church, and Regius Professor of Divinity.

[1] Heath, p. 72. This writer always styles colonel Mytton major-general. Mr. Carte, iv. 510, is singularly succinct in his account of the fall of Shrewsbury. He hurries over the disastrous ruin of the King's affairs, with an evident sensation of pain—

———animus meminisse horret, luctuq; refugit.

[2] Of Lee Hall and Acton Burnell, £3719.
[3] Of Boreatton, £1542.
[4] Of Caus Castle, £3554. His son was created Viscount Weymouth.   [5] Of Condover, £314.
[6] Town-clerk of London, and seated at Willey, which he purchased of the Lacons, £1121.
[7] Of Rowton.   [8] Of Shelvocke, £720.
[9] The town-clerk; he was seated at Dinthill.
[10] Of Oteley, £1500.   [11] Of Adbrighton.
[12] Of Sandford.
[13] Perhaps second son of Arthur.
[14] Of Leigh and Adbright Hussey, ancestor of the Corbets of Sundorn.
[15] Of Shrewsbury and Sandford, afterwards chief-justice.

"L‍t Coll. Ed. Owen [1], and L‍t Coll. Thomas Owen [2].
"Major Francis Ranger.
"Doctor Lewyn, Dr. Arnewey [3].
"T. Raynsford, Wm. Lucas, John Cressy, Thoˢ Collins, Wm Long, Pontesbury Owen [4], and Henry Harrison, Captains.
"John Pey, Feodary [5].
"Cassey Benthall [6], Edwd Talbot, Richd Lee, Ed. Stanley [7], Francis Manwaring, John Jones, John Bradshaw, Ed. Littleton, Peter Dorrington, Thoˢ Barker, John Whitacars, Jos. Taylor, Fran. Sandford, Richd Gibbeons, Geo. Manwaring, and Char. Smith, Gentlemen.
"Ed. Palmer and Mathew Whitwick, Ensigns.
"Vincent Tayler, Thoˢ Dew, Hum. Davis, Richd Breyn, Serjants.
"Nic. Proud, Cleark.
"James Lacon, Master Lendall, Moses Hotchkies, Geo. Bucknal, Corporals. Patrick Lacepaid, Irish, and 49 other Irish prisoners.
"N. B. The reason we found no more Commanders was because Prince Maurice had drawn them out for his design at Chester."

---

[1] Of Condover, £207.
[2] Of Whitley.
[3] John Arnway, D.D., rector of Hodnet, and archdeacon of Salop in the diocese of Litchfield. He wrote, while an exile for his loyalty, "The Tablet, or Moderation of Charles I. Martyr." 12mo. printed 1661. See Walker's Sufferings of the Clergy.
[4] Of Eton Mascot, £601.
[5] The Feodary was the officer whose business it was to attend upon all inquisitions after the death of tenants in chivalry under the feudal system, and watch over the dues thence arising to the crown.
[6] A younger son of Laurence Benthall, esquire, of Benthall; he fell fighting for Charles I. at Stow in the Wold, and is said to have been then a colonel.
[7] Of Knockin, £132.

SECTION THE SECOND.

FROM THE TAKING OF SHREWSBURY BY THE PARLIAMENT FORCES TO THE RESTORATION.

The fall of Shrewsbury into the power of the Parliament was not unimportant even in a national view. It had long been the object of their most anxious desires; it had even been the subject of prophecy[1]: and they omitted no means of animating the spirits of their party, by announcing its value. The House of Commons ordered a gratuity of £20 to the first messenger, and half that sum to the second that brought the news[2]; and they took care to tell their friends, that it was " one of the strongest inland garrisons in England, and of farre greater concernment than Oxford[3]," in the fruitless siege of which they had for some time been engaged. They directed £4000 to be provided out of the excise for its defence[4]; which, however, was subsequently reduced to half that sum[5]. They commanded the 12th of March to be kept as a day of solemn thanksgiving throughout the city of London, for this among other blessings and good successes of the Parliament's forces[6]: and the gallant leader of the enterprise, colonel Mytton, who, as our authority has it, " performed an unparalleled service in taking of Shrewsbury," having reached London on the 28th of March, was " called into the House of Commons on the following day, and master Speaker, in the name, and by the command, of the whole House, gave him hearty thanks for his many and faithfull services done to the state; giving him all encouragement to persist in the same: and especially for that gallant service of Shrewsbury; assuring him that he shall never want the encouragement of the House of Parliament in his undertakings[7]."

In the mean while the effects of this capture upon the town itself were, as might be expected, considerable. The persons of rank and fortune, whose asylum it had so long been, and who now lost their freedom, were soon sent off to London[8]: and the Committee, too conscious of the advantages

---

[1] Monthly Account of March 31, 1645. " A prophesie was made by the old Welshwoman about three moneths since, that before the then present year was ended, Shrewsbury should be in the Parliament's hands, and Chester shall not hold out long after. I put it not here," says the compiler, " to *traduce* any to put belief in old wives tales; but take notice how shrewdly she guessed at that which was then so unlikely to come to passe."

[2] Perfect Diurnal, 27 Feb. [3] Id. 25 Feb.

[4] Id. 27 Feb. [5] Id. 11 March.

[6] Id. ib. In Shrewsbury the anniversary was kept with great solemnity, probably through the whole Interregnum. On Feb. 20, 1651-2, is a resolution of the Corporation: " Agreed that in regarde the day of thankesgivinge for takinge this Towne by the Parliament forces falls upon the nexte Lord's daye, that the daye be observed on Tuesday next." [7] Id. 29 March.

[8] Id. 10 Mar.

they had received from a co-operation within the walls, to permit their adversaries to enjoy the same, "put about fifty families out of the town for malignancy." Sir William Brereton, eager to claim the merit of the enterprise, and jealous, as it seems, of colonel Mytton, hastened hither as soon as he learned the success of it: for he was here on the 26th of February, and reinforced the Parliament garrison with three regiments of Cheshire foot[1]. There were grounds for these precautions. The royalists, deeply wounded by so severe a loss, were active in their endeavours to recover it. Prince Rupert and sir Jacob Astley endeavoured to bring a force from Ludlow for this purpose; General Langdale was said to be advancing from another quarter[2]; and it was reported in London that these enterprises had been successful[3]. But the contrary soon appeared; and it was "ascertained that the town was in very good condition, and had a brave garrison there, the Committee having taken great pains for the well ordering and securing of it"[4]: indeed, there can be little doubt that the abandonment or demolition of royalist fortresses in Shropshire[5], which took place just at this time, was entirely owing to the consternation occasioned by the fall of Shrewsbury, and to the occupants of those fortresses despairing of its recapture, in spite of some transient alarms to that effect[6].

Among the families compelled to seek another home on account of their attachment to the cause of their sovereign, were, doubtless, some leading members of the corporation, who had hitherto kept that body steady to the cause of royalty. By their forcible extrusion it experienced an entire change, of which the first result was the following resolution. "18 Feb. 21 Car. (1644-5) In regarde of the great love and affection which Andrew Lloyde of Aston, Samuel Moore of Linley, Robert Clive of Stiche, and Robert Charleton of Apley, esquires, four of the comittyes of parliament for the county of Salop, with the rest of the Committee, who were borne burgesses, have expressed to this corporation, they" [i. e. the mayor, aldermen, and assistants] "are aggreed and do bestowe on them their burgesseship." On the 2d of June, Thomas Niccolls, Hump. Mackworth, and Tho. Hunte,

---

[1] Perfect Diurnal, 3 Mar.
[2] Id. 6 and 10 Mar.
[3] Id. 3 Mar.
[4] Id. ib. Thus too the Weekly Account, Mar. 4. "Notwithstanding Aulicus's flourish of P. Maurice's retaking of Shrewsbury, it is (and like to continue) in the Parliament service"
[5] Id. ib. "Out of Shropshire it is certified that the enemies' forces have quitted divers garisons in that county, as Rouse Castle [probably Red Castle, near Hawkstone] Medley House, and burnt downe Tongue Castle, Sea Hall, [Lea Hall] and Morton Corbet Castle, least they should be advantageous to the Parliament."
[6] Perfect Passages, 28 Ap. 1645. "We have this day intelligence from Shrewsbury, that the Committee there have apprehended some who had a plot in hand about the betraying of that place againe to the enemy, Rupert being to march that way: and that it is newly discovered, and some in examination at the date of the letters: but because they had not been then examined, it being newly discovered, they sent not the particulars." Colonel Massey, in his Letter to the Speaker, 25th April, 1645, relating the affair at Ledbury, says, "Prince Rupert's army, by the report of the country, is noysed about to be six or seven thousand horse and foote; who are now upon their march againe towards Ludlow, and so, as I heare, intend for Salop, if they be not prevented againe." Perf. Diurnal, May 1.

esquires, whom we saw before removed, were, together with Thomas Knight, gent., restored to the office of alderman; and sir Francis Ottley, knight, and Timothy Tourneur, esq. were removed from the same *for non-residence*.

The post of Governor was now too to be filled. As early as the 27th of February, when the House of Commons first received intelligence of their new acquisition, this matter came under debate; and it was then ordered to be referred to the Committee of the county of Salop[1]; the gentlemen, some of whose names have just been specified. Colonel Mytton, whose ancient relation to the town, of which his ancestors had been inhabitants and burgesses for four centuries; whose ample estates in its immediate neighbourhood; and, above all, whose active and zealous services for the Parliament through the whole war, and in this particular conquest; gave him so many titles to their notice, naturally looked forward to it. An article of intelligence of March 19, asserts, that he was actually appointed[2]. This, however, was premature: and the observations of a succeeding number of the same paper intimate the opinion of the writer, that it would never be realized; for, having related the thanks delivered to the colonel by the Speaker, " giving him all possible encouragement for the prosecution of the Parliament service," the writer goes on, " the government of that town is one thing which he expects; which was at first left to the Committee pro tempore to dispose of. If they find reasons of weight to put another there, he will be recompensed some other way: for such men ought to have their merit rewarded. And so the business is referred to further consideration; for these things must not hinder the publick service[3]." The Committee did find such reasons; and at least as late as the 15th day of the following October, had retained the government of Shrewsbury in their own hands[4].

---

[1] Perfect Diurnal, Feb. 27.

[2] 1645. Wed. March 19. Weekly Account. " By letters out of Shropshire, it was this day certified that prince Rupert was on Friday last at Ludlowe, and sir Jacob Astley at Bewdly, and some of their forces at Clybury, Tenbury, and Burford, and prince Rupert sent out his warrants to summon in the country as a convoy for his Majesty, (a subtle way to put them upon service). They intend to have a fling at Shrewsbury, but, if they attempt that town, they are like to find hot entertainment, for col. Mitton is Governor, and hath a considerable strength to defend it," &c.

[3] Weekly Account, March 29. The Mercurius Britannicus, No. 76, from 24 to 31 March, 1645, says, " Col. Mitton hath had thanks given him for his many good services, especially that of Shrewsbury. *Indeed Shrewsbury is worth thanks at any time.*"

[4] Symonds's Pocket-books. Harl. MSS. 944, p. 67, vel idcirca. They evidently wished to exalt another commander at the expence of Mytton. In the Kingdom's Weekly Intelligencer, No. 99, from 26 to 31 May, 1645, is the following letter from them " To the Right Honourable the Committee of both Kingdoms," the object of which is very discernible.

" Right Honourable,

" The bearer of this, lieut.-col. Reinking, ever since his entertainment in the service of this county, we have found most faithfull and usefull. His activeness and skill hath chiefly conduced to the taking of Mourton Castle and Shrewsbury; in which designes he had the chief command. Besides, by his directions, Wem is refortified, and made far more strong than before. Our humble desire is, you would be pleased to take notice of him as a souldier demeriting much for his civil discourse, demeanour, and judicious valour, in all which we know none outstrips him. And be

The truth is, colonel Mytton's politicks were getting very fast out of fashion. He had sided with the Parliament only for the limitation of prerogative, not for the subversion of monarchy. The Presbyterians, to whom he appears to have belonged, had no insurmountable objection to the office of a king, provided he was under their controul; or to a national establishment of religion, if its revenues were at their disposal. But those who commence important changes in a state have seldom the satisfaction of reaping the fruit of their labours. Spirits more ardent, with views more extensive, step in between them and the consummation of their designs; and thus it proved in the period now under consideration. The Independents, gaining the ear of the soldiery, reared a fabric upon the foundations laid by the Presbyterians, which astonished and confounded their precursors in reform: and thus, one of the ablest and most successful commanders of the latter persuasion, sir William Waller, gives vent to his complaints, on their disappointment, for the instruction of posterity. "The army has freed us from King, Lords, and Commons; and from whatsoever was of honour or worth in the nation: and we may brag of the same liberty which the inhabitants of Corfu were said to enjoy; Ελευθερα Κορκυρα, χεζ' οπε θελεις. 'A man may be free to untruss where he will.' Witness our very churches, so polluted by them, that if Athenodorus were alive again, he might make a judgment of the diseases of his time *ab excrementis*. To be short, after the expence of so much blood and treasure, all the difference that can be discerned between our former and present estate is but this, that before time, under the complaint of a slavery, we lived like freemen; and now, under the notion of a freedom, we live like slaves, enforced by continual taxes and oppressions, to maintain and feed on our own misery[1]."

The truth of this last remark is amply verified by the records of Shrewsbury; the inhabitants of which experienced no alleviation of their burdens from the change of masters. On the 4th of June, " Mr. Maior, sir Richard Prynce, and others, were commissioned by the corporation to treat with the gentlemen of the Committee about the monthly cessment on the town and liberties." There was a garrison to be supported[2]: and besides this,

---

pleased to be not only ayding to him in the obtaining some special gratification for his service; but to give him that dispatch, that his speedy returne to us may further us in carrying on our several designes both for perfecting our fortifications of this towne, which are yet defective, and removing the several garrisons of the enemy, which are yet very many, and doe much infest us. And hereby you will engage your most humble servants, Hum. Mackworth, And. Lloyd, Tho. Hunt, Sam. More, Rob. Charlton, Leighton Owen. Apr. 17." Colonel Reinking was soon after taken prisoner in an attack upon the royalist garrison of High Ercall.

[1] Vindication of sir W. Waller, by himself, p. 29.
[2] The Perfect Diurnal of June 16 mentions the good services of "a party from Shrewsbury" against "several parties from Worcester, Litchfield, and other garrisons," assembled to "besiege sir William Whitmore's house, a garrison of the Parliament." The detachment from Shrewsbury "encountered with them, slew and took prisoners between three and four hundred of them, and disperst the rest. In this service sir Williams Crofts, the great Herefordshire malignant, was slaine." The house here mentioned must be Apley, though the Whitmores were themselves royalists. It had

there was, which could not be very pleasing to any English heart, and must have been especially odious to every lover of the monarchy, there was a foreign army to be supported at their charge. The Parliament had called in the Scots to aid them in dethroning their sovereign; and on the 9th July, " the House spent much time in debate for raising of money for the army of our brethren of Scotland, who now advance cheerefully to the worke: and wee hope, by God's blessing on them and our other armies, if our sins prevent not, a period will be put to our troubles this summer: and ordered, that the ordinance for raising moneys by a weekely assessment for the maintenance of the Scotts army in England shall be renewed, and the counties assessed again in like proportion as before: and because the counties of Worcester, Hereford, Salop, and Stafford, formerly exempted from this taxe, do now receive much benefit, and may in a short time receive more, by the advance of that army, in bringing them out of the slavery of the enemy, the House ordered that those counties should bee charged with this weekely taxe as the rest of the counties."

These northern invaders, under the command of the earl of Leven, sate down before Hereford on the 30th of July: and on the 13th of August our corporation was obliged to "agree, that a cessment of 30s. per diem be raised to paye the Scottish army now against Hereford, according to the warrant from the Comittyes of Parliament for this town and county." It is impossible not to observe the greater liberty taken with their friends by these last gentlemen; and, in consequence, the greater vigour and firmness with which they enforce obedience to their commands, far exceeding any thing which had been exhibited by the royalists while they had the conduct of the town. Such was the awe inspired by their proceedings, that Shrewsbury continued for the whole of the following year in a state of tranquillity, and the " malignants," as the loyalists, who had been expelled from its walls, were called, were eager to make their submissions, and obtain leave to return to their former habitations. The steps taken by one of these shall be given in a note as a specimen of the measures pursued in such cases[1].

---

been assailed by the Parliamentarians from Wem and Longford in the spring of 1644, at that time unsuccessfully: (Mercurius Aulicus, March 20, 1643-4): but in 1645, Symonds (ut supra), among the "rebel garrisons," enumerates a house "about three miles from Bridgenorth," in all probability this

[1] The person, whose attempts to expiate his delinquency (as loyalty was then called) we are here to recount, was John Harding, gent., attorney-at-law, one of the original assistants nominated in the charter of 1638. The papers were obligingly communicated by his great great grandson, the rev. J. Harding, vicar of Hope Say.

The first of them, dated Shrewsbury, Jan. 21, 1645-6, permits him to "repaire to this garrison to make his defence and answears to such matters of delinquency as are chardged against him." The next paper is dated Goldsmiths'-hall, London, at the Committee for compounding with delinquents, 8 May, 1646; recites the order of the House of Commons, Feb. 23, 1645, authorizing " the Committee at Goldsmiths'-hall, to suspend the sequestrations of such delinquents as shall compound with it, after they have paid the moyetie of such fine, and having given securitie to pay the

But the times were unfavourable to measures of conciliation. The war, indeed, was at an end: the King a prisoner in the hands of his House of Commons; and the authority of that assembly apparently supreme. It was, however, only in appearance. The elements of discord were at work. The Independents were secretly employed in setting the army against the houses of Parliament; and the nation was beginning to range itself under one or the other of these parties. The Governor of Shrewsbury at this time was Humphrey Mackworth, esq. of Betton, grandson of the John Mackworth spoken of at p. 309. From his subsequent history he appears to have been an Independent: but his authority here was, at this time, extremely limited; and the government of the town was really vested in the Committee, who seem to have been generally Presbyterians; and as such, supporters of the Parliament. Such at least is the language of the following resolution of the corporation, which we cannot doubt was in conformity with the sentiments of the Committee. It belongs to the spring of 1647.

"Agreed that a petition be exhibited to Parliament that no disaffected person *to the Parliament* who hath formerly been turned out and lefte the towne by reason of his disaffection may be permitted to reinhabite with the said town: and to desire to have £1000 allowed the corporation out of such delinquent's estates as hereafter shall be discovered within the countye, towards making of stronge stone walles about the towne: and in case of any further insurrection the towne will undertake to keep it for the Parliament."

This is the language of alarm, and bespeaks at once attachment to the House of Commons, and apprehension of danger to its power. In fact, matters were upon the very eve of an explosion. The House having manifested a disposition to cashier the army, the leaders of the latter resolved to deprive their adversaries of the sanction which they derived from possessing the royal person. The seizure of Charles at Holmby by Cornet Joyce (June 3) was the signal for further hostilities against the Parliament, and for the proscription of its principal leaders to the number of eleven (16th).

other moyetie; and certifies, that John Harding of Shrewsbury, gent., hath appeared, submitted, paid, and secured as above, and commands all sequestrators, &c. to forbear all proceedings upon his sequestration, unless there shall be any further estate discovered.

Aug. 8, 1646, is a pass subscribed by the Shrewsbury Committee (with the exception of Leighton Owen, for whom the name of Robert Clive is substituted) authorizing Mr. Harding to pass all their scowtes of guard, and scowts from Shrewsbury, to the Cittie of London, and from thence back, without any lette or interruption.

The 29th of August following is a receipt from Richard Waring and Michael Herring, treasurers of the monies to be paid into Goldsmiths'-hall, for £25, in full of £50 imposed upon John Harding by the House of Commons as a fine for his delinquency to the Parliament. Notwithstanding which, it is not until May 15, 1649, that an order issues from Goldsmiths'-hall, ordering, that the sequestration of the said John Harding his estate be henceforth discharged, and he admitted to the possession thereof: and that hee bee no further troubled ... for any delinquency charged upon him for any thing said or donne in relation to the first warr: unless he have bin since ingaged in the latter warr."

Such were the lustrations and delays through which our fathers were made to purge their crime of loyalty to their king.

The "*latter war*" mentioned in the last of these papers, was that which broke out in 1648; the abortive effort of the Scots in behalf of the King.

Proceedings such as these threw the kingdom into consternation; accustomed as it had been to regard all the measures of the House of Commons with implicit submission. The following letters from the Governor of this town seem to bespeak, that neither himself, nor either of the gentlemen to whom it was addressed, two leading members of the Committee, were at that time at all favourable to the ulterior views of the army.

"Gentlemen,
"I heare, how true I know not, that the King, with the commissioners at Holmby, are fetcht away by a 1000 horse to the army. What thinges may come to, God onely knowes. Wherfore, I propose to you whether it may stand with your likeinge, 1st, That I speedily put this towne into a posture, and have a maine guard in the towne at least every night, if not some in the day: which, if you assent, I shall doe speedily. 2. That all the troope bee sent to Ludlow forthwith, to convey the ordinaunce and magazin away with as much speede as may bee hither: and some of the troope to lodge constantly in the Castle here, at least till all artillery and macgazin bee brought away. 3. That all the armes in all places of the county bee speedily seised, and brought hither and kept, to bee delivered to the owners when the danger cease; and that none in the county be permitted to sell armes or powder without an order from the Committee. 4. That all the delinquents that have not compounded bee presently seized. To these, or what else you thinke needfull, I desire your subscriptions and this letter returned. What you advise I shall see immediately executed, and remain

"Sa.   "Your assured loveinge friend to serve you,
"5 June, 1647,   "H. MACKWORTH.
"9 in the morneinge.

"1 desire you to set downe an order for Atcham bridge alsoe, before you ...... I shall concurre with you.

"For his honored freind, Coll. Andrew Lloyd
    and Capt. Leighton Owen, these."

"Gentlemen,
"I received this inclosed this morneinge from Stafford, the other from Mr. Moore not longe before, both which I send you that you may consider whether a meeteinge were not convenient to morrow, and if you shall conclude it, that then you send the messenger away to Mr. Harcourt Leighton [desiring] him without faile to meete you, when hee and you shall appoint to meete. For truly I app[rehend] when danger is suspected noe time is to bee delayed, and if the parliament of England bee like to suffer violence, I thinke our lives and estates are not to deere to spend in that quarrell where and when soever bee the opponents, shall be the resolution of

                              "Y^r assured loveinge friend to serve you,
"Salop, Tuesday, 8 June, 1647.   "H. MACKWORTH.

"For his honored friends, Coll. Andrew
    Lloyd and Capt. Leighton Owen, or
    either of them, at Aston, these."

Notwithstanding these demonstrations of vigour, it was far from the design either of the Governor or the Committee to secure Shrewsbury to the Parliament. Such at least was the opinion of an inhabitant of the town, whose representation of this conjuncture has reached us under the title of "A Narration of the business at Shrewsbury, called by some the raging of a New Warr." According to him,

"Upon the armie's refusall to disband, the forcing of the King's person, marching up to London, and demanding the eleven members, mighty feares and distractions arose in the countrey, and the cavaliers grew very bold and insolent. Many of us in the towne," says the writer, " did humbly move the Committee that they would take speciall care of it, as its importance was so well known: and in consequence of this application, the Committee appointed some faithfull men to be captains in the town, who should take such names as should be given them to be their companies, and to watch under them: which captaines did execute their comand and orders, and many men of the towne did duty many nights; but the captaines finding divers of the inhabitants of the towne very backwards to doe any duty under them, and not being enabled by any order from the Comittee to enforce them to doe duty, were discouraged, and left of to watch. Our feares in the towne still continuing, by reason of cavalliers rising in some parte of Wales, and flocking together in divers meetings, we desired the Comittee to pursue their first order, and to encourage the captaines that they had named, by giving them power to bring in the men that would not watch, and that one may be designed by them to keepe the keyes of the towne. Nothing being donne upon this motion, some weekes after, divers of the chiefe men of the towne did goe to the Comittee, desiring that in pursuance of their former orders, they would secure the towne; which did then grant an order for the delivery of some armes and ammuniçõn out of the Castle for the safety of the towne; which order was the next day shewed to the Governor by some of the towne, who gave a dilatory answer, soe nothing was donne upon it, nor any further moving in the business.

" All this was donne before the army entered London, the truth of the pticulars will, wee doubt not, bee affirmed, and proved by many suffitient witnesses."

And if what is here stated be true, it is scarcely possible to doubt that the governing part of the inhabitants were in some collusion with the enemies of the Parliament: the more so, as this alledged slackness to defend the town lasted no longer than the conjuncture that produced it. For the Independents having finally gained the ascendancy, and being threatened at once with an invasion from Scotland, and with a rising of the royalists, the subsequent proceedings of the Committee for Shropshire, who now assumed the title of the Committee for Safety, evince much promptitude and vigour for the preservation of this important post.

" At the Comittee for Safety of the county of Salop, 25 June, 24 Car. It is ordered that the towne of Shrewsbury bee forthwith put into a posture of defence . . . and that capt. John Prowde, capt. Adam Webbe, capt. John Betton, and capt. Charles Doughty, doe speedily enlist such men within the said towne as are fitt to beare armes . . . and present the lyste of theire names to this Comittee . . . and that the walles of this towne (now fallen downe) bee speedily repaired.

" At the Comittee for Safetye of the countye of Salop, 6 Augt. a^o. r. r. Carol. Angl. &c. 24to. It is ordered that the towne of Shrewsbury bee forthwith put into a posture of defence, to prevent suddaine insurrecçõns of malignants and cavelliers; And that it bee referred to the care of the well-affected of the towne to recomend to this Comittee sixe comaunders, which comaunders are to enlist all such well-affected persons as are willing to beare armes for the defence of the towne: and that the mayor for the tyme beeinge, Rowland Hunt, esq., John Lowe and capt. John Betton aldermen, have twentye barrells of powder forthwith delivered them out of the Castle by the Governor, with match and bullett proporconable, And that fower hundred musquetts and pikes bee alsoe delivered to the said Mayor, R. H., J. L. and capt. J. B., out of the Castle, for the use of such persons as shall bee enlisted according to this order.

" Vera cop. ex^d. Rich^d. Mason,
" Clre to the Com^{ttee}."

The activity displayed in the government of our town appears to have preserved it in tranquillity during the stormy period that ensued: nor have any incidents respecting it occurred till the dreadful plague of 1650. This broke out, as St. Chad's register states, at John Come's house in Frankwell, on the 12th day of June; and that is the first day when any one is entered therein as having died of it. But it is not mentioned in the London papers till the 8th of July, when we are told[1] that "God's heavy visitation of this garrison with His sore judgement of the pestilence still continues, although it is as yet with gentleness, not more than twenty having hitherto died of it." Its increase was, however, greatly apprehended, in consequence of which above half the inhabitants, most of them of the gentry, had left the town. Some forces, also, were drawn out of the Castle: but enough were left to secure both that and the town, and from the "sedulity of the Governor," no fear was entertained "of the disaffected either within or without." Two days after, a similar account occurs, with the addition "that the Governor had drawn most of the soldiery that were free from the contagion into the Castle, and confined them there: having commanded those that were either ill, or inclinable to any indisposition, into the field, where they are to lye till he sees how the Lord will dispose of them."

Early in the following month, the condition of Shrewsbury attracted the notice of government, and produced the following letter from the Council of State[2].

"Sir,

"Wee are informed the plague continues much in Shrewsbury, for which wee are very sorry, desireing God to put a speedy end to it: while it continues wee feare it may bring danger to the place, if it shall fall among the Guarrison, or that for feare thereof they shall desert the place. You are therefore to take order, that all the houses that have beene, are, or shall bee infected, neere the Castle or the Gates of the Towne, may be emptied of the people, that the Souldiers being there upon their duty may not be endangered by them. And you are also forthw[th] to dissolve both the Schooles in yo[r] Towne, and see they continue soe till it shall please God the infection shall cease.

"Signed in the name and by order of the Council of State, appointed by Authority of Parliament.

"White Hall, 9 Aug. 1650. "Jo. BRADSHAWE, P[r]sident.

Indorsed, "For the Mayor of Shrewsbury, Whitehall, 10 Aug. 1650."

This disease continued to rage through the months of September[3] and

---

[1] Perfect Diurnal, July 8–15, 1650.

[2] From the original, obligingly communicated by the late rev. John Hayes Petit of Coton, a descendant of Thomas Hayes, who at this time filled the office of mayor. This gentleman conducted himself in so exemplary a manner as chief magistrate during this dreadful visitation, that the corporation presented him at the conclusion of his mayoralty with a silver tankard and high cup and cover, on which are engraven the arms of the town, and which are still preserved in the family.

[3] Perfect Diurnal, Thursday, Sept. 5. "The sickness still encreases here in our garrison; there being seven or eight houses broke out thereof. But God's mercy hath hitherto surrounded us and our soldiers, so that none of them, though we have sixty at the several posts, and eighty in the Castle, are infected." This article, probably written by

October[1]: but by the 21st of November[2], we read that the place was in a hopeful way to be freed from this grievous judgement, there being not one at that time "known sick of that disease within the suburbs;" and on the 11th of December, it is stated to have "ceased, the inhabitants resorting apace to their habitations[3], and the market kept as freely as in former times." These accounts, however, do not exactly concur with the register of St. Chad, which, it is remarkable, is the only one of our parishes that notices this visitation, though that of St. Julian affords internal evidence of its existence, by the increased number of its burials[4]. According to the former document, it did not entirely cease till the 16th of January, which is the last day on which any burial is entered as having been occasioned by the plague. During this space of time, two hundred and fifty persons became its victims in St. Chad's parish; viz.

June,	8.	October,	42.
July,	47.	November,	14.
August,	76.	December,	7.
September,	54.	January,	2.

Being thirty-three per month, without including the ordinary burials of the period, the average number of which for several preceding years appears by the register to have been somewhat under ten a month[5]. The disease appears to have been peculiarly fatal in some families[6]. The pest-houses, one of which was situated in Frankwell, must have been dreadfully crowded[7]: one hundred and twenty-three persons of the two hundred and fifty abovementioned died in them, and a few, about six, were buried there.

---

the governor, is of some importance, as presenting us with the peace establishment of the garrison of Shrewsbury.

[1] Ibid. Oct. 16. "The sickness doth still encrease, and it is spread into all parts of the town, and lately came into the suburbs next the Castle, into a victualling house, where many of the Castle souldiers were used to resort; so that I am now much afraid of them: though the same God can still preserve them, that hath done it hitherto marvellously."

[2] Perf. Diurn. of that date.

[3] From an expression in that newspaper for Nov. 21, it seems as if some permission from the police, perhaps some certificate of physicians, was requisite to enable a person who had shut up his house on account of infection, to regain possession of it: after having stated, as in the text, that there are none known sick in the suburbs, and that most of those in the pest-house are somewhat well recovered, it goes on, "that if new breaking-out hinder not, most of them, within few days, will be *admitted* to their own dwellings."

[4] There is a tradition that the butchers were not attacked by the plague, and it is true that the burials in St. Alkmund's register for the year are rather fewer than ordinary.

[5] The whole number of burials from June 12 to Jan. 16, is two hundred and seventy-seven: from which, if we deduct two hundred and fifty marked as dying of the plague, there will remain but twenty-seven for the ordinary burials of the period: i. e. not quite four a month, whereas the average monthly mortality of that era is, as we have said, nearly ten. Hence we can scarcely doubt, that several are set down as having died of the plague whose deaths ought not properly to have been ascribed to that distemper.

[6] Five servants of Mr. Rowley's are recorded to have died of it. At St. Julian's, out of twenty-one interments during the period of the plague, fifteen are out of four families.

[7] The Perfect Diurnal, Nov. 21, speaks of near two hundred as being then in the pest-house, "most of whom," it says, "are somewhat well recovered:" which may reconcile the apparently contradictory statements of that paper, (which asserts, on Dec. 11, that the sickness had ceased)

In the summer of 1651 the tranquillity of the kingdom was again disturbed by the Scottish covenanters under the nominal command of Charles II. To excite the population of the country to a vigorous resistance of this aggression, the government had recourse to their customary expedient of religious exercises. "Yesterday," says a writer from Shrewsbury of July 12, " the Governor, and many other Christians, kept a fast to seek the Lord for a blessing upon our armies and soldiers by sea and land. We found much of God in carrying on the duty of the day. On Thursday the high sheriffe and the commissioners met, in order to the security and peace of this country, which is carefully laboured after by our wise Governor[1]." There was need of all this precaution; for the western side of the kingdom, and, of course, Shropshire, was the point against which the attack of the Scots was directed. Their army broke up from Stirling on the last day of July, and advanced southwards with expedition. From Warrington the King proceeded with a hasty march through Cheshire, by Drayton[2] and Newport[3], to Tong Norton, where we find him on the 20th of August. Shrewsbury, however, was, as we are informed[4], " in a good posture, and the countreymen at an hower's warning to be in readines with what horses and arms they have[5]." All, however, in the town and county, were not steady to the Commonwealth; for "Cornet Kinnersley," one of three brothers, sons of Hercules Kinnersley, esq. of North Cleobury, all of whom had served in the Parliament armies, joined his Majesty " with a party of horse," as did " captain Benbow from Shrewsbury[6]:" and it was probably this last officer, whom we have seen signalize himself in the capture of our town for the Parliament, and who had subsequently served with distinction in the same cause[7], that suggested to Charles, the measure which he adopted at Norton[8], of dispatching a summons to Shrewsbury, inviting colonel Mackworth to deliver up to him the town and castle. The summons was accompanied by a very civil letter, in which, after complimenting the Governor as "a gentleman of an ancient house, and of very different principles," says the King, " as I am informed, from those with whom your

and of the parish register, which proves that seven persons died of it in the course of that month. It might have ceased in the town, and yet have proved fatal to some of the inhabitants of the pest-house. [1] Perfect Diurnal, 14—21 July, 1651.
[2] Phillips, p. 53.   [3] Heath.
[4] Perf. Diurn. Aug. 18—25. " From Shrewsbury Castle, Aug. 16." There can be no doubt that the intelligence from this town was dictated by colonel Mackworth, or at least written under his eye.
[5] It is added, " Worcestershire and Herefordshire have sent to us, and desire to joyn with us."

This shews the high consideration in which Shrewsbury and its governor were held by the neighbouring counties.   [6] Baxter, Life, p. 68.
[7] Sept. 16, 1648, in the attack on Anglesey by sir Thomas Myddelton and major-general Mytton, captain Benbow, and Vavasor Powell, a military preacher, were wounded on the round-head party. Account of the rising in Anglesey: in the Appendix to Beaumaris Bay, a poem, p. 52.
[8] Heath makes Charles to summon Shrewsbury from Newport; Phillips from Drayton: but the summons, as printed by himself, is dated from Tong-Norton.

employment ranks you at present," his Majesty engages not only to pardon what is past, but also to reward so eminent and seasonable a testimony of loyalty with future trust and favour: and leaves it to himself to propose his own conditions, if he will peaceably comply with the terms of the summons. Mr. Mackworth addresses his reply "To the Commander-in-chief of the Scottish army;" thus evading a recognition of his royal title, which had been voted down by parliament, without offending his Majesty by the bare appellation of Charles Stuart, which was all that vote allowed him. "I resolve," says he, "to be found unremoveable the faithful servant of The Commonwealth of England: and if you believe me to be a gentleman, you may believe I will be faithful to my trust. What principles I am judged to be of, I know not: but I hope they are such as shall ever declare me honest; and no way differing from those engaged in the same employment with me,—unless *they* should desert that cause they are imbarqued in:" a glance, by no means concealed, at the late defection of Kinnersley and Benbow. Charles, finding all his endeavours to seduce the fidelity of the Governor unavailing, continued his march to Worcester, which he reached on the 22d of August.

On the 3d of September was fought the fatal battle, or rather rout, which gave a death-blow to all the present hopes of the royal party, and opened an immediate way to Cromwell's assumption of the vacant throne. The Lord General, as he was then called, in order to repress such risings for the future by an example of terror, determined to summon a court-martial for the trial of the earl of Derby, who had been taken at Newport[1], and several other commanders of distinction, among whom was captain Benbow. The court assembled at Chester in the month of October, Governor Mackworth being president. The prisoners were soon found guilty, and five of them ordered for execution. On the 15th, the same day on which the earl was beheaded in his town of Bolton, Benbow was shot at Shrewsbury, where he is said to have first joined the late King in 1642[2], which he had been afterwards mainly instrumental in securing for the Parliament, and whence he had now deserted to serve under the standard of Charles II. The scene of his execution was the garden under the Castle Mount, between that and the Council House: it was then called the Cabbage Garden, was afterwards used as a bowling-green; and, in all probability, was chosen for the present fatal purpose, as having been the very spot on which the prisoner had most eminently distinguished his zeal for his former masters; when he headed the scaling party which on that memorable morning mounted the walls, and succeeded in gaining the town. His body was

---

[1] Heath, p. 299.

[2] For this we have no other authority than Dr. Campbell, as quoted hereafter.

interred in St. Chad's churchyard on the following day: and the humble stone placed over his remains still bears the following inscription[1].

> HERE LIETH THE BODY
> OF CAPTAINE IOHN
> BENBOW WHO WAS
> BURIED OCTOBER Y^E
> 16. 1651.

Dr. Campbell, in a note on his life of Admiral Benbow[2], writes thus. "When the civil wars broke out, King Charles I., relying strongly on the affection of the inhabitants of this county, repaired in person to Shrewsbury ..... and made public declaration that he did not carry on this war from a thirst of blood ... &c. Upon this declaration the lords Newport and Littleton, with the greatest part of the gentry of the country, came in, and offered his Majesty their services. Among these were *Thomas Benbow and John Benbow, esquires, both men of estates, and both colonels in the King's service.* After the King's affairs fell into confusion, such gentlemen as had served in his army retired to their own countries respectively, and lived there as privately as they could: but though their interests were much reduced, and their fortunes in a great measure ruined, yet their spirits remained unbroken, and they acted as cheerfully for the service of King Charles II., as if they had never suffered at all by serving his father: so much better a principle is loyalty than corruption. When, therefore, that Prince marched from Scotland towards Worcester, the two Benbows, amongst other gentlemen of the county of Salop, went to attend him; and after fighting bravely in the support of their Sovereign, were both taken prisoners by the rebels;" and then he goes on to relate how colonel Thomas Benbow was adjudged to be shot on the 19th at Shrewsbury. The whole

---

[1] Phillips gives this as if it bore "Colonel:" but any reader resident in Shrewsbury may satisfy himself to the contrary by an inspection of the stone. [2] In the Biographia Britannica.

note is so well written that it is a pity so little of it should be true. But, in the first place, the biographer mistakes, as we have seen, both the christian name and the military rank of the officer executed here. Then as to the estates possessed by the two Benbows, whom he dignifies with the addition of *esquires*, it is all purely gratuitous. Their father was, as we shall shew hereafter, from undoubted evidence, an honest tanner; nor does the name once occur in the " List of the Noblemen and Gentlemen who compounded for their estates." From sequestration, indeed, captain John, whom Dr. Campbell calls *colonel Thomas* Benbow, was effectually protected by the side which he espoused in the civil wars; and as to his brother, called by the Doctor, colonel John Benbow, and father, as he asserts, of our brave townsman admiral Benbow, it is quite certain that no such person ever existed. As to the *rank* of the unfortunate sufferer, it is equally clear that he could not be a colonel in 1642, for he was then scarcely nineteen years of age; having been baptized at St. Julian's, as the register of that parish attests, on the 20th of August, 1623: and that he never rose higher than *captain* is put beyond a question by the authorities we have quoted, his sepulchral stone still remaining, and the register of his burial[1]. Even the accurate and laborious Carte commits two errors in his account of this gentleman: " Captain Richard Benbow," says he, " was shot on the 15th of October, at Shrewsbury, for high treason against the pretended commonwealth, in assisting the King contrary to an ordinance of the rump passed on the 12th of August last[2]." There wanted no ordinance of parliament to shoot a deserter taken in arms against his commanding officer.

We have already stated that the capture of Shrewsbury in 1645 had ever since been observed here as a day of devout thanksgiving. On the anniversary that occurred in 1652-3, it appears to have been celebrated with more than usual solemnity, perhaps as a political expedient, to impress the people with a sense of the blessings they derived from the government of the parliament, now tottering to its downfall. " Yesterday," says an article from Shrewsbury of Feb. 23, " our Governor, with the wel-affected of this place, solemnly kept the whole day in commemoration of the great mercy in taking this garrison. Many petitions were put in the behalfe of our councels and armes, and to strengthen the resolutions of those whom God hath made instrumentall for his glory and the propagation of the Gospel, that they may be carried on for the welfare of them that are faithful in and to the Commonwealth[3].

---

[1] " 1651, Oct. 16. John Benbowe, Captaine, who was shott at the Castle, B." St.Chad's Register.
[2] iv. 652.
[3] Perfect Diurnal of the day.

If this anniversary had any such design as we have suggested for it above, it proved wholly inefficient. On the 20th of the following April, general Cromwell broke up the House of Commons by force: and before the end of the year (Dec. 16) was inaugurated Lord Protector of England, Scotland, and Ireland. The Governor of this town, his devoted adherent, caused him to be proclaimed here " with great rejoicing" on the 28th[1].

Governor Mackworth died in December, 1654, and having been one of Cromwell's privy council, was buried in King Henry VII's chapel in Westminster Abbey on the 26th, with a very magnificent funeral. He seems to have been succeeded in office here by Thomas Hunt, esq., representative of the town in Parliament, and a colonel in the army. This gentleman had soon occasion for all his vigilance and activity, of which he displayed no inconsiderable share. Every party in the nation was become disgusted with Cromwell's dominion. The royalists were indignant to see the ancient monarchy usurped by an upstart who had no hereditary claim upon their allegiance: the republicans were mortified to see all their blood and efforts, which had been spent for the setting up of a Commonwealth, lavished only for the support of a government which, in every thing but the name, was a most despotic monarchy: the presbyterians were chagrined at the favour of their rivals the independents, and at a general toleration of every religious denomination (excpt the church of England). Under these circumstances we cannot wonder that a conspiracy should arise against Cromwell's government. Yet it was confined to the royalists. It had been fermenting during the whole of the preceding year, and broke out into action at the beginning of 1655. The exiled King removed to Zealand, that he might be ready, on the shortest warning, to join his friends. But Cromwell was too crafty and vigilant to be taken unawares. Among his secret pensioners was sir Richard Willis, whom we saw, during the wars, in an eminent command at Shrewsbury[2] under Charles 1., and who being now admitted into the councils of his son, divulged the critical moment when it became necessary for " his Highness" to interfere. Among the important places which the conspirators proposed to secure, the town of Shrewsbury was one. Their plan, as the Protector himself states it in his Declaration put out a few months later[3], was to rise first in the West, Wales, the North, and other remote parts of the nation, hoping thereby to draw the army, or a great part of it, from London; whereupon Kent, Surrey, and their party in London, were to rise, &c.," and among the " garrisons and strong places which they intended first to surprize and seize upon," the Declaration expressly mentions this town.

Two zealous friends of monarchy, sir Thomas Harris, bart. of Boreatton, and Ralph Kynaston, esq. of Llansanfraid[4] in Montgomeryshire, undertook

---

[1] Perfect Diurnal of the day.
[2] Vide supra, p. 439.
[3] Parl. Hist. xx. 453.
[4] He was son of the rev. Ralph Kynaston, rector

this enterprise. Their plan was to surprise the Castle, on the 8th of March, by sending six gentlemen, about four o'clock in the afternoon, two of them in female attire, and two as servants to the others, who should beg leave to view the fortress. This company was " to keep the gate open, and the bridge down," under some pretence which is not related, " untill a party designed to seize upon the Castle should rush out of certain alehouses near at hand, where they were to be ready at the discharge of a pistol, and overpower the garrison, which consisted of no more than 70 men." Sir Thomas Harris was to have had a rendezvous in his own park about five miles off, of several persons he had engaged, " at one o'clock in the afternoon[1]," and was very confident of the town and Castle that night. But the whole of this scheme, which does not seem to have been very well laid[2], was entirely frustrated by the extreme imprudence of Mr. Kynaston; who, at the distance of only ten miles from Shrewsbury, had publicly listed 50 troopers for the service of Charles II., on the day preceding that on which the attempt was to have been made. Intelligence of this; of the intended rendezvous at Boreatton Park; and of a projected attack upon Chirk Castle that same night by " one sir Arthur Blaney, at the head of the Montgomeryshire forces;" reached the Governor of Shrewsbury on the morning of the 8th. He had been put upon his guard four days before by a messenger from the lord Protector and his council[3], who, in all probability, had information of this design from sir Richard Willis: and he had, in consequence, sent off to Hereford for a troop of horse. As that did not arrive, he had nothing left but to act upon the defensive. " He immediately called in all his men into the Castle; planted the guns as advantageously as he could; set a file of soldiers at every gate of the town, that no one might stir out of it: seized twenty of the best horses he could find in any stables, and mounted that number of his friends, with orders to secure all persons in sir Thomas's house, and search it for arms: which accordingly they went about. At their coming to Boreatton, they found some trying to escape[4]: two got clear away: some endeavoured to make

of Middle, and had himself been a mercer in Shrewsbury, before he succeeded to his patrimony in Montgomeryshire.

[1] Our authority, the Mercurius Politicus for March 17, says, " one o'clock at night:" but it is plain, from the words immediately following (that sir Thomas was confident of gaining the town *that night*) that this might be a mistake. A meeting at midnight could never co-operate with an enterprise which was to be undertaken in the preceding afternoon.

Stratagems very similar have, however, often succeeded. It was almost exactly thus that Pampeluna and Barcelona were seized by the French in 1808. Southey's Hist. of the Peninsular War, i. 156, 158. But the English governments of the Interregnum were in the highest degree watchful and able: every department in Spain supine and infatuated.

[2] The Faithful Scout, Mar. 16.

[4] The " Faithful Scout," ut supra, says, that two of these were slain in the pursuit after them: as was one who endeavoured to escape out of Shrewsbury over the river, though many others got off safe that way." The Mercurius Politicus of April 5, relates, that " on Sabbath-day at night, Mr. Eyton, an agent that sir Thomas Harris used to draw in his several friends in his late design, escaped out of the house of correction, though he had irons upon his legs, and we can hear nothing of him."

resistance; but finding themselves overpowered, surrendered upon quarter. Sir Thomas himself, and about five gentlemen more were taken; about fifteen horses, as many cases of pistols; seven of them hid under straw in the barn; a little barrel of gunpowder; a great quantity of bullets in his study, new made of lead took from off his house. He confidently denies, for all this, any design against this garrison: but Ralph Kynaston being taken by Redcastle forces[1], hath confessed the whole business[2]." So confident were the cavaliers of success, that a party of 700 horse, besides infantry, advanced towards Shrewsbury the day after, and gave it an alarm: but finding that the design had not taken effect, they retreated back again towards the farther part of North Wales, where they proclaimed the King, and from thence were reported to have taken shelter in Anglesey[3].

The government of Cromwell was unconstitutional and severe; but it does not appear to have been cruel. Very little blood was spilt upon the occasion of this insurrection. None at all in Shrewsbury. Mr. Kynaston, and another conspirator, Mr. Armstrong, were, it is true, sent prisoners to London " by order of his Highness[4];" and the Governor seized on all the eminent cavaliers in the country. But no lives were sacrificed on the occasion. Indeed the news-writer intimates, that the malignants " had acted very warily, though the Governor found good cause of suspicion against most of them, and had certain intelligence that those who had been left unseized were very high, and had taken new courage seeing so small forces in the town." Yet it is some merit in an illegal government not to act upon suspicions, as if they were proofs. All usurpers have not been so scrupulous. But if the Protector spared the lives of the royalists, he had no mercy on their purses. He raised a new and standing militia of horse in every county[5], and laid the burden of maintaining these forces upon that party. The tax was called *decimation*, because it took from them the tenth part of their property. Still further to rivet their chains, he parcelled out the kingdom into twelve districts, over each of which he placed a major-general with very extraordinary powers; which, while they were ostensibly directed against the cavaliers alone, did in fact aim a deadly blow at the whole fabrick of British freedom. These military magistrates were authorized to compel every householder whom they thought fit to suspect of disaffection, to give such security as they should judge expedient for their good behaviour: no person was permitted to ride post without a special warrant; nor could any one of whom security had been taken, remove to another place, without giving previous notice. It must be admitted, that

[1] i. e. Powis Castle.
[2] Mercurius Politicus, March 17.
[3] Faithful Scout, ut supra.
[4] Mercurius Politicus, April 5.
[5] Parl. Hist. xx. 456.

with these and the like vexatious restraints, were intermingled several wholesome regulations; such as a suppression of bear-baiting, cock-fightings, and other dissolute assemblies: a controul over idle and loose persons who had no visible way of livelihood; provision for the apprehension of robbers and murderers; and for security of the roads[1]. But it is easy to see that so coercive a system, which comprised restrictions of daily occurrence, and impeded in so many ways the intercourse of social life, would excite great dissatisfaction, and expose the new major-generals appointed to enforce it, to general detestation. One writer calls them "an obscure company of mean fellows[2]:" and it may be true that most of them were persons of low extraction. Another, with less probability, stiles them "a companie of *silly* meane fellows[3]:" Cromwell knew mankind too well to select persons of that description for his instruments. A third says, that "they carried things with unheard-of insolence in their several precincts[4];" and Ludlow not inaptly calls them "bashas."

Colonel James Berry, now appointed major-general for this county, with the adjoining ones of Hereford and Worcester, and the whole of North Wales, had been originally either a woodmonger[5] in London, or as Baxter, who is likely to have known, assures us, clerk in an iron-work. He had been the old bosom friend of that eminent non-conformist; had "lived in his house and been dearest to him; of great sincerity before the wars; affectionate in religion; and while conversant with humbling providences doctrines and company, carried himself as a very great enemy to pride." But when Cromwell "made him his favourite," (for he represented the counties of Worcester and Hereford in 1656, and was afterwards one of the lords of the Protector's "Other House,") "his mind, his aim, his talk, and all was altered. And as ministers of the old way were lower, and sectaries much higher in his esteem than formerly, so he was much higher in his own esteem when he thought he had attained much higher, than he was before, when he sate with his fellows in the common form[6]." Whatever he were, when intimate with Baxter, and after he had left that divine for the "new light" of the "sectaries," he commenced his administration at Shrewsbury by a judicious act of lenity and favour. Several gentlemen of this county had been put into confinement, in the course of the year, not under suspicion of having been implicated in the late insurrection, but for general disaffection to the government. Three of these are mentioned[7] as having been apprehended in June last, sir William Owen, [of Condover],

---

[1] Parl. Hist. xx. 461.
[2] Roger Coke, Detection, p. 392.
[3] Mem. of Col. Hutchinson, p. 337.
[4] Parl. Hist. xx. 468.   [5] Noble.
[6] Baxter's Life, p. 57, ubi plura. The pamphlet called "England's Confusion," (abridged in Parl. Hist. xxi. 409) calls "Bury the worst of major-generals except Butler:" but little reliance is to be placed on such party effusions.
[7] Certain Passages of every day's Intelligence. Friday, June 22, 1655.

Mr. Roger Owen [his son and heir], and Mr. Edward Wen, and they had been lying in prison ever since. The first thing which our major-general did, upon his arrival in Shrewsbury, in the beginning of December, was to set these gentlemen at liberty ; first taking security from them for their good behaviour[1]. He had done the same at Worcester[2]; perhaps also at Hereford; and as he went from Shrewsbury into Wales, it is probable that he marked his progress by a similar exercise of clemency in his journey through the principality. It produced its intended effect ; as these parts were kept in quiet during the remainder of Cromwell's life; and the succession of his son was admitted in Shrewsbury with apparent acquiescence.

"Monday, Sept. 13, 1658," says a paper of that day[3], "the Mayor and Aldermen, in their scarlet robes, the common councel and assistants in their liveries, the sheriff and governor of the Castle, and some gentlemen and ministers, proclaimed Richard Cromwell Lord Protector of this Common wealth, with firing great guns; afterwards the Mayor and Aldermen entertained the sheriff and gentlemen with a great banquet: and the sheriff and governour entertained the souldiers. The whole business was mannaged by the Governour, the sheriff, and Major Wareing, captain of the county troop[4]."

The expression, "*some* gentlemen," does not denote a numerous attendance ; and the concluding observation seems intended to imply that the ceremony was a mere official act of the constituted authorities, without any concurrence of the general population, or perhaps even of those authorities themselves.

This was undoubtedly the case. The protectorate of Richard quickly came to an end (April 22, 1659) : and general Berry was one of the principal actors in pulling him down[5]. The slender remains of the Long Parliament, with whose meeting this chapter commenced, resumed their session (May 7). The contempt into which they had sunk encouraged

---

[1] Mercurius Politicus, Dec. 8, 1655.
[2] Nash, ii. 44, n.
[3] The Diurnal.
[4] From a scarce pamphlet in the possession of W. Hamper, esq., entitled "A true catalogue ... of the several places .... where ... R. C. was proclaimed, &c. Taken out of the second and fifth dayes (heathen-like called Monday and Thursdays) Diurnals, &c. Printed in the 1st year of the English armies small or scarce beginning to return from their almost six years apostacy," 4to. pp. 76. The work contains a most high-flown address from the county, Feb. 7, 1658-9 : in which the late Protector is called "a Moses who led the Lord's people out of the land of Egypt, attained to more than a Pisgah sight of the land of Canaan, and gave to them more than a taste of the clusters of its grapes ;" and "his highness," whom they address, i. e. Richard Cromwell, is styled their "Joshua, who has so signally taken of the spirit of their Moses," and who has received "a certain pledge that God ... will not fail him nor forsake." In little more than ten weeks poor Joshua's sceptre had crumbled to dust.

[5] On the eve of the Restoration, Mr. Berry was imprisoned at the instigation of Monk: "and was closely confined in Scarborough Castle: but being released, he became a gardener, and lived in a safer state than in all his greatness." Baxter, ut supra. Hence it has been supposed that he was reduced to the necessity of that manual occupation, to earn a livelihood. Orme's Life of Owen, p. 365. Quarterly Review, No. 50. p. 320. Such, however, could not be the case. The order at his liberation "that he should retire to *such of his seats as was* farthest from London," seems to bespeak him a man of fortune. No doubt he solaced his declining years with horticultural amusements, and in that sense "*became a gardener*." He had been, when Baxter's intimate associate, "of very good natural parts, especially mathematical and mechanical."

both royalists and presbyterians to join, for the purpose of bringing in the King. Charles advanced to Calais to meet the ardour of his subjects, and a day in the middle of July was named for the general rising. But Willis, who still continued the same correspondence with the republican government which he had carried on with that of Cromwell, perfidiously suggested the postponement of rising for ten days, and in the mean time disclosed the important secret to his employers. As early as the 12th of July, we find the House of Commons authorizing the Council of State to take up some suspicious persons[1], and towards the close of the month directing troops to be raised in London, and calling upon the citizens to do all in their power for " the safety and good of this Commonwealth in this time of imminent danger[2]." Sir George Booth, however, took up arms in Cheshire on the day finally agreed upon (Aug. 1); and " old sir Thomas Middleton, then near eighty years of age," says Ludlow, " proclaimed the King at Wrexham. This rising encouraged the enemy," (i. e. *the royalists*) " so much[3], that they immediately sent out a party to seize Shrewsbury: but, though the malcontents" (*royalists*, again) " were very numerous in that town, yet captain Waring, with the militia troop, prevented their design, and secured that place for the Parliament[4]."

The officer here styled captain, and, a little above, major, was Edmund Waringe, esq., of Humfreston near Shifnal, a very active Commonwealth's man, who was now, and had been for the two preceding years, sheriff of the county. He was also, but from what period we have not found, governor of this town; and a letter from him in that capacity to the Right Honourable the Lord President of the Council of State, dated Shrewsbury 21st Aug. 1659, ten at night, was printed at London soon after[5]. It gives a short account of "lord" Lambert's defeat of sir Geo. Booth, and of the flight of sir Thos. Middleton and the lord Kilmorrey to Chirk Castle. It appears that the Governor of Shrewsbury had sent the horse " from this garrison," the day before, on some service which he does not specify. " Just now at writing," says he, " a boy of this town, now fled home, confesseth he was under one capt. Shenton, who dismist his company last night at Chester, and bad them shift for themselves. I crave your favour for my rude lines, remaining engaged to serve you." The zeal of the colonel, for such it appears he was by this time become, proved so satisfactory to the house, that it was resolved, 23 Aug., " that col. Edmund Waring, Governor of Shrewsbury,

---

[1] Parl. Hist. xxi. 434.
[2] Ibid. 436.
[3] Sir Charles Lyttleton, bart. of Frankley in Worcestershire, and of Upper Arley in Staffordshire, appears to have been one of the leaders of this party, for in a letter of lord Mordaunt to Charles II., printed in Collins (art. Lyttelton) the writer says, " Charles Lyttelton had undoubtedly carried Shrewsbury, but that one misfortune on another happened." Lord Clarendon (b. xvi.) adds the lord Newport and other gentlemen of Shropshire as engaged in this design.
[4] Ludlow's Memoirs, p. 390. edit. 4to.
[5] It is also printed in Parl. Hist. xxi. 445.

be captain of a foot-company in Shrewsbury; and that a commission be brought in accordingly; as also for the officers of his company[1]."

But the rule of this shadow of a Parliament was fast melting away. No discouragements could damp the ardour of the royalists: and before the end of the year, sir Thomas Middleton, who had begun the war as a Parliamentarian, but now found monarchy indispensable to the settlement of the nation, undaunted by his late very narrow escape, was again forming designs for the seizure of this town[2]. It is less pleasing, but not at all less curious, to observe, that the ambitious aspirations after the post of Governor of Shrewsbury, which had been afloat at the beginning of these troubles, continued to prevail even at their close: so uniform is human nature under all circumstances. Sir Thomas was to receive a commission as Commander-in-chief of the counties of North Wales; but he aimed likewise at the government of this town; and this pretension embarrassed sir Edward Hyde, chief minister of the exiled King, as likely to clash with the views of his friend lord Newport; " in whose excellent spirit, and cordial desire to promote the King's service," he felt, however, the most entire confidence. " What is to be done," says he to his correspondent, " with reference to the proposition concerning Shrewsbury, must be left to my lord Mordaunt, and the rest of the commissioners to adjust. If it were included in his [Middleton's] commission, it must draw that whole county likewise under his power and command: and how that will suit with the good acceptance of my lord Newport, and the rest of the commissioners of that countrey, is not hard to guess; and yet, no doubt, they will be glad of any sure way to take Shrewsbury, and to have so good a neighbour in North Wales as sir Thomas Middleton: therefore, there is no way to prevent all jealousies and mistakes, but by bringing my lord Newport, or Andrew Newport, and sir Thomas Middleton together: who will easily agree, and prosecute any noble design, and secure one another[3]." And again, on the 20th of February, the same statesman, still at Brussels, " What I said concerning Shrewsbury, was not that I thought it unfit to be in sir Thomas Middleton's hands: I know very well, how it lies to North Wales, and the great advantage they may receive from each other; and no man is so fit to be Governor of it as sir Thomas Middleton, who offers to contribute so much to the possessing of it: but what I said upon that occasion, concerning my lord Newport, was, that it would be fitter to be transacted and consented to, by an association with Shropshire, than by an absolute disposition of the King's. And I named my lord Newport only, as the principal person of that county, and one very much affected to the King's service, not as Commander-in-chief;

---

[1] Merc. Pol. Aug. 25.
[2] Sir Edward Hyde, Brussels, Jan. 12, 1660, to the rev. Mr. (afterwards Dean) Barwick. " If sir Thomas Middleton can make himself master of Shrewsbury, ... it would be an excellent post." Vita Johannis Barwick, Appendix, p. 384.
[3] Hyde (Brussels, 14 Jan.) to Barwick, Appendix, ut supra, p. 389.

which I do not believe he will ever affect to be. He is too wise a man to keep any thing in his mind of former passages" (alluding to the early disaffection of Middleton) " that may breed a disturbance in the present service; and no body can be so fit to negotiate such an association as Andrew Newport: and therefore I pray, let my lord Mordaunt and Mr. Rumbald dispose Andrew Newport in such a manner, as you will do sir Thomas Middleton, that they may meet together, and settle the association : and I shall then wonder if the Shropshire gentlemen shall not be very willing that sir Thomas shall be Governor of Shrewsbury, when he hath been the principle means to take it : and that is all I shall say of that matter."

But all the arrangements for wresting Shrewsbury by force of arms from the Parliament, had been rendered unnecessary before this letter was written, by Monk declaring (Feb. 11) for the King. Upon that joyful event all ranks hastened to return to their allegiance: the Long Parliament broke up (March 16); the King returned (May 29); and the following letter, written on that very day, by Richard Ottley, esq. of Pitchford, (son of the former governor, now deceased) who hastened in the direction of Dover, to meet and congratulate his Sovereign, depicts the universal joy which prevailed, in a manner more lively, because more natural, than the most studied periods of the historian.

"My most deare and evere honored Mother,

"I prayse God we are safe come to towne, and his Matie, with his two brotheres, the duke of Yorke and duke of Glouster, are now at White hall. I met them at Canterbury, and had the happinesse to be of the life guard since Fryday last; wherein my content over ballanced the paynes I underwent. I most humbly thanke yor La^p for your py which I shall enquire after. I beg pardon that I am soe short in wrighting, being weary at p'sent: I humbly crave yor blessing: wth my duty and thanks for yor goodnesse to mine, for whom my hearty prayers to God are: I rest

"Yo^r La^{pp} most dutiful sonne and servant,

"May 29,
  60.   " These
RIC. OTTLEY.

  "For my most deare Mother,
   the Lady Lucy Ottley, at
   Pitchford in Shropshire.

  "Leave this at Mr. Banister, the
   King's Head, in Shrewsbury."

CHAPTER XI.

FROM THE RESTORATION TO THE REVOLUTION.

NEARLY two centuries remain to complete our annals; and, executed in the detail which we have felt ourselves bound to give to the former periods, they could not fail to exhaust the patience of every reader, and of most writers. But such minuteness is no longer necessary. Modern times afford few incidents for local histories such as the present. The seat of government is now confined to the metropolis. Our Kings seldom quit that immediate vicinity: and neither civil warfare nor foreign invasion interrupt the repose of a provincial town. From these causes Shrewsbury has scarcely once been brought into contact with any event that can be properly deemed historical, since the convulsive period from which we are just emerged. We shall, therefore, no longer attempt a continuous narrative, but merely set down, often with long intervals, such incidents or remarks as seem to possess somewhat of general or local interest.

One of the first acts of the corporation, after the King's return, was, of course, to reinstate such of its members as had been displaced for their attachment to his father. On July 6th it was " aggreed that those aldermen and assistants that were excluded this house after this town was taken by the Parliament forces bee restored:" and the royalists, now in their turn triumphant, would not be slow to seize any opportunity of annoying their late masters. Governor Waring, and Vavasor Powell, a seditious preacher, who, according to his enemies, had run through each degree of conformity and non-conformity, and been stained with every immorality and crime, were thrown into prison in Shrewsbury. Powell, being " much haunted by his own party," was removed into Montgomeryshire, and there kept in close custody till he was committed to the Fleet prison[1]. Waring

---

[1] So Wood, Athenæ, in v. This author places Powell's seizure at Shrewsbury " on the approach of the King's restoration," and " about the latter end of February 1659," by which must be intended, 1659,60. He was, however, at large in August 1660, when a petition of the Justices of Merionethshire against him was read at the Council-board, complaining of the numerous congregations to which he preached in North Wales, " admitting none but such as will swear against magistracy and ministry." Kennet's Register, p. 241. This, it is hoped, justifies us in departing, on the present occasion, from the chronology of the Oxford Antiquary.

was set at liberty after a short confinement. But this was done contrary to the opinion of the lord lieutenant (Francis lord Newport): and the insurrection of Venner and his Fifth Monarchists (Jan. 6, 1660-1) seems to justify that peer in the rebuke which he addressed to sir Richard Ottley, one of his deputy-lieutenants, for the lenity shewn by him and his colleagues to the ex-governor of Shrewsbury. Hume[1] represents the madness of those enthusiasts as affording the ministry "a *pretence* for departing from their neutrality." But this is scarcely a fair statement: and the measures of the administration were marked by considerable forbearance.[2] On the 8th of January the privy council write to the lord lieutenant, reciting the existence of "unseasonable meetings," and desiring him and his deputies "to *observe* dangerous persons." On the 22d of the same month, they refer to the "late barbarous, bloody, and rebellious attempts in London," and authorize him "to arrest suspicious and leading persons," employing therein the civil power. Lord Newport communicated these orders to sir Richard Ottley, on the 24th.

"I send you enclosed," says he, "a letter from the Councell, and a proclamation for the moderating of your proceedings. Though it may bee conceived a very ineffectual way for the securinge of persons to send warrants to a constable, yet if souldiers bringe the warrant to him, your ends may seeme accomplishable. You see the letter speakes of leadinge men. Therefore you did ill in releasinge Waringe, and you needed not have apprehended his ranting demand of a mittimus, which will serve him for discourse in his two pot houses. I would advise you to send for him agen, though not as a criminal by proofe, yet as a dangerous person, especially havinge the comand of the Councell for it...."

The remainder of this letter alludes, with some soreness, to the severe frugality of the administration, and their resolutions to disband the army; measures which are justly to be ascribed to the patriotick and constitutional views of their leader, the great lord Clarendon; whose long and faithful services to the father and the son, and endeavours to restrain the profusion, and limit the authority of the latter, were ultimately rewarded by exile and disgrace;—such disgrace as worthless kings have it in their power to bestow. "All the inland garrison-forces," continues the lord lieutenant, "are to be disbanded, and among the rest us at Shrewsbury and Ludlow . . . . neither would they allow a Governor in the establishment of Shrewsbury, soe frugall they are[3]. And what will become of Shrewsburye now, God knowes. They are very well content to bee safe, but not to pay for it . . . . When our companyes at Shrewsbury are disbanded, the deputy lieutenants had best comitt the prisoners in the Castle to the provost marshall; where Mr. Waringe must alsoe bee, unlesse hee give securitye to bee true prisoner at other quarters, and for his good behaviour there. By Sherington Tal-

---

[1] Sub anno.
[2] The following information is derived from the Ottley papers.
[3] This was not correct. It will appear presently that there was a governor.

bott's[1] letter to mee, which I sent to G. Hosier[2], it is to bee doubted hee had bin dablinge in this late businesse."

On the 4th of March the council write again to lord Newport; reminding him of their former letters, for observing and securing dangerous characters, " upon which account," say they, " very many persons under the notion of Quakers have been secured," but, " the danger being well over," the present letter " permits all persons to be discharged who were secured only on suspicion in the late insurrection, except the ringleaders of faction:" and it is presumed that these documents effectually vindicate both the real lenity and the necessary circumspection of the first administration of Charles II.

Much of both these qualities appears in the next transaction which we have to record respecting our town. In the latter end of 1661 an act passed for the well-governing and regulating corporations: (13 Charles II. stat. 2. cap. 1.) The preamble recites, that questions are likely to arise concerning the validity of elections of magistrates, both in respect of some who were removed, and others who were placed during the late troubles, contrary to the charters, and that, notwithstanding his Majesty's unparalleled indulgence in pardoning all that is passed, many evil spirits are still working, so that it is necessary to perpetuate the succession in corporations in persons well-affected to the established government. The act then empowers the King to appoint commissioners, to administer the oaths of allegiance and supremacy, together with a third oath, expressive of the unlawfulness of taking arms against his Majesty on any pretence, to all persons who shall on the 24th of December hold any office in corporations, and to exact from them a declaration of the nullity and illegality of the Covenant. Those who refuse to take the oaths or subscribe the declaration are, of course, removed: and besides this, the commissioners have power to remove any other persons from office in corporations, " if they shall deem it expedient for the publick safety," though such persons may have complied with the above enactments.

Thomas Jones, esq., whom we have seen first on the list of aldermen of Shrewsbury, in the charter of 1638, occupied at this time the situation of town-clerk. He must have come into office during the interregnum: for Charles II., in a letter (16th July, 1660) to the mayor, speaks of the office as " being in your gift:" and recommends Adam Ottley, esq., son of the

---

[1] There was a Sharington Talbot seated at Rudge in 1630: if he were the son of Sharington Talbot, esq., of Salwarpe in Worcestershire, (cousin-german to John Talbot of Grafton, father of the ninth earl of Shrewsbury,) he was of principles very different from those of his father, who was mulcted in no less a sum than £2011, for his loyalty to Charles I.

[2] George Hosier, sometimes called captain Hosier, was son of Richard Hosier, esq. of Cruckton. He appears to have been Governor of Shrewsbury Castle in 1663, 1670, and 1673, and to have dwelt there.

former Governor, to be appointed; taking no notice of its being filled by Mr. Jones, but stating it to be void " by the resignation of our faithful subject Thomas Owen, esq." Mr. Jones, however, notwithstanding this royal letter, retained possession till the 9th of August, 1662. On that day lord Newport, sir Francis Lawley, bart. of Spoonhill, Richard Fowler, of Harnage Grange, Francis Thornes, of Shelvocke, Robert Sandford, of Sandford, and James Lacon, of West Coppice, esquires, as commissioners under the new act, tacitly remove him, by appointing the above-mentioned Mr. Ottley to the office: and a letter from lord Newport[1] to the brother of the new town-clerk, written under evident apprehension that lord Clarendon would disapprove of such severity to so eminent a lawyer as Mr. Jones, seems to justify what we have said of the conciliating temper understood to belong to that great and excellent person.

" Sir Richard,   " 30 Aug. 62.

" I rec̃ed yours of the 26th, and give you thanks for the trouble you have taken upon you concerning my seale. I believe your brother has given you an account how his bussinesse stands in Shrewsbury. I haue wrytten this poste to the Chancelor about it; and I thinke it were not amisse if you speedily wayted on the Chancelor, and to make as if you came to know if hee would comand you any service into Shropshire (though you goe not soe soone, which hee will not know). He knowes by my letter that your brother is chosen Town Clark, and perhaps will speake to you of that bussinesse: if he does, and seeme to be unsatisfyed, I w`d` advise you to tell him how great a Countenancer of the Presbyterians Mr. Jones has bin in Shrewsbury, how he had all their voices last election who are turnd out now; how he made Mr. Proude compound with Mr. Talence; the bussinesse of Waring when he was comitted at the time of Venner's insurrection, and what things you can remembr ag`t` him; that my Ld. Ch. may finde others speake ag`t` him as well as I. He declared himselfe ag`t` the comission of array in the time of the Warre, and refused to finde a horse for the King, for which your father comitted him; and unworthily supplanted your brother in this very place a yeare and halfe since, though he were not duly elected by those people that now have refused to subscribe, and are turnd out, who could not make a full number to choose him neyther according to their charter. These things, if you can finde an opportunity to speake to him of, if administred by him, you will doe very well in the opinion of

              " Y`r` very affect. cosen and servant,
" I am very glad Dick Screven mends.   " FRA. NEWPORT.

  " For my much honord friend,
   S`r` Richard Ottley, kn`t`, at his
   Lodgings over against the Rose
   and Crowne in Petty France in
      Westminster,
       these."

Either sir Richard Ottley declined the commission thus assigned him, which, to speak the truth, was not quite an ingenuous one, or lord Clarendon did not receive full satisfaction, or Mr. Jones, who would scarcely sit down quiet under such an affront, was loud in his expressions of complaint. The

---

[1] The writer subscribes his Christian name, though a baron of the realm. This was almost the universal practice of the peerage before the troubles; but gradually wore out after the Restoration, which introduced many French customs, and among others, this.

commissioners found it expedient to justify themselves at length, and their paper deserves attention, though, perhaps, not implicit credit; for Mr. Jones's name occurs in the list of prisoners when the town was captured by the Parliament forces, and therefore he had, at least up to that period, adhered to the King: and if, after the ruin of the monarchy, he submitted to the ruling powers, he did so in common with the great majority of the nation. The document, however, throws some light on the state of the town, not yet fully composed after the storms of the late agitated period; and it paints the feelings of those who had so recently suffered most severely for their loyalty, and who were very naturally jealous, that persons who had not, like them, borne the burden and heat of the day, should share, on equal terms, in the emoluments and rewards of the new government.

" The reasons that induced the Commissioners for regulating the Corporations within the County of Salop to think it expedient to the publicke safety to displace Mr. Tho. Jones of Shrowsbury from the office of Townclerke there.

" 1. Mr. Jones, though in possession of the place, had no right at all to it, being unduely elected according to the charter: and not only soe, but for the most part by ill-affected persons whoe have beene since turned out themselves . . . .

" 2. He hath been a great countenancer of the Presbyterian partie of that Towne since the King came in, . . . which is generally beleev'd gave incouragement to the factious ministers there (hee being a Parliament man) to preach soe boldly and seditiously as they did, and to refuse all along to reade the common prayers.

" 3. After the act for regulation was past, Mr. Jones (knowing that noe members of corporations co^d by the act be displaced but such as were in office upon Dec. 24, 1661) came downe from London to Shrewsbury, viz. upon that very day: and there solicited the Presbyterian Mayor (Bagott) and his brethren the aldermen (whoe were since turned out for refuseing to subscribe) very earnestly to fill up their number of aldermen and common councill men, of which they wanted then at least the one halfe: and afterwards, the 2d of Jany following, made a long speech in the Towne hall to the same end, by which he had persuaded them to consent to his desires, and the mayor had appointed a day of meeting for the same purpose, but were prevented by the deputy lieutenants, who foreseeing the evill consequences of soe pernicious a designe, confined the mayor and aldermen to their howses when they were about to assemble. If it had taken effect, the act of parliament had beene totally eluded as to the greatest part of the governors of that corporation: and consequently that towne, which has been ever held of the most factious in England, had remained soe to posterity. For it is not to be presumed that that mayor and those aldermen that then were in, and are since turned out (haveing been all in armes against the King) would have chosen honester men then themselves, and then what the consequence of this had been—to other corporations—is left to the judgement of those who made the act. In this new intended election, Mr. Jones did designe to have one Joseph Prowd and Edw. George, the one a sequestrator, and both notoriously ill-affected, to be chosen common councell men. The Comm^{rs}, therefore, could not hold it expedient to the publique safety to continue a person in such office in that towne whoe was guilty of soe dangerous a practice and machination there.

" 4. At the tyme of Venner's insurrection in London, letters being sent from the Lords of the Conncell to the severall lords lieutenants, to give order for the secureing dangerous persons in all countyes, and there beinge at that tyme one Major Waring, who was thought the most dangerous person in the County of Salop, Quarter-Mr Litchfield, and one Harrison, an active and violent Anabaptist, committed by the deputy-lieutenants of that county, the same Mr. Jones then sent Major Waring advice that he was unlawfully committed, and that he should eyther take noe notice of his confinement (he being committed only to a private house) or move for a habeas corpus, the terme being neare at hand, which advice some of the persons abovementioned say at this present they resolved to follow, but that they heard the next day that they should in a short tyme be released if noe accusation came in against them.

"5. The Commissioners looked upon Mr. Jones as a person they could not confide in, in regard that if his judgement be for the King's prosperity, as he sayes it is, he prostitutes that judgement to his interest upon all occasions where they come in competition: as, in particular, he endeavoured with all his might, since the King came in, to make one Captaine Hunt (a man that had beene in armes against the King under all the usurped powers from the begining to the very last, and a bitter enemy to all the King's party) to be post master of the Towne of Shrewsbury: whereby all the intelligence and all dispatches both from King and councell, in those dangerous tymes, must have come through his hands, and this, he being tenant to him of an Inne there, to increase his rent 40 or 50s. yearely.

"6. Though Mr. Jones sayes he was alwayes for the King, yet he was never sequestred for the King; declared himselfe against the Commission of Aray in the tyme of the warrs, which was the dispute betweene the King and Parliament, and refused to find a dragoone for the King's service; for which he was committed by Sir Francis Ottley, then Governor of Shrewsbury; which committment Mr. Jones afterwards brought twoe men to testifie before the Parliament's committees in that Towne, as an argument of his good affection to them.

"His brother, that was of the Parliament's partie and recorder of the towne in the tyme of rebellion, declared him then publiquely upon the Bench at a quarter sessions a man well affected to the Parliament.

"If Mr. Jones hath the confidence to deny all or any of these allegations, they will be proved upon oath.

"If he demand why they were not proved before he was displaced, 'tis answered, the Commissioners had noe power to give an oath, but were well satisfied otherwise of the truth of them.

"If Mr. Jones complayne he was not heard, or had noe notice of the Commissioners' meeting, 'twill be proved upon oath that (though they were not bound to give him notice, yet) that he knew of their meeting, and that they sent twice that day they first mett, and twice the next, to his house to summon him: but he was out of towne, whereby they conceive themselves not obliged to give any further stop to their proceedings upon his accompt.

"If he alledge some of the Commissioners had noe notice of the meeting, 'tis answered that all had notice except 2 or 3 which lived at the furthest part of the county, whoe were principally intended in the commission for other corporations wch were better knowne to them.

"If he alledge that Waring now denyes that he had that advice from Mr. Jones; it is answered he does not deny it, but is unwilling to confesse it, or to have his name brought upon the stage to accuse a man that gave him advice soe agreeable to him: but it is offered to be proved upon oath by 2 suff^t witnesses, whoe have given it under their hands that Waring confessed to them he received that advice from Mr. Jones."

In August 1663 another visitation of Shropshire was made by the heralds; the last of the sort that has ever occurred. The following families then entered their pedigrees as residents in Shrewsbury. Betton, Billing, Bowdler, Burley, Capell, Clarke, Cole, Doughty, Downes, Edwards, Hatton, Jenkes, Jevon, Jones, Langley, Lowe, Prince, Proude, Rocke, Scot, Severne, Turner, Vaughan, White, Williams, Wingfield, Wright.

The summer and autumn of 1663 were disturbed by alarms, and by the actual explosion of an insurrection of "the bigots for schism and a commonwealth to conspire for the good old cause[1]." It was chiefly confined to the North of England; but agents were employed in most other counties,

---

[1] Complete History of England, iii. 247.

and among other places, as was reported, in Shrewsbury. As early as the 11th of June, lord Newport writes to his friend sir Richard Ottley; "It is believed there was a design lately for the surprise of Chester Castle, and by what Geo. Hosier wrytes to me this last post, I believe no lesse for Shrewsbury." He then states himself to have heard of factious meetings of ministers in Shrewsbury, and desires Sir Richard

"to employ, if possible, one of the brotherhood to give an acco' of their designs: otherwise to find out their next meeting, and when they are assembled, to go to them, and enquire their motives, and take down their names; and demand if those that reside in the towne will be engaged for the appearance of the rest: if soe, you may dismiss them for the present if you see cause, and within a day or 2 may get 2 Deputy Lieuten[ts] more to signe a warrant to the marshall for their committment, which, in case they meet any more, I advise be done: but if you can learn that they have any seditious or treasonable designes on foot, and are able by any testimony to make it out, I have wrytten to G. Hosier that in that case he be aydinge to you w[h] his souldiers for their present securing in the Castle."

After these measures of precaution no fresh alarm seems to have arisen in Shrewsbury for several months; but by a letter of Oct. 6th, from lord Newport to sir Richard Ottley, it appears that this last had communicated to his lordship "some fears of an insurrection." Lord Newport now informs his correspondent that the King thought not much of it;

"However you may doe well to advise the Governor of the Castle to be carefull. Present my affectionate services to the rest of the deputy lieutenants, and let them know my opinion is, that unlesse they make further discovery of danger at home, they neede only give orders to Capt. Prince and Capt. Jones of Ludlow, to have their companyes in a readinesse, that the Towne Gates be shut for a forthnight, or some such time, in the night time, with a small guard at them, which I hope will bee sufficient without putting the country to any further charge in callinge the militia together: for if those two townes bee securd, I thinke wee should not bee ill satisfyed to see them in the field."

The wish expressed in the concluding sentence of this letter was very near being gratified: for the 12th of this month was agreed upon by the conspirators for the day of rising, which they had given assurance to their friends should be general. The passages over the Severn were to be secured[1], and therefore it is natural to believe that Shrewsbury would not be forgotten. Lord Newport intimates in the following letter that this was the case: and even expresses his belief that the puritan clergy who had lately been dismissed from their benefices in the town, were concerned in the plot:

"Sir, "Lon. 24 Oct. 1663.

"There beinge such discourses come up hither out of the North of a reall designe to give new disturbances in the kingdome, some of the confederates havinge met according to appointment (about 200) but speedily dispersed, and many more havinge agreed to joyne with them, which they had done, as is confessd, if the 2 companyes of foot and the 2 troopes of horse sent hence had not deterr'd them; I thought fitt noe longer to forbeare acquaintinge

---

[1] Complete History, ut supra.

you and the rest of the Deputy Lieutenants that I have long had intelligence of a correspondence held by some persons of our countrey with these new plotters both in the north and at London, and that they have had severall private meetings and consultations about carryinge on their wicked worke, and that they have made provision of armes and other necessaryes for the beginninge of a warre. The persons are the ejected ministers residing still in Shrewsbury, Mr. Brian, and Mr. Talence, likewise Mr. Laurence, Captaine Doughty, Capt. Betton, Capt. Buttrey, Jo. Bromley, Richard Price, Ed. George, and severall others that Capt. Hosier can informe you of, who can likewise acquaint you of severall particulars that evidence with great plainesse they had a designe on foot. I desire, therefore, the Deputy Lieutenants, that they give present orders for the securinge the persons before mentioned, and such others as they shall finde cause for, some to the Marshall's, and others, which shall bee conceivd most dangerous, to the Castle, with strict orders that none of them bee permitted to speake with one another upon penalty to the Marshall of loosinge his place if hee suffer it: and that they bee, immediately upon their confinement, examined severally (that they may not have the same reason to complaine which wee were used to have) what the cause of their frequent meetinges was, and of such other particulars as you shall bee informd of by Capt. Hosier or any other person. 'Tis possible that some of them may have the grace to confesse their designe (though it bee not much to be hop'd) if they be threatned: and particularly it must bee pressd to them to confesse who was to command in that county in cheife. Though Major Waringe possibly may not bee confederated with the presbyterians of that Towne, yet it is not to bee thought that there càn bee soe generall a wicked designe on foot as this is certifyed to bee from many places, to which hee is not privye: and hee may with more reason bee thought to bee associated with those in London, who have confessd their designe was to kill the King, then with such as onely aymed at the fettering of him and setting up the presbyterian government; therefore I advise hee bee secur'd in the Castle. [The rest of this letter is not material.]

" I was lothe to doe this before, because I was willing these gentⁿ should first have given some more open evidence of their treason, in order to their conviction. But since the neck of their designe is I hope broke, I hold it not fitt they should bee passd by as innocent persons who were soe active in it.

" For my much respected freinde Sr Richard Ottley, kn^t, one of
the Deputy Lieutenants of the County
of
" Haste   Salop.
   F. NEWPORT."[1]

" Sir,
" Y^r kinsman and servant,
    " FRA. NEWPORT.

" The Queene is somwhat better, but not yet out of danger.

---

[1] As this rising is passed over very slightly, or wholly omitted, in our general histories, the reader may not be displeased to read some account of the evidence respecting it which was laid before the upper house by the earl of Clarendon, and which, as he will see by its contents, belongs strictly to our subject. It is preserved among the Ottley papers, is directed "These for my most deare mother the Lady Lucy Ottley at Pitchford in Shropshire. Leave this at the pheasant in Shropshire (sic) to be sent Franck R. Ottley," and entitled the Lord Chancellor's Additionall Report of the Trayterous designs.

He named Mr. Moyer, Lenthall, Major Haines, Nevill Parker and Salmon. Salmon confessed a pass was desired for them. Wildman said he knew nothing of it.
160 officers.
' There sho^d have been a meeting in London about the 10th or 11th of December. And intended about the end of Jany or Feby to have made sure of Shrewsbury, Coventry, and Bristoll. Where they were prevalent, they sh^d begin with assassination, which moved one of them to relent.
A letter from Mr. Walden at Huntington, that many mett under the name of Quakers that were

In further pursuance of the measures for the regulation of corporations, a new charter was drawn up, bearing date 6th July, 16 Car. II. (1664) the chief, if not the only purpose of which seems to have been a new modelling of our municipal body: for it merely confirms the charters of the 28th of Elizabeth, (our *progenitor*, as it oddly stiles her) and the 14 Car. I.—(reserving, however, to himself, his heirs, and successors, "all that our Castle of Salop, and all ditches, fosses[1], lands, tenements, and hereditaments, with their and each of their appurtenances, to Us lately surrendered,") and adding the usual appendage of formal clauses: after which the King assigns, nominates, constitutes, and confirms his beloved subject Jonathan Langley, now MAYOR, and his beloved subjects *Timothey Turneur*, Richard Prince, Andrew Vivers, Edward Kinaston, Francis Burton, Thomas Bawdwin, Samuel Wingfield, Francis Newton, Richard Warring, Robert Betton, John Harding, Samuel Lloyd, Richard Taylor, Thomas Cotton, Gabriel Wood, Roger Griffies, Daniel Jevon, Thomas Merrick, Rowland Middleton, John Gardner, Will. Thyn, Daniel Brigdale, and John Seaverne, now ALDERMEN, and his beloved subjects Richard Wright, Will. Hill, Rowland Pritchard, George Hosier, Robert Forster, jun., Edward Phillipps, Thomas Barnestone, Will. Pears, Rich. Lloyd, Arthur Hincks, Rich. Bowdler, John Shelvock, Edw. Griffees, Rich. Griffees, jun., Edw. Bayton, Michael Wilding, Hugh Plungeon, Tho. Bowdler, Stephen Davies, Collins Woolridge, James Vaughan, Rowland Jenks, Tho. Lloyd, Tho. Tipton, John Harwood, Geo. Llewellin, William Lloyd, Rowland Collins, James Bathoe, sen., Rich. Cox, John Gowin, Will. Watkins, Tho. Ryton, John Whittakers, Edmund Mansell, John Hoggins, Richard Bayton, Will. Farmer, Tho. Jackson, John Butler, Samuel Prichard, Edward Wolfe, Joseph Stone, Tho. Baker, John Phillips, John Latewood, Tho. Bright, and Richard Gravener, now the COMMON COUNCIL (commune consilium ejusdem ville), and the said Tim. Turner (sic) now RECORDER, the said Tho. Bawdwin, now STEWARD, and Adam Ottley, now COMMON-CLERK, to continue in their said offices: and enjoins the mayor, aldermen, recorder, common clerk, and all other officers and ministers of the town, to take the oaths of obedience and supremacy before they execute any office. This charter, however, though extant among the archives, was never acted upon, and indeed has never passed the great seal.

The following order of the corporation forcibly depicts the terror prevailing in the town during the continuance of a dreadful scourge, for its deliverance from which the present age ought to be deeply thankful.

not so, and ridd in multitudes by night to the terror of his Majesty's subjects. That there was there a dangerous inne and a seditious preacher, who uttered the same thing there as was here by Seaman, who used the late King barbarously at the Isle of Wight.

[1] Fossis, fossatis.

" 18 Sep. 1665. Agg. y⁺ y⁰ aldermⁿ and assist⁰ shall, dur⁰ such tyme as y⁰ City of London shall remaine infected w^h the plague, 3 of them day and night take upon them the chardge of the wardes and watches and at each gate .... and to give an oath to all strangers to declare from what part they come...."

This was the last time the metropolis was ever infested by this tremendous visitation. The dreadful conflagration of the succeeding year effectually exterminated it: and this, perhaps, may account for its general disappearance over the whole kingdom: for it seems to have been always an importation from London into the country.

In the second volume of the Antiquarian Repertory is a translation of the travels of a M. Jorevin de Rocheford through England, printed at Paris in 1672.

His description of Schrosbery, as he writes it, shall here be given.

" The Severn is navigable to Schrosbery, I passed it over a large stone bridge. At the entrance there is a suburb, the church of which appears to me to have formerly belonged to some fine abbey. I ascended from thence to the town; which is mounted on the platform of a rock, scarped on almost every side, which renders its situation naturally strong. Besides which, the wall that encloses it made it difficult to be scaled. The environs consist of large woods, and high mountains. Nevertheless, the town is filled with people and rich shopkeepers, who dwell in two large streets, one leading to the market-place, and the other turning from this place towards the left. Near which are the Great Church, the Exchange, and Town-hall. They are in a street called Aystrit, which is so broad, that it seems a long market-place, terminating at one of the ends of the town, where stands the Castle and commands it; being more elevated, and by so much the stronger, as it is environed on one side by broad ditches, closed with good walls, and on the other there is no approach to it, on account of the steepness of the rock. But it has been ruined by the late wars, insomuch that, excepting a few towers, and some lodgings within, I see nothing remarkable.

" I met nothing more pleasing to me than the funeral[1] ceremonies at the interment of a My Lord, which mine host procured me the sight of. The relations and friends being assembled in the house of the defunct, the minister advanced into the middle of the chamber, where, before the company, he made a funeral oration, representing the great actions of the deceased, his virtues, his qualities, his titles of nobility, and those of the whole family; so that nothing more could be said towards consoling every one of the company for the great loss they had sustained in this man, and principally the relations; who were seated round the dead body, and whom he assured that he was gone to heaven, the seat of all sorts of happiness, whereas the world that he had just left, was replete with misery: (It is to be remarked, that during this oration, there stood upon the coffin a large pot of wine, out of which every one drank to the health of the deceased;) hoping that he might surmount the difficulties he

---

[1] Funerals at Shrewsbury about this time were conducted upon a scale of great expence, to which the friends of the family were expected to contribute. There is now before us " a noate of what wyne was sent to the funerall of John Hardinge, gent., March 26, 1669 :" who may have been the very " Milord" at whose interment M. de Rocheford attended. The contributors are *seventy-six* in number: among whom are Mr. Adam Ottley, the old lady Edwards, Mr. Rowland Middleton, Mr. George Severne, Mr. William Thynn, Captain George Hosier, Mr. Edward Kynaston, Mr. Robert Pemberton, Mr. Jonathan Scott, Mr. John Harwood, Mr. Maior, Roger Brigdale, &c.; and the contributions consist of 19 quarts, 22 pottles, and a " gallant" of clarett, 8 quarts and 3 pottles of sack, 2 quarts and 2 pottles of white wine, five sugar loaves, 12 pound and a half of sugar, 17lb. of white sugar, 11lb. of loaf sugar, 1lb. of powder sugar, one pound of mackaroomes, and four dozen of " sugar cakes," probably our well-known Shrewsbury cakes.

had to encounter in his road to Paradise, where, by the mercy of God, he was about to enter: on which mercy they found all their hope; without considering their evil life, their wicked religion, and that God is just. This being finished, six men took up the corpse, and carried it on their shoulders to the church. It was covered with a large cloth, which the four nearest relations held each by a corner with one hand, and in the other carried a bough. The other relations and friends had in one hand a flambeau, and in the other a bough: marching thus through the street, without singing or saying any prayer, till they came to the church: where, having placed the body on tressals, and taken off the cloth from the coffin,—which is ordinarily made of fine walnut-tree handsomely worked, and ornamented with iron bandages chased in the manner of a basket,—the minister then ascended his pulpit; and every one being seated round about the coffin, which is placed in a kind of parade in the middle of the church, he read a portion of the holy scripture, concerning the resurrection of the dead, and afterwards sang some psalms;—to which all the company answered. After this he descended, having his bough in his hand, like the rest of the congregation. This he threw on the dead body when it was put into the grave, as did all the relations; extinguishing their flambeaus in the earth with which the corpse was to be covered.

" This finished, every one retired to his home without further ceremony : and I departed from Schrosbury for Chester: and having passed over a large desert plain, I reached Addar, Morton, and a Castle. The country here is barren: passed a river near a wind-mill. From thence to Pries and Vitechurch on a river. Here is a manufactory of woollen cloth. The road lies afterwards over some mountains, &c."

This is the place to notice such tradesmen's tokens as were struck in, or for the use of, Shrewsbury. Something of the sort, in lead or tin, appears to have existed in former reigns, from the time of Henry VIII. to that of James I.[1] But those of copper or brass do not seem to have been introduced till after the Restoration. At least, the earliest date that occurs upon any of the Shrewsbury tokens is 1660. The latest is 1671; for in the following year (July 25, 1672) an official notice was issued in the gazette, that no person would for the future be permitted to make, coin, exchange, or use, any farthings or tokens, except such as should be coined in his Majesty's mint[2]. A plate is subjoined of such Shrewsbury tokens as our most diligent search has been able to procure.

No.	Date.	Metal.	Obverse.	Reverse.
1	—	B	BENIAMIN HINDE (Shrewsbury arms)	IN SALOP. (B. H.)
2	—	B	BENIAMIN HINDE (arms)	IN SALOP. (B. H.)
3	—	C	SAMVELL MACHIN (a wheat-sheaf between S^M H)	BAKER IN SALOPP. (HIS HALF PENY.)
4	—	C	MICHAELL WILDINGE (Mercers' arms)	MERCER IN SALOP. (M^{W}I.)
5	—	B	IOSHVA WILLIS (Shrewsbury arms)	IN SALLOP MERCER. (HIS HALF PENY.)
6	1660		IOHN THOMAS (Mercers' arms)	OF SALOP MERCER. (I T.)

---

[1] Ruding, ii. 69, 162, 209, &c.

[2] Id. ib. 343.

CHARLES II.

No.	Date.	Metal.	Obverse.	Reverse.
7	1663		THO: MEYRICKE (Vintners' arms)	IN SALOPP 1663. (HIS HALF PENY.)[1]
8	1663	B	THOMAS MEYRICKE (Vintners' arms)	IN SALOPP 1663. (T.M.)
9	1663	C	CONSTANTINE OVERTON (Shoemakers' arms)	IN SALOPP 1663. (HIS HALF PENY.)
10	1664	C	MICHAELL WILDING (Mercers' arms)	IN SALOP 1664. (HIS HALF PENY.)
11	1666	C	WILLIAM THOMAS MERCER (Mercers' arms)	OF SALOP 1666. (HIS HALF PENY).
12	1666		WILLIAM HARRISON (HIS HALF PENY)	OF SALOPE 1666. (a chevron between three ......)
13	1666	C	OWEN ROBERTS (a wheat sheaf between O R)	IN SALOPP 1666. (HIS HALF PENY.)
14	1667		IOB SELBY DISTILLER (HIS HALF PENY)	IN SALLOP 1667. (probably a distillatory between I S.)
15	1667	C	IOHN BRIGDELL 1667 (Chandlers' arms)	IN SALLOP CHANDLER. (HIS HALF PENY.)
16	1667	C	IOHN MILWARD 1667 (A still)	DISTILLER IN SALOP. (HIS HALFE PENNY.)
17	1668	C	IOHN HOLLIER 1668 (Mercers' arms)	IN SALLOP MERCER. (HIS HALF PENY.)
18	1669	C	IOSEPH BENYON IN (a wheat sheaf between I^{B}E)	SALLOP HIS PENY 1669. (I^D between a pair of scales.)
19	1669	C	SAMVELL CONEY INKEEPER (a star of six rays)	OF SALOP 1669. (HIS PENNY.)
20	1669	B	PETAR MACHEV BAKER (a wheat sheaf)	IN SALOP 1669. (HIS PENY.)
21	1670		THOMAS ACHELLEY 71 (a wheat sheaf between T I^D A)	IN SALLOP 1670. (a fleur de lis between T A.)
22	1671	C	SAMVELL RIDGEWAY (Grocers' arms)	IN SALOP 1671. (HIS HALF PENY.)
23	1664	C	IOHN MILLINGTON (a pair of scales between three wheat sheaves and I^{M}M)	OF SHREWSBURY 1664. (HIS HALF PENY.)

Besides the above, two others appear in a catalogue of these tokens compiled by the late M. C. Tutet, esq. formerly in the library of the late Mr. Gough, and now transferred, with the rest of his collection, to the Bodleian, viz.

| 1 | — | B | ROBERT DAVIES (Mercers' arms) | IN SALLOPP. (R D.) |
| 2 | — | C | THOMAS STVDLEY (his peny) | OF SHREWSBVRY. (T^{S}E.) |

---

[1] Another variety of this is described as struck by THOMAS MAYRICK, IN SALOP 1668. This we have not seen, and it is perhaps only an erroneous reading of the last numeral.

and a third appears in the catalogue of a modern collector,

No.	Date.	Metal.	Obverse.	Reverse.
3	—		EDMOND CLARKE (arms)	IN SALOP. (E C.)[1]

In Ritson's "Ancient Songs," is one entitled "Shrewsbury for me:" being

> A song in praise of that famous town
> Which hath throughout all England gain'd renown,
> In praise thereof let every one agree,
> And say with one accord, Shrowsbury for me.

It is reprinted by the editor from an old black letter copy in the Pepysian collection, but does not contain a single line deserving to be recorded.

In 1673 was published the Britannia of Blome; a very respectable work for the time in which it was executed. It contains a detailed account of Shrewsbury, of which it says, that

"For largeness, (numbring five parish churches, besides a chapel; two of which, St. Marie's and St. Alckmond's, are fair structures, and beautified with lofty spires,) neatness of buildings, both publick and private, largeness and variety of streets, and populousness, may be ranged in the number of cities of the first rank.

"It is a town of a good strength, as well by nature as by art; being fenced about with a strong wall; besides another bulwark ranging from the Castle unto, and in part along, the Severn; through which there are three entrances into the town: on the East and West, by two fair stone bridges, with gates, towers, and barrs: and on the North by a strong gate, over which is mounted the said Castle, once exceeding strong.

"It is a place of a great resort, and well inhabited both by the English and the Welsh, who speak both speeches: and enjoyeth a great trade for cloths, cottons, frizes, and a variety of other commodities: this being the common mart between England and Middle Wales."

Notwithstanding the general joy of the kingdom at the restoration of its ancient institutions, there were some, most probably, in every county

---

[1] In the plate are added two Shrewsbury tokens of modern date, viz.

			Obverse.	Reverse.
1792		C	SHREWSBURY HALF HALFPENNY. (Shrewsbury arms)	SALOP WOOLLEN MANUFACTORY. (a woolpack.)
1794		C	SHREWSBURY 1794 HALFPENNY (Shrewsbury arms)	SALOP WOOLLEN MANUFACTORY. (a woolpack). on edge PAYABLE AT LONDON, LIVERPOOL OR BRISTOL.

The chief coinage of this halfpenny took place in 1793; though the specimen here engraved happened to be struck in the succeeding year.

[2] P. 299.

who still sighed for the Commonwealth; and republicans were not likely to be weaned from their prejudices in favour of that form of government, by the late measures of the King and his brother. So hostile had these been to the liberties, the religion, and even the honour of their country, since the banishment of Clarendon, that many, even of the best affected, as our lord Newport, had gradually relaxed from the ardour of their loyalty: and others of the best intentions, as his nephew[1] lord Russel, went great lengths to obtain a more limited form of government. This plot, or rather this combination of plots, was on the point of breaking out into action in the summer of 1683: the views of those concerned were very comprehensive, extending to various parts of the kingdom: and our town, which, as we have seen[2], had been for some time esteemed "factious," was not forgotten. "Colonel Rumsey," says a contemporary authority[3], "discovered that Shrewsbury was to be seized, which is a walled town, *ill affected;* and in the Castle were thirty-eight barrels of powder, one hundred and twelve pounds to the barrel, and arms for three hundred men; and great guns. The Castle is strong by situation: and lies so conveniently, that either from the North, or West, or Midland, or Wales, the party might easily resort thither: and if they could baffle the militia, and draw the King's forces out of town, they gained their end." A former occasion has occurred, in which it was proposed, by the seizure of Shrewsbury, to draw the regular troops out of the metropolis; and thus leave the seat of government exposed to attack; and the same stratagem seems to have been projected in the present case. The violent measure adopted by the court just at this juncture, of annulling the charter of the metropolis, cannot be alleged as the cause of this conspiracy, for that illegal sentence was passed on the very same day (June 12) on which the plot was revealed to the secretary of state; but it was doubtless, a complete proof how totally incompatible with the liberties of the kingdom was the rule of the Stuarts. Indeed, the great bulk of the population seemed ready to submit to the yoke. All the municipal bodies of the realm, terrified by the example of London, made haste to surrender those charters which they had received from former monarchs into the hands of the sovereign, with the last hope of the victim to despotick power;

Ut liceat *paucis* cum dentibus inde reverti.

Our ancestors stood out for a twelvemonth. At length, on the 13th of June, 1684, " at a full assembly, it was agreed unanimously, that the charter of the town should be surrendered and yielded up to his Majesty,

---

[1] Lord Newport's wife was aunt to lord Russel.
[2] See above, p. 483.
[3] Lord Keeper Guilford, in his History of the Pye Plot, printed in the Examen, p. 389. The passage respecting Shrewsbury does not appear in those parts of Rumsey's depositions which are given by Dr. Spratt in his "True Account and Declaration of the Horrid Conspiracy, &c."

when his pleasure is to require it." This was followed up by resolutions passed on the same day, " that Mr. Recorder and Edward Kynaston[1], esq. draw up a petition to his Majesty, signifying the contents of the order for surrendering the charter; and it was " Agreed and desired, that Collins Woolrich, esq. mayor, will please to attend my lord chief justice Jones with the order; and to take with him such persons of quality as he shall think fit." On the 29th of August, it was " Ordered, that the mayor and committee attend the lord chief justice Jones to discourse him touching the renewing of the charter: and unanimously agreed, that in the new charter, there shall be only twelve aldermen and twenty-four assistants." It was further " agreed on the 20th of September, that the councell learned in the law. for this corporation attend Mr. Mayor about surrendering the charter, when he attends sir Thomas Jones; and in case that he cannot, Mr. Mayor choose other councell:" and on the 11th of October, the corporation found it necessary to borrow the sum of £200, for the purpose of defraying the expences which would attend the renewal of their charter.

The king's death, (Feb. 6, 1684-5) prevented this instrument from passing the great seal in his name. Within a week after that event, viz. on the 13th of February, the corporation sent up an address to their new sovereign, expressive of their " joyfulness in his succession, and humbly thanking him for his gracious declaration in preferring the protestant religion;"—no obscure intimation of their wishes on that momentous subject, which then engaged all ranks with an intensity of interest difficult to be conceived by the present generation.

On the 17th of the following March, the corporation received their new charter, a few of the provisions of which deserve attention, as indicating the real views of the infatuated monarch. After expressing his gracious affection for the melioration of his town of Salop, his will that there may be henceforward a certain and undoubted manner of governing its inhabitants to the terror of the evil and sustentation of the good, and his hope, that if the burgesses and inhabitants have more ample liberties and privileges by his concession, they will be the better enabled and the more bound to render him the more special service, he grants that the town shall be a free town of itself, and the burgesses and inhabitants shall be a body corporate, and sue and be sued, &c.; that there shall be one good and discreet man of the aldermen of the town who shall be mayor; twelve good and discreet men, the mayor being one, who shall be, and shall be

---

[1] He was of Hordley; but having married a great heiress, Amy, daughter of Thomas Barker, esq. of Haghmond, by whom he obtained the very extensive estates of her family surrounding, and once appertaining to that monastery, he fixed his residence within the liberties of Shrewsbury, at Abrightlee, another ancient mansion of the Barkers, and took, as we see, an active part in the concerns of the corporation. His son John, the leader of the Shropshire tories, was grandfather to the rev. sir Edward Kynaston, bart. now of Hordley and Hardwicke.

called, aldermen; and twenty-four good and discreet men, assistants; also one famous man (preclarus vir) recorder; one good and discreet man, steward; and one good and discreet man, common clerk: and he nominates John Wood, esq. first and modern MAYOR to continue till the Friday after Michaelmas: Edward Kynaston, esq., Francis Edwards, baronet, Tho. Bawdewin, esq., Roger Griffes, Robert Forrester, Edw. Phillipps, Collins Noldrich[1], the aforesaid John Wood, Rob. Wood, Rich. Salter, John Hill, and Jonathan Scott, gentlemen, to be first and modern ALDERMEN; and John Hollyer, Samuel Adderton, Geo. Lewellin, Tho. Bowdler, Rob. Sheppard, Edw. Kynaston, Will. Corbett, John Kynaston, John Wood, junior, Tho. Biggs, Tho. Phillipps, Humf. Tomkyns, John Brickdale, Richard Williams, Andrew Johnson, Rowland Bright, Samuel Thornton, Cornelius Poyner, Rich. Plimley, James Crosse, Henry Corser, Simon Hanmer, John Davis, and Richard Atkins, gentlemen, to be the first and modern ASSISTANTS; his most beloved and most faithful cousin Charles earl of Shrewsbury, to be first and modern RECORDER, *to execute the said office by himself or by his sufficient deputy*[2]; his beloved Robert Price, esq. first and modern STEWARD; and his beloved Thomas Edwards, esq. first and modern COMMON CLERK. Then follows a clause empowering the corporation to supply vacancies occasioned by death, amotion, or departure, in the manner used in the town for the last ten years; the King reserving to himself, his heirs, and successors, power to amove the mayor, recorder, or other officers, and any of the aldermen or assistants, at the will and good pleasure of us, our heirs, &c. by any order made in privy council, and signified to them under the seal thereof: whereupon the said mayor, &c. so signified to be amoved, shall be declared to be so amoved "*ipso facto*, really, and to all intent or purpose whatsoever, without any further process," and this *toties quoties*, as often as the case shall happen.

The corporation of Shrewsbury, and it was not more hardly dealt with than other towns, was thus laid prostrate at the feet of the sovereign; and we may imagine the secret execrations with which such an aggression would be received. But it is at all times a serious matter to overturn an existing government; and our forefathers, who had felt the tyranny eventually resulting from an attempt to obtain liberty, were slow in resorting to a resistance which might bring back those oppressions to which civil warfare had so recently exposed them. Hence, when James made a progress through this part of his dominions, in August 1687, either to gain such popularity, or to inspire such terror, as might secure elections of parliament-men calculated to ensure success to his attempts for the gradual re-establishment of popery and absolute power; whatever might be the private sentiments of the inhabitants respecting the measures he was then

---

[1] Sic. Woldrich was the name intended.   [2] The words in italicks are interlined.

pursuing, there was no want of the external marks of respect. Burnet, indeed, tells us, that wherever " he went, he saw a visible coldness both in the nobility and gentry, which was not easily borne by a man of his temper. In many places they pretended occasions to go out of their countries. Some staid at home. And those who waited on the King, seemed to do it rather out of duty and respect, than with any cordial affection." How far all this applies to the gentry of Shropshire we are not informed, and it would be very unsafe to rely upon the testimony of so warm a partizan as this writer. Lord Newport, to whom they would naturally look up, had taken no pains to conceal his dislike of the King's aggressions upon the liberties and religion of his people[1]: had in consequence been removed from the lieutenancy in the February preceding this royal visit, and not long after it, formed one of the splendid *cortège* of peers who attended the bishops to the court of King's Bench, upon their extraordinary trial. But we shall find some reasons which make it very uncertain whether even he absented himself from paying his respects to the King upon this visit to Shrewsbury; and the corporation were by the existing charter wholly dependent upon the crown, and could not, consequently, display, if they felt, any resentment. They " resolved (Aug. 23) to expend £200 in entertaining and making a present to the King, and such further sum as shall be thought reasonable," thus evidently making the expence unlimited: they dispatched two gentlemen[2] to Gloucester and Worcester for the purpose of ascertaining the manner in which the royal traveller was entertained in those cities; they resolved that the conduits should run with wine on the day of his Majesty's entrance, and that the corporated companies should appear with their drums, colours, flags, and streamers. They further determined to meet in their gowns on the following morning under the market-house at the toll of the bell; which, as the King was not expected till the day after, was probably for the purpose of rehearsing their several parts. Forty-five years had elapsed since the town had been honoured by a royal visit. Our ancestors might prudently distrust

---

[1] James's ministers, at least one of them, made no secret of their master's views. Lord Newport told the second lord Dartmouth, who has recorded it in his notes upon Burnet, that " he dined in a great deal of company at the earl of Sunderland's, who declared publickly that they were now sure of their game, for it would be an easy matter to have a House of Commons to their minds:" and when lord Bradford (for so he was, when he related this anecdote) intimated that he would have some opposition in the House of Lords, lord Sunderland turned to lord Churchill, who sate next him, and in a very loud shrill voice, cried, "O silly, why your troop of guards shall be called to the House of Lords." Sunderland was, as is now well known, urging on the King for the purpose of ruining him; but what must we think of a king who permitted himself to be so urged?

[2] Mr. Scott and Mr. Kynaston. Probably Jonathan Scott, esq. of Betton, alderman, and Mr. Edward Kynaston, draper, a younger son of Edward Kynaston of Lee, near Ellesmere, assistant. They must have rode hard to enable their employers to profit by the information which they collected: for the King reached the first of these cities on the 22d, and the second on the 23d. Only two days later he arrived in Shrewsbury.

their abilities to conduct themselves properly on an occasion so grand, and so unusual, without a little previous training; and an incident[1] which is said to have happened at one place in the course of this progress, may have induced them to adopt this wise measure, for the purpose of preventing a repetition of that awkward scene. Lastly, to hide, perhaps, their pavement, which might not be much better then than it is at present, they resolved that the streets should be gravelled just before his Majesty's arrival, every inhabitant to throw it before his own doors.

The King left Ludlow on the morning of August 24, and passing through the Strettons[2], arrived in Shrewsbury about five o'clock in the afternoon. He took up his abode at the Council House, which he might have remembered as the residence of his father during the civil wars, and where the corporation presented him with a purse of gold containing one hundred guineas. No particulars of his behaviour here are recorded. Burnet, however, tells us, that "through the whole of his progress, he was very obliging to all that came near him, and most particularly to the dissenters, and to those who had passed long under the notion of Commonwealth's-men. He ran out on the point of liberty of conscience, saying, this was the true secret of the greatness and wealth of Holland; and every

---

[1] The scene of this tale is laid at Winchester; and it is certain that James II. passed through that city on his road from Portsmouth to Shrewsbury. The mayor is said to have been both illiterate and dull, incapable of reading or remembering an address. It was settled, therefore, says the tale, that the recorder should stand behind him to set him right, if he happened to be out. When they were ushered into the royal presence, and the chief magistrate was about to commence his harangue, as he appeared somewhat sheepish and embarrassed, his friendly monitor whispered in his ear, "*Hold up your head, Sir, and look like a man.*" Mistaking this for the beginning of his speech, he boldly stared the King in the face, and audibly repeated, "*Hold up your head, Sir, and look like a man.*" The recorder, chagrined, again whispered, "*What the d—l do you mean?*" This was likewise repeated with proper emphasis. The recorder, out of all patience, muttered, "*By heavens, Sir, you'll ruin us all.*" His worship, still taking this to be a continuance of the speech, and still staring his Majesty full in the face, with a yet louder voice repeated, "*By heavens, Sir, you'll ruin us all.*" James, conscious how little his measures were approved by some of his subjects, now rose, in much anger: but being informed of the cause of this rough address, passed it by with a smile. We do not vouch for the truth of this story: but even the report of it might induce the corporation to come to the resolution recorded in the text.

[2] An idle tradition derives the etymology of one of them from an incident which occurred on this journey. When the King reached Little Stretton, he enquired, it is said, the name, and was told "Stretton;" coming soon after to Church Stretton, he asked the same question, and received the same answer, "Stretton:" shortly after, arriving at a third village, and enquiring its name, he was again told "Stretton:" whereupon, says the story, the King exclaimed, "What, *All* Stretton?" and hence we are expected to believe, it has borne that name ever since. But this deserves no credit. The name is merely a slight corruption of Eald Stretton, and points it out as the *oldest* of the three *tons*, or enclosed collections of houses, which was set up, according to an usual practice of the Romans, at a short distance from the *street*, or paved way, which they formed from Uriconium to Bravinium. It is more likely to be true, what another tradition records, that the king, passing through a beautifully limpid and copious stream which crosses the road at the entrance into All Stretton, intimated a desire to taste the water, and stopped while a glass was procured from a neighbouring house for that purpose. This last tradition we derive from the late rev. James Atcherley, head-master of Shrewsbury School: and if the King had been a member of the established church, and if the day on which this happened had been the 23d instead of the 25th, one might have conjectured that he intended an allusion to the psalm of the morning service, "He shall drink of the brook in the way; therefore shall he lift up his head." cx. 7.

where recommended the choosing such Parliament-men as would concur with him in settling this liberty as firmly as Magna Charta had been." On the following morning he exercised the gift of healing formerly attributed to the kings of this realm as successors of Edward the Confessor[1], by touching various persons for the king's evil[2], but left the town soon enough to reach Whitchurch that night.

A late writer has endeavoured to persuade his readers that the leading object of James's reign was the acquisition of despotick sway, to which, according to him, the promotion of his faith was quite a secondary concern. Unquestionably, Charles II., who cared nothing at all about religion, was very desirous of absolute power, and felt degraded in his own eyes when he compared his limited authority with the plenitude of power exercised by Louis XIV. But certainly the great aim of James was the restoration of popery, and, with a view to *that*, the securing of such a House of Commons as would vote for a demolition of all the tests which guarded the established church. Accordingly, soon after his return to London, determining to convene a new parliament, he applied himself to the regulating of corporations by the exercise of that power which he had reserved to himself in their new charters; substituting either papists, or dissenters, or persons indifferent on the subject, or such as thought no security requisite, for those who, as he found, would not concur with his views. To Shrewsbury he dispatched a mandate under his sign manual, dated Jan. 1, 1687-8, in the third year of his reign, and countersigned by lord Sunderland, president of the council, informing them that he had removed Charles earl of Shrewsbury

---

[1] Bishop Percy (notes on Northumberland Household, p. 334) attributes the claim of this healing power to the Stuarts: but it is certain that the Tudors, Henry VIII. and his daughter Elizabeth, exercised it. See Reed's note on Macbeth, iv. 3. Bishop Gardiner defending the efficacy of holy water in driving away devils, from the objections of Ridley, cites the case of the royal touch " as the special gift of curation ministered by the Kings of England, which, not of their own strength, but by invocation of the name of God, hath been used to be distributed in rings of gold and silver. If the strength of the invocation of the name of God to drive away the devils cannot be distributed by water, why can it be distributed in silver to drive away diseases, and the dangerous one of the falling evil?" Gloster Ridley's Life of Bishop Ridley, p. 201. There is address in this: for Ridley would not venture to deny the power of the royal touch, and without such denial it is not easy to see how he could evade the argument; unluckily, his answer is lost. The claim of this healing power was by no means peculiar to England; having been practised by the kings of Scotland (Dalrymple's Annals, i. 301) and France (Sully, iii. 209): with whom, indeed, it is most probable that the notion originated. For Clovis is said to have received this miraculous faculty immediately after his baptism, A. D. 499, and it is more likely that our kings would derive the idea from them, than they from us. See, in the Continuation of Monstrelet, vol. xi. chap. 51, vol. xii. ch. 1. p. 11, and elsewhere, how Charles VIII. touched for the evil at Rome and Naples, " to the great astonishment of the Italians who witnessed the miracle."

[2] Other persons afflicted with tedious or incurable diseases occasionally thrust themselves in, as might be expected, among the scrofulous. R. Gough, in his History of Middle, mentions a poor woman seized with pains and lameness in all her limbs occasioned by a cold, who, after many years ineffectual trial of various remedies, being at length assured by a skilful surgeon, that her case was hopeless, " went to little more charges: only when King James II. came his progress to Shrewsbury, she was admitted by the King's doctors to his Majesty for the touch: *which did her no good.*"

from the office of their recorder, Robert Pryce, gent. from that of steward, Thomas Bawdewin, esq. Robert Wood, John Hill, Nehemiah Scott, and Jonathan Scott, from being aldermen; Samuel Adderton, Rich. Williams, Rich. Corbett[1], John Hollier, Rob. Cozier[1], Edw. Kynnaston, John Kynaston, Samuel Thornton, and James Cross, from being common council men; and he required them to elect William marquis[2] of Powis, recorder, Thomas Burton, councillor-at-law, steward; Charles Doughty, Edw. Gosnell, Rich. Muckleston, Timothy Seymar, and Samuel Adderton, aldermen; and Arthur Chambers, John Cooke, Joseph Tipton, John Tomkins, Samuel Thomas, Howell Brown, Will. Clemson, John Arther, and Rich. Twiss, common council men; " without administering unto them any oath or oaths (but the usual oathe for the execution of their respective places) with which we are pleased to dispense in this behalf."

The mayor informs the lord president, that immediately after he received the royal order, he caused it to be served upon all the persons named therein, except the earl of Shrewsbury and Mr. Nehemiah Scott, who reside out of the county: and "to demonstrate the reddyness of the corporation to comply with the order, the very next day after I received his Majesty's letter, they elected and admitted" all the persons ordered to be elected, "*although this corporation is very sensible that upon the death or removall of any person, the right of election of a new member doth by charter belong unto, and is vested in this corporation.*" The mayor then informs his lordship that since the said election, as he calls it, all the persons soe elected have taken the usual oaths for the execution of their places, except the marquess of Powis, T. Burton, esq., C. Doughty, E. Gosnell, and S. Thomas; three of whom, Burton, Gosnell, and Thomas, mean to apply to the King to be excused from serving in the same offices, and Mr. Doughty prays to be excused on account of his age, (upwards of seventy-eight years) and his infirmities of body[3].

---

[1] These Christian names were mistaken, and should have been William Corbett and Henry Corser, as Mr. Salter the mayor informs the earl of Sunderland.

[2] In the entry of this nobleman's election on the corporation book, he is called earl, though the King expressly styles him marquiss: and he had been so created March 24, 1686,7. James II. after the abdication made him duke of Powis. His religious principles had attracted the notice of government in his earliest infancy. Mr. Garrard writes to lord Wentworth, Feb. 14, 1637,8, that there was "a proposition made at the council-table, to take away the eldest sons of all who were popishly affected, and breed them up in the religion of the church of England. My lord chamberlain [Philip Herbert, earl of Pembroke and Montgomery] moved to have Percy, Herbert's son, who is heir to his [the chamberlain's] estate, should his son fail, taken from his father, and bred up in the protestant religion. My lord Powis was not much pleased with this motion: gets access to the King: pleads hard for his son; humbly desires that his son may not be held the most jesuited papist of England, and made the only example in this kind. Nothing is done of this kind, yet." Strafford Papers, ii. 147. The lord Powis mentioned in this extract, father of Percy Herbert, and grandfather of the duke, was cousin-german of the lord chamberlain.

[3] The remainder of Mr. Salter's return to the lord president relates to a dispute about the fees of admission which the newly appointed corporators refused to pay; and which is "wholly referred to his lordship's determination."

What effect these changes would have produced on the Shrewsbury election cannot be known. The King found so little success from all the pains he had taken, as still to postpone the convening of a parliament: and in fact none was ever summoned during the short remainder of his infatuated reign. James, indeed, found it now necessary to retrace his steps. The prince of Orange was known to be embarking an army; and to this we must attribute the proclamation which the King issued on the 17th of October, for restoring corporations to their ancient charters and franchises; and the orders which were the same day made in council for removing all corporate officers, mayors, aldermen, recorders, &c., who had been put in by the crown since 1679. Richard Muckleston was at this time mayor of Shrewsbury under the new charter of 1685; the proclamation was delivered to him on the 29th of October, whereupon he was discharged from his office, and John Hill, esq. was elected in his room, under the charter of 1638.

If the following draft of a letter, without signature or address, among the corporation archives, were written by the mayor, and sent to lord Newport, as seems probable, it throws some light upon the state of publick opinion in our town at that most momentous conjuncture in the whole of our history, when, the King having been frightened away, the prince of Orange, with the sages and patriots who called him over, were laying the foundations of that glorious system which was destined to ensue, in which a CONSTITUTIONAL MONARCH was to reign over a FREE PEOPLE. The peer addressed, and it could scarcely have been any one but him whom we have indicated above, seems to have designed to occupy Shrewsbury at this precarious crisis.

"My Lord,

"I received your letter by Mr. Moore, and forthwith communicated the same to Mr. Recorder, Mr. Steward, the Aldermen, and Common councell of this corporation: who give your lord^p an account of the state of our towne, that itt is open and ungarrisoned, and that your Lordship may enter without any opposition by us or any others, to the best of our knowledge, which we hope is a satisfactory answer to your Lordship's letter att present from your Lordship's most

"Humble Servant."

"8 December, 88.

CHAPTER XII.

FROM THE REVOLUTION TO THE PRESENT TIME.

In February 1695-6, the kingdom was thrown into a general consternation by the discovery of a conspiracy to assassinate the King. This, which is generally known by the name of sir John Fenwick's plot, is so fully recounted in all our histories, as to render any detail of it in these pages quite unnecessary. On the 24th of February, an association was drawn up reciting the existence of the conspiracy, recognizing the title of the King, engaging to defend his person, and to avenge his death. It quickly spread through the country, and was read in the "house," i. e. at a meeting of the corporation of this town, on the 13th of March: when it was "agreed, nem. con., that it should be signed by the members of the house, and tendered to all absent members: and persons were also appointed to tender it to all gentlemen, burgesses, and other inhabitants: viz. for the Welsh ward, Mr. William Leighton and Mr. John Williams: for the Stone ward, Mr. William Bowdler and Mr. William Clemson: and for the Castle ward, Mr. Sam. Hinde and Mr. Joseph King." Lord Newport had been created earl of Bradford (11 May, 1694) and by him it was resolved that this association should be presented to the King.

The sprightly but licentious comedy of *The Recruiting Officer* is said to have been written when its author George Farquhar was resident here in that capacity. The scene is certainly laid in Shrewsbury; and as the play contains more than one allusion to our great victories under the duke of Marlborough, particularly to the battle of Hochstet, or Blenheim, which was fought August 1704; and as the epistle dedicatory "To all Friends round the Wrekin" is, in part, an answer to Durfey's complaint that the piece came out on the third night of his *Wonders in the Sun*, which was printed in 1706, we may infer that it was written in the latter end of the first of these years, and brought upon the stage at the close of the theatrical campaign of 1705: for he says in the epistle aforesaid, that "the season was far advanced, and the officers that made the greatest figure in his play, all commanded to their posts abroad." We are not to suppose that the plot, light as it is, had any foundation in fact: but the writer is known to have had "living originals in his eye[1]."

Justice Ballance was Francis Berkeley, esq. barrister-at-law, and recorder of Shrewsbury and Bridgenorth: he died 1710.

John Hill, esq. of Shrewsbury, the mayor of 1689, who lived in the old house in Hill's Lane, and died March 29, 1731, was one of the other *justices*.

Worthy was a Mr. Owens of Rhiwsaison in Montgomeryshire; probably Athelstane Owens, esq. who married Anne, daughter of Vincent Corbet, esq. of Ynysymaengwyn, and had by her a daughter, eventually his heiress, married to Price Maurice, esq. of Lloran.

Melinda was meant for a Miss Harnage: no doubt, Dorothy, daughter of Edward Harnage, esq. of Belswardine. She died at Tewkesbury, 1743, aged sixty-eight, and, as serjeant Kite oddly anticipates in the play, unmarried.

Sylvia was Laconia Berkeley, the recorder's daughter, by Muriel, daughter of sir William Childe and his wife Anne Lacon, (whence her christian name). This young lady was in her twenty-third year when the comedy was written. She married Edward Browne, esq. of Caughley, and died 1736, at the age of fifty-three.

In *Plume*, our informant said, Farquhar was thought to mean himself; and it is in accordance with what the biographers relate of his thoughtless dissipated character. He died in April 1707.

For the very happily imagined character of *Brazen* he might draw upon his own fancy, or, perhaps, upon many of his associates in and out of the army.

It need not be told, how Dr. Sacheverell, for two scurrilous intemperate sermons, very undeserving such exalted notice[2], was impeached at the bar of the House of Lords (Dec. 13, 1709): and that foolish measure of queen

---

[1] This information is derived from Anne relict of Thomas Blakeway of Shrewsbury, attorney-at-law: she died Feb. 1766: and communicated this information to her husband's nephew, the rev. Edward Blakeway. See Tatler, edit. 1786, vol. i. p. 425. In her youth she had lived as companion with Mrs. Honour Dryden, and from that lady received the letter of her cousin-german, the great poet, which stands at the head of his Prose Works in Mr. Malone's edition, and contains the first specimen of his verses known to exist.

[2] "One weak step, in trying a fool for what he said in the pulpit with all the pomp that could be used, cost the most able ministry that ever England was honoured with, its being: and anarchical fury was carried so high, that Harry Sacheverell swelling, and Jack Higgins laughing, marched through England in a triumph more than military." Steele's Letter to Sir Miles Wharton.

Anne's whig ministry, condemned even by Burnet, was followed by a sentence (March 20, 1709-10) whereby he was enjoined not to preach for three years. A termination so impotent to a proceeding so solemn was deemed by those who espoused his cause to be equivalent to an acquittal, as it did not preclude his acceptance of any church-preferment. Robert Lloyd, esq. of Aston, who had been his pupil[1] at Magdalen college, Oxford, presented him to the rectory of Selatyn near Oswestry, which fell vacant at this time. The benefice in question lying in a remote part of the kingdom, the high-church party had thus an opportunity, and they did not neglect it, of keeping up the spirits of their friends, by welcoming the doctor in the most distinguished manner on the course of his journey to take possession of it. "In May," says the tory Salmon, " he entered upon his triumphant progress to Shropshire. He was magnificently entertained at Oxford by the university, and received in the other great towns he passed through [Banbury, Warwick, Coventry, and Shrewsbury, are particularly specified] with the loud acclamations and joyful congratulations of the people, upon his deliverance from whiggish persecution." "As he passed through the countries, both going and returning," says the whig Burnet, " he was received and followed by such numbers, and entertained with such magnificence, that our princes, in their progresses, have not been more run after than he was. Great fury and violence appeared, on many occasions, though care was taken to give his followers no sort of provocation. He was looked on as the champion of the church: and he shewed as much insolence on that occasion, as his party did folly." To the same effect, Steele, in the person of Pasquin, alluding to the prosecution then impending over the duke of Marlborough; "Heroes in your service are treated with calumny, while criminals pass through your towns with acclamations[2]." In a pamphlet[3] of the day, his reception in this town is particularly described; and from that it seems as if he came here on his return from Selatyn. He notified his intention of entering Shrewsbury, says that authority, on Tuesday the 3d of July[4], about noon. Hereupon " the cryer was sent about to make proclamation through the town and adjacent villages. The bells began to ring to call the rabble together, and the gentry assembled in the market-place, and went out of town in this order to meet him." Then follows an account, evidently caricatured, of the procession. K—ston,

[1] So Sacheverell himself says in a letter to Swift, dated Jan. 31, 1711-12, printed in the dean's works, xiii. 150. Hawkesworth's edit. In this letter he calls secretary St. John, his "great countryman." Lydiard Tregoze, the seat of lord Bolingbroke's ancestors, is in Wiltshire; and the doctor is supposed to have sprung from the Cheverells of that county. One of his immediate ancestors is said to have prefixed a syllable to his name, in order to assimilate it to the ancient Derbyshire Sacheverells, who, however, owned him as a kinsman, and left him an estate. See Lysons in that county, cxliv.
[2] Tatler, No. 187.
[3] A new map of the Travels of our High Church Apostle. London, 1710, pp. 16. price 2d. It is a very poor performance.
[4] Here is a mistake. The 3d of July in 1710 was on Monday.

O——n, Cr—set, Cr—well, and M——n[1], are particularly mentioned as "chief townsmen," who formed part of the cavalcade. "At the town's end they were joined with several parties of horse from the adjacent villages, and when they came to Monford Bridge, where they had a sight of the pulpit hero, there were no less than seven thousand horse[2]. He was safely conducted to his inn, where he was kindly entertained with wine and sweetmeats, and the mob with strong drink and tobacco; and the evening concluded with ringing of bells, and bonfires, and other demonstrations of joy." Leonard Hotchkis, afterwards head master of our free school, is said to have led his horse into town[3]: but this information is somewhat questionable: if true, it was a mere boyish frolick: for he was then only an undergraduate of St. John's in Cambridge. The ministers of St. Chad's and St. Mary's, Mr. Bennett and Mr. Dawes, of maturer age, (for they had been more than thirty years possessed of their respective livings,) did not think fit to make so open a disclosure of their sentiments. They sent a message to the Raven, desiring leave to wait upon the doctor at night; but he sent for answer, "that he would have no Nicodemuses[4]." From Shrewsbury he went to Condover, and so to Bridgenorth, Kinlet, Ludlow, and Mr. Berkeley Green's near Worcester, but met with a rebuff in that city by the direction of bishop Lloyd. Nor were all the inhabitants of Shropshire unanimous in their admiration of this "ecclesiastical drummer;" for there is a violent invective against him in rhyme, entitled, "The Wolf stript of his Shepherd's clothing: addressed to Dr. Sacheverell by a Salopian gentleman[5]." Government thought the affair so important, that the secretary of state wrote to the lord lieutenant of Shropshire (the earl of Bradford) that it was her Majesty's pleasure that his lordship and the gentlemen of the county should prosecute the offenders on this occasion with the utmost severity[6].

On the death of queen Anne (Aug. 1, 1714) and the peaceful accession of George I., the populace in many parts of the kingdom were inflamed to a high pitch of resentment: for which no adequate cause can be assigned,

---

[1] These blanks appear to denote John Kynaston, esq. of Hordley, Hardwicke, and Abrightley, or his son, Corbet Kynaston, Roger Owen, esq. of Condover and the Council House, Edward Cresset, esq. of Cound, Richard Creswell, esq. of Sidbury, and Robert Myddelton, esq. of Shrewsbury, eventually heir of Chirk. The pamphlet gives a letter from Mr. Cresswell, signed R. C. junior, (for his father was then living) informing his friends, "Dr. Sacheverell comes from Condover on Wednesday the 5th of July, and doth me the honour to dine that day at the Cock and Castle in Bridgenorth. I beg the favour of all clergymen, and others, that are well-wishers to him or his doctrine, to accompany him into town about twelve aclock."

[2] The Life and Reign of Queen Anne, p. 541, says five thousand.

[3] MS. note in the late Dr. Hart's copy of Phillips's history.

[4] From the information of the late rev. John Rowland, fourth master of Shrewsbury school.

[5] London, 8vo. 1710, pp. 8.

[6] Wherever the doctor went, people were desirous to have their new-born infants christened with a name so revered: and, having been transmitted through succeeding generations, it is not yet extinct in this town.

but the defeat of the Pretender's hopes; and the return to power of a whig ministry, from whom they apprehended danger to the church. In an ebullition of fury, they directed their attacks very generally against the places of dissenting worship. The meeting-house in our High Street was demolished, and the materials carried, as is said, to Frankwell, and there burned with great exultation. The sufferers related, that the mayor, though obliged by his office to discountenance such riotous proceedings, yet, in his heart, approving the zeal of the mob, approached the scene of action, and in a very gentle voice, scarcely audible, only said, "Good people, this is very wrong." To what degree of credit this story is entitled cannot be known. Times inflamed by party are little favourable to truth. It is certain that a law of the first parliament of George I., which met on the 17th of March, 1714-15, called the Riot Act, recites, that "of late many rebellious riots and tumults have been in divers parts of the kingdom, to the disturbance of the publick peace, and the endangering of his Majesty's person and government, and the same are yet continued and fomented by persons disaffected to his Majesty:" and the following letter from the secretary of state to one of the county magistrates, Thomas Severne[1], esq. of Wallop, instructing him to be aiding in the introduction into the town of the posse comitatus, bespeaks a distrust which the government entertained of the steadiness of the chief magistrate of Shrewsbury. Mr. Severne resided here at The Bell Stone.

"Sir, "Whitehall, 14 July, 1715.

"The King having received information of a Riott being lately committed at the town of Salop, and that several outrageous proceedings ensued thereupon, which ought to be timely suppressed, in order to prevent further mischiefs of the like nature, I have this day, by his Majesty's command, wrote to the High Sheriff of that County, to take care that the Laws against Riotts be duely put in execution, and that in pursuance thereof, he, or the under-sheriff, together with two or more of the Justices of the Peace, taking along with him the Power of the said County, if need be, should repair to the said Town of Salop, and in case the said riott and disturbance is still subsisting, to take the best care he can to suppress the same, and to give his assistance to his Majesty's Justices of the Peace in making strict enquiry concerning the riotous proceedings aforesaid, in order to the prosecuting and punishing the offenders according to the utmost rigour the Law will allow. His Majesty has therefore commanded me to signify his Pleasure to you, as being a Magistrate in whose Loyalty and true Zeal for his service the King has an entire confidence, that you do repair with such other Justices of the Peace as can be conveniently got together to the said Town of Salop, and there exert your utmost Power and Authority in suppressing all such unwarrantable practices, and likewise that you do take exact Informations of the mischiefs which have already been done, and of the chief actors therein. I am,

"Sir,

"P. S. I have wrote the like letter to the Mayor of Salop, and to Thos. Edwards and John Lacon, sen^r. Esq.

"Your most humble servant,
"TOWNSHEND.

"Thomas Severne, Esq."

---

[1] Mr. Severne was of an ancient family long seated in Worcestershire, and possessed of extensive property at Shrawley, Powick, &c. His father, John Severne, was the first who settled at

In the year 1715, a very serious attempt was made by the adherents of the Pretender, James III. as he was called, to place him upon the throne. The earl of Mar raised his standard in the shire of Aberdeen on the 3d of September; as Thomas Forster, esq., M. P. for Northumberland, did in that county on the 6th of October, and began to march southwards, being joined by the earl of Derwentwater, grandson of Charles II., lord Widdrington, the Scottish earls of Nithisdale, Carnwath, and Wintoun, lord viscount Kenmuir, &c. The militias of the northern counties retired upon their approach; and the affair wore so serious an aspect, that the government found it necessary to dispatch a considerable army against them. Brigadier Dormer's regiment, which was at that time quartered in Shrewsbury, for the maintenance of good order, was ordered to march to Preston in Lancashire, where the rebels arrived on the 10th of November. To defend Shrewsbury in case of emergency, its gates were put into repair, several passages were stopped up, and the trained bands, as the militia was then called, were assembled. In aid of these, and to evince their attachment to the house of Hanover, the loyal part of the population of the town and neighbourhood entered into a voluntary association. The following paper contains the names of the officers.

"The Association, or Artilary Regiment of Shrewsbury, raised voluntarily by the inhabitants in the year 1715, in defence of the town in opposition to the rebells, consisted of one Troop of Horse and four Companys of Foot, all uniformly cloathed in fine blew cloth with gilt brass buttons.

Horse Officers.
Henry Viscount Newport, Colonel and Captain[1].
Sir Charles Lloyd, Major[2].
William Kinaston, Esq. Lieutenant[3].
Edward Donne, Esq. Cornett[4].

Foot.
Thomas Gardner, Esq. Captain[5].

Shrewsbury, and is called in the admission to his burgesship, son of John Severne, of the College of Worcester, gentleman. One of his sisters, Catharine, became the wife of John Somers of Clifton-upon-Severn in the same county: and mother of the great lord Somers.

[1] Henry viscount Newport, was grandson of the first earl of Bradford, of whom so much has been said in a former part of our history.

[2] Sir Charles Lloyd, bart. of Garth, in the county of Montgomery, married, at St. Julian's, Shrewsbury, 1694, Victoria, daughter of sir Richard Corbett of Longnor, bart. by whom he had no issue: by his 2d wife, Jane, daughter of sir Edward Leighton, bart. and relict of Thomas Jones, esq. of Shrewsbury, he left a daughter named after his first wife, who became the wife of Edward Kynaston, esq. of Hardwick and Hordley.

[3] William Kinaston, esq. was son of William Kinaston of Lee, by Jane, daughter and heir of Thomas Kynaston, esq. of Ruyton. He was a master in chancery, and represented Shrewsbury in parliament from 1734 to his death in 1749.

[4] Edward Donne, esq. was son of Edward Donne, esq. of Place-A-Court in that part of the parish of Alberbury which lies in the county of Montgomery. He was at this time a LL. B. of Queen's College, Cambridge: but soon after took orders, and became, by the interest of lord Bradford, a prebendary of Canterbury, where he died 15th Jan. 1745, aged 59.

[5] Thomas Gardner, esq. of Sansaw, a barrister, who died 17th Nov. 1763, aged 83. He was grandfather to the late John Gardner, esq. of Sansaw.

GEORGE AMLER, Esq. Lieutenant[1].
JOHN SKRYMSHER, GENT. Ensign[2].

JOHN FOWNES, Esq. Captain[3].
HENRY JEUKS, GENT. Lieutenant[4].
RICHARD LOXDALE, GENT. Ensign[5].

DR. JOHN HOLLINGS, Captain[6].
RICHARD WHITMORE, Esq. Lieutenant[7].
RICHARD DICKIN, GENT. Ensign[8].

EDWARD GOSNELL, Esq. Captain[9].
JOHN LACON, GENT. Lieutenant[10].
SAMUEL ELISHA, GENT. Ensign[11].

GEORGE BOWDLER.
EDWARD GRANT."

From this time nothing has occurred requiring notice in our history before the institution of the SALOP INFIRMARY; which, though to be detailed more at length in our future pages, must not be entirely passed over here; as Shrewsbury had the distinguished honour of very nearly leading the way in this career of benevolence; being, at least in the conception, second only to Winchester: for in a printed address, dated July 24, 1737, and entitled "A proposal for erecting an Infirmary for the poor, sick, and lame, in this county and neighbourhood," that "recently" established in the city just mentioned, is the only one referred

---

[1] George Amler, esq. of Shrewsbury, a wealthy draper, was son of John Amler, gent. of Ford, and died in 1754, aged 87.

[2] John Skrymsher, gent. of Shrewsbury, clerk of the peace, was son of Richard Skrymsher of Forton, and grandson of John Skrymsher, a younger son of sir Thomas Skrymsher of Aqualate in the county of Stafford.

[3] John Fownes, esq. was of Onslow, which his father, John Fownes, esq. of Stoke Prior in the county of Worcester, barrister-at-law, obtained by marriage with the heiress of Thomas Harper, esq. of that place.

[4] Henry Jeuks, gent. was an attorney of Shrewsbury, to whom the inhabitants are much indebted for their beautiful walk, the Quarry, which was laid out and planted in his mayoralty, 1719. He was of an ancient family, long seated at Wolverton near Drayton; and his grandfather Thomas is called, on what authority we know not, governor of Ludlow Castle to Charles I.

[5] Richard Loxdale, gent. son of John Loxdale of Meartown, in the parish of Forton and county of Stafford, was the first of his family who settled in Shrewsbury.

[6] Dr. John Hollings was an eminent physician, as his father was before him, and his son after him.

[7] Richard Whitmore, esq. was of Shrewsbury, and admitted a burgess in 1718. To his brother William, of Slaughter in the county of Gloucester, his father's cousin-german, sir William Whitmore of Apley, left his estates. The present lieutenant had a son, Weld Whitmore, and was himself buried in St. Chad's, March 1733, aged 48.

[8] Richard Dickin, gent. was of Leaton, in the county of Stafford, and of Preen in this county.

[9] Edward Gosnell, esq. was of Rossall, which his father, also Edward Gosnell, a merchant of London, purchased after the dreadful conflagration of that city, by which he was a great sufferer. Mr. Gosnell, the captain, was steward of the corporation.

[10] John Lacon, gent. attorney and clerk of the peace, lived at Bridgenorth as late as 1695, but removed to Shrewsbury before 1700, and resided at the College.

[11] Samuel Elisha was an attorney, and father of Edward, steward of the corporation, and a member of the same profession, who bestowed much attention on the history of the town: for his papers on which subject we are indebted to the rev. Archdeacon Corbett.

to. But no steps were taken to accomplish the design before 1744. A general meeting of the contributors took place at the summer assizes of 1745, when the laws by which the institution should be conducted were agreed upon; and notwithstanding the distracted state of the country in that memorable year, the work proceeded so vigorously, that the house was actually opened in the spring of 1747, and has ever since maintained a course of unabated and encreasing usefulness.

The advance of the Scottish invasion in 1745, under the command of the grandson of James II., as near to Shrewsbury as Ashborne (sixty miles), Dec. 4, excited much uneasiness in this town. This was encreased four days after into a violent alarm, when intelligence arrived at eleven o'clock P. M. that the Highlanders were on their march hither, and would be here in the morning. Hereupon many of the principal inhabitants, members of the corporation and staunch whigs, quitted the town with precipitation. Even those who were the most strongly attached to the exiled family, were not less anxious than the warmest adherents of the house of Hanover, to secrete their valuable effects from the anticipated depredations of their friends. Lord Herbert, lord lieutenant of the county (afterwards earl of Powis) had been commissioned (Oct. 1) to raise a regiment of fusileers in Shropshire, which he completed in a very short time. They were lying in Shrewsbury at this time, and, on the news of the enemy's advance, marched out to meet them: but having been just raised, and quite undisciplined; and being, indeed, totally inadequate in numbers to cope with the Highland army, they soon fell back. Sir Thomas Whitmore, of Apley, K. B., marched as a volunteer in the grenadier company, and is recorded[1] to have shewn more courage and resolution than many of the officers. The information which excited so much bustle was a mere joke of some mischievous jacobite: for the Scots were so far from any thoughts of advancing to Shrewsbury, that they were on that very night (Dec. 8) marching northwards, from Leek to Macclesfield. Having received no encouragement from their friends in England, they commenced their retreat homewards on the second day after their arrival at Derby; and the inhabitants of Shrewsbury quickly returned to their former tranquillity.

One of the last executions which took place in these realms for attachment to the Stuarts, occurred in Shrewsbury, seven years after the transaction last referred to. Mr. Thomas Anderson, a Yorkshire gentleman from the neighbourhood of Richmond, had risen to the rank of lieutenant in sir John Ligonier's regiment of dragoons, and had deserted from it. This offence, so unusual in an officer, must, it is probable, have been repeated

[1] MS. contemporary chronicle, whence this account is taken.

more than once, or it would scarcely have been visited with the extreme severity of military law. It originated in his attachment to the exiled family, for whose service he was also charged with enlisting men. His trial, which lasted three days, commenced at Worcester on the 16th of November, 1752, and after the sentence, he was removed to this town, where orders were received for his execution. Several petitions for mercy were laid before the King, from Yorkshire, Lancashire, Worcester, and Shrewsbury, but these are supposed to have been very far from doing him any service, as the political principles of the petitioners were more than suspicious. On Monday, Dec. 11th, about ten in the morning, he was conducted from the gaol to Kingsland, under a guard, attended by the regiment. The mayor, with his usual attendants, was also present. Mr. Anderson was dressed in a suit of black velvet, and behaved with great composure. His dying speech consisted chiefly of religious sentiments very properly expressed: but a few passages of it indicate his political tenets. He prays God "to strengthen the ancient church," (by which it should seem that he had imbibed an attachment to the religion[1], as well as to the descendants of James II.): "to encrease the number of the *Royal Family*, and to protect and guard the dearest P—— (doubtless Prince Charles Edward) wherever he goes. As to the late account from London," he says "that he is pre-advised of it, and can justly say, that he is guilty only of one of the faults charged upon him."

In his letter delivered to the sheriff on the morning of his execution, he holds the same language: "Nothing laid to my charge has been proved except desertion." He requests the sheriff to cause all that befell him at Shrewsbury, and the friendship shewed him by its worthy citizens during his confinement, to be inserted in the London evening paper[2]. "The whole town, and you[3], with lady Kynaston in particular[4], have an assurance of my

---

[1] Unless by the *ancient church* Mr. Anderson intended, as he very likely did, *that* set up at Manchester in 1734 by the reverend, or, as his own flock styled him, the right reverend Dr. Thomas Deacon; and which professed to be formed upon the model of the four first centuries of the Christian æra. The orthodox British church, for so it was called, grew up among the descendants of those non-jurors who refused allegiance to king William, and retained their affection for the abdicated family. Thomas, Robert, and Charles Deacon, officers in the Manchester regiment, taken in Carlisle by the King's troops, December 30, 1745, were sons of Dr. Deacon, and were all condemned to death; which the first of them actually suffered. They, no doubt, were members of the "ancient church," of which their father was bishop: its principles are known to have extended into Yorkshire; and may have been adopted by lieutenant Anderson's family.

[2] *Four* evening papers were at that time published in London: but from this expression of the lieutenant's, it should seem that only *one* was taken in at Shrewsbury. There are now (Nov. 1823) about *four hundred and sixty* London papers received at our post office in a week, for inhabitants of the town, besides our own two and other provincial papers.

[3] The sheriff for that year was Thomas Sandford, esq. of Sandford.

[4] The lady thus designated can have been no one but Anne, daughter of Thomas Harwood, esq. by a sister of Mr. Hill the envoy, known in Shropshire as *the great Hill*, and second wife of John Kynaston, of Hordley, esq. knight of the shire for Shropshire, on whose death, in Sept. 1733, she took up her abode in Shrewsbury, where she survived her husband more than forty years, deceasing in Oct. 1773. At an earlier period of her widowhood, she is said to have been very frequently employed in

sincere thanks. The rest is to assure you that I'm entirely resigned to die, annexed to an assurance that nothing gives me any material concern, solely a reflection that I have offended a GOD who has always treated me so tenderly." His last words were a request for silence, that he might exculpate Mr. Wilding, his governor[1], from a malicious accusation of having used him unkindly. "I now declare, upon the word of a dying man, that both he and his wife used me with the greatest tenderness and humanity during my confinement with him."

Mr. Anderson then composed himself to death. Five soldiers were appointed to shoot him, but only three fired. The balls from two entered one into each breast: the third shot him through the head. Some signs of animation still remaining, the commanding officer stepped forward with a pistol, and released him from all sensation; an action which was considered by the spectators, who deeply sympathized with the sufferer, to indicate a ferocious resentment against the deceased; but which may, perhaps, be more candidly ascribed to the humane desire of terminating his agonies[2]. He was buried in St. Mary's churchyard on the same day, with an inscription of his own inditing, which will be seen in our account of that cemetery.

Though the bill for putting the militia upon its present footing received the royal assent June 28, 1757, it was not carried into effect in Shropshire before 1763: for which delay, a writer of little credit gives a reason which we trust is founded in error[3]. The militia properly belongs to the history of the county; and would not have been noticed here, but for a ludicrous incident respecting it[4], which occurred in the town, and for a sportive effu-

carrying over to Flanders the contributions of the Shropshire jacobites for the court of St. Germain's.

[1] Samuel Wilding had recently (in 1751) been appointed gaoler in the room of his father Thomas. He and his wife here spoken of died within two days of each other, 1786.

[2] A strong feeling of indignation was, however, excited in the regiment, by the apostacy of Mr. Anderson. They would not permit the funeral procession to enter the church, that part of that fine service might be suppressed. In return, the curate, Mr. Brooks, pronounced it all, without curtailment, at the grave. From the information of John Scott, esq.

[3] The author alluded to is Tate Wilkinson, an actor, and patentee of the theatres at York and Hull. In his Memoirs of his own Life, vol. i. p. 173, he mentions his joining Whitley's company of comedians, who were playing at Shrewsbury, in September 1763. The county militia were then assembled for the first time, though the war was over, during the whole of which it had not been embodied: and he accounts for this extraordinary delay, by observing, that on a former occasion, this county had raised a regiment, consisting of creditable farmers' sons, for the internal defence of the kingdom; which regiment was immediately marched off to the sea-coast, was taken by surprise, forced on board transports, and sent to the Indies,—which breach of faith so disgusted the inhabitants of the county, that they threw every obstacle in the way of the militia.

[4] The first day of the militia's assembling, proceeds Mr. Wilkinson, was the annual fair for cattle; and after describing, and perhaps exaggerating, the rout to which the recruits were put by the oxen and sheep, he relates the offence which he gave to the officers by his inadvertent performance on the succeeding evening of the part of major Sturgeon, in Foote's farce of the Mayor of Garrat,

sion to which it gave rise, and with which we have ventured to enliven our pages.

1.

Since the Shropshire militia is now to be rais'd,
The Shropshire militia by me shall be prais'd:
While others but trot, my muse rides full gallop,
To sing to some tune the militia of Salop.

2.

The great earl of Bath, the county's lieutenant,
Has gathered together the very best men on't.
All ready, with swords in their hands, to advance
'Gainst popish invasion from Spain and from France.

3.

Lord Pulteney, the col'nel, so bold and so brave,
To Portugal's gone, his country to save.
Like a lion he fought at Valentia they say [1],
For true glory all, without profit or pay.

4.

The lieutenant-col'nel, the great squire Lawley,
In courage as great as a Huske, or a Hawley [2],
From Staffordshire comes, with pleasure, we hear,
To head the militia of merry Shropshire.

5.

Equipt with a major you'll be in a trice,
And who is so proper as major Chase Price?
In the parliament-house he has got great renown;
And he beat squire Gorges at fair Lem'ster town.

6.

Captain Hall [3] is a soldier we all must applaud;
Captain Hill [4] has got knowledge by going abroad;
And the brave captain Morhall there's no one can doubt on,
For he's cousin to good 'squire Lyster of Rowton.

7.

When captain Wat Williams [5] recruiting appears,
They ballot no men, but all list volunteers:
Captain Maurice [6] and he the brave Welshmen will bring,
To join the Salopians, to fight for their king.

---

then just come out, in which is contained a ridiculous account of a similar circumstance. He was extricated out of this emergency, as he says, with some difficulty, by the exertions of Mr. Littlehale, of that town, and the good-humour of Chace Price, esq. colonel of the militia; who invited him afterwards to dinner at the mess, and got him to recite the part before all the company. "The good-humoured intention was smoked, and it ended with an afternoon and evening all in perpetual harmony,—animosity or discord was no more thought of." By Littlehale is meant Mr. Edmund Littlehales, an eminent and much respected draper upon Mardol-head.

[1] The battle of Valencia d'Alcantara in Portugal, where general Burgoyne commanded, and lord Pulteney served as colonel of the royal volunteers, was fought Aug. 27, 1762. This fixes the date of our song within a few months, for that young nobleman died Feb. 16, 1763.

[2] Lieutenant-general Hawley and major-general Husk commanded at the affair of Falkirk, Jan. 17, 1746, where the King's troops did not particularly distinguish themselves; though both officers behaved very gallantly soon after at Culloden.

[3] William Pearce Hall, esq. of Downton-hall in the parish of Staunton-Lacy. His daughter and heiress married sir C. W. Boughton Rouse, bart.

[4] Samuel Hill, esq. elder brother of the first lord Berwick. He died unmarried, 1766.

[5] Watkin Williams, esq. of Penbedw, in the county of Flint, and Trenewydd in the county of Salop.

[6] Edward Maurice, esq. of Lloran, in the county of Montgomery: he afterwards took the name of

8.
The lieutenants and ensigns to name in my song
Most folks will allow would make it too long;
In short, they are all such brave gentle-men,
That the like in all England you'll not meet again.

9.
I think in my heart 'twould beat Shrewsbury show
To see these brave officers all in a row:
When so gallant a sight upon the parade is,
Take care of your hearts, ye fair Shropshire ladies.

10.
But my bold country lads, let none fear to go,
With such noble commanders to face the proud foe:
Who boldly will venture their fortunes and lives,
To fight for your property, sweet-hearts, and wives.

11.
Then join in this reg'ment, all lads of true spirit,
Where preferment will always attend upon merit.
And by Act of Parliament, as you well know,
There's no one can force you from England to go.

12.
And now of my ballad pray don't make a jest,
To honour the country I have done my best.
Then fill up a glass of Joe Laurence's[1] beer,
And drink to the lads of the merry Shropshire.

The Welsh-cloth trade of Shrewsbury will be considered hereafter: but its termination was an event of too much importance to the town to be passed over in this place. We enjoyed this branch of commerce for more than three centuries, and during the two last it had been carried on in the great room over the market-house. Every Thursday[2] the central parts of the town were all life and bustle. Troops of hardy ponies, each with a halter of twisted straw, and laden with two bales of cloth, poured into the market-place in the morning, driven by stout Welshmen in their country coats of blue cloth, and striped linsey waistcoats: and the description given by Dyer[3] may boast an accuracy seldom to be found among the poets.

> The northern Cambrians, an industrious tribe,
> Carry their labours on pygmæan steeds
> Yet strong and sprightly; over hill and dale
> They travel unfatigued, and lay their bales
> In Salop's streets, beneath whose lofty walls
> Pearly Sabrina wafts them with her barks,
> And spreads the swelling sheet.

Corbet on succeeding to the estate of Ynysymaengwyn, in the county of Merioneth, and died December 1820.

[1] He kept the Raven inn, and was father of Robert mentioned hereafter.

[2] The market was originally holden on Friday, the change took place in 1649.

[3] Fleece, b. iii.

After dinner, i. e. at two o'clock, the drapers, with their clerks, and shearmen, assembled under the market-house, and proceeded up stairs in seniority, having, by ancient usage, the right of pre-emption in that order. The market being over, drays were seen in all directions, conveying the cloths to the several warehouses: and more than six hundred pieces of web have been sold in a day. The whole was a ready-money business, and as the Welshmen left much of their cash behind them, in exchange for malt, groceries, and other shop goods, the loss of such a trade to the town may be easily conceived. The first blow levelled at the market may be dated from about the year 1790; when, or soon after, individuals, not members of the drapers' company, began to travel into the countries where these goods were made (Merionethshire, and the Vale of the Dee above Llangollen) and taught the farmers, that they might find a mart for their manufactures at home, without the trouble and expence of a journey to the walls of Amwythig.

Ex illo retro fluere ——.

About 1795 the market was most materially impaired, and almost ceased with the century. Till at length, in March 1803, the company relinquished the great room in which they had so long carried on their business; and though much business in this branch is still carried on within our walls, the town has entirely lost the advantage which it derived from the weekly visits of the Cambrian farmers, which produced so much emolument to the drapers, and raised so many families who now shine in the foremost ranks of our gentry.

The cessation of our cloth-market may in part also be ascribed to the improvement of the roads in Wales, which opened a more free communication to these interlopers, and this again reflected back some compensation upon the town for the loss of this branch of its trade. For, if Shrewsbury was no longer the emporium of North Wales, it was becoming the centre of communication between London and Dublin: and the agriculture of the neighbourhood, and the trade of the town, received a new impulse from the vast increase of posting and stage-coaches, which was thus diverted into this line of road. The subject is sufficiently curious to justify a brief deduction.

Stage-coaches were introduced into England shortly before the Restoration[1]. Ellwood the quaker, in his curious life[2], mentions that his sister went to London in one in the *tenth* month, 1659. They were evidently new things in Nov. 1663, when a young gentleman writes thus to his father in Lancashire[3]. "I got to London on Saturday last: my journey was noe ways pleasant, being forced to ride *in the boote*[4] all the way. The company

---

[1] Anthony Wood mentions the warden of Merton coming to Oxford in a stage-coach in 1661. Life, sub ann. [2] P. 19. [3] Archæologia, xx. 443.

[4] The boots of the coach were two seats practised in the sides of it by making the doors project. The persons occupying those uncomfortable

that came up with mee were persons of greate quality, as knights and ladyes. This traval bath soe indisposed mee, that I am resolved never to ride up againe in the coatch."

This town did not long remain without such a convenience: for it appears from the MS. diary[1] of sir William Dugdale, that in June 1681, having occasion to remove from London to his country seat in Warwickshire, he came down by "*Shrewsbury coach.*" The first night it stopped at Woburn: for in those times so imperfectly settled, and in the then wretched state of the roads, no coach thought of travelling all night. The second night it stopped at Hill Morton (near Rugby), and thence proceeded on the third day for Coleshill, where Dugdale would of course alight. This, it will be evident, was not the nearest line from London to Shrewsbury: but it might be deemed the best road: or the coach might even go out of its way[2] to accommodate the antiquary, whose seat lay close to Coleshill.

This first stage-coach to Shrewsbury did not probably long continue. The town lay remote from any of the great roads, and led to little beyond it but Montgomeryshire, then a county of small resort. All traces of the existence of such a coach had vanished from recollection, and as late as 1750, it is remembered that a lady, whom a sudden emergency of business required to go in haste to London, was obliged to ride to Ivetsey-bank to meet the coach which travelled between Chester and the metropolis. In default, therefore, of any earlier account of Shrewsbury stage-coach travelling, we present our readers with an authentick description of it, as practised from the last named city, which is only twenty miles further from London, written by the gentleman who himself underwent the journey. "In March 1739-40," says he, "I changed my Welsh school for one nearer to the capital, and travelled in the Chester stage, then no despicable vehicle for country gentlemen. The first day, with much labour, we got from Chester to Whitchurch, twenty miles: the second day, to the Welsh Harp: the third, to Coventry: the fourth, to Northampton: the fifth, to Dunstable: and, as a wondrous effort, on the last to London, before the commencement of night. The strain and labour of six good horses, sometimes eight, drew us through the sloughs of Mireden, and many other places. We were constantly out two hours before day, and as late at night: and in the depth of winter proportionably later[3]." As post-chaises were then unknown, persons of the first distinction had no means of reaching London but the *family coach and*

---

seats rode sideways, as in a modern car. See the cuts in La Serre's account of the entry of Mary of Medicis into London, 1639; reprint of 1775.

[1] In the possession of W. Hamper, esq.

[2] Such deviations for the convenience of individual passengers were not unusual at that time. Dryden, describing his journey in the Oundle coach from Northamptonshire to London, in September 1699, says, "The master of the stage-coach has not been over civill to me: for he turn'd us out of the road at the first step, and made us go to Pilton." Letter xxxv. in Malone's edit. of Dryden's prose works. This journey (seventy-eight miles) occupied two days. They slept the first night "at Silso, six miles beyond Bedford:" having travelled thirty-seven miles that day: dined at Hatfield the next day, "and came to town safe at seaven in the evening:" having travelled forty-one miles that day.

[3] Pennant's Journey to London, p. 143.

six so admirably depicted by Vanbrugh[1], or riding on horseback[2]. "The single gentlemen," says Mr. Pennant, "then a hardy race, equipped in jack-boots and trowsers up to their middle, rode post through thick and thin, and guarded against the mire, defied the frequent stumble and fall: arose, and pursued their journey with alacrity." Their boots were well covered with tallow before they set out, and the unctuous integument, with the superinduced incrustation of each day's mud, rode unmolested by the brush, till the wearer,

Stain'd with the variation of each soil,

was safely housed in the metropolis.

As to the carriage of goods to London, it is said[3] to have been only by pack-horses as late as 1730. After a few years, however, a common stage-waggon was set up, in which travellers of meaner rank were glad to find a place[4]; and the first step towards any thing like improvement was to place a large leathern box, something like a coach, and hung upon chains, in the middle of the waggon. Persons of a bettermost class were thus separated from their inferiors. This was sometimes called the *Gee-ho*. It was drawn by eight horses; with two more to drag it through sloughs and up hills. Seven, eight, and even nine days, were sometimes consumed in the journey. Such a conveyance existed in 1740, and perhaps earlier; and no other was known at Shrewsbury till 1750.

At the close of that year a new carriage started; the Caravan; fitted up within with benches against the sides for eight, twelve, and even, as other accounts have it, for eighteen persons: and very much resembling those conveyances of the same name, in which wild beasts are now transported to country fairs. It was drawn by "six able horses," and professed to per-

---

[1] See sir Francis Wronghead's journey to London, in the admirable comedy of the Provoked Husband. In these delineations of manners, plays and novels are sterling authorities.

[2] We have now before us a letter dated, Shrewsbury, Feb. 16, 1730, in which the writer informs her husband, then in London, that on the following Monday, a party of fourteen, three ladies, five gentlemen, whom she names, and their six servants, were to set off on horseback for that city. Such a cavalcade, which would set an ordinary troop of robbers at defiance, almost reminds one of Chaucer's pilgrims to Canterbury in the reign of Edward III.

[3] For this information we are indebted to Mr. Robert Hill, coroner of the corporation. The pack-horses were kept by a widow Warner, of the Pheasant, under the Wyle. A soldier named Carter, who was quartered at her inn, married his hostess, removed to Mardol, and began the first London waggon in ten or more days, and after a short time, *the Gee-ho*. Such is the verbal information which we have received, and on which we confidently rely; but the first *written* notice of any London waggon which we have discovered, is in Aris's Birmingham Gazette of Dec. 18, 1749, when Pryce Pugh advertises from "the Red Lion on the Wild Cop," that at his house "there is stable-room for a hundred horses, and a stage-waggon goes from thence to London." This is not spoken of as if it was a new thing: though it is the first time that it occurs in that provincial paper, which commenced eight years before. The time occupied by Mr. Pugh's waggon does not appear. But on Oct. 22, 1750, it is announced that "the Shrewsbury flying stage-waggon will begin to *fly* on Tuesday next, in five days, winter and summer." This is the waggon by which such great fortunes have been made.

[4] If Smollet intended, as is asserted, to depict the early incidents of his own life, under the name of Roderick Random, that novel will furnish a complete idea of the mode of travelling per waggon in 1739.

form the journey in four days, but often occupied the whole of five. The caravan travelled the old Chester road till the beginning of 1752, when we find it "lying on Tuesdays," which was the day it left Shrewsbury, "at the Castle Inn, Birmingham;" fare 15s.

The roads were now beginning, under the operation of various turnpike bills, and the general act of 1745[1], to lay aside somewhat of their pristine horrors. In April 1753, "the Birmingham and Shrewsbury Long Coach, with six able horses, in four days," started from "the Old Red Lion" here, to the Bell in Holborn; fare 18s. There was even an opposition: for in the following June, Fowler's "Shrewsbury stage-coach, in three days and a half," began to run from the Raven to the George and White Hart Inn in Aldersgate-street; fare 1l. 1s. Outside passengers half price. This is the first mention we have found of this class of travellers: and they, as it seems, must have ridden in an immense wicker basket of the kind delineated in Hogarth's print of *Night* published in 1738, and which, though now exploded, continued even to our own time.

The communication between Shrewsbury and London was, however, as yet but trifling; for none of these conveyances seem to have gone more than once a week; but in April 1764, a new carriage started, the Machine, which went thrice a week, and performed the journey in two days; fare 30s.; resting at Coventry for the night. This celerity of motion could not, however, be maintained during the winter. The journey was at that season extended to three days; and when, in the spring of 1766, the Machine returned to its former reduced time, it received, from its *extreme rapidity*, the new name of the "*Flying* Machine in two days." This continued in 1769, then sleeping at Dunchurch; the fare being raised to 36s. In August 1772 the time was reduced to a day and a half, and the fare to 34s.: the passengers sleeping at Wolverhampton on their journey from London[2].

In 1776, there were, as will be seen in the note, three modes of getting to London. The supply, however, was evidently as yet too great for the demand. The Fly, as well as its rival, was obliged to drop one journey in

---

[1] We find no example of an act of parliament authorising the imposition of a toll for the repair of roads before 1696; from that time, few years elapse without one or more acts being passed for that purpose. At the end of forty years they were increased so much, as to excite great dissatisfaction in the country, and tumults in which some lives were lost. But it was not until 1745 that a general highway act was passed: an innovation which occasioned loud complaints.

[2] These improvements were the fruits, as usual, of an opposition. Mr. John Payton, a spirited inn-keeper at Stratford-upon-Avon, (who had signalized himself by projecting the jubilee celebrated there in honour of Shakspeare, 1769) announced, in May 1772, " a *new Fly on steel springs*,"

fare 12s., from Shrewsbury to Birmingham; to communicate with "his London coaches." It set off from the Raven here at eight in the morning, and from Birmingham at six in the evening, and seems to have been the first coach that travelled *all night*. From the mention of *steel springs*, we infer, that former coaches had been suspended upon leathern braces, as it is said they were.

The new Fly was superseded in the following year (May 10, 1773) by the *new Machine* through Oxford, in two days; fare 36s. This was conducted by Mr. Payton, in conjunction with Mr. Robert Lawrence of the Raven, to whom Shrewsbury was afterwards indebted for many most important improvements in this department.

In April 1774, he announces his "London and

a week during the winter, and the Diligence soon ceased to run at all; but it would be uninteresting to pursue these minor details any further: and the speculative genius of the spirited master of the Raven[1] soon after struck out a new line of travelling, which brought a fresh accession of visitors to the town, and gradually increased this branch of business to an extent which former ages had never seen.

The road from London to Dublin had been invariably direct from Chester; and from Chester by sea, while North Wales continued to be ruled by its native princes. No "*Saeson*" might venture to travel by land to Holyhead: and even after that obstacle was removed, natural ones remained in " uncertain fords, unsafe ferries, and roads on the sides of the mountains, with precipices into the sea[2]." The inspection of any map will shew that Chester lies to the north of the right line; Shrewsbury much nearer to it: and that by adopting this latter road, a ferry at Conway, not always safe, and always unpleasant and productive of delay, might be avoided. Nor did this remark, so important to Shrewsbury, escape the notice of its inhabitants fourscore years ago. We have now before us a paper on the subject drawn up by the late Mr. Elisha. His favourite plan was to embark for Dublin from Carnarvon, and to lead the road to that port from London through Shrewsbury. But he proposes another route, very similar to that which was afterwards realised, through Oswestry, Cerrig y Druidion[3], Llanrwst, Conway, and Bangor ferry[4].

This paper appears to have been drawn up between 1730 and 1740: but nothing was done in consequence of it for forty years. In the beginning of 1779, occurs the first notice which we have found of any serious attempt at travelling through North Wales. It is an advertisement (April 3) from the innkeepers at Holyhead, Borth Ferry, Conway, St. Asaph, Ruthin, Llangollen, and Oswestry, who, styling themselves " the proprietors of the New Company for reducing the rates of travelling on the Welsh roads," return thanks to " the nobility, gentry, and others, travelling

---

Shrewsbury New Fly, in *one day and a half*, three times a week, on steel springs, and quite in the modern taste;" fare £1. 10*s*.: and he begs the publick to " observe, that notwithstanding this Fly sets out after the old coach, it will be in London as soon." Both went all night in their journey to London, but lay at Wolverhampton on their way back: and were, in fact, the best part of two days on the road.

To encounter the new intruder, " The original London and Salop Machine, in the modern taste, on steel springs, and bows on the top," called upon all travellers to observe, " that the road through Coventry being several miles nearer than through Oxford, will fully demonstrate the most speedy conveyance to London." The *bows* were doubtless for the accommodation of the outside passengers, who now were enabled to relinquish the rumbling,

though secure basket, for easier seats, which are in subsequent advertisements called " chairs " on the roof of the coach.

But all these attractions were unsuccessful. In April 1776, the Machine was no longer able to perform the journey under two days, and in the November following was obliged to reduce the number of its journies to two in a week; while Mr. Lawrence, in addition to his Fly in a day and a half, set up (April 13) a " new Diligence, which carries three people commodiously, at £1. 11*s*. 6*d*. in one day," three times a week.

[1] See the last note.
[2] Mr. Elisha's paper quoted below.
[3] His road from Oswestry to Cerrig y Druidion is through Llanarmon and Cynvyd.
[4] " Sixty-two miles, bad roads and inns."

between Holyhead and London, Bath, Bristol, &c., either by way of Shrewsbury or Chester,—for the very great encouragement and support they have received, which has enabled them to carry on their plan of fixing the rates of travelling on this road to the same rates as in England." They state their determination " to run chaises with pairs at 9*d*. a mile; post-coaches with four horses at 1*s*. 3*d*.," and " to render travelling through Wales agreeable and expeditious." Mr. Lawrence is no party to this advertisement: but, on the 3d of July following, he, in conjunction with the others, set up a post-coach from this town to Holyhead, in a day and half, thrice a week, by the way of Wrexham, Mold, St. Asaph, and Conway; fare £2. 2*s*.[1]

This coach, it is plain, could never be a formidable rival to those through Chester, as it retained all the disadvantages under which they labour, of the double ferry. But in May 1780, Mr. Lawrence started a new one by way of Oswestry, Corwen, Llanrwst, and Conway, without, however, relinquishing his concern in that through St. Asaph. He was, perhaps, unwilling to break, as long as he could avoid it, with the persons interested in the old line of road. But the proprietors of the Chester coaches immediately took the alarm: and in the very next paper after his announcement of his new coach (May 11), in which, after thanking the publick for the support already shewn to his carriages, he entreats their further patronage, " without which," says he, " several years' labour, and great expence he has been at in endeavouring to open a communication between Holyhead and London by way of Salop, as well as Bath and Bristol, and also the great benefit that must arise from travellers to the town of Shrewsbury, and the country through which such carriages pass, will be entirely lost:" and he adverts, in terms of resentment, to the conduct of his opponents in threatening Mr. Payton with an opposition to his coaches from Birmingham through Oxford, if he did not abandon his connexion with Lawrence.

This threat of the Chester proprietors was, in the following month, carried into effect: and The Defiance, from the Raven and Bell, took the Worcester road to London, thus avoiding Stratford. But this competition, while it was a benefit to Shrewsbury by affording an increased communication with the metropolis, was of no injury to the Irish road, or to Mr. Lawrence, who on removing to the Lion (Nov. 4, 1780) announced his determination to pursue with unremitting industry the object he has for so many years laboured to accomplish, and expressed his hopes that " the gentlemen commissioners, and every other well-wisher to these towns and country will exert themselves, in improving the roads," so as to convince travellers " of the great saving and advantage which must accrue to them upon these roads in preference to any other, and of the superiority of the accommodations." This enterprising character did not stop here. He used

[1] This coach appears to have ceased running in the summer of 1783.

great personal exertion to improve the roads, and prevailed on several persons who had been upper servants in great English families to establish inns at the several stages: thus inducing the principal Irish travellers, by the prospect of superior accommodations, to prefer the Shrewsbury line, which saved them Conway Ferry, and was about two miles shorter.

These exertions were not made in vain. The editor of the Shrewsbury Chronicle, Feb. 3, 1781, is "happy to inform the publick, that the travelling through this town daily increases:" and his paper for two or three years, at various intervals, records the names of travellers of any note who came this way. Soon after (Apr. 14) Mr. L. extended his views still further, "and we have not a doubt," says the Chronicle, "from the rapid increase of business on this road, if proper application is made, one, if not both, of the Irish mails will pass through this town." April 13, 1782, care is taken "to inform the publick that the new road through Wales, via Llanrwst, has, by the activity of Mr. Lawrence, been kept open during the late inclement weather, notwithstanding most other roads were rendered impassable by the heavy falls of snow." These infant struggles of a measure, the completion of which we now witness, will not be uninteresting to those who love to contemplate the prosperous issue of industry and talent directed with perseverance. On the 3d of September, the new lord lieutenant of Ireland, earl Temple, arrived at the Lion, and was attended by the corporation in their formalities[1]. "*His lordship said he was extremely glad the Shrewsbury road had been recommended to him, as he found it, not only considerably nearer, but the accommodations were in every respect perfectly to his satisfaction.*"

The indefatigable Lawrence, in Feb. 1784, determines "to use every effort to establish effectually what he has so long laboured at a great expence to accomplish." Yet as late as Oct. 5, 1792, it was deemed not inexpedient to state that "the posting business from Ireland, by way of Holyhead through Shrewsbury, has of late increased prodigiously." But the Union of the kingdoms (1800) and the consequent annual journies of the members of the Irish legislature to the metropolis of the empire, made this road an object of still greater moment, and still further stimulated his exertions. About the year 1802, he procured the commencement of a shorter line of road, which was completed in the autumn of 1804[2], through Capel Curig and Bangor, to the exclusion of Llanrwst and

---

[1] Chronicle of that date. "His lordship," it adds, "complimented the mayor with a banner of his arms elegantly emblazoned, which, we hear, is to be fixed in the county hall when completed." We learn from Isaac Walton's Life of Sir Henry Wotton (p. 45), that in the reign of James I. ambassadors (at least English ambassadors) did the same thing: as was the usage of all the German nobles in the days of Erasmus. See his pleasant Colloquy On Inns. And Montaigne, when at the baths of Plombieres in Lorraine, "me commanda," says his secretary, "à la faveur de son hostesse, selon l'humeur de la nation, de laisser un ecusson de ses armes." Journal du Voyage, &c. t. i. p. 36. It was the established practice for all lords lieutenants to leave behind them, at the inns where they slept, their coat of arms and titles.

[2] It is not till June 28, 1805, that we find a coach advertised by that road.

Conway; thus effecting a saving of eight miles. In this undertaking he found an active and munificent patron in the late lord Penrhyn, to whom, indeed, the idea is by some, and perhaps justly, ascribed. The new road was a very favourite scheme of that nobleman; who, in furtherance of it, erected a very large and handsome inn at Capel Curig. This road has since received the last improvements of Mr. Telford, and is now, perhaps, the finest in the world. It has hitherto placed the route through Shrewsbury beyond the reach of competition from Chester: and the road now maintains a mail coach, and two other daily coaches.

In the mean time, to the Machine and Fly coaches to London, which we have seen the only coaches to London in 1776, and those confined to two journies a week, was added, in January 1780, a post-coach from the Raven, at first once, but soon afterwards thrice a week. It travelled in "two easy days," and lay at Stratford; but in the following spring was advertised at one day. This was followed (June 1780) by the Defiance. In the summer of 1785, Mr. Lawrence succeeded in "procuring a mail upon Mr. Palmer's plan," and the first mail coach from London to Shrewsbury began to run on the 5th of September: and from this period it would be tedious to enumerate the gradual accession which has been made to the number of these conveyances. The journey which thirty-five years before required four days, and only ten years before that, double the number, might, in August 1788, be performed in twenty-two hours, and by later improvements (Oct. 1822) is now reduced to eighteen: while the two London coaches, twice a week, of 1776, are multiplied to seven every day, besides daily mail coaches to Chester, Hereford, Welsh Pool, and Newtown, and other coaches, thirteen in number, to Chester, Manchester, Worcester, Aberystwith, Holyhead, and Birmingham, thus creating such an influx of travelling through Shrewsbury, as greatly supplies, if it does not quite compensate, the injury it has sustained by the diminution of its trade in Welsh woollens.

In the course of the preceding history we have noted all such instances as have occurred of visits paid to this town by branches of the royal family. In pursuance of those examples, it is proper to record, that on Saturday, July 30, 1803, prince William of Gloucester, the King's nephew, came here on his road to Liverpool, to which he was repairing, for the purpose of taking the command of the north-west military district. His highness, having been applied to for information at what hour he would permit the corporation to have the honour of waiting upon him, was pleased to appoint the following morning at half-past ten o'clock, at the Lion inn: when, after an appropriate address pronounced by the high steward, Joseph Loxdale, esq., to which the prince made a suitable return, extremely well expressed, and pretty much at length, on the existing circumstances of the country, a circle being formed, he paid his compliments to each individual of the body. He then, accompanied by the mayor and other officers, proceeded to divine service in St. Chad's church; and left a very pleasing impression on the minds of the inhabitants who witnessed the propriety of his demeanour. He was the first prince of the blood that had visited Shrewsbury since the Revolution.

On Tuesday, Oct. 9, 1804, his royal highness the duke of Gloucester passed through this town on returning from a visit to his son at Liverpool.

And on the evening of Tuesday, Sept. 9, 1806, his royal highness George prince of Wales, accompanied by the duke of Clarence, passed through Shrewsbury on his way to Rossall and Loton, the seats of Cecil Forester, esq. M. P. (now lord Forester), and sir Robert Leighton, bart. His royal highness made no stay in the town; but having changed horses in the Abbey Foregate, passed under the walls by St. Chad's church and Barker-street to Rossall, where, on the following morning, he was, according to his royal highness's pleasure signified to that effect, attended by a select deputation of the corporation, consisting of the mayor, senior alderman, and high steward[1], which last gentleman delivered a loyal address, and received a gracious answer.

A considerable event respecting Shrewsbury, intimately connected with the comfort and health of its inhabitants, has recently occurred, and will form an appropriate conclusion to the present history. While most other towns, many of very inferior pretensions, had advanced in the scale of internal improvement, this remained stationary. Its streets continued almost as narrow and crooked as they had been for centuries before: its pavement of the rudest description, its thinly scattered lamps diffusing little more than a *visible darkness*, and its air polluted by the exhalations of open kennels. These and similar nuisances were occasioned by the scanty provisions of our Street Act of 29 George II.; the funds created by which were so limited as to prevent the possibility of incurring any expence to remove those grievances. Many ineffectual attempts had been made to obtain a new act: but the town-meetings convened for that purpose had uniformly withheld their consent from such a measure.

At length, on the 28th of May 1821, a bill received the royal assent, which, though not so perfect as it might have been, has conferred such powers upon a Committee of Management, as have already produced considerable effects. The committee was selected on the 18th of June, and immediately proceeded on their task. Their first step was to make an agreement with the new gas company, which had been incorporated by act of parliament in the preceding year. The town began to be supplied with that species of light on the 8th of September: and this great improvement was carried through all the streets before the commencement of the next

---

[1] William Wilson, William Smith, and Joseph Loxdale, Esquires.

winter: with an extension of the period of lighting from seven months to eight, and from seven hours, or scarcely that, to eleven. In the same winter of 1821, the watch was regulated upon an improved system. The narrowest parts of several streets have been progressively widened and their corners rounded; as at Lee Stalls on Mardol Head; at the turning from Pride Hill into High Street; from Carrier's End towards Murivance and Barker Street; from Swan Hill into Cross Hill. The line of houses has in many places been rendered straight, by the removal of projecting steps and windows. A path for foot passengers, which before existed only in a few parts, has been secured by curb-stones, and flagged, or paved with brick, or small pebbles. More than all these, as conducing to the comfort of the town as an healthy and agreeable residence, it was resolved, at the commencement of 1823, to under-drain the streets by common-sewers; and this grand measure is, in great part, accomplished. Other improvements are carrying on or contemplated: particularly in the widening of Dogpole, and Ox Lane; the removal of St. Mary's almshouses; and the opening a thoroughfare through that churchyard at fair-times: and if the Committee of Management continues to be judiciously chosen, and faithful to its trust, our town may, in time, assume its due place among the cities of the empire.

Yet it must be owned, when the Committee have done all they can, Shrewsbury will still remain far distant from the cleanliness and comfort which the declivity of its streets renders so practicable, and the pre-eminent beauty of its situation so well deserves. Greater powers than the new act confers are requisite to provide a spacious market, by which the streets shall be relieved from the encumbrance of booths, sheds, and shambles, and the meat no longer exposed in an offensive butchers' row; and to banish to an eligible contiguous situation the monthly cattle-fairs, by which the lives and limbs of passengers are endangered, and more than one of their senses grievously annoyed. The pavement, too, must ever continue rugged, jolting, and full of deep holes, as long as three-ton waggon-loads of coal, which might be carried across the Raven meadow, drag along our streets in ponderous succession. Till these and some other enormities, such as numerous and dangerous trap-doors, and the shooting down of coal in the streets at all hours, are redressed, of which there appears no present likelihood, we are compelled to conclude that Shrewsbury is, in some respects, very imperfectly rescued from the barbarism of ancient Pengwern, and that what the poet says of the drama of his country, may be applied, with little variation, to the subject before us:

> Horridus ille
> Defluxit numerus Saturnius, et grave virus
> Munditiæ pepulere: SED IN LONGUM TAMEN ÆVUM
> MANSERUNT, HODIEQUE MANENT VESTIGIA RURIS.

CORPORATE OFFICERS.

To the preceding history we subjoin lists of the corporate officers, as far as they can be recovered.

PRÆPOSITI.

It has been sufficiently stated in the preceding pages[1], that the chief magistrate of Shrewsbury in the Norman times was a provost (præpositus); whose office it was to collect the burgesses' rents.

REINER the provost, or, as he is sometimes called, prefect, who gave land in the town fields of Shrewsbury (campis urbis) to the abbey of Shrewsbury, pro filio quem fecit monachum, in the time of Henry I., when Richard de Belmeis was steward, is the first upon record.

AILRIC RUFFUS, who gave the same monks other land in the same fields, was perhaps another, and may have been the same with EDRIC the provost.

ROBERT the prefect, the son of Andrew the clerk, bequeathed the same monks all his land in the fields after his mother's death.

EDRIC.

PETER the provost appears to have been brother of John son of

[1] Page 39.

Clement son of Peter burgess of Shrewsbury: which John was a benefactor to the abbey.

RICHARD Rusticus. Chartulary of Haghmond abbey. He occurs both singly and as colleague with another: and may have been the connecting link between the single and double provosts.

We find no other names of provosts while the office was held by a single person: i. e. while the appointment was in the earl or king. In whom it was vested when Henry II. gave or restored to the burgesses of Shrewsbury free customs, does not appear. But from the time (1199) that king John empowered them to elect *two* of their body annually to hold the *prepositure* or provostship of the town, we are sure that it was governed by two provosts till the middle of Edward I.'s reign, when that title was changed to *bailiff*: and though the regular series of our FASTI CONSULARES does not commence till 1372, yet the attestations of private deeds preserve the names of a considerable number of these annual officers under both their titles. Unfortunately, the practice of dating deeds was not fully established in England before the close of Edward I.'s reign: so that of many of these magistrates we are unable to fix the year with certainty.

PROVOSTS OF SHREWSBURY.[1]

*King John began his reign
6 April, 1199.
Among our earliest provosts are probably*
Richard Rusticus, and William son of William.
Gamul, and Reiner: H.: called also
Gamel de Romoldesham, and Reiner son of Martin. H.
Richard Pride, and Walter son of Feirwin. H.
Reiner Ruffus, and Robert son of William: perhaps the same with
Robert Infans, or le Child, who occurs colleague of Reiner Ruffus, or, as he is elsewhere called, Reiner son of Ruffus.
Robert de Sulton, and Warin son of William.
1212. Alan Villanus, or the Villein, and Robert Pally:
  probably a mistake, as they occur again after 1256.
Thomas son of William, and John son of Robert, between 1204 and 1217.

The following probably belong to this reign:
Roger son of William, and John son of Hugh.
Lucas de Coleham, son of Walter, and Walam Poncer. S. 186.
William son of John, and Clement son of Peter. S. 202.
John Seimbel: John son of Agnes. H.
John Poncer: John Seimbel. S. 175. }
John Villan: John Louhe.   }

*Henry III. began his reign
19 Oct. 1216.*
Roger son of Pagan or Payn, and John son of Hugh.
Hugh son of Ethel, and Warin son of William.
Alan son of Ivo, and Hugh Champeneys or Chaponoys.
The above before 1224.

---

[1] In the ensuing lists S. denotes the chartulary of Shrewsbury Abbey, and the figures after it, the *number* of the deed in that manuscript; and H. that of Haghmond. The deeds in this last are without any number. P. stands for the list in Phillips. Those without a reference are chiefly copied from the papers of Mr. Elisha, who took great pains with this part of our antiquities. With some of them we are not, however, quite satisfied: and must intreat the indulgent acceptance of our readers. The year prefixed to any names denotes *that* in which the respective provosts or bailiffs were elected, which was, at that time, on the Sunday after the 1st of September. The names connected by a *brace*, seem to have followed in a consecutive series, or nearly so.

PROVOSTS.

The following probably belong to an early period of this reign:

Andrew son of Hubert, and Reiner Ruffus. H.
Peter son of Clement, and Roger son of Reyner. S. 410.
    called also Roger Reiner. H.
Andrew son of Hubert, and Robert le Child. H.
Alan son of Gamel, and John de Norton. S. 195.
Warin Infans, and Hugh son of Hugh Hathebronde. H.
Alan Shitte: Richard Crawe. H.
John de Hibernia: Simeon son of Thurstan. S. 175.
Richard Pride[1]: Henry son of Ivo.
William son of John: Clement son of Peter.
Richard Pride: Richard English. S. 175.
Alan son of Herbert, and John de Hibernia. H. perhaps the same with
John de Forieta, who occurs as colleague of Alan son of Herbert. S. 434.
Robert son of John: Richard Crawe. H.
William son of Robert: Robert Sitte.
Ernald Corde: Gilbert son of Wimund. S. 424.
Peter Juvenis: Hugh Villanus. H.
Richard Winnepeni: Adam son of Thurstan, or as he is elsewhere called,
Adam Kinge. S. 198. 428. H.
Thomas son of William: John son of Robert.
Laurence Cox: William Gogh. H.
Robert Pride: William Goch, son of Warin. H.
Hugh le Vileyn: Reiner Porchet. H.
Richard, son of Reiner: Alan Sitte. S. 207.
Robert Poncer, and Richard son of Reiner. S. 411. c.
Adam Cox: Reginald or Reiner Porchet. H.
John le Vileyn: John Burgh. P.
John Villanus: Simon Granegos. P.
Hugh Colle: John le Willeyn. H.
John Villanus: Hugh Colley. P.
Roger Russel: William Goch. H.
Peter son of Clement, and Roger Reyner: between 1241 and 1252.
Galfrid Rondolfe: Richard Borrey: between 1241 and 1252. H.

1246. Hugh le Vileyn, and Peter son of Martin: the same in 1261.
Alan le Vileyn and Robert Paelli.
Ric. Pride, et Ric. fil. Reineri. (S. 164. 429. tempore Reginaldi Pinzun.)
Rog. Russel: Will. Goch: prepositus. S. 165.
Rich. Schitte, et Lucas fil. Walteri. S. 169. et H.
Andreas fil. Hubert, et Hen. fil. Ivonis. (S. 167. 175. 188. where they attest a charter of Goronovw abbot of Pole: in 173 called Prætores.)
Alan Villanus and Rob. Pally or Paely: after 40 H. 3. (H. art. Derefald.)
Clement son of Peter occurs after 1256.

Edward I. began his reign 16 Nov. 1272.

1277. Richard Borry and Richard Stury.
The following seem to belong to an early period of his reign:
John Palmernis, and Laurence son of Edwin. S. 196.
Peter Villanus, and John. S. 196. 412. 203.
Henry de Hereford, and Peter Villanus. H.
John son of Hugh, and John Russel. P.
Galfrid son of William Randolf, and Thomas Colle. P.
Richard Villanus, and William son of William: succeeded by
Henry Wildegos: Roger de Hibernia. S. 190.
Henry Wildegos: Roger Clericus: probably the same.
William son of William son of John: Clement son of Peter. H.
Henry Palmarius: Henry Wildegos. H.
Ralph le Kente, and Richard son of Robert Stury. H.
William son of Nicholas: Robert Pride. S. 172.
1282. Thomas Champeneys and William Vaghan.
1283. Andrew son of Hubert, and Reiner Ruffus.
1288. Hugh Bernard and William Vahhan. H.
1293. Johannes Roberti: John Gamel[2].

BAILIFFS.

1294. John de Ludlow, jun.: Richard Stury. H.
1295. Nicholas Ive: Nicholas de Picheford: they call themselves *Bailiffs of the Liberty of the Town.*
1296. John de Perla and Henry le Wildegose[3].
1298. Thomas de Bykedon and Alan Clement.
1300. Richard son of Richard Pride, and Geoffrey Rondulph[4].

---

[1] Richard Pride occurs also as provost after 40 H. III.   [2] In office 18 Jan. 22 Edw. I.
[3] They are stiled *bailiffs or provosts.*
[4] In office Feb. 1300 (i. e. 1300-1).

BAILIFFS.

The following appear to be about this time:
Geoffrey Rondulph: Richard Borrey.
John Stury: William le Parmenter. P.
Thomas de Bykedon: William le Parmenter.
Ralph le Kente: Richard son of Robert Stury.
Richard Pride junior: Laurence son of William.
John Roberd[1]: John de la Pole. P.
1304. William Vaghan: John Gamel.
1305. Hugh le Donfowe: Tho. de Bykedon.
1306. Simon de Stafford: William le Parmenter.

Edward II. began his reign 7 July, 1307.
1309. Thomas de Bykedon: John Baldwin.
1311. William Vaghan: John Gamel.
1312. Roger Pride: Nicholas Spicer[2].
1314. Hugh le Donfowe: Nicholas le Child.
1315. Tho. de Bykedon: Reginald Perle.
1316. Roger Pride: Nicholas Spicer[3].
1318. Thomas de Bykedon: Hugh son of Robert le Donfowe.
1319. Tho. de Bykedon: John Reyner[4].
1321. Gregory Montisgomeri: John Hagwas.
1324. Geoffrey Rondulph: John Baldwin.
Geoffrey Rondulphe: Robert Spicer.

Edward III. began his reign 25 Jan. 1326,7.
1330. Hugh son of Robert le Dunfowe: John de Weston.
1332. John Reyner: Tho. Colle junior.
1334. John Reyner: John le Walische.
1336. John de Weston: Tho. Ive.
1337. John Stury: John Tour.
1340. John Stury: Tho. Colle[5].
1342. John de Upton: Reginald Perle.
1343. Thomas le Foremon: ....
1344. John Stury: Will. le Skynner.
1345. John de Upton: John de Foriate.
1346. Tho. Gamel: Richard de Weston.
1347. Reginald Perle: John Tour.
1348. John de Loddelowe junior: Richard Stury[6].
1349. John Stury: Will. son of Roger de Withyford[7].
1350. Walter de Smythecote: Rob. de Upton.
1351. John Stury: Will. le Skynner, called also le Parmenter.
1352.
1353. Thomas Gamel: Will. de Smythecote.
1354. Reginald Perle: Roger de la Yate.
1355. John Stury: Will. de Byrinton.
1356.
1357. William Vaughan: John Gamel.
1358. John Stury: Will. de Byrinton.
1359. John Stury: Will. le Skynner.
1360. Tho. de Mutton: Rog. de la Yate.
1361. John Stury: Will. de Longenolre.
1362. Will. de Birinton: ....
1363. Robert de Thornes: Will. de Longenolre.
1364. John Stury: Richard Russel.
1365. Reginald Perle: John de Schotton.
1366. John Stury: Tho. de Birinton.
1367. John Stury: John Schotton.
1368. Will. de Longenolre: Tho. le Skynnere[8].
1369. John Geffery: Will. de Biriton.
1370. Rich. de Beorton: Reginald le Skriveyn.
1371.
1372.[9] Tho. de Byryton.
S. 3 greyhounds A. collared G. within a border of the last.
Roger atte Yate.
Quarterly S. and A. on a bend of the 1st 3 mullets of the 2d.

---

[1] This marks the manner in which patronymics gradually slid into surnames. This person a little higher up is called in Latin Roberti: a few years before it would have been *filius* Roberti, *son of* Robert. [2] In office 25 July, 7 Edw. II.
[3] In office on the feast of St. Peter ad Vincula, (1 Aug.) 11 Edw. II.
[4] In office Friday before St. Simon and Jude, 13 Edw. II.
[5] In office Feb. 8 and Aug. 15, 15 Edw. III.
[6] In office on the Purification of B. V. M. 23 Edw. III.
[7] On Friday after St. Matthew's day, 23 Edward III.: they are styled bailiffs elect.
[8] In office on Monday before the Nativity of St. John the Baptist, 43 Edw. III.

[9] From this year the names of the bailiffs are regularly entered in the first book of our corporation, marked A., the orthography of which is adopted in the ensuing list; and which carries us down to the middle of the sixteenth century. The armorial bearings subjoined to the several bailiffs are taken from a curious MS. in our School library; in which Robert Owen, gent. " bearing singuler affection to the place of his nativitie," collected the " escouchions" of the several bailiffs. Though Mr. Owen was "·authorized by the court marshall of England a deputy herald of this and severall other adjacent counties," we must not give implicit credit to all the coats which he has set down. It is little likely that many Shrewsbury burgesses bore such distinctions, in the fourteenth and fif-

VOL. I. 3 Y

1373. John Stury¹.
: A lion rampant G. tail fourchee.
Regin. de Mutton.
: Per pale B. and G. an eagle with two heads displayed O.
1374. Richard de Pontisberie².
: Per chevron S. and B. in chief two leopards' faces O. in base a dolphin naiant A.
or,
G. on a fesse O. between 3 martlets A. as many fleurs de lys B.
" The first is upon a tombe in the parish church of St. Almond's betwene the quier and the aulter."
John Geffrey.
: Ermine a lion rampant and dexter canton S.
1375. Will. de Withyforde.
: Paly of 8 O. and G. on a chief A. 3 pellets.
Rog. de Foryate.
: O. a triple pile S. issuing from the dexter chief in bend towards the sinister base.
1376. Regin. de Mutton³.
Thomas Pride.
: B. 3 preeds (small lamperns) in pale hauriant A.

Richard II. began his reign July 16, 1377.

1377. Will. de Longenore.
: A. 2 pallets G. over all on a bend S. 3 crescents of the field.
John Geffry.
1378. Will. de Biriton.
James le Dyer.
: Gyronny of 8. O. and G.
1379. Ric. de Beorton.
: A. 2 bars S.
Will. de Weston.
: S. a lion rampant A. collared G. chained of the field.
1380. Will. de Biriton.
Tho. Pryde.
1381. Tho. le Skynner.
: Per chevron O. and B. 3 fleurs de lys counterchanged.
Ric. Russel.
: A. a fesse between 3 water bougets S.

1382. Will. de Biriton.
Hugh le Donfowe.
: A. on a chevron between 3 cross crosslets fitchee S. 3 mullets pierced O.
1383. Tho. Skynner.
Thomas Pryde.
1384. Will. de Biriton.
Regin. de Mutton.
1385. Will. de Biryton.
Hugh Wygan.
: A. 3 pallets B. over all a fesse G.
1386. John Geffrey.
Regin. de Mutton.
1387. Richard Stury.
Will. de Byryton.
1388. Robert de Thornes.
: S. a lion rampant gardant A.
Hugh Wygan.
1389. Hugh Donfowe.
James le Dyer.
1390. Regin. de Mutton.
Robert de Grafton.
: Per saltire S. and Erm. a lion rampant O.
1391. Sim. de la Towr.
: S. 3 towers embattled A. 2 and 1.
Radulf de Forde.
: O. 2 bars wavy B.
1392. John Geffrei.⁴
Will. de Byryton.
1393. Thomas Pryde.
Will. Willylei.⁵
: A. a chevron Erm. between 3 escocheons V. each charged with 2 bars and a border of the field⁶. In Le Neve the escocheons are G. and charged with a fesse V.
1394. John Tylere.
: Per saltire S. and O. a saltire Erm.
Ric. de Alduscote.⁷
: Per pale indented O. and G. a chevron party per pale S. and A.
1395. Will. de Biryton.
Regin. Skryveyn.
: A. guttée de sang a lion rampant S.

---

teenth centuries, when they were by no means generally introduced even among gentlemen of family. Very few of our bailiffs could have had them from the first: but the descendants of many obtained them by subsequent grants, and these are here ascribed to their ancestors. Whence Mr. Owen derived the rest we cannot say. The collector died in 1632, and his burial is recorded in St. Chad's Register on the 8th of November, as " Robert Owen, gentleman, an herald at armes :" but the book has been continued to 1724, and it is a valuable heraldical monument. Among Rawlinson's MSS. in the Bodleian library, in a volume of Peter Le Neve's, are the armorial bearings of our bailiffs, taken from collections made by Rob. Owen of Salop deputy to Clarenceux, down to 1624. They occasionally differ from those here given; but it is not worth while to note the variations. Where the arms are not specified, they are the same as when that name was last mentioned. ¹ In office June 48 Edw. III.
² In office Wednesday after the Nativity of B. V. M. Sep. 8, 48 Edw. III.
³ In office Sunday after St. Andrew, 50 Edw. III.
⁴ In office 21 Sept. 1392. ⁵ Alio loco *de*.
⁶ When this coat is repeated, the escocheons look more like inverted beehives.
⁷ Alio loco sine *de*.

BAILIFFS.

1396. John Geffrey.
James Dygher.
    Arms as Dyer.
1397. Will. Williley.
Nicholas Jerard.
    G. a lion passant gardant A. crowned O.
1398. Robert Thornes.
Will. Byriton.
    They were removed[1] on the Tuesday before Whitsuntide, 22 Rich. II. (1399) and
Tho. Paunteley,
    S. a fesse A. between 3 mascles voided O.
Ric. Alduscote,
    Elected the same day. They appear to have continued in office only to the next election day.
1399. James Dygher or Dyer[2].
Thomas Porter.
    S. 3 bells A. tongued O.
    Henry IV. began his reign 29 Sept. 1399.
1400. Thomas Skynner.
Reginald de Mutton.
1401. Robert de Grafton.
Will. Biryton.
1402. Robert Thornes.
John Scryveyn.
1403. Sim. de la Tour[3].
William Forster.
    Quarterly per fesse indented A. and S. in the first and fourth a bugle-horn strung of the last.
1404. Thomas Skynner.
Richard Stury.
1405. William Tour, he was the 2d bailiff.
Will. Biryton, senior,[4] Died.
John Perle junior, Elect.
    B. on a chevron between 3 leopards' faces O. as many mullets of the field.
1406. John Skryveyn.
John Perle junior.
1407. John Glover.
    S. 2 gloves pale-wise, dexter and sinister A.
David Rathebon.
    G. on a fesse A. 3 roses of the field.
1408. Richard Stury.
Nicholas Schetton[5].
    Erm. 3 chevrons S.; or B. a cross O.
1409. Robert Thornes.
Sim. de la Tour[6].
1410. John Perle[7].
William Tour.

---

[1] The circumstances attending the removal of Thornes and Byriton are singular, and deserve to be noticed. In the oldest book of the corporation marked A. are articles of accusation against one John Raves, one of the underbailiffs (i. e. what are now called serjeants-at-mace) of Shrewsbury. One of them runs thus: "And that the said J. R., on the 16th day of April, 22 Rich. II. at Shrewsbury, excited and procured many men of the community of the aforesaid town to rise and kill R. Thornes and W. Biriton bailiffs, and other good and lawful men having the government and rule of the town. By pretext (i. e. reason) of which excitation and procuration the said bailiffs and the rest despaired of their lives." The election of Paunteley and Aldescote is thus entered in the same book:

"Electio Ballivorum de novo A°. xxij do."

"Memorand. quod die mart' prox' ante fest' Pentecost' anno r. r. Ric'i secundi xxij do Robert' Thornes & Will' de Byriton remoti fuer' de officio Ballivor' virtute composicois ville Salop in presencia Hugonis Burnell militia unius Justic' d'ni Reg', Joh'is Beostan, Mathi del Mer & alior' generosor' tunc ibid' existencium ac omnium burgencium & communitatum ejusdem ville. Et eodem die & loco Thomas de Paunteley & Ric'us Aldescote ellecti sunt ad officium Ballivorum ville predicte & coram prefatis personis jurati, prout dicta composicio exigit & requirit."

How sir Hugh Burnell, baron of Holgate, and a justice of peace for Shropshire, at a time when that commission was confined to a very few of the very highest personages in every county, and how the gentlemen mentioned above, with all the governing part of the town, yielded to a compliance, which appears to us so weak, with the demands of a furious rabble, we are left to conjecture. A slight glance at the great events which were now passing in the kingdom may afford a probable one. Tuesday before Whitsuntide, 22 Rich. II., the day when these bailiffs were turned out in consequence of the riotous proceedings, was the 20th of May, 1399, not a week before the King embarked for Ireland, leaving the kingdom very generally disgusted by his gross injustice to the banished duke of Lancaster, who, availing himself of that popular feeling, soon after thrust his oppressor from the throne. Burnell was a secret but warm adherent of the duke; but whether the Shrewsbury tumult was connected with that great revolution must be left to the judgment of the reader. The bailiffs would of course support the legitimate government of Richard: Raves and his associates broke forth perhaps in favour of the usurper Henry IV.

[2] These are omitted in Taylor's MS. which makes Dyer and Porter elected in 1400: but this is certainly wrong.
[3] Al. l. sine *de la*.
[4] Al. loc. 2d bailiff.
[5] Al. loco *Shotton*.
[6] Al. loc. sine *de la*.
[7] Al. loc. *jun*.

1411. Nicholas Gerard.
William Hord.
G. on a chief A. a raven proper.
1412. David Holbache.
A. a cross S. and dexter canton Erm.
Richard Stury.

*Henry V. began his reign
March 20, 1413.*

1413. John Gamell senior.
O. 3 hammers S.
John Glover.
1414 Nicholas Shetton.
Robert Horsley.
S. 3 cinquefoils pierced A.
1415. David Rathebon.
John Schetton.
1416. Roger Corbet.
O. a raven proper.
John Perle.
They continued in office two years.
1418. Roger Forster.
William Hord.
1419. David Rathebon.
John Northampton.
O. a chevron disjointed G. between 3 pellets.
1420. John Glover.
Rob. Whytcombe.
S. 3 plates in fesse between 2 combs A.
1421. John Shelton.
Robert Horsley.

*Henry VI. began his reign
August 31, 1422.*

1422. John Perle.
Nic. Schetton.
1423. John Tour.
Vryan Seintpier, alias St. Piere.
A. a bend S. over all a label of three points G.
1424. John Gamell.
John Glover.
1425. John Schetton.
William Forster.
1426. Rob. Wytcombe.
Will. Boreley.
A. 3 tilting spears erected in fesse S.
or, A. a lion rampant S. debruised by a fesse checky O. and B.
1427. William Tour.
William Hord.
1428. Nicholas Schetton.
John Paunton.
Barry of 6. O. and G. a bend S.
1429. Roger Corbet.
Richard Hord.
1430. Thomas Forster.
Vrian Seinpier.

1431. William Hord.
John Schetton.
1432. Rob. Whitcombe.
Thomas Thornes.
1433. Nich. Schetton.
John Knyght.
A. 3 pales G. within a border engrailed B. on a canton of the 2d a spur with the rowel downwards O. leathered of the third.
1434. Thomas Forster.
Will. Burleigh.
1435. Richard Hoorde.
John Falk'.
V. a fleur de lys A.
1436. Thomas Thornes.
John Begget.
A. a chevron G. between 3 martlets S.
1437. Rob. Wytcombe.
John Scryven.
1438. John Gamel.
Rich. Boerley.
1439. Will. Boerley.
Thomas Otley.
A. on a bend B. 3 oat-sheaves O.
1440. Thomas Thornes.[1]
Thomas Mytton.
1441. Rob. Wytcombe.
John Mutton.
1442. Richard Boerley.
John Gamel.
1443. John Falke.
Thomas Oteley.
1444. Will. Boerley.
Richard Stury.
1445. Robert Eyton.
O. a fret B.
William Bastard.
O. a chevron engrailed between 3 cocks G.
1446. Thomas Forster.
Adam Goldsmyth.
G. a fesse A. between 3 pellets.
1447. John Knight.
John Falke, Died.
John Gamell, Elect.
1448. Will. Boerley.
Richard Stury.
1449. Roger Eyton.
John Hoord.
1450. Robert Scryven.
Thomas Lyd or Luyt.
A. an eagle with two heads displayed S.
1451. John Gamell.
William Bastard.
1452. Richard Stury.
Richard Boerley.

---

[1] Occ. 20 Jan. 1440,1.

BAILIFFS.

1453. John Colle.
A. a chevron G. between 3 scorpions S.
Phillip Grace.
O. a fesse G. between 3 leaves slipped V.
1454. William Boerley.
Robert Scryven.
1455. Roger Eyton.
John Trentam.
A. 3 griffins' heads erased S. 2 and 1.
1456. Richard Stury.
John Horde.
1457. Nic. Fitzherbert.
G. 3 lions rampant O.
Roger Adis.
G. an antelope's head erased at the neck O.
1458. Robert Scryven.
Nicholas Stafford.
A. a griffin segreant S. his beak and fore-legs O.
1459. John Trentam.
Tho. Byrington.
1460. John Knyght.
John Grafton.

Edward IV. began his reign
March 5, 1461.

1461. Thomas Wynnes.[1]
B. a fesse bretessed O.
Thomas Stone.
A. a cross G. in the dexter chief a catharine-wheel of the 2d.
1462. Thomas Lloyd, arm.[2]
William Ottley.
1463. John Baxter.[3]
A. a bat S.
Hugh Hosier.[4]
Per bend sinister ermine and ermines a lion rampant O.
1464. Richard Stury.
Thomas Mytton.
1465. Roger Knyght.
John Colton.
G. a fesse O. between 3 pellets.
1466. John Cole.
Edward Easthope.
Per chevron S. and Erm.
1467. John Trentam.
Thomas Ottley.
1468. Thomas Mytton.
Tho. Goldsmith.
1469. William Ottley.[5]
Tho. Pontesbury.

1470. Roger Knyght.[6]
John Baxter.
1471. Hugh Hosier.
Richard Wantnor.
A. chevron S. and chief B.
1472. Thomas Mytton.
John Trentam.
1473. Thomas Otteley.
Tho. Pontesbury.
1474. William Otteley.
Roger Horton.
Quarterly A. and B. a cross O.
1475. John Colle.
Rob. ap Egnion or Beynyon.[7]
Per pale O. and G. a pale indented counterchanged.
1476. Thomas Mytton.
Thomas Thornes.
1477. John Hoord.
Roger Knyght.[8]
1478. Thomas Ottley.
Tho. Byrinton.
1479. Tho. Goldsmith.
William Sugdon.
G. 6 billets A. 3, 2, and 1.
1480. Thomas Mytton.
Tho. Pontesbury.
1481. Thomas Thornes.
John Baxter.
1482. John Hoord.
John Guttyns.
Lozengy sinister bendwise A. and G

Edward V. began his reign
April 9, 1483.

Richard III. began his reign
June 22, 1483.

1483. Rich. Wantnor.
John Ottley.
1484. Thomas Mitton.
Roger Knyght.

Henry VII. began his reign
August 22, 1485.

1485. Thomas Thornes.
Nic. Pontesbury.
1486. John Hoord.
John Baxter.[9]
1487. Rich. Wantenor.
John Otteley.

---

[1] In office on Ascension-day 1462.
[2] In office Feb. 1462,3.
[3] In office Monday after St. Nicholas 3 Ed. IV. and Feb. 1463,4.
[4] He is called also Trevor and Pimley.
[5] In office July 1470.
[6] Annus 49 H. VI. & readpeois regie potestatis 1[mo], also 11 Ed. IV.
[7] Occ. July 1476.
[8] In office 17 Jan. 17 Ed. IV. i. e. 1477,8.
[9] Occ. Mar. 1486,7.

BAILIFFS.

1488. Thomas Mitton.
Roger Knyght.
1489. Thomas Thornes.
Tho. Pontesbury.
1490. John Guttyns.
Robert Thornes.
1491. Thomas Trentham.
Florence Seymper.
1492. Thomas Mitton.
Nic. Pontesbury.
1493. Will. Cole.
Will. Pontesbury.
1494. John Guttyns.
Lawrence Hosyer.
1495. Nic. Waryng.
G. on a fesse engrailed O. between 3 bucks' heads cabossed A. as many bugle-horns sans strings S.
Hugh Walker.
A. a chevron engrailed Erm. between 3 pellets each charged with a trefoil of the field.
1496. Thomas Mitton.
Edward Hosier.
1497. Roger Thornes.
Richard Forster.
1498. William Colle.
Lawrence Hosier.
1499. Nic. Pontesbury, Died.
Nic. Waringe, Elected.
John Lloyt.
1500. Thomas Mitton.
Thomas Trentham.
1501. Thomas Knight.
Edward Hosier.
1502. William Coll.
Richard Dicher.
Quarterly per fesse indented A. and S. 4 pellets counterchanged.
1503. Richard Mitton.
Tho. Withyford.
1504. Roger Forster.
Thomas Mytton, Died.
William Mytton, Elected.
1505. Roger Thornes.
Thomas Knight.
1506. Richard Lyster.
Erm. on a fesse S. 3 mullets O.
Edward Hosier.
1507. Tho. Trentam.
Edward Knight.
1508. William Mytton.
Tho. Wythyford.

*Henry VIII. began his reign
April 22, 1509.*

1509. Roger Thornes.
Thomas Knight.

1510. Nic. Waringe, Died.
Edward Hosyer, Elected.
David Ireland.
G. 6 fleurs de lys A. 3, 2, and 1.
1511. Tho. Trentham senior.
Thomas Kynaston.
A. a chevron engrailed between 3 mullets S.
1512. Tho. Trentam junior.
William Mytton, Died.
Richard Mytton, Elected.
1513. Thomas Knight.
William Jenyns.
A. a chevron G. between 3 levels S.
1514. Richard Pursell.
A. 2 bars nebulee G. over all on a bend S. 3 boars' heads couped A. tusked O. langued G.
Roger Luter.
B. a plate on the fesse point between 3 marquisses' coronets O. 2 and 1 within a border A.
1515. Robert Dudley.
O. a lion V. with 2 tails armed and langued G.
Roger Thornes.
1516. Tho. Trentham junior.
Tho. Hosyer.
1517. Thomas Knight.
William Jenyns.
1518. Richard Mitton.
Richard Pursell.
Barry of 6, A. and G. a bend, &c. as at 1514.
1519. David Ireland.
Tho. Wytheford, Died.
Rog. Luter, Elect.
1520. Randle Biston.
A. a bend between 6 bees S.
Edward Bent.
A. 2 bars G. within a border engrailed S.
1521. Roger Thornes.
Thomas Hosier.
1522. Roger Dudley.
Edward Cole.
1523. Adam Mitton.
William Bayly.
1524. David Ireland.
Randle Biston.
1525. Roger Thornes.
Thomas Hosier.
1526. Robert Dudley.
Edward Bent.
1527. Adam Mytton.
As before, with a crescent for difference.
William Bailie.
V. a chevron O. between 3 unicorns' heads erased A. horned of the 2d.
1528. Edmund Cole.
David Ireland.
1529. Thomas Hosyer.
Randolph Beyston.

BAILIFFS.

1530. Roger Thornes.
Richard Brickdale.
G. a fesse indented between 3 cross crosslets fitchee O.
1531. Robert Dudley.
Adam Mytton.
1532. Tho. Byrington.
Nicholas Purcell.
1533. Edward Cole.
Thomas Hosier.
1534. Richard Hussey.
Barry of 6. Erm. and G.
Will. Bayly, died at Bartlemewtyde.
John Watur, Elected.
B. a castle embattled A.
1535. John Thornes.
David ap Owen.
V. a chevron between 3 hinds' heads erased A.
1536. Roger Lewis, alias Pope.
O. 2 chevrons the uppermost G. the under one B. a canton of the last.
Nicholas Purcell.
1537. Edmund Cole.
Adam Mytton.
1538. Tho. Byrington.
Thomas Ireland.
1539. Richard Atkis.
A. a cross cotised of a tressure of half a fleur de lys between 4 mullets S.
David ap Owen, Died.
Rich. Brickdale, Elected.
1540. Nich. Purcell.
John Mackworth.
Barry Paly S. and Erm. on a chevron G. 3 crosses patee O.
1541. Adam Mytton.
Edward Hosier.
1542. Richard Mytton.
Tho. Byrington.
1543. Thomas Ireland senior.
Roger Luter.
1544. Humph. Onslowe.
A. a fesse G. between 6 falcons S. armed and belled O.
Nicholas Purcell.
1545. Tho. Montgomery.
G. a chevron Erm. between 3 fleurs de lys O.
Richard Dawes.
A. on a bend B. cotised G. 3 swans proper.
1546. Adam Mytton.
Roger Lewis, alias Pope.
*Edward VI. began his reign
Jan. 28, 1547.*
1547. Edward Hosier.
Will. Whittakers.
S. 3 mascles voided A. 2 and 1.

1548. Tho. Byrington.
John Mackworth.
1549. Richard Mitton.
Humph. Onneslowe.
1550. Nicholas Purcell.
Thomas Ireland.[1]
1551. Roger Luter.
Rich. Whittakers.[2]
1552. Sir Adam Mytton, knt.
Roger Lewys, alias Pope.[3]
*Mary began her reign
July 6, 1553.*
1553. Richard Mytton.
Richard Dawes.
1554. Nicholas Purcell.
Robert Ireland senior.[4]
1555. Hump. Onslowe.
Tho. Byrington.
1556. Tho. Montgomery.
John Dawes.
1557. Richard Mytton.
John Mackworth.
*Elizabeth began her reign
Nov. 17, 1558.*
1558. John Evans.
B. a chevron between 3 spears' heads A.
John Holliwell.
O. a bend A.
1559. Robert Allen.
S. a bend engrailed A. cotised O.
Rich. Owen, jun.
S. 3 nags' heads erased A.
1560. Tho. Montgomery.
William Tenche.
A. on a chevron between 3 lions' heads erased G. as many cross crosslets O.
1561. Richard Mytton.
Richard Dawes.
1562. Roger Luter.
Rich. Owen jun.
V. a chevron between 3 wolves' heads A. a crescent for difference, thereon a label of three points.
1563. Hump. Onslowe.
George Higgons.
V. 3 cranes' heads erased A.
1564. Rich. Owen sen.
Arms as 1559.
George Leighe.
A. a lion rampant G.
1565. Richard Purcell.
William Peers.
Quarterly O. and B. 4 pheons counterchanged.
1566. Robert Allen.
Rob. Ireland jun.

---

[1] In office 24 March, 1550,1.
[2] In office 2d Feb. 1551,2.
[3] In office 29 Sept. 1 Mariæ, 1553.
[4] In office 1st Oct. 2 and 3 P. and M. 1555.

BAILIFFS.

1567. Richard Mytton.[1]
Thomas Stury.
1568. George Leighe.
Ric. Owen senior.
1569. George Higgons.
George Proude.
O. a chevron barry of 6. G. and S.
1570. Hump. Onslowe.
Hugh Baynes.
G. 2 chevrons, in chief 3 escalop shells O.
1571. William Peers.
Thomas Burnell.
A. a lion rampant S. armed and langued G. crowned O. within a border B.
1572. Thomas Sherar.
A. a fesse G. between 3 torteaux each charged with a mullet O.
William Lowe.
Arms torn out. [G. 2 wolves passant A.]
1573. Richard Owen senior.
Richard Powell.[2]
A. 3 boars' heads couped S. tusked O. langued G.
1574. George Leighe.
George Higgons.
1575. David Lloyd.
S. 3 nags' heads erased A.
John Okell.
G. a chevron A. between 3 garbs O.
1576. John Dawes.
Richard Owen.
1577. Thomas Sherar.
Thomas Charlton.
G. 10 besants 4, 3, 2, 1.
1578. William Weale.
G. a bend gobony O. and B. between 6 crescents of the last.
Roger Harris.
O. 3 hedgehogs V.
1579. Rob. Ireland jun.
John Perche.
G. on a chevron O. between 3 fleurs de lys A. as many chess rooks S.
1580. William Jones.
A. a lion rampant V. vulned in the shoulder G.
William Heringe.
A. semee of cross crosslets 6 herrings hauriant O.
1581. Thomas Sherar.
Thomas Lewis.
G. a chevron Erm. between 3 Saxons' heads proper couped at the neck.
1582. William Tench.
Edward Owen.
A. a lion rampant and canton S.
1583. George Higgons.
Michael Chambre.
B. a dexter arm in fesse couped at the elbow and armed O. cuffed A. holding a rose G. stalked and leaved V.

1584. John Dawes.
John Webbe.
Quarterly A. and G. 4 crosses counterchanged.
1585. Richard Owen.
As 1576.
Richard Dawes.
1586. Thomas Sherar.
David Lloyd.
1587. George Higgons.
William Jones.
1588. John Perche.
Nicholas Gibbons.
Paly of 6 A. and G. on a bend S. 3 escallop shells O.
1589. Thomas Lewis.
John Davies.
A. a cross fleury engrailed S. between 4 Cornish choughs proper. On a chief B. a boar's head couped at the neck, of the field.
1590. Thomas Sherar.
Thomas Burnell.
1591. Richard Powell.
Edward Ireland.
1592. Robert Ireland.
Michael Chambre.
1593. Edward Owen.
As 1582.
Humphry Hughes.
S. a pile O.
1594. David Lloyd.
Thomas Lewis.
1595. William Jones.
Thomas Charlton.
1596. John Webbe.
Nicholas Gibbons.
1597. Thomas Burnell.
Rich. Cherwell.
S. a fesse O. between 3 plates.
1598. John Perche.
Richard Dawes.
1599. Thomas Edwards.[3]
G. a chevron engrailed between 3 boars' heads erased at the neck A. a crescent for difference.
Edward Owen.
1600. William Jones.
Thomas Lewis.
1601. Richard Higgons, tanner.
Thomas Jones.[4]
1602. John Perche.
Roger Marshall.
G. a bend engrailed O.
James I. began his reign March 24, 1603.
1603. Edward Owen.
John Hunt.
Per pale A. and S. a saltire counterchanged. A crescent for difference.

---

[1] He was bailiff six times: ob. Nov. 1591, æt. c. 100. [2] In office 3 April, 1574.
[3] "Mr. Edwards refused to weare scarlet, or to use the accustomed feasting in Christmas."
[4] Son of Mr. Wm. Jones, draper.

BAILIFFS.

1604. Richard Cherwell, Died.
Tho. Lewis, Died.
Edward Donne, Elect.
Arms torn out. [B. a wolf rampant A.]
Rob. Betton, Elect.
A. 2 pales S. each charged with 3 cross croslets fitchee O.
1605. Rowland Langley.
A. a fesse S. in chief 3 pellets. A crescent for difference, thereon a mullet.
Robert Stevens.
Per chevron B. and A. in chief 2 falcons rising O.
1606. William Wilkes.
Paly of 8, O. and G. on a chief A. 3 mascles voided of the 2d.
Arthur Kynaston.
A. a lion rampant S. armed and langued G. crowned O.
1607. William Jones.
Andrew Lewis.
As before, a crescent for difference.
1608. Richard Higgons.
John Nichols.
S. a pheon A. the point downwards.
1609. Robert Betton.
As before, a mullet for difference.
John Garbett.
G. a griffin segreant O. supporting a standard A. the staff twisted.
1610. Thomas Jones.
Hugh Harris.
1611. Thomas Wolley.
V. a bend counter-embattled A.
John Hawkeshead.
S. 3 tons O.
1612. Rowland Langley.
Rowland Jenks.
A. 3 boars' heads couped at the neck and a chief indented S. a mullet for difference.
1613. Richard Hunt.
As before, a martlet for difference.
Richard Betton, Died.
Thomas Gardner, Elected.
Per fesse A. and S. a pale counterchanged, 3 griffins' heads erased of the 2d.
1614. John Gardner.
Thomas Fawkener.
S. 3 falcons rising A. armed O.
1615. Thomas Jones.
Roger Blakeway.
A. on a bend engrailed 3 besants.
1616. John Nichols.
Richard Wynne.
A. an escallop shell S.
1617. Edward Donne.
As 1604.
Tho. Wingfield.
A. on a bend G. cotised S. 3 pair of wings conjoined in allure of the field.
1618. Arthur Kynaston.
John Garbett.

VOL. I.

1619. George Wright.
O. 3 trefoils slipped V. on a chief A. 2 pallets G.
Richard Gibbons.
1620. Roger Pope.
Howell Vaughan.
O. a lion rampant S.
1621. Sir William Owen, knight.
As 1582.
Thomas Jones.
1622. Robert Stevens.
Richard Hunt.
As 1613.
1623. Tho. Wingfield.
Leonard Hinckes.
G. a lion rampant A. within an orle of besants.
1624. John Studley.
G. on a chevron A. 3 cross croslets fitchee S.
Tho. Matthews.
Erm. a cross G.

Charles I. began his reign
March 27, 1625.

1625. Thomas Knight.
Charles Benyon.
Vaire A. and S. on a chief O. 3 mullets of the 2d, a crescent for difference.
1626. Richard Pershouse.
A. a fesse between 3 cross croslets fitchee S.
Richard Llewellin.
O. 3 chevronels G.
1627. Thomas Jones.
A. a lion rampant V.
Robert Stevens.
1628. William Rowley.
A. on a bend S. between 2 Cornish choughs proper, 3 escallop shells of the field.
Edw. Donne, Died.
Richard Gibbons, Elect.
1629. Robert Betton.
Daniel Lewis.
1630. George Hunt.
As 1603, a mullet for difference.
Simon Weston.
S. a lion rampant A. collared and chained G.
1631. Richard Hunt.
As 1603, without the difference.
Thomas Knight.
1632. George Wright.
Owen George.
S. a goat erect A. attired O. supporting a tree on a mount in base both V. at its foot an infant proper, vested G. swaddled A.
1633. John Poyner.
Torn out. [A. a parrot V.]
Andrew Griffiths.
A. a cross fleury engrailed between 4 Cornish choughs S. a chief B. a crescent for difference.
1634. Charles Benyon.
Thomas Hayes, draper.
A. on a chevron between 3 wolves' heads erased at the neck G. 5 besants.

3 z

534 MAYORS.

1635. Thomas Jones, esq.
As 1627.
John Proude, draper.
1636. Thomas Nichols, esq.
Simon Weston, draper.

1637. Richard Llewellin.
John Wightwick, draper.
B. on a chevron A. between 3 pheons points down O. as many crosses patee G.

MAYORS.

1638. Thomas Jones, first Mayor.
As 1580.
1639. Robert Betton, mercer.
1640. Hugh Harris, Died 16th June 1641.
Tho. Wingfield, Elected.
1641. Richard Gibbons.
1642. John Studley, draper.
1643. Robert Betton junior.
1644. Charles Benyon, gent.
1645. Thomas Niccols, esq.
1646. Thomas Knight, draper.
1647. Richard Llewellin, tanner.
1648. Owen George, mercer.

The Commonwealth of England,
Jan. 30, 1649.

1649. Thomas Hayes, draper.
1650. John Prowde, draper.
1651. Charles Benyon, gent.
1652. Richard Cheshire, draper.
G. 2 lions' paws A. issuing chevron-wise from the sides of the shield between 3 lures O. 2 in chief and 1 in base.
1653. Jonathan Rowley, draper.
1654. John Cooke, dyer.
Quarterly G. and O.
1655. Adam Webbe, draper.
As 1584.
1656. John Lowe, draper.
A. on a bend cotised B. 3 lions' heads erased of the first.
1657. Thomas Hunt, esq.
As 1631.
1658. John Betton, gent.
1659. John Walthall, draper.
Per pale A. and S. a saltire surmounted of another engrailed, both counterchanged.

Charles II. began his reign
May 29, 1660.

1660. Andrew Vivers.
Per pale O. and Erm. on a bend G. 3 unicorns' heads erased at the neck A. horned and maned of the 1st.
1661. Richard Baggott, draper. Displaced.[1]
Robert Forster, bookseller, Elected.
Quarterly per fesse indented S. and A. 1st and 4th a pheon point downwards, 2d and 3d a bugle-horn strung, all counterchanged.

1662. Sir Rich. Prince, knt.
G. a saltire O. surmounted of a cross engrailed Erm.
1663. Jonathan Langley, gent.
As 1605, without the difference.
1664. Edw. Kynaston, esq.
A. a lion rampant S. armed and langued G.
1665. Francis Burton, esq.
Quarterly, 1st and 4th party per pale B. and G. 2d and 3d G. and B. a cross engrailed O. between 4 roses A. barbed and seeded O.[2]
1666. Richard Waringe, gent.
1667. John Harding, gent. attorney-at-law.
G. 3 greyhounds current in pale O. collared of the field.
1668. Samuel Lloyd, draper.
B. a lion passant gardant O.
1669. Richard Taylor, gent. attorney-at-law.
A. 3 martlets S. 2 and 1.
1670. Thomas Cotton, draper.
B. a chevron Erm. between 3 hanks of cotton A.
1671. Roger Griffiths, gent.
As 1633, without the difference.
1672. Daniel Jevon, draper.
O. a torteau between 4 saltires G.
1673. Rowl. Middleton, mercer.
A. on a bend V. 3 wolves' heads erased at the neck of the field.
1674. William Thynne, gent.
Barry of ten O. and S.
1675. John Severne, gent.
A. on a chevron S. nine besants.
1676. George Hosier, gent.
1677. Robert Forster, bookseller.
1678. Edward Philips, draper.
A. 3 trefoils in pale between 2 flaunches V.
1679. Arthur Hinckes, gent. attorney.
1680. John Harwood, gent.
G. a chevron A. between 6 cross croslets fitchee O.
1681. George Llewellin, draper.
G. 3 chevrons A.
1682. Edward Gosnell, gent.
Per pale indented O. and B.
1683. Collins Woolrich, apothecary.
G. a chevron between 3 wild-geese volant A.
1684. John Wood, attorney. Died 31st Aug. 1685.
Robt. Wood, apothecary, Elect.
G. 3 demi wild-men A. holding in the right hand over the left shoulder a club O.

---

[1] Displaced by the act for regulating corporations.

[2] The field of this coat should be per pale B. and P.: but we describe it as in the MS.

MAYORS.

James II. began his reign
Feb. 6, 1684,5.

1685. Sir Fra. Edwards, bart.
As 1599, without the difference, charged with the arms of Ulster.
1686. Thomas Bawdewin, esq. barrister-at-law.
A. a saltire S.
1687. Richard Salter, draper.
S. 10 billets O. 4, 3, 2, and 1, within a border B. besantee.
1688. Rich. Muckleston, Displaced Oct. 29.
V. on a fesse between 3 greyhounds' heads erased at the neck A. as many crosses patee G.
John Hill, gent. Elected.
Erm. on a fesse S. a castle triple-towered and embattled A.

William III. and Mary II. began their reign
Feb. 13, 1688,9.

1689. Jonathan Scott, gent.
G. 3 Catharine wheels O. 2 and 1.
1690. Samuel Thomas, mercer.
G. a lion rampant regardant O.
1691. Charles Kynaston, gent.
As 1664.
1692. John Hollier, mercer.
A. on a chief B. 3 mullets O. within a border engrailed G.
1693. Arthur Tong, attorney, ob. 21 Sep. 1729.
G. on a bend A. 3 Cornish choughs proper, each holding in his beak a sprig of palm V.
1694. Samuel Adderton, draper.
A. 2 bends and a border S.
1695. Simon Hanmer, gent.
A. 2 lions B. statant gardant in pale, a crescent for difference.
1696. John Kynaston, esq.
As 1664.
1697. Robert Shepard, mercer.
S. on a chevron engrailed O. between 3 fleurs de lys A. as many etoiles of 6 points G.
1698. Andrew Johnson, dyer.
S. on a bend O. between 2 tirrets A. 3 pheons G.
1699. Moses Reignolds, attorney. Died 1700.
S. 3 nags' heads erased at the neck A.
Richard Presland, draper. Elected 11th May.
S. a lion rampant A. debruised by a bend counter compony O. and B.
1700. John Kinaston, draper.
As 1664, with a mullet for difference.

1701. Robert Phillips, draper.
Arms omitted. [Erm. a chevron between 3 falcons A.]
Anne began her reign
March 8, 1702.
1702. Rowland Bright, glover. Died March 1702,3.
B. a fesse wavy Erm. in chief 3 crescents A.
Thomas Harwood, Elected.
Arms omitted. [A chevron between 3 bucks' heads cabossed G.][1]
1703. William Bowdler, tanner.
Arms omitted. [A. 2 Cornish choughs proper.]
1704. William Leighton, mercer.
Arms omitted. [Per fesse indented O. and G.]
1705. Thomas Bowdler, draper.
1706. John Twiss, clothier.
Arms omitted. [.... a vine sprig slipped V. fructed O.]
1707. John Felton, brazier. Died.
Arms omitted. [G. 2 lions passant Erm. crowned O.
William Smith[2], apothecary. Elected.
S. a bend between 6 martlets A.
1708. Samuel Cooke, draper.
As 1654.
1709. William Clemson, barber.
A. a fesse dancette in chief 3 crescents G.
1710. Walter Pateshull, draper.
B. on a chevron A. between 3 hearts O. as many escallop shells G.
1711. William Turner, draper.
Ermines on a cross A. quarter-pierced of the field, 4 fer de moulins S.
1712. Jonathan Scott, draper
1713. Edward Jones, ironmonger.
G. 3 chevrons A.
George I. began his reign
Aug. 1, 1714.
1714. James Blakeway, mercer.
As 1615.
1715. Thomas Phillips, attorney.
B. a chevron between 3 falcons close A.
1716. Joseph Muckleston, grocer.
As 1668.
1717. William Kinaston, esq.
As 1664.
1718. Sir Chas. Lloyd, bart.
S. 3 nags' heads erased at the neck A. and the arms of Ulster.

---

[1] The arms within brackets are from a MS. of Mr. Elisha.
[2] Mr. Smith may have been the person alluded to in the following passage of "The Ancient Physician's Legacy to his Country, by Thomas Dover, M.D. 4th edit. 1733:" "I was lately called to an only son of a nobleman of the first quality, six months old. He had four physicians: *the famous Shropshire gentleman, fortunate to a proverb, quondam mayor of Shrewsbury*, at the head of them. He had been twice vomited, twice blooded, an issue out in his neck: his head, his back, his arms, his thighs, his legs, the soles of his feet, all blistered in four days time; when it pleased God, by death, to take him out of the hands of his tormentors." Dr. Dover's remedies are placed, in Medical Essays, v. ii. p. 406, (Edinburgh 1734) among the improvements made since the beginning of 1732.—The case he alludes to had "lately" occurred, and no other medical character appears among our mayors since 1684.

MAYORS.

1719. Henry Jenks, gent. attorney.
  As 1612, without the difference.
1720. Thomas Morhall, mercer.
  A. on a fesse embattled G. between 6 ravens proper, 3 palm branches of the field.
1721. Michael Brickdale, furrier.
  A. a chevron between 3 garbs of 5 arrows each, their points downwards G. banded O. a mullet for difference.
1722. Edward Gregory, ditto.
  O. 2 bars, in chief a lion passant B.
1723. Matthew Travers, grocer.
  S. a chevron between 3 boars' heads A. tusked and langued G.
1724. Thomas Lindop, malster.
  A. on a saltire B. 5 roses of the field.
  This is the last coat in Robert Owen's MS.
1725. Samuel Elisha, attorney.
  [G. 3 bulls' heads A. armed O.]
1726. John Adams, ironmonger.
  [Erm. 3 cats passant B.]

George II. began his reign
June 11, 1727.

1727. Joseph Jones, gent. attorney.
  As 1627.
1728. John Fownes, esq. barrister.
  [B. in chief 2 eagles displayed, in base a mullet A.]
1729. Godolphin Edwards, esq.
  [G. a falcon proper preying on a martlet A. a border engrailed O.]
1730. Rich. Woolaston, mercer.
1731. Abraham Davies, tin-plate worker.
1732. Richard Lloyd, draper.
1733. John Lacon, esq.
1734. John Rogers, bookseller.
1735. Sir Rich. Corbett, bart. of Longnor.
1736. Charles Bolas, gent. attorney.
1737. Robert More, esq. of Linley.
1738. Edward Corbett, esq.
1739. Brockwell Griffiths, esq.
1740. Edward Twiss, wool-merchant.
1741. Trafford Barnston, esq.
1742. William Turner jun., draper.
1743. Edward Elisha, gent. attorney.
1744. Francis Turner Blithe, esq.
1745. John Langley, gent. attorney.
1746. Isaac Pritchard, mercer.
1747. James Downes, esq. barrister.
1748. William Atkiss, gent.
1749. Thomas Fownes, esq.
1750. John Adams jun. ironmonger.
1751. William Oswell, malster.
1752. Thomas Wynne, grocer.
1753. Richard Jones, esq.
1754. John Cotton, bookseller.
1755. Edward Blakeway, draper.
1756. Baldwyn Leighton, esq.
1757. John Oliver, gent. attorney.
1758. John Bennett, goldsmith and toyman.
1759. John Ashby, gent. attorney.

George III. began his reign
Oct. 25, 1760.

1760. John Rocke of Trefnanney, co. Montg.
1761. Henry Adams.
1762. Robert Lord Clive.
1763. Pryce Owen, M.D.
1764. Richard Vaughan.
1765. Charles Bolas.
1766. John Kinchant.
1767. Thomas Wingfield of Alderton.
1768. Edward Vaughan.
1769. William Oswell.
1770. William Smith of Hinton.
1771. Edward Atkis.
1772. John Vaughan.
1773. James Winnall.
1774. Thomas Loxdale.
1775. Captain William Owen.
1776. Robert Corbett of Longnor.
1777. Charlton Leighton of Loton.
1778. Noel Hill of Tern.
1779. Edw. Cludde of Orleton.
1780. Joshua Blakeway.
1781. Robert Pemberton.
1782. John Flint.
1783. John Oliver.
1784. Samuel Harley.
1785. James Holt.
1786. Richard Rocke of Trefnanney.
1787. Thos. Kinnersley of Leighton.
1788. Wm. Oakeley of Tanybwlch co. Merioneth.
1789. Bold Oliver.
1790. John Bishop.
1791. Thos. Eyton of Eyton.
1792. Rev. John Rocke.
1793. Rev. Edw. Blakeway.
1794. Captain Thos. Pemberton.
1795. William Cludde of Orleton.
1796. Henry Bevan.
1797. Joseph Loxdale.
1798. Nathaniel Betton.
1799. Joseph Carless.
1800. Richard Bratton.
1801. Edward Stanier.
1802. Edward Burton.
1803. General Baldwin Leighton.
1804. Philip Michael Williams.
1805. William Wilson.
1806. William Prissick.
1807. Charles Bage.
1808. Robert Pemberton.
1809. Joseph Bromfield.
1810. Thomas Lloyd.

1811. Sir John Hill, bart. of Hawkstone.
1812. John Lee.
1813. William Coupland.
1814. Richard Philips. Died.
   William Harley. Elect.
1815. Samuel Tudor.
1816. Sir John Betton, knt.
1817. Joshua Peele.
1818. William Egerton Jeffreys.
1819. Rev. Hugh Owen.
   George IV. began his reign Jan. 29, 1820.
1820. Edward Cullis.
1821. Samuel Harley.
1822. Rice Wynne.
1823. Jonathan Perry.

RECORDERS.

The charter of Henry VI. 12 Jan. 24º regni, (1445,6) gives the bailiffs of Shrewsbury authority to hold sessions of gaol-delivery, associating with them some sufficient person, learned in the law, Recorder or Steward of the said town, ("quodam sufficiente legis perito recordatore vel seneschallo dicte ville.") This is the first mention which we have found in our records of the office or title of Recorder[1]: and it will be seen by the list of town-clerks, that nearly thirty years more elapsed before it was actually called forth into existence. *Legis peritus* is doubtless the Latin translation of the French term *Appris de la lei, Learned in the law,* the denomination of barristers in that age[2]. We cannot affirm, however, that John Phelyppes, who appears with the title of Recorder in 1473, 1482, and 1485, and is the first that we can find who bore it, was invested with that legal degree. But his successor Roger Mountgomerie, elected 1491, is proved to have been such by the following letter among the collections of Mr. W. Mytton, in which Richard Pontesbury, abbot of Haghmond, engaged in a law-suit with one Fowke, (probably Fulke Lee, esq. of Langley,) requests his professional advice, and reminds him that he had received the *general retainer* of a piece of cloth to make him a gown,—no incurious note of ancient manners.

"Most trusty beloved Sir,

"I recomend me unto you most hartely, dyssiring to here of your welfare, etc. Moreover, Sir, shewyng to you how that Fowke bee late time haue taken possession in the grownde at Hawrthon, the which ye haue the evidence therof, and he thynkythe to make a trobull in the cause thereof: wherefor I heartily pray your cowncell as I shall desire hyt unto you. Ye promysyd me at Shroysbury for a gowne clothe that ye wold undertake hyt while ye lyved: the which I shall be ready to performe, yf hyt please you that I may haue any

---

[1] London appears to have had a recorder as early as 1298. They were at first aldermen: but the qualifications for the office are thus set down in one of the city books, the date of which Maitland has neglected to give. "He shall be, and is wont to be, one of the most skilful and virtuous apprentices of the law, of the whole kingdom: whose office is always to sit on the right hand of the mayor in recording pleas, and passing judgements," &c. Maitland's Hist. of London, p. 1205.

[2] Our legal antiquaries have generally given *apprentice de la ley* as the ancient name of barristers: but Mr. Barrington proves, from the year books, that the title really was as stated in the text. Obs. on Stat. p. 311. It is, indeed, as he observes, very little likely "that the law, which was so liberally professed in England, and had such noble establishments, should have borrowed for one of its degrees in science, a term of mechanics and trade."

writyng from you betwixt this and Sonday night at Lychefeld for the cause, for I must be with my Lord of Chester at Ludlowe be Tewsday night: and yf your cowncell wer that I shuld do any thyng ther for the cause, I wold do hyt: and yf ye think hyt be not expedient to have eny thing don, that I may haue your cowncell be my servant at his cumyng to Shroysbery, which shall be hastely, as God knowethe, who keepe you. Amen. Wrytten at Lychefeld the xvii day of January.

"Item. Sir, yf hyt plese you to write me of your mynde, Thomas Gylder, my servand at Haughmond, will be with me on Sonday next; and I woll reward hym that bryngeth your writynge to the seide Thomas Gilder for his labor.

"Your owne thabbot of Haghmond.

"To my trusty beloved freende Roger Mountgomere, Recorder of Shroysebery [be] this bylle deliverd."

John Phelypps. In 1456 and 1468 he is called Common Clerk. His name is subscribed to the burgess roll, 1459: and it appears to have been his duty to enter the admissions of burgesses. In 1473, 1482, and 1485, he occurs as Recordator. He lived in Dogpole. See the list of Town-clerks.

1491. - - - Roger Mountgomerie. Elected.

1508. - - - George Bromley. In 1511 it is ordered that he have a fee of £1. 6s. 8d. as recorder, and that his former grant be resumed. He was still recorder in 1527.

George Harebrowne, esq. son of Thomas Harebrowne of Lyrpoole, in the county of Lancaster, was made a free burgess of the town of Shrewsbury in 1520. He could have been recorder only a few years.

1532. - - - Thomas Bromley, elected on Wednesday after Easter, with "£4 fee as long as he is abiding in the town, and that he shalnot be of counsell with thabbot of Salop, ner no burgess or inhabitant, and so doying to have £5 of fee."

Reginald Corbet. We have not found the date of his appointment, but it is entered on our books 27 Dec. 2 Eliz. (1559) that "Mr. Reynold Corbett, recorder, is made a justice of the Court of Common Pleas."

Sir John Throgmorton, 1569, 1574.
Sir George Bromley, 1582. ob. 1588.
Thomas Owen, esq. serjeant-at-law, 1592.
Richard Barker, esq. barrister-at-law, 1603, 1613.
Sir Edward Bromley, knight, baron of the exchequer, ob. 2 June, 1626.

1626. Sept. 25. Sir John Bridgeman, knight, serjeant-at-law, chief justice of the council in the Marches of Wales, ob. 5 Feb. 1637.

1637,8. Feb. 9. Timothy Tourneure, esq. barrister-at-law, and chief justice of South Wales, elected with a fee of £4. Displaced 17 Nov. 1645, "being by ordinance of parliament adjudged a delinquent, for which he now stands committed."

1645. Nov. 17. Humphrey Mackworth, esq. learned in the law. He appears to have resigned.

Edward Moseley, esq. On his being sent by parliament one of the judges into Scotland,

1652. July 14. Mr. Humphrey Mackworth, son of Humphrey Mackworth, esq. It seems as if neither of these gentlemen accepted the office; for

1654,5 March 1. William Jones, esq. is elected in the room of Humphrey Mackworth, esq. deceased: now the Humphrey Mackworth who died in December 1654, was certainly the same who was elected recorder in 1645: and the other, elected recorder in 1652, was certainly alive in 1659.

Sir Timothy Tourneur, knight, restored. He was made King's serjeant in 1670, and died in January 1676,7, aged 94.

RECORDERS—STEWARDS.

1676,7. Jan 2. Thomas Bawdewin, esq. of Diddlebury. He married a daughter of Humphrey Mackworth, esq. the recorder of 1645.
1685. - - - Charles Earl of Shrewsbury: removed by sign-manual, Jan. 1, 1687,8.
1687,8. - - William Marquis of Powis.
1690. - - - Thomas Burton, esq. of Longnor, barrister-at-law, and a Welsh judge, ob. 24 Apr. 1695.
1695. - - - Francis Berkeley, esq. See p. 501. ob. 1710.
1710. - - - Robert Middleton, esq. of Chirk Castle, ob. 5 April, 1733.
1733. - - - William Kinaston, esq. of Ruyton, barrister-at-law, master in Chancery, and M.P. ob. 24 Jan. 1749.
1749. - - - Henry Arthur Earl of Powis.
1771. - - - Robert Lord Clive. ob. 22 Nov. 1774.
1775. - - - Edward Lord Clive, created Earl of Powis 12 May, 1804.

DEPUTY RECORDERS.

1734. - - - Henry Jenks, esq. ob. Nov. 1753.
1754. July 17. Charles Bolas, esq. ob. 1758.
1759. April 27. John Oliver, esq. ob. 20 Sept. 1780.
1781. - - - William Harris, esq.
1786. July 12. Joseph Loxdale, esq.

STEWARDS.

Thomas Colle, seneschal, occurs as a witness with Hugh .... and .... de Weston, bailiffs, in the 5th year of .... (probably Edward III.)

Thomas Newport, senescall, 13 Richard II. After him is a long interval.

7 Hen. VIII. Thomas Cowper appointed.

William Fowler, esq. of Shrewsbury, and of Harnage Grange, which he purchased from the Greys, occurs as steward in 1594. He was the third son of Roger Fowler[1] of Broomhill in Staffordshire, by the sister of Rowland Lee bishop of Lichfield. It appears that in his time capital offences were usually tried at our town sessions: for the MS. chronicle of Shrewsbury relates, that "on the 29th day of October, 1594, was the town seassions of Salop of gaole delivery, Master Fowlar beinge stuard and sittinge there withe the baylifes. In the whiche sessions were condempnid Hughe Preece, servant with Robart Taylor of Salop, sherman, and Will. Morris, soon unto Will. Morris of Salop, sherman, for wilfull murther of one Thomas Lakon, servant unto Mr. Rychard Cherwill, draper, a proper youth and come of good frinds. They were executid at the Olld Heathe the next day following." Mr. Fowler was buried at Cound, 1 Mar. 1597.

Henry Townshend, esq. of Cound, third son of Sir Robert Townshend, chief justice of Wales, was elected in his room. "March 13, 42 Eliz. 1597,8, aggreed that Henry Townsend, esq. is more fit to supplie the place of stewardshippe in place of Will. Fowler, esq. deceased." "Thursday the 13th day of July, 1598, the towne sessionns of Salop of gaol delivery was kept there. At whiche seassions Master Townsend his wooorshipp beinge of late chosen to be steward, sate as judge, and there were three executid." And the next year our Chronicle relates that "there was but one executid, for Mr. Towneshend, that worthy esquire, being stuarde and judge over them, was so full of pitie and mercy, that his worship did what was possible for them." Sir Henry (for he was afterwards knighted) was buried at Cound 9 Dec. 1621. His daughter Elizabeth married Edward Cresset, esq. of Upton Cresset.

1622. May 16. Edward Jones, esq. elected in the room of Sir Henry Touneshend, knt. decesed, with a fee of 40s. He was buried at West Felton (in which parish his estate of Sandford is situate) 1 April, 1648.

1648 (24 Car.) Apr. 7. Thomas Niccolls, esq. ob. April 1662.

---

[1] James Fowler, the fourth son of Roger, and younger brother to our steward, was seated at Penkford in the parish of Tettenhall, where his descendants yet reside.

1662.	Aug. 20.	Thomas Bawdewin, esq. *vice* Niccolls. Resigned 1676.
1676,7.	Jan. 2.	Thomas Burton, esq. *vice* Bawdewin.
1684,5.	Mar. 17.	Robert Price, esq. appointed by the charter of James II. Removed by the King 1 Jan. 1687,8, and
1687,8.	Jan. 1.	Thomas Burton, esq. restored. Resigned 1690.
1690.	- - -	Edward Barrett, esq. ob. 1699.
1699.	Nov. 10.	John Fownes, esq. utter barrister. ob. 1713.
1714.	April 3.	James Hanmer, esq. He had been recommended to the Queen for her approbation Nov. 9, 1713, and was now admitted upon producing such approbation. ob. 11 July, 1726.
1726.	- - -	Edward Gosnell, esq. barrister: occurs 1746.
		James Downes, esq. 1749. ob. 1750.
1750.	- - -	Edward Elisha, esq. Resigned 26 April, 1768.
1768.	Sept. 20.	John Langley, esq. Resigned 1787.
1787.	Aug. 31.	Joseph Loxdale, esq.

TOWN CLERKS.

On the bailiffs' rolls of 45 Henry III. is an entry: "Paid to *Henry Borrey*, clerk, for his labour of the preceding year, half a mark." This sum in 1260 was at least equal to £9 at present. Mr. Borrey may have been town clerk of Shrewsbury.

We are sure that *Thomas*, called sometimes (such was the unsettled state of surnames) *Russel*, from his complexion, and sometimes *de la Clyve*, from the place of his birth, was so; for he stiles himself *clericus burgi Salop*, in his will made on Wednesday the feast of St. Leonard the abbot (Nov. 6) 1336, and extant in the oldest book of our exchequer, marked A. This instrument, which is much at length, contains all we know of our earliest undoubted town clerk. He bequeaths his soul to God and St. Mary, "et omnibus sanctis ejus:" and his body to be buried in the church of St. Mary of Salop, "where my father and mother and sons *(pueri)* lye buried. Also I will that the whole choir of the said church assist *(intersint)* at my obsequies, and also two chaplains, a deacon, and two clerks from every parish church of Salop. Also I bequeath to the fraternity of the said church of St. Mary, 2s.: and to the fabrick of the same, 2s.: and to the fabrick of the church of Lichfeld, 6d." He also bequeaths four pounds of wax to make four wax lights to burn round his body on the day of his interment: two of which are to remain in the church, and a third at the light *(luminare)* of St. Mary there, and the other at the chapel of la Clyve, and 12d. to the behoof *(opus)* of that chapel. He bequeaths 20s. to the poor at his burial; 2s. to the friars preachers of Salop: 1s. to the friars minors, and the same to the Augustine friars. Among numerous other bequests, he leaves to his son John for life the tenement which he bought from Thomas Bonel, on condition, that if he takes priests orders, *(si in ordine sacerdotali sit constitutus)* he shall celebrate daily one mass in St. Mary's church before the cross and the images of St. Michael and St. Thomas the Martyr (Archbishop Becket) " for my soul, and for the souls of my wife and my sons, and particularly for the souls of those to whom I am bound in any debt, with or without my knowledge." If the devisee shall not take orders, he shall provide that the mass be celebrated by some other honest chaplain " *honus ab alio magistro non habente,*" *having no burden from any other master :* i. e. as it seems, whose services are not already engaged[1]. Our town clerk died possessed of considerable property, and had numerous descendants and relations among whom to divide it. The following brief pedigree is collected from the will :

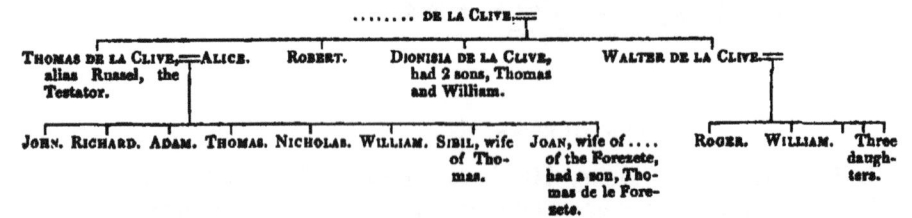

```
                        ........ DE LA CLIVE.
    ┌──────────────┬─────────┬───────────────┬──────────────────┐
THOMAS DE LA CLIVE,=ALICE. ROBERT. DIONISIA DE LA CLIVE,    WALTER DE LA CLIVE.
alias Russel, the                  had 2 sons, Thomas
Testator.                          and William.

JOHN. RICHARD. ADAM. THOMAS. NICHOLAS. WILLIAM. SIBIL, wife   JOAN, wife of ....   ROGER. WILLIAM. Three
                                                of Tho-       of the Forezete,                    daugh-
                                                mas.          had a son, Thomas                   ters.
                                                              de le Fore-
                                                              zete.
```

And there was a seventh son, not noticed in the will, " Rogerus filius Thome (Russel interlined) de la Clyve," who appears upon the " rotulus de forinsecis " (the foreigners' roll) of the " gild merchant of the liberty of the town of Salop," 18 Edw. III. as then admitted, " sans fine :" in compliment, we may suppose, to the memory of his deceased father.

The next town-clerk with whom we meet is John de Tolleford, who occurs in 1372 and 1373 : the 46th and 47th of Edward III. But before we proceed further, it is proper to mention another species of publick clerk that had risen up in Shrewsbury, *the Clerk of the Statute Merchant:* and as the two offices were very generally held by the same person, and at length became consolidated, we must in this place explain the nature of this last.

The statute of Acton Burnell (11 Edw. I. 1283), after reciting the injury sustained by the realm, in consequence of the refusal of merchants to trade here, " because there was no ready law provided by the which they might hastily recover their debts," ordains in remedy of this grievance, that " the merchant who will be sure of his debt, shall cause his debtor to come before the mayor of London, York, or Bristowe, and before the mayor [*of other towns*], and *before a clerk whom the King will attorn* (appoint) for this purpose, and there acknowledge the debt : and the said clerk shall enroll the said recognizance," &c. And the process by which the merchant shall

---

[1] It was a doubt among the doctors of the Romish church, whether a priest who had taken money to say a mass, could take fresh money for the same mass. The casuistry by which this was held lawful may be seen, if the reader is curious, in the sixth of Pascal's celebrated Lettres Provinciales. Our Shrewsbury Town-clerk, we see, determined to have the whole benefit of the mass to himself.

recover his debt upon this *recognizance of statute merchant* is regulated by this act, and by another two years later, in which any doubts which might have arisen, from the omission of the words included within brackets, as to the towns to which this privilege was intended to be extended, are done away, and it is enacted, that " the merchant shall cause his debtor to come before the mayor of Appleby¹, or before other chief warden of the town, or *of other good town where the King shall ordain*, and before the mayor, or chief warden, or other *prodhome* (good man) chosen and sworn thereunto, and before one of the clerks whom the King will attorn thereto," &c. That Shrewsbury was one of the *good towns* which Edward I. appointed for taking recognizances of statute merchant is clear from our having possessed a seal for that purpose. It bore a well-executed bust of Edward I., beardless, and crowned, with a kind of necklace: and imports that he must have had a fine countenance: on his breast lies a lion couchant and gardant. On each side of the head is a castle triple-towered, in compliment to his queen, a princess of Castile. Legend: S. Edw. Reg' Angl' ad Recogn' debitor' ap'd Salop ☆. i.e. The seal of Edward king of England for recognizance of debts at Salop.²

From this time the town-clerk was also generally the clerk for taking recognizances of statute-merchant, as long as that method of security continued in fashion: though the appointments were different: for the common clerk was appointed by the corporation, but the clerk of the statute-merchant by the crown; till the charter of Elizabeth, which ordered, that in future the offices should be united, and left the appointment to the corporation. But we find no name of any clerk of the statute-merchant in Shrewsbury before that of Roger Pride, who filled the office in 17 Edw. III. 1343.

William de Weston was clerk of the statute-merchant in 1373: the same year in which we have seen Tolleford town-clerk.

In 1393, 16 Rich. II., the said Weston was elected town-clerk " in the presence of the earl of Arundell, the lord Strange, the lord Talbot, and other lords, and of the whole community." He was still in office 21 Rich. II.

In 1404, 6 Hen. IV., Richard Swetenham, son of Thomas Swetenham of Middlewich,

---

¹ The introduction of Appleby, for an example, is odd: because there is no appearance that Edward was in the north in 1285, and the parliament at which this supplementary statute-merchant passed, was certainly holden at Westminster. The printed translation of the statutes substitutes London for Appleby.

² This seal is now lost, and the figure here given is from one in Gent. Mag. vol. lxxii. p. 209. Similar ones are engraved by Dr. Milner, in his History of Winchester (who erroneously supposes it to have been peculiar to that city), by Mr. Seyer in his Memoirs of Bristol, and perhaps in other topographical works.

was appointed town-clerk. He continued in office to the end of this reign, and perhaps later. He occurs as clerk of the statute-merchant 9 Hen. VI. 1430.

John Gamel was town-clerk in the reign of Henry V. He occurs as clerk of the statute-merchant 1 and 19 Hen. VI. 1422 and 1440.

In 1456, 35 Hen. VI., John Phelyppes, son of *Philip* Glover (whence his surname) and probably brother of Roger Phelyppes warden of the Battlefield college, was appointed town-clerk, or as at this time it came to be called, *Common-clerk*. He lived in Dogpole.

In 1457, David Ferror was appointed. This must have been but a temporary appointment, or soon superseded or vacated; for

The name of Mr. Phelyppes is subscribed to the burgess roll of 1459, and he occurs again as clerk in 1462 and 1470. About this time the corporation determined to have a Recorder, and he was the first appointed to the office. He occurs with that title in 1473, 1482, and 1485: yet in an intermediate year he appears with his old one; there being an entry, 1483, " solut' Johanni Phelyppes communi clerico in plenam persolucõem feodi sui hoc anno xli.s." The inference from this is, that the two offices were at this time identified.

And so they must have been in 7 Hen. VII. 1491, when Roger Montgomery was elected town-clerk, for that was the very year in which he was elected Recorder.

In 1503, 19 Hen. VII., Thomas Cowppere was common clerk and clerk of the statute-merchant. He occurs as town-clerk, 12 Hen. VIII. 1520.

In 1567, Thomas Bromley, gent. was appointed town-clerk. He seems to be the same who was admitted a burgess in 1556, and who was son of William Bromley, gent. of Stoke-upon-Tern, the elder brother of lord chief justice Bromley.

Hugh Woolten is stiled " formerly town-clerk" in a deed of 1592: he must have vacated the office, by death or otherwise, before

1578, 20 Eliz.; for then Adam Mytton, gent., son of Richard Mytton, esq. of Shrewsbury and Habberley, was appointed town-clerk. Soon after, viz. in 1586, it was ordained, by queen Elizabeth's charter, that the common clerk should thenceforth be also the clerk of statute-merchant. Mr. Mytton's last signature in that capacity is 14 Dec. 1608.[1]

31 Jan. 1609,10, is the first signature of Thomas Owen: his last, 13 Jan. 1644,5. A few weeks after, Shrewsbury was taken by the parliament forces, and he was displaced Nov. 17, " being by ordinance of parliament adjudged a delinquent, for which he now stands committed."

1645, Nov. 17. Rowland Hunt, gent., learned in the lawes, (i. e. a barrister) younger brother of colonel Thomas Hunt, was appointed in his room. He occurs in office 14 Mar. 1645,6 and in 1649.

1650. Mar. 3. Edward Moseley, esq. elected vice Rowland Hunt, esq. occurs 20 May and 5 June, 1651.

Humphrey Mackworth, esq. junior, occurs in 1652, 1 Aug. 1653, and so down to 28 Apr. 1660. He was a younger son of colonel Humphrey Mackworth of Betton Strange, governor of Shrewsbury. Mr. Mackworth probably retired upon the prospect of the Restoration: his father having been very active in opposition to Charles II.; for in

1660, Apr. 26, Thomas Jones, esq. was elected on the resignation, as it is stated, of Thomas Owen, esq. The ruling powers, however, did not approve of this intrusion: and the following letter was directed hither, in which no notice is taken of Mr. Jones, but the office is considered to be vacant by Mr. Owen's resignation.

" Charles R.

" Trusty and well beloved, we greet you well: Whereas we are informed that the Office of Town Clerk of the Town of Shrewsbury, being in your gift and disposal, is now resigned by our faithfull subject Thos. Owen, esq. into your hands, we being mindfull of the fidellity and good service done us and our Royal Father by Sir Francis Ottley, and of the integrity of Adam Ottley, esq. his son, to us and our service, we do therefore recomend the said Adam

---

[1] In the Harleian MSS. 2105, is a letter from James I. in 1604 to our corporation, recommending them to grant the reversion of the office of Town-clerk, after Mr. Mytton's death, to his Majesty's trusty and well-beloved counsellor Thomas Unton: with their humble answer, by way of petition, giving their reasons why they could not comply with his Majesty's letter.

Ottley unto you as a fit person to serve us in that office, and so not doubting of your Compliance with this our desire, we bid you farewell.

"Given at our Court at Whitehall this 16 day of July in the twelvth year of our Reign.
"By his Majesty's command,
"WILL. MORICE.
"To our trusty and well beloved
the Mayor of our Town of Shrewsbury."

But Mr. Jones was not so easily dislodged; he continued in office, and signs as town-clerk as late as 26 Mar. 1661,2. On the 9th day of the following August, he was, as has been already stated, positively, though silently removed: the commissioners for regulating corporations then appointing Adam Ottley, esq. of Pitchford.

Mr. Ottley was sworn in Sept. 7; he was afterwards knighted and appointed a master in chancery. He resigned 29 Sept. 1681.

1681, Sept. 29. Thomas Edwardes, esq. barrister-at-law. He was buried at St. Chad's, 1 Feb. 1726,7.

1720, 14 Dec. Henry, afterwards Sir Henry Edwardes, bart. son of the preceding, on this day produced his Majesty's approbation of his election, and took the oaths. ob. 26 Mar. 1767.

1767, Apr. 2. John Ashby, esq. ob. Jan. 29, 1779.

1779, Apr. 12. Thomas Loxdale, esq. ob. 20 Apr. 1793.

1793, May 6. Thomas Loxdale, esq. son of the preceding.

BURGESSES OF THE PARLIAMENT.

It has been seen above, that the year 1283 was the first time that the representatives of boroughs had a seat in parliament by legal authority, and that Shrewsbury was one of the towns on which that privilege was then conferred. We cannot doubt that it received the same mark of distinction at every future parliament to which the commons were called. But they were by no means, as yet, a necessarily constituent part of those assemblies. There seems good reason to believe that they were not summoned to several subsequent parliaments: at least, there is no proof that they were; and a well-informed writer has fixed upon that of 13 Nov. 1295, 23 Edw. I. as " the earliest epoch of acknowledged representation[1]," by which he probably intends the period since which no parliament has been holden without the presence of the Third Estate of the Realm. The names of the members for Shrewsbury are not, however, preserved till three years later than that date: and the following is the best list of them which we have been enabled to compile from Prynne, Browne Willis, and manuscript authorities. We have set down the date of every parliament which has been since convened, collected from the Parliament Rolls and Statute Book, and the series may not be without its use to the readers of our general history. The year is understood throughout to commence on January the 1st.

EDWARD I.

25	1297 Oct. 10.	London.		
26	1298 Easter.	Ib.	Richard Pride.	Geoffrey Raundulfe.
27	1299 Apr. 2.	Westminster.		
28	1300 Lent.	London.	Richard Stury.	John de Ludlow.
29	1301 Jan. 21.	Lincoln.		

[1] Middle Ages, ii. 325.

BURGESSES OF THE PARLIAMENT. 545

30	1302	July 2.	Westminster.	Geoffrey Randolfe.	Thomas Champeneys.
—	—	Oct. 13.	Ib.		
33	1305	Feb. 28.	Ib.		
—	—	Sept. 16.	Ib.[1]		
35	1307	Jan. 21.	Carlisle.	Thomas de Byketon.[2]	Roger de Stanton.[2]

EDWARD II.

1	1307	Oct. 13.	Northampton.	Geoffrey Randolfe.	Simon de Stafford.
2	1309	Easter.	Westminster.	The same.	Thomas de Bikedon.
3	1310	Mar. 16.	Ib.[3]		
—	—	August.	Stanford.	Nicholas le Spicer.	William Pryde.[4]
5	1311	November.	Westminster.	Hugh Gregory.	Richard de Westbury.
6	1313	July 9.	Ib.	Thomas Colby.[5] John de Ludlow.	Roger Pryde. Richard Stury.[6]
8	1315	January.	Ib.	Geoffrey Randolphe.	Nicholas, son of Nicholas of Salop.
9	1316	January.	Lincoln.	Nicholas le Spicer.	William de Golden.
12	1318	Oct. 20.	York.	John Reyner.	William de Lodelow.
—	1319	May 8.	Ib.		
14	1320	Sept. 30.	Westminster.		
15	1322	May 2.	York.	William Skinner.	Roger Pryde.
—	—	July 15.	Westminster.[7]		
16	—	Nov. 14.	York.	John Staunton.	The same.
17	1323	Nov. 19.	Nottingham.		
—	1324	Feb. 2.	Westminster.		
18					
19	1325	Nov. 19.	Ib.	Laurence Prichet.	The same.[8]

EDWARD III.

1	1327	Feb. 3.[9]	Ib.	Thomas Foremon, John Reyner.	The same. The same.
2	1328	April 24.	Northampton.	John Wottonhull.	The same.
—	—	Oct. 17.	New Sarum.	John Reyner.	The same.
3	1329	....	Westminster.		
4	1330	March 11.	Winton.	John de Weston.	The same.[10]

---

[1] The statute-book contains various statutes of 34 Edw. I.; but they seem all to have been royal ordinances. The rolls have no mention of any parliament assembled in that year.

[2] The writ for their expences is dated from Lanercost, Jan. 20, 35 Edw. I., and addressed "majori & ballivis ville Salop."

[3] See Rot. Parl. i. 281, 445. No. 6.

[4] There is some inaccuracy here. Prynne sets down N. Spicer and W. Pryde, as in the text, members to the parliament 4 Edw. II. But the statute-book and parliament rolls have no parliament in that year. Nicholas le Spicer and Richard Pride were members in this king's fifth year: for there is a liberate of 68s. 7d. to them for being "ad parliament' tent' anno 5to."

[5] Probably a mistake for Colle.

[6] Prynne makes two parliaments in 6 Edw. II., and these persons to have been members to them, two to the first and two to the second. The statute-book and parliament rolls have no such second parliament: nor have they any parliament in 7 Edw. II., to which Prynne gives Hugh son of Robert and Roger Pryde as returned.

[7] The statute-book also mentions a parliament at Carlisle in this year.

[8] Prynne gives John Reyner and Roger Pride as members to a parliament 20 Edw. II. We can find no trace of such parliament.

[9] The statutes of this parliament were passed Mar. 7.

[10] Writ to the bailiffs of Salop to allow these burgesses £4. 4s. for their expences in attending twenty days at the parliament at Winchester. This is rather more than 2s. 1d. a-day for each burgess. In this very year, as we know from the Haghmond Chartulary (art. Trefeglus), corn was estimated at 4s. a quarter, i. e. 6d. a bushel. Taking it now at 64s. (a low estimate) 2s. 1d. then would have gone as far as 35s. at present. Knights of the shire were paid nearly twice as much. The difference of the two classes is herein strongly marked. We can find no parliament at Winchester in the 4th year; but there were two at Westminster.

BURGESSES OF THE PARLIAMENT.

4	1330	Nov. 27.	Westminster.	Richard Walleforde.	Richard Pryde.
5	1331	Sept. 30.	Ib.	William Russell.	Roger Pryde.
6	1332	March 16.	Ib.	William Skynner.	John Reyner.[1]
—	—	Sept. 9.	Ib.		
—	—	Dec. 4.	York.	Nicholas de Sale.	
—	1333	January.	Ib.[2]		
8	1334	Feb. 21.	Ib.	John de Watenhull.	
—	—	Sept. 19.	Westminster.	Will. le Skinnere.	John de Weston.
9	1335	May 26.	York.	William Skinner senior.	William Skinner junior.
10	1336	March 11.	Westminster.	William Skinner.	Thomas Gamel.[3]
—	—	Sept. 24.	Nottingham.		
11	1337	March 3.	Westminster.	Thomas Colle	William Pryde.
—	—	Sept. 27.	Ib.		
12	1338			{ Richard Russell.[4] Geoffrey Randolfe. William Pryde.	Robert Upton. William Randolf. Richard Russell.
13	1339	Feb. 3.	Ib.	William Skynner.	William Brownley.[5]
—	—	Oct. 14.	Ib.		
—	1340	Jan. 21.	Ib.		
14	—	March 29.	Ib.	{ Roger Pryde. John Weston.	John son of John. Richard Weston.
—	—	July 12.	Ib.	William le Skynner sen.	William de Bromeley.
15	1341	April 23.	Ib.	John Stury.	Thomas Colly.
17	1343	April 28.	Ib.	Thomas Fermon.	John Reyner.
18	1344	June 7.	Ib.		
20	1346	Sept. 11.	Ib.	John de Forgate.	William de Lodelowe.
21	1348	Jan. 14.	Ib.	Richard Weston.	Reginald Perle.
22	—	March 21.	Ib.[6]	{ Thomas Lodelowe. John Stury.	John Pryde. John de Crompeden.[7]
25	1351	February 9.	Ib.		
—	1352	Jan. 13.	Ib.		
27	1353	Sept. 23.	Ib.[8]	John Stury.	Robert Reyner.
28	1354	April 28.	Ib.		
29	1355	Nov. 12.	Ib.	John Stury.	Reginald Perle.
31	1357	April 17.	Ib.	{ John Stury. William Vaghan.	Robert Thornes. Thomas Biketon.[9]
34	1361	Jan. 24.	Ib.	{ Robert Thornes. Reginald Perle.	John Stury. John Stury.
36	1362	Oct. 14.	Ib.	John Gaumbedon.	John Stury.
37	1363	Oct. 7.	Ib.	William Longenolre.	Richard Cooke.
38	1365	Jan. 21.	Ib.	John Stury.	Robert Thornes.
40	1366	May 4.	Ib.		
42	1368	May 1.	Ib.		

---

[1] 6 Edw. III. "Will'o le Parmenter & Johanni Reyner electis ad parliamentum apud Westm'." Skinner & Parmenter (i. e. parchment-maker) are in effect the same name.

[2] This parliament continued into the king's seventh year.

[3] 11 Edw. III. "Expens' Will'i le Parmenter & socii sui ellecti apud parliament' cu' allocac'oe unius equi IV.s. pro liberata dicto Will'o pro expensis suis XVI.s."

[4] The statute-book and parliament rolls have only one parliament this year, though Prynne gives three sets of burgesses. The adjustment of this difficulty would require a laborious search of the records, and would little reward the trouble.

[5] Qu. Bromley?

[6] The statute-book has a statute 23 Edw. III.; but the Commons do not appear to have been summoned, on account of the pestilence.

[7] Prynne sets these down for the 24th year, in which year we do not find a parliament.

[8] This must have been a parliament, though it is only called a "great council" on the rolls.

[9] Prynne sets these down for the 33d year, in which we do not find a parliament.

BURGESSES OF THE PARLIAMENT. 547

43	1369 June 3.	Westminster.	Roger Atte Yate.	John Geoffrey.
45	1371 Feb. 24.	Ib.		
46	1372 Nov. 3.	Ib.	Thomas Skinnere.	Philip Godberd.
47	1373 Nov. 21.	Ib.	Richard de Pontesbury.	Reginald de Mutton.
50	1376 April 29.	Ib.	William de Longenolre.	Thomas Skinner of Salop.
51	1377 Jan. 27.	Ib.		

RICHARD II.

1	1377 Oct. 13.	Ib.	Will. de Longenolre.	Reginald Mutton.
2	1378 Oct. 19.	Gloucester.	John Geoffrey.	Thomas Pryde.
—	1379 April 25.	Westminster.	Thomas Skinner.	William Beorton.
3	1380 Jan. 16.	Ib.		
4	—— Nov. 5.	Northampton.	Thomas Skinner.	Richard de Beorton.
5	1381 Nov. 4.	Westminster.		
—	1382 May 7.	Ib.		
6	—— Oct. 7.	Ib.	William Burton.	Robert Thornes.
—	1383 Feb. 23.	Ib.		
7	—— Oct. 26.	Ib.	Will. Burton.	Thomas Skinner.
—	1384 April 29.	New Sarum.		
8	1384 Nov. 12.	Westminster.	Will. Burton.	Tho. Skinner.
9	1385 Nov. 20.	Ib.	Thomas Pryde.	Tho. Skinner.
10	1386 Oct. 1.	Ib.	Robert de Grafton.	Hugh Wygan.
11	1388 Feb. 3.	Ib.	Roger Thornes.	....
12	—— Sep. 9.	Canterbury.	Robert de Acton.	Hugh Wygan.
13	1390 Jan. 18.	Westminster.	Robert de Grafton.	Thomas Pryde.
14	—— Nov. 12.	Ib.		
15	1391 Nov. 3.	Ib.		
16	1393 Jan. 21.	Winton.	Thomas Gamill.	Tho. Pryde.
17	1394 Jan. 28.	Westminster.		
18	1395 Jan. 28.	Ib.	Richard Aydstote.[1]	Roger de Thornes.
20	1397 Jan. 22.	Ib.	Thomas Skinner.	John Geoffrey.
21	—— Sept. 17.	Ib.[2]		

HENRY IV.

1	1399 Oct. 6.	Ib.	Nicholas Gerard.	Thomas Berewyk.
2	1401 Jan. 20.	Ib.		
3		Cambridge.	Roger Thornes.	Thomas Pryde.
4	1402 Sept. 30.	Westminster.		
5	1404 Jan. 14.	Ib.	Simon Toure.	Thomas Price.[3]
6	—— Oct. 6.	Coventry.		
7	1406 March 1.	Westminster.		
9	1407 Oct. 20.	Gloucester.		
11	1410 Jan. 27.	Westminster.	Roger Thornes.[4]	John Thornes.
13	1411 Nov. 3.	Ib.		

HENRY V.

1	1413 Three weeks after Easter.	Ib.	David Holbach.	Urian Seint Pyer.
2	1414 April 30.	Leicester.	Robert Horsley.	William Horde.
—	—— Nov. 19.	Westminster.		
3	1415 Nov. 3.	Ib.		
—	1416 March 16.	Ib.		

[1] This should be Ardescote or Aldescote.
[2] This parliament had a second session at Shrewsbury, Jan. 28, 1398: and it was the first that ever had two sessions: and thus our town, as it had exhibited the first legitimate example of a parliament in its full integrity of three estates, so now witnessed the next important change in its constitution, by which the duration of the assembly was continued beyond its first meeting.
[3] Probably an error of the press for *Pride*.
[4] Printed *Robert*.

BURGESSES OF THE PARLIAMENT.

4	1416	Oct. 19.	Westminster.	Robert Horsley.	William Horde.
5	1417	Nov. 16.	Ib.	David Holbach.	Will. Horde.
7	1419	Oct. 16.	Ib.	Robert Thornes.	John Perle.
8	1420	Dec. 2.	Ib.	John Whitcomb.	Richard Bentley.
9	1421	May 2.	Ib.	William Horde.	Robert Whytcomb.
—	—	Dec. 1.	Ib.		

HENRY VI.

1	1422	Nov. 9.	Ib.	John Perle.	Rob. Whytcomb.
2	1423	Oct. 20.	Ib.	{ Roger Eyton.[1] John Perle.	John Horde. Urian Sempyer.
3	1425	April 30.	Ib.	Roger Corbet.	John Gamnill.
4	1426	Feb. 28.	Leicester.		
6	1427	Oct. 13.	Westminster.	Will. Boerley.	Will. Horde.
8	1429	Sept. 22.	Ib.		
9	1431	Jan. 12.	Ib.		
10	1432	May 12.	Ib.		
11	1433	July 8.	Ib.		
12				Robert Whytcomb.	Will. Horde.
14	1435	Oct. 10.	Ib.	Thomas Thorne.	Will. Burton.
15	1437	Jan. 21.	Ib.		
18	1439	Nov. 12.	Ib.		
20	1442	Jan. 25.	Ib.	Rob. Whytcomb.	Will. Burton.
23	1445	Feb. 25.	Ib.		
25	1447	Feb. 10.	Bury.	William Bastard.	Thomas Beget.
27	1449	Feb. 12.	Westminster.	Will. Bastard.	John Horde.
28	—	Nov. 6.	London.[2]	Thomas Luyt.	John Horde.
29	1450	Nov. 6.	Westminster.[3]	Thomas Luyt.	Will. Bastard.
31	1453	March 6.	Reading.[4]		
33	1455	July 9.	Westminster.[5]		
38	1459	Nov. 20.	Coventry.		
39	1460	Oct. 7.	Westminster.		

EDWARD IV.

1	1461	Nov. 4.	Ib.[6]		
3	1463	April 29.	Ib.[7]		
7	1467	June 3.	Ib.[8]		
12	1472	Oct. 6.	Ib.[9]	Thomas Mitton.	John Hord.[10]
17	1478	Jan. 16.	Ib.	Robert Ap Eyn'	John Guttyne.[11]
22	1483	Jan. 20.	Ib.		

RICHARD III.

1	1483	Jan. 23.	Ib.	Robert Wantenoure, bailiff.[12]	

---

[1] Printed *Gyton*.

[2] This parliament had a second session at Leicester, Apr. 29, 1450.

[3] This parliament had a second session 20 Jan. 1451, and a third, May 5, 1451.

[4] Second session (after three prorogations) 14 Feb. 1454, at Westminster.

[5] Second session 12 Nov.; prorogued 13 Dec. to 14 Jan. 1456. [6] Dissolved 6 May, 1462.

[7] Second session (after four prorogations) 21 Jan. 1465, at Westminster.

[8] Second session 12 May, 1468, at Westminster.

[9] Second session 8 Feb. 1473; third session 6 Oct.; fourth, 20 Jan. 1474; fifth, 9 May; sixth, 6 June; seventh, 23 Jan. 1475; dissolved 14 Mar.

[10] Printed *Ford*. But on the bailiffs' accounts 14 Edw. IV., is an entry, "In denar' solut' Joh'i Hoord uni burgensium existentium ad parliament' in partem soluco'is vadior' suor' 53s. 4d."

[11] The indenture of their return, in which they are called Rob. Beynyon and John Gyttons, is 7 Jan. 17 Edw. IV. (1478.) They are said, in Phillips, to have been returned by the inhabiting burgesses.

[12] In the bailiffs' accounts, from Michaelmas 2 Rich. III. (1484) to the same day 1 Hen. VII. (1485), it is entered, "Et de xx.s. i.d. allocatis Ric'o Wantenor in partem soluco'is debiti sui & cost' ad parliament'."

BURGESSES OF THE PARLIAMENT. 549

HENRY VII.

1	1485 Nov. 7.	Westminster.		
3	1487 Nov. 7.	Ib.		
4	1489 Jan. 13.	Ib.[1]		
7	1491 Oct. 17.	Ib.[2]	Will. Mutton.	Lawrence Hosyer.
11	1495 Oct. 14.	Ib.		
12	1497 Jan. 16.	Ib.		
19	1504 Jan. 25.	Ib.		

HENRY VIII.

1	1510 Jan. 21.	Ib.	Roger Thornes.	Thomas Knight, bailiffs.[3]
3	1512 Feb. 4.	Ib.[4]	Thomas Kynaston.[5]	Tho. Trentham junior.
7	1515 Nov. 12.	Ib.[6]	The same.[7]	The same.
—	1520 [8]		Edmund Colle.	Adam Mutton.
—	1522		The same.	The same.
14	1523 April 15.	Ib.[9]	The same.[10]	The same.
21	1529 Nov. 3.	London.[11]	Robert Dudley.	Adam Mitton.[12]
28	1536 June 8.	Westminster.[13]		
31	1539 April 28.	Ib.[14]	Nicholas Pursell.	Robert Thornes.
33	1542 Jan. 16.	Ib.[15]		
37	1545 Nov. 23.	Ib.[16]		

[1] Dissolved 27 Feb.

[2] Prorogued 4 Nov. to 26 Jan. 1492; dissolved 5 March.

[3] Accounts of Roger Thornes and Thomas Knight, bailiffs for the year from Michaelmas 1 Hen. VIII. (1509) " Pro expens' ballivor' existenc' burgensium ad parliament' inchoat' xxi die Jan' & finit'   hoc anno, viz. per 50 dies eundo, redeundo & ib'm morando £10." This is 2s. each per diem: so that the wages of a member for Shrewsbury was nearly 1d. less than it had been one hundred and seventy-nine years before: though 2s. 1d. in 1330 would have gone as far as 35s. at present; and 2s. in 1509 only as far as 16s. One can scarcely account for these wages continuing thus stationary, or, indeed, rather retrograding, but on the supposition that a seat in parliament was now becoming somewhat an object of ambition.

[4] Prorogued to 4 Nov. when it met, and was afterwards prorogued to Jan. 29, 1514, when it again met for the dispatch of business, and was afterwards prorogued to Feb. 5, 1515. The Parliamentary History (iii. 16) makes this a new parliament: but the statute-book expressly says that it met on "the 5th day of February in the 6th year of his most noble reign, after the prorogation."

[5] "Mem. that T. K. and T. T. junior, burgesses in parliament, set out thither last of Jan., and returned March 4th, and had each £6. 10s. in fees." This is 3s. 9¾d. a-day.

[6] The Parliamentary History (iii. 22) makes this a prorogation of the parliament which met Feb. 5, 1515; but this is not so expressed in the statute-book.

[7] 6 H. VIII. "Agreed, at the instance of the King's letters, to elect the same members of parliament as were last chosen."

[8] It does not appear that any session of parliament was holden in 1520 or 1522.

[9] It met then, and was afterwards adjourned to July 31. Our town records contain a notice of a parliament which does not occur on the statute-book. Bailiffs' accounts from Michaelmas 19 Hen. VIII. (1527) for a year. "Sol' Roberto Dudley arm' pro expensis per ipsum factis *tempore parliamenti* circa negotia ville, 9s. 6d."

[10] Date of return 28 March.

[11] Adjourned and prorogued then to Westminster palace, and there continued to 17 Dec.; and thence prorogued to 27 April 1530; and thence, by sundry prorogations, to 16 Jan. 1531, when it met for dispatch of business; and was thence adjourned to March 31; and thence to 13 Oct.; and thence to 15 Jan. 1532, when it again met. It afterwards met, upon prorogation, 4 Feb. 1533, and passed sundry laws; and again on 15 Jan. 1534, when it did the same. It again met, on prorogation, 3 Feb. 1535, and passed laws; again 4 Feb. 1536, and did the same; and was dissolved 4 April.

[12] These members are placed by Prynne in 1530, but we have the assessment of the inhabitants of the town and liberties to send them to the parliament of 3 Nov. 21 Hen. VIII. 1529.

[13] Dissolved 18 July following.

[14] Met again, after sundry prorogations, 12 Apr. 1540; passed laws, and was dissolved 24 July.

[15] Holden again, by prorogation, 22 Jan. 1543, and 14 Jan. 1544.

[16] Prorogued to Nov. 4, 1546; and again to 14 Jan. 1547, when it met for the dispatch of business, and was dissolved by the King's death on the 28th of the month, which being notified to the peers, "they could not refrain from tears."

VOL. I.   4 B

550   BURGESSES OF THE PARLIAMENT.

EDWARD VI.

1	1547	Nov. 4.	Westminster.[1]	Reginald Corbet, esq.	John Jenens, gent.[2]
7	1553	March 1.	Ib.	Nicholas Purcell, alderm.	George Lye, merchant.

MARY.

1	1553	Oct. 5.	Ib.[3]	Nicholas Purcell, burgess and alderman.	Reginald Corbett, esq.[4]
—	1554	April 2.	Ib.[5]	The same.	Thomas Mytton.[6]
2	— Oct. 21.		Ib.[7]	Robert Dowe.	Thomas Dewe.
	1555			Nicholas Purcell, esq.	Reginald Corbett, esq.[8]
4	1557	Jan. 21.	Ib.	The same.	George Lye, gent.[9]

ELIZABETH.

1	1559	Jan. 23.	Ib.	Nicholas Purcell, esq.	George Lye, gent.
5	1563	Jan. 12.	Ib.	Robert Ireland jun. esq.[10]	Richard Purcell, gent.
13	1571	April 2.	Ib.	William Ireland, jun. esq.	George Leigh, esq.
14	1572	May 8.	Ib.[11]	Richard Purcell, esq.	George Lee, esq.
27	1584	Nov. 23.	Ib.	Thomas Owyne of Lincoln's Inn, esq.[12] 366.	Robert Barker, esq. 299. *Thomas Harris, esq.* 176.
28	1586	Oct. 29.	Ib.	Reginald[13] Scriven, esq.[14]	Thomas Harris of Lincoln's Inn.
31	1589	Feb. 4.		The same.	Andrew Newport.[15]
35	1592	Nov. 19.	Ib.	The same.	Robert Wright.[16]
39	1597	Oct. 24.	Ib.	Reginald Scriven, esq.[17]	Roger Owen, esq.
43	1601	Oct. 27.	Ib.	The same.[18]	John Barker of Hamond, esq.

---

[1] Met again, by prorogation, Nov. 24, 1548; and again 4 Nov. 1549; and again 23 Jan. 1552; and was dissolved 15 April.   [2] Elected 25 Oct.
[3] Met again, on prorogation, 24th of the same month; and dissolved 6 Dec.
[4] Indenture dated 29 Sep. 1 Mariæ (1553.)
[5] Dissolved 5 May.
[6] Willis calls him Richard: but our bailiffs' accounts for a year from Mich. 3 and 4 P. and M. (1556) have " Solut' Thome Mytton pro feodo suo tempore quo fuit burgensis parliamenti pro villa Salop; secundum tenorem brevis dominorum Regis & Regine inde nobis directi £8. 16s.:" i. e. P^d *Thomas* Mytton for his fee when he was burgess of the parliament.   [7] Dissolved 9 Dec.
[8] The statute-book has no parliament of 1555: but there was certainly one summoned; for the indenture of Purcell and Corbet's return is extant, dated 1 Oct. 2 and 3 Ph. and Mary.
[9] Mr. Lye was one of the members who seceded from this last parliament of Qu. Mary, in dislike of their proceedings; and who were prosecuted for that their contempt.
[10] Second session 13 Sept. 1566.
[11] Second session 18 Feb. 1576.   Third session 16 Jan. 1581.
[12] Return 6 Nov. From this place the names in italicks denote unsuccessful candidates.
[13] Taylor's MS. calls him *Charles*.
[14] Return 13 Oct.
[15] The election was on the 19th Oct. 1588.

[16] This election did not take place till 10 Feb. 1593. It was settled by the earl of Essex. Mr. Wright was his steward, and the following letter from that great peer proves the high sense which he entertained of the obligation:
" After my verie hartie comendacons. I do verie hartleye thank you for your frendlie readines in the accomplishment of my late letters, and thinke my self so much the more beholding unto you, in that you made choyse of my servant Wright to be one of your Burgesses, notwithstanding earnest sewt made for others. Wherein to geve you some testimonie of my acceptance thereof: althoughe I do not doubt but my servant Eynes hath some good reason for that which he hath done, nevertheles what soever interest I have, or may have in those geldings, I will not contend with you, but do freelye release the bands which he hath taken of you in that behalfe, to which purpose I have willed Wright to take order with hym. And if in any other matter I may stand you in steede hereafter, in fuller requitall of this curtesie towards hym, you shall be assured to fynd me readie. So I commit you to God. From the Cowrt the xith of Marche 1592.
" Y^r very loving frend,
" To my verie lovinge   " Essex.
frends the Bayleffs of the
town of Shresburye."
[17] Return 22 September.
[18] Return 10 Oct. " In this election was much ado." Taylor's MS.

BURGESSES OF THE PARLIAMENT.   551

JAMES I.

1	1604 March 19.	Westminster.[1]	Richard Barker, esq. recorder.	Francis Tate, esq.
12	1614 April 5.	Ib.[2]	Sir Roger Owen, knt.[3] On his death, 1617, Francis Berkeley, esq.	Lewis Prowde, esq.
18	1621 Jan. 30.	Ib.[4]	Francis Berkeley, esq.[5]	Sir Richard Newport, knt.
21	1624 Feb. 19.	Ib.	Thomas Owen, esq.	Francis Berkeley, esq.

CHARLES I.

1	1625 June 18.	Ib.[6]	Thomas Owen, esq.[7]	Sir William Owen, knt.
—	1626 Feb. 6.	Ib.[8]	The same.[9]	The same.
3	1628 March 17.	Ib.[10]	The same.[11]	The same.
16	1640 April 13.	Ib.[12]	The same.	Francis Newport, esq.
—	—— Nov. 3.	Ib.[13]	Will. Spurstow, merchant. On his decease, Thomas Massam, esq. Writ issued 19 Jan. 1646.	The same. Disabled by vote 22 Jan. 1644; and in his room, Thomas Hunt, esq. return 10 Nov. 1645.

OLIVER CROMWELL.

	1653 July 4.[14]			
	1654 Sept. 4.	Ib.[15]	Rich. Cheshire, gent.[16]	Humphrey Mackworth junior, gent.
	1656 Sept. 17.	Ib.[17]	Samuel Jones, esq.[18]	The same: then a colonel.

RICHARD CROMWELL.

	1659 Jan. 27.	Ib.[19]	William Jones, esq. recorder.	The same, then town-clerk.

INTERREGNUM.

	1660 April 25.	Ib.[20]	Samuel Jones, esq.[21]	Thomas Jones, esq. afterwards chief justice.

---

[1] Second session 5 Nov. 1605; third session 18 Nov. 1606; fourth session 9 Feb. 1610, prorogued in July; fifth session Oct. 23; dissolved 31 Dec. Book of Orders, 1 James I., "Ordered that at all future elections of burgesses in parliament for this town, the election be made of such persons as shall then be inhabiting within this town or suburbs, being burgesses of the town, and known to be men fearing God, of sound religion, lovers of the estate of this town, and able to speak in that place as occasion may require."

[2] Dissolved 7 June. No laws received the royal assent in this parliament.   [3] Return 29 Mar.

[4] Adjourned June 4 to 14 Nov.; met 20 Nov.; dissolved 8 Feb. 1622.   [5] Return 28 Dec. 1620

[6] Adjourned 11 July to Oxford; met there 1 Aug.; dissolved the 12th.   [7] Return 6 May.

[8] Dissolved June 15.   [9] Return 24 Jan.

[10] Prorogued 26 June to 20 Oct., and then to 20 Jan. 1629. Dissolved 10 March.

[11] Return 8 March.—" 3 Car. Ordered that Mr. Thomas Owen have his charges borne by the corporation for serving as a burgess of the parliament for this town."

[12] Dissolved 5 May, without any laws being passed.

[13] Voted the house of lords useless, Feb. 1649: house of commons "purged" by col. Pride 6 Jan. 1653; expelled by Cromwell April 20; restored 7 May, 1659; again expelled by Lambert 13 Oct.; restored 26 Dec.; the members who had been secluded by Pride resume their seats Feb. 21, 1660; long parliament (i. e. the house of commons) dissolved themselves March 16.

[14] There were no members for boroughs at this pretended parliament, commonly called that of Barebone.   [15] Dissolved 22 Jan. 1655.

[16] Return 15 July.

[17] Adjourned 16 June, 1657, to 20 Jan. 1658. Dissolved 4 Feb.   [18] Return 20 Aug.

[19] Dissolved April 22.

[20] Called without the king's authority, but recognised by him, and turned into a legal parliament. He dissolved it 29 Dec.   [21] Return 17 April.

BURGESSES OF THE PARLIAMENT.

CHARLES II.

13	1661	May 8.	Westminster.[1]	Robert Leighton, esq.[2]	Thomas Jones, esq.
31	1679	March 6.	Ib.[3]	Sir Richard Corbett, bart.[4]	Edward Kynaston, esq.
—	—	Oct. 17.	Ib.[5]	The same.[6]	The same.
33	1681	March 21.	Oxford.[7]	Sir Rich. Corbett, bart.[8]	Edward Kynaston, esq. of Abrightlee.

JAMES II.

1	1685	May 19.	Westminster.[9]	Sir Francis Edwards, bart.	The same.

INTERREGNUM.

	1689	Jan. 22.	Convention. The same.	Honourable Andrew Newport, esq.

WILLIAM AND MARY.

1	1689	Feb. 23.		
2	1690	May 20.[10]	Richard Mytton, esq.	The same.

WILLIAM.

7	1695	Nov. 22.	John Kynaston, esq.	The same.
10	1698	Aug. 24.	The same.	Rich. Mytton, esq.
13	1701	Dec. 13.	The same.	The same.

ANNE.

1	1702	Aug. 20.	The same.	The same.
4	1705	June 14.	The same.	The same.
7	1708	July 8.	Sir Edw. Leighton, bart. *John Kynaston, esq.*	Tho. Jones, esq. *Richard Mytton, esq.*
9	1710	Nov. 25.	Richard Mytton, esq. 224. *Sir Edw. Leighton, bart.* 131.	Edward Cresset, esq. 222. *Thomas Jones, esq.* 177.
12	1713	Nov. 12.	Corbet Kynaston, esq.	Edward Cresset, esq. *Thomas Jones, esq.*

GEORGE I.

1	1715	March 17.	The same.	Thomas Jones, esq. On his death, July 31, Andrew Corbet, of the Park, esq. elected.
9	1722	Oct. 9.	Sir Richard Corbett, bart. 644. *Corbet Kynaston, esq.* 722.[11]	Orlando Bridgman, esq. 643. *Richard Lyster, esq.* 695.

GEORGE II.

1	1728	Jan. 23.	Richard Lyster, esq.	Sir John Astley, bart.
8	1734	June 13.	Sir Richard Corbett, bart. 265. *John Mytton, esq.* 201.	William Kinaston, esq. 269. *Richard Lyster, esq.* 199.
15	1741	Dec. 1.	Sir Richard Corbett.	William Kinaston.

---

[1] This parliament sate every year (except 1676, in which there was no session) to Jan. 24, 1679.

[2] Return 17 April.

[3] Prorogued 13 March for two days, to settle the dispute about a speaker. Second session Mar. 15, prorogued 26 May, and dissolved 10 July.

[4] Return 3 Feb.

[5] This parliament did not meet till Jan. 26, 1680, and then only for one day. It first met for the dispatch of business 21 Oct. and was dissolved 10 Jan. 1681.

[6] Return 2 Aug.

[7] Dissolved 28th following.

[8] Return 17 Feb.

[9] From this time it is unnecessary to specify the place of meeting, which has been invariably Westminster.

[10] From this time it is unnecessary to specify the sessions of each parliament, as a session has been holden every year.

[11] Voted out upon petition by the disfranchisement of the Abbey Foregate.

BURGESSES OF THE PARLIAMENT. 553

21	1747 Nov. 10.	Sir Richard Corbett. 150. *Robert Pigott, esq.* 140.	William Kinaston, esq. 155. *Richard Prince Astley, esq.* 135. On Mr. Kinaston's death, 1749, Thomas Hill, esq.
27	1754 May 31.	Robert More, esq.	The same.

GEORGE III.

2	1761 May 19.	Colonel Robert Clive. created, Dec. 1, Lord Clive.	The same.
8	1768 May 10.	The same. 149.	Noel Hill, esq. 233. *William Pulteney, esq.* 97.
15	1774 Nov. 29.	The same. 210.	William Pulteney, esq. 171. declared sitting member on petition. *Charlton Leighton, esq.* 178.
		On Lord Clive's death, Nov. 22, John Corbet, esq. elected 17 March, 1775.	
21	1780 Oct. 31.	Sir Charlton Leighton, bart.	William Pulteney, esq.
24	1784 May 18.	The same. On his death, Sept. 9. John Hill, esq.	The same.
31	1790 Nov. 25.	The same.	The same.
36	1796 July 12.	Honourable William Hill. 242. *John Hill, esq.* 153.	The same. 370.
41	1802 Nov. 16.	The same.	The same. On Sir W. Pulteney's death, June 5, 1805, John Hill, esq.
47	1806 Dec. 15.	The same. 589.	Hon. Henry Grey Bennett,[1] 370. *Thomas Jones, esq.* 351.
—	1807 June 22.	The same. 538.	Thomas Jones, esq. 345. *Hon. Henry Grey Bennett.* 321. On the death of Sir T. Jones, Nov. 26, 1811, Honourable Henry Grey Bennett.
53	1812 Nov. 24.	Lieut.-Gen. Sir Rowland Hill, K. B. 512. On his elevation to a peerage, May 3, 1814, Richard Lyster, esq. 551. *Benjamin Benyon, esq.* 286.	Hon. Henry Grey Bennett. 724. *Benjamin Benyon, esq.* 336.
59	1819 Jan. 14.	Richard Lyster, esq. On his death, May 3, John Mytton, esq. 384. *Panton Corbett, esq.* 287.	Honourable Henry Grey Bennett.

GEORGE IV.

1	1820 March 9.	Panton Corbett, esq.	Honourable Henry Grey Bennett.

---

[1] Mr. Bennett's election was declared void, April 24, 1807, on account of an informality in his qualification: but the writ which had been issued for a new election in his room, was superseded by the dissolution of parliament on the 29th.

CORPORATION INSIGNIA.

The vignette which precedes these lists of Corporate Officers is intended to represent the ensigns of office, and other decorative appendages of the corporation. The former are very handsome, and consist of the sword of state, five maces, and the marshal's staff. The first of these is in the form of an ancient broad-sword, with a highly polished steel blade, two inches in breadth. The hilt, guard, and pommel, are of silver double gilt, and richly enchased. On one side of the pommel is a small figure of Justice, and on the other, of Fame, well executed in relief. At the points of intersection of the guard and blade, are the arms of Charles II. within the garter; and on the reverse, those of the borough. The scabbard is covered with crimson velvet, adorned with four broad *chaps* or bracelets, and a deep ferula, of silver double gilt, beautifully embossed with figures of Cariatides, masks, and flowers. This highly elegant piece of cutlery is four feet four inches in length; the hilt being one foot two inches and a half, the guard one foot and half an inch, and the pommel three inches and an half. In the corporation accounts it appears, that " a new sword was purchased" in 1670 for £34. 2s. " to be used on scarlet days." This was doubtless the sword just described. It is in the costly style of that day, and would now probably not be bought for less than treble the original price. The enchased work was repaired and newly gilt during the mayoralty of the Rev. Hugh Owen in 1820. At the time the sword was purchased, the sum of £9 was allowed for a gown to the sword-bearer; so that this officer must at that day have been most superbly attired. There is a more ancient sword in the Guildhall, much like one of the great two-handed weapons of our ancestors; the guard, pommel, and hilt of this are iron, but have been gilt. There was a new sword bought for £9. 2s. in 1638, when our chief magistrate obtained the title of mayor, but this, from its rudeness, seems more ancient than that date.

The *mace*, as an ensign of office, derives its name and origin from the ancient *massa, maxuca, massue*, or *mass*, a rude weapon of offence. It was perhaps used at first, like the Roman fasces, to make a way for the chief magistrates through the surrounding crowd. From an odd custom[1] in Switzerland, it appears probable that the mace was an ensign of magistracy in that country during the dark ages. That seems to have been a tall

---

[1] When a magistrate became unpopular, the people proceeded against him by a species of ostracism called La Mazza, from the heavy club, or mace, cut at one end into the form of a man's head, which was carried about as a rallying point for the enemies of the obnoxious individual. Every person disposed to enter the ranks against him planted a nail in *la mazza*. Simond's Switzerland, t. ii. p. 207. This looks as if the mace was thought to stand for the magistrate.

ponderous club, such as the Kenilworth porter bears in Laneham's curious letter, and such as are still borne by church beadles in London, and at the Temple and Lincoln's Inn. Even in modern times the dignity of the mace appears to be commensurate with its size: those borne before the Lord Chancellor and Speaker of the Commons, being the largest we know, and requiring the shoulder to sustain them.

Our Shrewsbury maces are five in number: the two larger are modern, and were purchased by a subscription of the members of the corporation in 1820, at the cost of £76. They are of silver, double gilt. On one side of the bosses are the arms of England with the supporters, and on the other, those of the town; the whole surmounted by large imperial crowns, round which is engraven on each, THE REV. HUGH OWEN, MAYOR. WILLIAM SMITH, ESQ. SENIOR ALDERMAN. EDWARD EARL OF POWIS, RECORDER. A. D. MDCCCXX. LX. GEO. III. They are each two feet six inches in length.

The three smaller maces are of some antiquity. They are silver, made to be borne upright in the hand. The oldest is one foot four inches in length. On the summit of the boss are the arms of France and England, much worn, with the words VILLA SALOP. Below are the arms of Shrewsbury, with the union rose and portcullis. The pattern is old, and may be of Henry VII.'s reign. The second mace is nearly of the same form, but more modern. On the top are the arms of Charles I. with supporters, double gilt, and very neatly executed. Round the boss are the arms of the borough, with the thistle, crown, and portcullis, in high relief.

The smallest mace is only one foot two inches long, and very similar in shape to the others. On the flat summit of the boss are the arms of queen Elizabeth; and on its side those of Shrewsbury, with the portcullis, and double rose, crowned. Sir Henry Englefield, in his elegant topographical account of Southampton, remarks, that one of the smaller maces of the corporation of that ancient town, was, not many years since, carried before *the mayoress* when she appeared with her husband, as she did on all occasions of form, attired in a scarlet gown. The wives of the bailiffs of Shrewsbury were enjoined, in the reign of Elizabeth, " to wear scarlet gowns[1] on solemn days," and hence it may be inferred, that the small mace was borne before those ladies, as they walked in civic processions, on the right hand of their magisterial spouses, when " knolled with holy bells to church," or called to " good men's feasts." We are sure that in some corporations the ladies formerly took part on occasions of state. At Coventry, says an old custumale of that city, " the old Mrs. Mayoress, attended by the

---

[1] At Berwick House is the unknown portrait of a comely dame with the Elizabethan ruff and coif, and arrayed in all the honours of the scarlet furred robe, cut as near to the fashion of the aldermen's gowns as a lady's dress would permit.

wives of the sheriffs and other officers, cometh (on the day of swearing in) to the new mayor's house, and they fetch the new Mrs. Mayoress to the church of St. Michael, where was the new mayor, the new mayoress having the right-hand place."

The marshal's baton, or staff of office, has an acorn-shaped head of silver, encircled by an elegant rim of open leaves. On the top are the arms of England with the supporters, and beneath, the rose and portcullis crowned. The original baton was a slender ebony verge, about a yard in length; having been broken, the ancient boss was preserved, enlarged, and fixed on a strong staff of black wood, adorned with silver bracelets. In 1624 " a newe *mace*" was ordered for the " marshall, and £1. 6s. paid for the same;" and in 1669 " a new *verdge*" was purchased for that officer, at the expence of £2.

But the most costly and valuable part of the corporation ornaments are the magnificent tankard and salver which adorn the mayor's table, and are presented by the sword-bearer to the judges of assise; the one well stored with cakes, and the other with negus, when the mayor visits their lordships on their arrival. The former was given by Robert lord Clive; the latter, by his son the earl of Powis, as an appropriate appendage to his father's present. The tankard is a massy and highly beautiful piece of plate. On the sides are figures in high relief, representing Commerce, Agriculture, and Manufactures, and are finely executed. On the lid, within a highly embossed border, is a boy brandishing the child's toy called a *mill-reel*, the purport of which, in such a place, is not very apparent. The handle and base are in the same rich style of decoration. The enchased work is raised on a frosted ground; and the inside, handle, base, and border, are double gilt. Around the upper part is inscribed THE GIFT OF COLONEL ROBERT CLIVE TO THE HON. THE MAYOR AND CORPORATION OF SHREWSBURY. SEPT. 17, 1760. This fine civic cup will contain somewhat more than three quarts, is ten inches in height, and weighs one hundred and seven ounces.

The salver is extremely splendid. It is raised on eight silver claws, and inclosed by an elevated margin, enchased with Bacchanalian masks, connected with wreaths of vine leaves and fruit. In the centre are the arms of Shrewsbury, on a frosted ground within a foliated border; on the outside of which is engraven, THE GIFT OF EDWARD EARL OF POWIS, SON OF COLONEL ROBERT CLIVE, TO THE HONORABLE THE MAYOR AND CORPORATION OF SHREWSBURY, SEPT. 1820, THE REV. HUGH OWEN MAYOR. The remaining portion is overspread with fine enchasing of vine-leaves, grapes, cornucopias, &c. The diameter of this gorgeous piece of plate is twenty-four inches, and its weight one hundred and eighty-eight ounces nine pennyweights.

MINOR OCCURRENCES AND MISCELLANEOUS TRANSACTIONS.

We conclude this general history of the town with such remarkable occurrences as could not be conveniently introduced before. Mr. Phillips began his chapter on this subject with the prices of various articles, and therefore we continue the same, as some readers will expect to find them, though we know not what credit they deserve.

He tells us that land about the town sold in 961 for 1s. an acre; an ox, 2s. 6d., a cow, 2s., a sheep, 1s., a swine, 8d.

1225. Three gallons of ale sold for 1d. in the town, and 4d. out of it.

1315. Prices settled by the bailiffs. A corn-fed ox, £1. 4s. A grass-fed ditto, 16s. A cow, 12s. A fat mutton, 1s. 8d. A mutton shorn, 1s. 2d. A fat hog two years old, 3s. 4d. A fat goose, 2d. A hen, 1d. A capon, 2d. Two chickens, 1d. Four pigeons, 1d. Twenty-four eggs, 1d.

1326. Hay, 5s. per load.

1347. A fine horse, 6s. 8d. The best fed ox, 4s. A cow, 1s. A steer, or heifer, 6d. A wether, 4d. An ewe, 3d. A lamb, 2d. An hog, 5d.

1454. Corn was so plenty, that a quarter (8 strikes) of wheat was commonly sold for 1s. or 1s. 2d. Rye, for 10d. Malt, 1s. 4d. or 5d.

1490. Wheat, 1s. 8d. per bushel. [Our MS. chronicle gives this as the London price, " which then was counted dear;" but says nothing of the price at Shrewsbury.]

1492. Wheat, 6d. per bushel.

1493. Wheat, 4s. per bushel. [Our chronicle gives 6d. as the London price this year.]

1498. Wheat, 6d. per bushel. [Our chronicle gives this as the London price.] Wine £2. per ton.

These prices are from Mr. Phillips: what follow are from our MS. chronicle, and are restricted to Shrewsbury, except where otherwise expressed. We have accommodated the spelling to modern usage.

1524. Wheat, 4s. per bushel. Rye, 2s. 10d.

1526. August. Wheat, 3s. 4d. per bushel. Rye, 2s. 4d. This was owing to the bad weather, for it rained from April 12 to June 3, day and night continually. " In the following year the merchants of the Stillyard imported such store of wheat and rye into London, that they were better cheap there than in any part of England."

1557. Wheat, 8s. 6d. the bushel. Rye, 6s. "But by the end of harvest wheat came to 8d., and so of all grain alike manner; so that in this year was both plenty and dearth in Shrewsbury."

1585. "Corn grew to be very dear in most parts of England, in June and July, particularly in the North and West countries: in Shrewsbury wheat was 8s. 8d. the bushel, and rye, 6d. The queen directed the justices to cause corn-masters to bring corn to market, so that the poor subjects should not want corn for their money. In July, all kind of corn was at an excessive price in the town: to say rye at 8s. the bushel; wheat at 9s., and barley at 4s. 6d. and upwards. But the careful zeal of master James Barker, brought from foreign places 100 strike of rye, and sold the same to the poor, after the rate of 5s. the bushel, and so brought down the price. The corporation also provided store to ease the suspected want that was like to ensue. The Lord bless them for their merciful care, and send plenty. Amen!"

1587 "was a very quick and timely harvest; for before Bartholomew day the most part of corn was carried into barns: the which timely harvest, and the abundant plenty thereof caused wheat and rye, being before harvest, in the town of Shrewsbury, at 11s. and 9s. the bushel, to fall to 3s. 8d. and 3s. the bushel and under; which (God be praised) was a comfortable hearing."

October 1594. " By the reason of swiftness of rye, and unseasonableness of barley, and carriage out of rye and other grain from place to place, and stolen out of the land, corn waxed very dear in Shrewsbury, to say rye at thirteen and fourteen groats, wheat at 5s. and sixteen groats the bushel: and if help had not " comun" from Denmark, which brought it to 3s. 4d., the people had perished."

1708. Wheat, 9s. per bushel. Muncorn, 8s. Rye, 7s. This is set down as a very remarkable instance of high prices.

To this list of prices in ancient times, we shall add one in modern times. Mr. Orton writing October 15, 1759, to Dr. Stonhouse, who had then some intention of removing here, says, "This was formerly a cheaper place to live in than almost any large town in England. But now things are considerably advanced by the number of gentlemen who have taken houses in the town, for the sake of cheapness, or to retrench; and yet, for want of good economy, suffer their servants to give any price for what they want; by which our markets are considerably raised. You may guess of our present state by the following particulars. Beef and pork 2½d. per lb. Veal, 2d. Mutton, 3d. Butter, 6d. per lb., of from 18 to 20 oz. Good Welsh butter, 4s. 6d. per dozen, only 16 oz. to the lb. A goose, 1s. 6d. Two fowls, 12 or 14d. Two ducks, 14 or 16d. A turkey, 18 or 20d. A hare, 1s. 6d. Cheese, for 120 lb. of 1759, 18s. of 1758, 22s. Coals, 10s. per ton. Malt, 2s. 9d. per bushel. Wheat per bushel, (36 quarts) 2s. 10d. Oats, 20d. or 22d. per bushel of 6 pecks. Best hay, £1. 12s. 6d. per ton. Head-maid's wages, £3. Under-maids, 50s."

The MS. chronicle to which we have been so largely indebted, sets down many pestilences, earthquakes, floods, &c., which have occurred in Shrewsbury: these we omit, as possessing no longer any use, curiosity, or interest. But we shall copy a few remarkable incidents or casualties; dropping, however, the obsolete spelling, except in the first extract, where it is retained because we profess ourselves not to understand the passage, and insert it to exercise the ingenuity of Salopian antiquaries.

1455.
1456. } "This yeare my lorde of Shrewsbury and John Trentam dyd mary and eyther of them had slayne a man."

The earl of Shrewsbury at this time was the second earl, who succeeded his father in 1453, and died in 1460; but he must have married, at the latest, in 1445, as his son and heir the third earl was upwards of fourteen years of age at his death. John Trentham, Esq. of Shrewsbury, was a person of great figure and consequence in the town, bailiff this year, and may have married his lady, (the sister and heir of John Hoorde, Esq. of the same place) in the year first above set down, but no memorial has reached us of the homicide imputed to him and the earl.

1538.
1539. } "One Richard Brewer of Salop, being John Brewer's son, the brewer, was suddenly slain passing through the gate of the Welsh bridge, by the reason of a great flaw of wind[1] blew the gates together as he passed the same, that his head being between them received such a blow that his brains fell out, and so presently died, and never spake word."

1548.
1549. } "The Tuesday after Easter holidays, two young men were smothered under the Castle hill, hiding themselves from maids, the hill falling there upon them."

This extract is inserted as affording an opportunity to elucidate an ancient custom, formerly prevalent over most of the kingdom, latterly much confined to Shrewsbury,[2] and now fast declining even here: we mean that of *heaving*, from which we presume these young men were seeking to hide themselves when they came by their death. Heaving is performed by the men on Easter Monday, on which day they sportively hold down young women in a chair adorned with ribbons and nosegays, and heaving them up, turn them round: the young women do the same to the youths on Easter Tuesday. In 1548 it was, as we see, a week later; and this approached more nearly to the ancient festival, from which it was doubtless derived, of

---

[1] A Shakspearian word:
O that the earth which kept the world in awe,
Should patch a wall to expel the winter's *flaw!*
HAMLET.

[2] In Brand's Popular Antiquities, i. 155. is a description of it as practised in this town in 1799.

Hocktide, or Hoxtiwesdei (i. e. Hock Tuesday) which was on the Tuesday fortnight after Easter Tuesday.[1]

Of Hocktide, the derivations are various. The best opinion seems to be,[2] that it originated in the excessive joy of the English for their delivery from the oppressive dynasty of the Danes by the sudden death of Hardicnute; which event occurred on *Tuesday*, June 8th, 1042, after hard drinking at the *wedding* of Tovy Prudan, a Dane, to Githa daughter of the great Osgod Clap.[3] *Hoch-zeit* is German for a wedding, from *hoge*, joy, and *zeit*, tide, or time: so that *hock-tide*, in old England, may well have denoted *a high tide,* or *time of joy*: it is one of the numerous instances of affinity between the two languages, at an earlier period, when they had been more recently separated.[4] The other usages anciently practised on Hock Tuesday, of tying the men down in the chairs, (whence it was called *Binding Tuesday*, dies martis ligatorius,) stretching ropes across the streets, to entangle the passenger's feet[5], and the like, may probably have been designed to represent the stratagems which the English women employed on St. Brice's day 1002, to assist their husbands in murdering their Danish masters, *furtivo impetu*, as Matthew of Westminster has it.

It has been thought that this cruel massacre could have been no subject of exultation, and consequently could have no connexion with Hock Tuesday, because the Danes soon after so signally avenged it by laying waste this country; and at the time it certainly could not; but forty years after, when, on Hardicnute's death, the Danish yoke was actually shaken off, those stratagems, of which some tradition must have remained, might become the subject of joyful recollection. At what period these ceremonies were exchanged for that of heaving, the men admitted to a participation in them,[6] and the days changed to Easter Monday and Tuesday,[7] we no where learn; but the conjecture is by no means improbable, that the change was intended to *spiritualize* the frolick, and to represent the resurrection of our Lord, and the joy with which that event ought to be hailed.

---

[1] Archæol. vii. 246. Mr. Nares, therefore, (Gloss. in v.) is not quite correct in saying that it "commenced the fifteenth day after Easter:" it did not commence till the *sixteenth* day after that feast. One of our town records is express to the point. "Die lune proxima *post clausum pasche*," and " die lune proxima *ante hokeday*," are the titles of two consecutive weeks in a roll of accounts 14 Edw. I.

[2] This is that of Mr. Denne in an able paper quoted above from Archæol. vol. vii.

[3] Simeon Dunelm. sub ann.

[4] See below, ii. 267.

[5] Watts. Gloss. ad Matth. Paris.

[6] This had taken place at least as early as 1450; for then Bishop Carpenter endeavoured to suppress it in Worcestershire. "Uno certo die, hoc solempni festo paschatis transacto, mulieres homines, alioq. die homines mulieres ligare."—Leland Collect. v. 5, p. 298.

[7] In the book of the controller of the royal household 18 Edw. I. is an entry which may be thus translated. "Ladies of the Queen's chamber. Paid May 15, to seven of the Queen's ladies and damsels, who took our lord the King in his bed on the morrow of Easter, and made him fine to them for the King's peace, (et ipsum fecerunt finire versus eas pro pace regis), which he did of his gift, £14." Brand ut supra, p. 154.

1573. "From the beginning of November, until within fourteen days of Candlemas, the season was so pleasant and fair, without frost, or any snow to speak of, that there appeared leaves upon hawthorn and plum-trees before Christmas; and the cuckow was heard sing, and also seen ten days before Christmas: also, there was at New-year's-day, certain tenants in Shropshire presented their landlords with green geese."

1575. November. "There was a hart came by chance to Rowsell in Shrewsbury, and there hunted, and brought alive to the bailiffs. The like was never seen."

December 5. "The drapers had like to have been robbed, if they had not been privily warned thereof. Upon which warning, the bailiffs and a great number went strongly upon their usual trade towards Oswestry; at whose coming the thieves having intelligence shrunk away. They purposed to have robbed them in the dale betwixt Shelton and Shrewsbury; and over night they harboured themselves and their horses in Mr. Sherar's barn on the other side of the water, and in the morning baited their horses in the thicket over against Shelton's-hill, having boats to pass and repass to their pretended[1] purpose."

This deliberate plan of robbery in a spot so contiguous to the town evinces a most imperfect police, and will remind the reader of the scene at Gad's-hill in the first part of Shakspeare's Henry the Fourth.

1576. September 20, "was a plain cross seen in the element right over the north side of Shrewsbury, continuing a full half-hour, and then vanished away."

This appearance, which must have excited many superstitious notions at the time, arose, no doubt, from the setting sun projecting the cross of one of the spires upon a dense cloud; at least the writer of this observed something extremely like it on the 22d of November, 1823, about half-past three P.M., when, the upper clouds being very thick and lurid, the setting sun suddenly broke out, and threw the shadow of St. Mary's spire and its battlements upwards upon the clouds to a great height, which still increased as the sun declined. It is somewhere related, but we cannot now recover the passage, that during some nightly festivities at Milan, the attention of the people was forcibly excited by the figure of a cross suspended aloft in the air over the great square, and sundry speculations were formed concerning it, till it was discovered to be the image of a cross which surmounted an obelisk, cast upwards upon a cloud by the effect of the illumi-

---

[1] i. e. intended: so Shakspeare perpetually uses the word.

nations below. In the Memoirs of the Literary Society of Manchester, (vol. iii. p. 463), Dr. Haygarth has recorded, and given a plate of a curious nimbus, or glory, which surrounded his own head on a winter's evening, being the image of the setting sun projected before him on a very thick cloud.

1579-80. "One Master Richard Jones of Nottingham, gent. set up a common brew-house hard by the abbey in Shrewsbury, and began to brew beer for the town the 19th day of March, and inhabiteth in the same brew-house."

"In the said month of March, one Mother Garve of the Castle-foregate was punished in the corn-market for going about to bewitch and enchant a cat of hers a disease from her neighbour's sow; and yet, notwithstanding, the sow died of the said disease."

1581-2. March. "The famous house in the Abbey-foregate in the town of Shrewsbury, situate by a great barn called the Abbot's-barn, was builded by one Master Prynce, lawyer, called *Master Prynce's Place;* the foundation began in March 1578, so was it four years in building, to his great charge, with fame to him and his posterity for ever."

1582. April 25. "Came to Shrewsbury one named Anthony Frynpan, being a Fleming born at Antwerp, who was two yards and a half of height; and lodged at Master Thomas Mytton's house *Under the Wyle;* and many people resorted to see such rare sight; and departing towards London was robbed of all the money he had; for he had gotten a great piece of money, and would not be seen without money. Wherefore, for his covetous mind, he was prevented, and so lost all that he had."

Under 1583, is a long account of strange and wonderful sights brought hither by John Taylor, merchant, of London; as a dead child with two heads, a live sheep with six feet, &c.; "and if the party which kept him would ask him and say, "*Be those people welcome?*" he would lift up his fore-foot and cry, *heigh, heigh:* also a live eagle, a purpentine of the sea, dead, a wild live lynx, commonly called a wild cat, to whom the keeper would offer to strike, but she would fiercely defend the blow with her paws, rasing the staff mischievously." Other curiosities are described;[1] and there must have been an increased desire for information, and an increase of surplus wealth, before individuals would think of earning a livelihood by carrying such things about. Travelling into foreign countries, and the productions

---

[1] A glass artificially made, being but two candles therein, and a chain with two faces or pictures, which would represent inwardly sundry candles, chains, faces, jewels, and other things miraculously.

of such countries, were now become favourite amusements. "Were I in England now," says Trinculo in The Tempest, "and had but this fish painted, not a holiday fool but would give a piece of silver: there would this monster make a man."

1590. 27th March, "a man and woman were executed at Knockin-heath for murdering a child of the age of five years, for his lands, being an heir of £5. a year, or thereabout; which fell after the said child's death, if he died without issue, to his uncles, being three of them; which uncles procured and imagined the death of the said child ever since his birth. Two of the uncles were executed at Bridgenorth assizes, and the third pressed to death there.[1] But the woman, being grandmother to the child, and the man, named Geffery Elkes, being hired to do the deed, were executed at the said heath where the deed was done." Elkes, at his execution, affirmed that he did not kill the child, but brought a pail of water to the heath, and left it there with the child and the uncle that was pressed to death; "but he confessed that before the deed was done, and after, two ravens usually would meet him, follow him, and cry about him; and when he escaped and hid himself, the said ravens did cry and fled about the place, and descried him out, and so was found in a cock of hay by their means."[2]

A vague tradition of this melancholy tale, coupled with a mistaken etymology, has given rise to an opinion, that the murder of the two children by their cruel uncle, on which the affecting and popular ballad of *The Babes in the Wood* is founded, was perpetrated in Babby's Wood near Whittington. But that ballad varies in almost all its circumstances from the tale of our chronicler, and the scene of it is laid in Norfolk. The name of the wood near Whittington is derived from a very different source.[3]

---

[1] For this horrible punishment see below, vol. ii. p. 385.

[2] Gough, the historian of Middle, relates this story, as he had received it from tradition. He had never seen our Manuscript Chronicle, which, doubtless, gives the true account; and therefore his tale contains many material errors. According to him, Elkes was the uncle and the murderer, and fled towards London, but was pursued; and as the pursuers were passing on the road near Mimms in Hertfordshire, they saw two ravens sitting on a cock of hay, pulling the hay with their beaks, and making an hideous and unusual noise: upon which they alighted, and found Elkes asleep in the hay, who confessed, &c. as in the text, and was brought back, tried, and hanged in chains on Knockin-heath. Our chronicler concludes:—Elkes, at his death, warned all to take heed of privy murder, for the fowls of the air will descry them, as was well proved by himself.—That Providence may interfere for the detection of secret crime, we in no degree question; but the present case may be *immediately* ascribed, not excluding that higher consideration, to the cowardice and terrors of a guilty mind. When Ibycus invoked the cranes to avenge his death, (and exactly the same story is told by Luther as happening in his time,) the casual remark of the murderers, on seeing a flock of such birds, was certainly not intended by them to lead to their discovery, but may have had that direction from a SUPERIOR SOURCE. See Erasm. Adag. v. Ibyci grues; and Beard's Theatre of Judgments, b. 2. c. 11. p. 299.

[3] In Saxton's and Speed's maps it is written Babin-wood. Wood's is the first that has Babby's, and Kitchen, Babb; but Bavin's wood is the true name, as it is given in Baugh's map. A *bavin* is a faggot, and it denotes the low coppice of which that wood consisted. A similar reason has given name to Baveney-wood in the parish of Neen Savage.

1592. Tuesday, 13th of June, being the town court-day, one of the bailiffs, to say Master Edward Ireland, being forth of the town, and master bailiff Powell, being very sick, was carried from his house in a chair to the Booth-hall, and sitting therein, the court was *rejornid*; and so, in like manner, was carried again home to his house: which event hath not been seen or heard of before."

Thursday, August 24. "The bailiffs of Salop made a feast to the aldermen, common council, and to a number of the commons, in the Guild-hall, being at four tables above an hundred persons; where they had plenty of venison, wine, and other good cheer: the which venison was given by Mr. Richard Corbett unto the town, for to meet and assemble in friendly manner, and to make merry."

This must have been the gentleman who is called in the Visitation Sir Richard Corbet, of Morton Corbet, K.B.

"This year, about the end of August, there was made by the bailiffs a clock within the Guild-hall with a dial within the hall, and two dials without: the one to serve the heighe-streete, market, and passers-by; the other, towards the corn-market, in like manner: the which two dials do not only note how the hours of the day passeth, but also therein the picture of the moon, how it doth increase and decrease, very artificial and commodious to the beholders."

November 27. "In the night, Mr. Prynce his house or place in the Abbey-foregate, was broken by thieves: being frighted upon some noise, they departed upon a sudden to a cote hard by, where they left their horses; but when they came there, their horses were gotten out into the fields they knew not whither: so they took their heels[1] whither no man can tell; and in the morning, the horses, being two, were found, with their furniture; the which were brought to be seen both in this town and other places, if by the sight of them any knowledge might be had."

These horses occasioned much subsequent discussion. The bailiffs seized them as waifs, and delivered them to Mr. Prince to be taken round to Worcester and several other market-towns, to be viewed and proclaimed for the discovery of the felons. But at Lichfield, as our bailiffs write to the Earl of Essex, "one Eyns, a servant, or officer of your Lordship's," seized them as waifs belonging to that nobleman. The bailiffs, therefore, apply to the Earl for redress, "for that we assure ourselves so much of your honour's good will and favour to us, that your Lordship will rather

---

[1] We should now express this, "they took *to* their heels." The ancient phrase is much more significant: indeed the modern one has no meaning.

assist us and the said liberties and town of Shrewsbury in defence of our right, than to take any thing wrongfully from the same. And so committing your honour to the protection of the Almighty, we humbly take our leaves, the 24th of February, 1592." The Earl's answer, which this letter explains, may be seen above, p. 550.

Eyns, of whom both parties speak so familiarly as *servant* to the Earl of Essex, was a gentleman of family and fortune at Church Stretton, and, in all probability, a first cousin of Sir John Thinne, founder of the Marquis of Bath's family. The name is usually written Heynes.

" 1594. Tuesday July 30th, being the town court day, a matter between Master Francis Meredith, and Master Stury of Rossall, went to a jury. They were charged about 8 o'clock at night, and continued until the same hour on Thursday night, without meat, drink, or any other relief, and some of the jury, before they would yield, would die themselves, or famish others. Upon which extremity the bailiffs and worship of the town entreated both the parties to consider the lives of men, and to put the matter to friends. The which, in the end, they did, and so the jury came out, weak enough; some of whom, if they had tarried one night longer, had died."

In our General History under the year 1595, we have noticed the imposition of ship-money by the ministers of Queen Elizabeth. The sum actually paid was £40; but 100 marks (£66. 13s. 4d.) was at first demanded, and the following letter shews that this new species of imposition did not pass without great murmurs even in that obsequious reign. The reader will not fail to observe, that the sum imposed upon this town exceeded that demanded from Worcester by more than one-half.

Right Worship", my dutie remembred, etc. I have received yo' l'res of the second of March. Whereby I understande that the ll'. of her Matie. moste honrable privie Councell have wrote unto you, for the levyinge of one hundred markes towardes the Shippinge to be sett fourth for her Ma^{ts}. service by the Cittie of Bristoll, wch l'res (albeit they maie seeme somwhat to discourage you,) yet in so much as since the date of their l^{ps}. l'res we have byn manie tymes before their hono^{rs}, & aunswered the contents thereof, you shall not (I hope) by not retourninge anie answer incurr their ll^{ps} displeasure. And for yo' wrytinge to Bristoll I thinke it not amisse you adv'tise them that (by us) you have aunswered the ll'. of the Councell, and so not wryte anie further things unto them. The Cittie of Worcester hath alreadie paide their xl^{li}. I thinke, seinge that the ll'. have p'cured Worcester to yelde, they will require the like of us, Wherefore I beseech you, with all convenient speede, to sende me up word what I shall doe herein, and I doe verely thinke the sooner I heare from you, the better shall I proceed in o' sute, and with the lesse charge. I doubt not but Mr. Cherwell hath before this tyme p'ticularly unfoulded unto you what hath byn done herein upon the sev'rall meetinges of the ll'. of the counsell, referringe you wholly unto his sufficiencie to instructe you in all the p'ticulars. And thus exspectinge yo' speedie resolucon, in all dutie I humbly take my leave this eight of Marche, 1595.

Yo' assured to comaunde,
ROGER MARSHALL.

To the Right Worship[ll] William
   Jones & Thomas Charlton,
   Bayliffes of the Towne of
   Shrewsbury, give these.

1596. The market-house begun and finished.

1597. April 13. "It rained wheat in some small quantity in Ludlow. There did the like fall in Pontesbury, and some in Shrewsbury very shortly after. The said grain being three square, some in perfect form, and some blacker and softer than the natural form, but fine of flour, and thinner rinded than the natural. God for his mercy's sake turn all to the best, and give us all grace to repent and amend. Amen!"

We pass over a great match of fighting cocks, Shropshire against Cheshire and Lancashire, in 1598, persuaded that minds which can be gratified by the consideration of ancient manners, would derive no pleasure from any memorial of so cruel a diversion. In the room of this cock-fight, we substitute a petition which seems to belong to this period, and refers to amusements of a more manly description. Of the *silver Game* of which it speaks, and which has not occurred to us elsewhere, we can think of no better reason than some of the ingenious conjectures of the minstrels in Shakspeare.[1]

To the right worshipfull the baylyfs, aldermen and counsaile of the towne of Shrowsbury.

Humbly besecheth your worships your poore orator Thos. Lloyd of this towne fletcher and beinge one of the comburges of this towne, havinge had greet sicknes and his famyly of long time, and the mistery of fletchers decayed by the wiche he is to get his lyvinge....and nowe therby brought to great adversite and povertie and hopeth nevertheles to be comforted and releved by his frends and alies yf he might be permitted to proclaime a silver game within

---

[1] Romeo & Juliet, A. 4. S. 5.—" Why, *musick with her silver sound?*" &c.

the towne; & to thintent his frends & alies may mor freely have accesse to come to releve & helpe hym with yor worship's favor and priveleg for all persons, for the tyme of the said silver game resorting to the same & shewing or offrynge to do any mastry therein, to pass & repass withowt arest. In tender consyderacon wherof may it plase your worships to graunt thefect therof unto your pore orator, & that he may, by your licens, proclaime the same silver game; as shoting flight and standerd, *hoshell*, Roning, leaping, & wrastling, & such lik activities used in silver games, & the persons to have the privelig as aforsayd, & this for God's love.

Hit is licenced that he shall have his game withoute anye suche priveledge except uppon Mr. bayliffes discrecon.

1600. April 12. "A servant of Master Thomas Onslow of Borow Attoon, near Baschurch, stood upon the pillory with a paper as concerning a vehement suspicion in him to pretend the poisoning of his said master." This is the last extract we shall make from our MS. chronicle.

The rolls of bailiffs' accounts which we have perused since those which terminated at p. 399, contain a few more particulars, which shall be briefly inserted, in continuation of the minor events of our town.

The same system continued of welcoming all personages of distinction who visited Shrewsbury, with a refection or banquet in the town-hall, and at the expence of the corporation. Indeed this was so much expected by the nobility, that, when the Earl of Arundel arrived in Bristol in 1616, finding no entertainment of the city, he so much resented it, that he after refused the courtesy proferred him.[1]

Our rolls supply, among other instances, the following.—

1601. Bestowed on Mr. Price of the Newe Towne, and other gentlemen of worshipe having occasions with Mr. Bailiffs in the Bothe hall, a potell of muscadell and three fine cakes: 2s. 6d.

—— Wine bestowed upon Sir Edward Kynaston, Mr. Roger Owen, &c.

In the same year, £12. 9s. 10d. is set down as charges about the justices of assizes and high sheriff, in wine, sugar, beer, house rome, and all other necessaries and furnitures, (£3. 6s. 8d.) wood fagotts, rushes and flowers to dress the judges' seats, (1s. 8d.)

Half-a-dozen of wood kokes in 1602 are charged 2s. 6d.

1602. Aug. 19. Bestowed upon Sir Henry Bromley, knight, to bid him welcome into this contrey, 3 gallons of clarett wyne, 2 gallons of sacke, 16s., a hundred of peares, 1s., one sugar loaf weying 9lb. at 22d. the lb. 17s. 5d., two dosen of fine cakes, 4s., in all, £1. 17s. 5d.

Item given to the keeper of Shrawarden parke, for his fee, 5s.

Item geven to the other officers in Sir H. B. his house, 8s.

1603. Bestoed upon my Lord President two fatt oxene, with the charge of fetching & bringing them, £14. 16s. 11d.

[1] Seyer's Hist. Mem. of Brist. c. 27. § 26.

1603. Bestowed upon the preachers at a monthlie exercise, a quart of sack, and the same of clarrett, 1s. 8d.

—— Bestowed upon the Steward of the counsell, and other gentlemen of worship belonging to the Lord President, in wine and fine cakes, 10s.

—— Paid for captaine Blunt for himself and his gide, with 3 horse, 2s. 6d.

This was probably some near connexion of Sir Charles Blount, Lord Mountjoy, so eminent for his services in Ireland.

—— Given to the Kinge his majesties players, 20s.

The following is a bill of expences of R. Mountgomerie, town-clerk.

Spent on myself and my horse up to London and downe againe, and my charges there, being in the whole 22 days: and spent and bestowed upon gentlemen that shewed the towne extraordinary favoure in the said sute, £7.

It was a law-suit between the corporation and Mr. Alexander Wood.

Payd for the chardges of two Scotts, the one of them beinge suspectid to bee one of the Gowries, 2s. 4d.

Few readers require to be reminded of the fright experienced by James I. on the 5th of August 1600, from the extraordinary seizure of his person by two brothers, John earl of Gowry and Alexander Ruthven. As they were both killed on the spot, the Scot apprehended at Shrewsbury must have been taken up on suspicion of being one of their confederates.

—— Expended in provision for the intertaynment of Sir Robert Steward, knight, one of the kings majestie's privye chamber, the 18th, 19th, 20th, & 21st daies of November, expecting his coming to towne by the advertisement of Mr. Henry Tenshownde and Mr. Rich. Berker, our recorder, £10.

"In Januarie & ffebruarie A° 1602. [i. e. 1602-3.]

John Perche desireth alowans of that he disbursed in regard of busines by him done at London for the corporation, upon Mr. Bayliffs request, viz. for the deliverie of the certificatt & petition of the corporation unto the hands of the Lord keper, being ingrosed in parchement & sealed with the comon seale of this towne.

I did performe it, & had verie spetiall speech with his L. concerning it, & from him receaved verie favorable & kind words of his love & good regard of the good of this corporation, with his L. most curteowse comendations to the Bayliffs of Shrewsburie, upon mie taking mie leave.

I did attend verie spetially bie direction of a jentilman of good place neer abowt his Lordship, to find a fitt oportunitie for the purpose, at least 6. or 7. severall dayes, & some times was at some chardg upon this gent. for his kindnes.

The chardg bestowed owt of mie purse bie this occation, 9 or 10s.

I was at chardg of bote hire sondrie times to & fro at least, 3 or 4s.

And what it shall please Mr. Bayliffs & six men to allow unto mee in regard of mie travaile & time of attendancs I referr to them.—[In toto 20s. in a different hand.]

I do deliver into the Cheker againe herewith the box which I Rec' with the sealed writing. And the copie of the said writing to be safely kept p. M' Mytton.

p. me Jo. P'che."

1605. Wine to Sir Thomas Middleton and lady, 6s. 10d.

He had been lord mayor of London, and was founder of the Chirk family, having purchased that castle in 1595.

Bestowed upon Sir Robert Nedome and his lady in wine and cakes, 20s. 8d.

He had recently succeeded to his estate, and was created Viscount Kilmorey in 1625.

1606. The 8. of August bestowed on a nobell man won Frederick lancegrave and other knights & gentell men of his company, a pottell of Ipocrusse, a dossen of fyne cakes, & galon of clarett wyne & 2l. of shuger, 11s. 8d.

This should seem to be the same who was founder of the line of the landgraves of Hesse Homberg, and died 1636. We have not found any notices of his journey to England, in the course of which he visited our town.

—— Paid for the provition for the lord of Buckehurst, £2. 10s. 3d.
To Mr. Perch for his chardges in going to the lord Buckhurst to Shifnal, 2s. 10d.

This lord was Robert, son and heir of the first Earl of Dorset. He was probably on a visit to his wife's nephew, Thomas Earl of Arundel, who became possessed of the manor of Shiffnal by marrying the Lady Alathea Talbot.

1608. Geven to the King's Majesties players, & the queene & princes players, & other noblemens players, £3. 15s. 8d.

Edward Owen & John Hunt gent'. servinge the office of bailiwick in this towne in the most miserable & lamentable tyme of the contagious plague to the endaungeringe of their lyves, to their extraordinary charge, had allowans of £29. 1s. 2d. They now seeke for £48. 10s. more.

They had served the office five years before. It were vain now to inquire why they permitted so long an interval to elapse, before they preferred this ulterior claim.

—— Parcels for the Lord Harbute, his chardges, £1. 17s. 3d.

We are unable to specify this Lord Herbert. The Earl of Pembroke of that day had no son. His brother Philip had been made Earl of Montgomery two years before; and no other branch of the Herberts was then ennobled.

The following petition will shew that our corporation expended their revenues, which were then ample, upon' worthier objects than treats and players; that they assisted indigent scholars, and encouraged religious education:

To the right worshipfull Richard Higgons, and John Nicholls, gent⁸.
bailiffs, &c.

Whereas Richard Bythell, B.A. of the University of Oxenford, being enforced, through want of convenyent mayntenance, to discontynewe his residence in the said university: and having, by God's providence, and his industrye, attayned to some competent sufficiencie to serve in the ministry, but is yet unbeneficed; and now opportunity offred him for the obteyning of some staye of living in your neighbourhood, but is unfurnished with some necessarye, is emboldened with the reports he hath heard of your good inclination to learning and true religion, to acquaint your worships,—the petitioner therefore prays such small benevolence as you shall think fit, and shall, God willing, make often repaire to the town, to tender to your worships his dutiful service.

1611. Mar. 5. Geven unto Mr. Lightfoote, a precher, which made two sermons, 20s.

John Lightfoot, the great orientalist, was the son of a Staffordshire clergyman, who was most likely the divine so handsomely rewarded on this occasion.

1612. Aug. 10. Gevan unto twoe strange frenche gent. which did teache schole in towne, and then, for want of mayntenaunce, departe the towne, 20s.
Bestowed upon the Lord Bushoppe of the Ile of Maune in wine, 2s. 6d.

His name was John Philips.

1613. Paid to John Hill, jersy-worker, for his house rent this year, £3. 6s. 8d.

This was, doubtless, to set the poor to work.

Bestowed upon Mr. Edmonds, one of the clarks of the privy councell, 8s. 11d.

This gentleman, Clement Edmonds, Esq. afterwards Sir Clement, was a Shropshire man, being a native of Shrawarden, and son of Sir Thomas Edmonds, comptroller of Queen Elizabeth's household. It is remarkable, that he was preceded in his office by another Sir Thomas Edmondes, who was no relation to him. Sir Clement was an author: having published in 1600, a translation of Cæsar's Commentaries de Bello Gallico; and in 1609, of those de Bello Civili, with observations upon them. In the title-page of this last work he stiles himself *Remembrancer of the city of London*, so that he could not then have held the higher office of a clerk to the Privy Council. He bought an estate at Preston near Northampton, and died 13th November 1622, aged 58.

1613. Bestowed upon Sir Vincent Corbett two potells of maligo sacke, sugar, fine cacks, & calliwells, 8s. 4d.

Given to a Gretian, 5s.
Given to the Lady Elizabeth her players, 20s.
Paid what was bestowed upon Mr. John Griffithes a preacher & a prognosticator, 23d.

That even grave divines were in that age seduced by the folly of astrology needs not to be related. Lord Clarendon, in his fine character of William Herbert, the third Earl of Pembroke, tells of some persons of quality, friends of that earl, supping together on his birth-day. At supper, one of them drank a health to him: i. e. as we should now phrase it, *gave him for a toast*. Upon which another of them said, that his lord had now outlived the day which his tutor, Sandford, had prognosticated upon [considering] his nativity he would not outlive; for that this was his birthday. That very day he died. This Shrewsbury prognostication was not very expensive, for it appears to have cost only a penny.

1615. April 24. Paid towards a banquett bestowed upon my lord treasurers sone, £16. 10d.

The treasurer at this time was Thomas Howard Earl of Suffolk, possessor of a considerable property in Shropshire, at Oswestry and Clun. The son now entertained at Shrewsbury was probably his fifth, Sir Robert, to whom he gave the latter estate.

A present is charged for Mrs. Merriell Lyttleton.

Muriel daughter of Lord Chancellor Bromley, married John Lyttelton, esq. of Frankley, and was the great preserver of that ancient family after its ruin by her husband's unfortunate connexion with the Earl of Essex.

The accompt of Arthur Kynaston, gent. for the some of £38. 7s. 5d. by him recieved in November last, 1614, at his going to London shortlie after at their appoyntment to answere the lords of the councell their letters touching the gratuitie given to his Majestie.

The unbounded profusion of King James had, by this time, reduced him to great straits. He was extorting money all over the country by privy seals; and, as it appears, had applied to our corporation for a loan.

Journey to London and stay there, by promise of Mr. Bailiffs, £6.
Given to the Lord Treasurer's Secretary, to be myndful of the busynes in my absence, that no imputation should be laid upon the towne, 22s.
Second journey to London, towching the trayned soldgers, and remaining there upon that busynes, attending the Lord Presydents leisure from 21 Jan. 1614, to 12 March then next following, £6.

The object of this journey was to obtain permission that the corporation might muster their own soldiers, and be lieutenants for that purpose within the liberties. The Lord President, upon whom Mr. Kynaston was so long kept waiting, was, doubtless, Lord Evers, President of the Council of the Marches.

9 Dec. 1614. Spent by Mr. bailiffs upon Mr. Barckley, whoe was burges for this town at the last parliament upon his own chardge, and in regard of other paynes which he tooke for the corporation, 10s.

From this entry we must correct our list of burgesses of the parliament at p. 551. It is there stated, that Mr. Berkeley became representative of the borough in 1617, on the death of Sir Roger Owen. But we now see that Sir Roger, though undoubtedly elected, either never served at all, or only for a very short time, and that Mr. Berkeley was elected in his room. The entry also lets us a little into the motives which induced boroughs to depart from the ancient usage of choosing representatives from their own body, and electing strangers. Such *foreign members* were willing to serve without fee.[1]

For making a place of three stepes high and eight foote long, for the jury to stand upon, 2s.

This entry is extracted only to mark the subordination in which the lower ranks were kept in that age. Juries, who are now very properly accommodated with *seats*, were then, as we see, kept *standing* during the whole of a trial. Little incidental hints like this, which no historian would deign to record, indicate the revolutions of opinion better than many a laboured disquisition.

Robert Owen's MS. described at p. 525, records, that on the 4th of August, 1614, a person of the name of Coles rode from London to Shrewsbury between 3 o'clock A.M. and 5 o'clock P.M., a very extraordinary performance at any period; but more particularly so, when the roads, as then, were in a state of nature; for it cannot be less than eleven miles an hour,[2] without allowing any time for rest or refreshment. This feat, therefore, exceeds in speed that of the first Earl of Cork,[3] which has been deemed incredible; but falls somewhat short of the expedition of Mr. Carey, when, a few years before, he rode to Edinburgh[4] with the news of Queen Eliza-

---

[1] They were not, however, so much regarded in the house as the actual burgesses. Mr. Broughton, of Oldbury in this county, who was one of them, writing to his father-in-law, Mr. Bagot of Blithfield, in 1588, when a Spanish invasion was anxiously apprehended, says, " in this great extremitie, we, who care more for our countrey than ourselves ...are...willinge..to yeld to accomplishe this end," [of granting a double subsidy,] "and althoughe we *foren burgesses elected* are not so well acquainted with payments of subsidies as *the inhabitants of boroughs* are, yet we, having their *power and aucthority to assent*, shall be well dijested.—Bagot Memorials, p. 49.

[2] This is taking the distance at 154 miles, which, according to Carey, it exceeds by half-a-mile, and according to Paterson falls short of by about a mile.

[3] Richard Boyle, afterwards Earl of Cork, left Shannon Castle about 2 o'clock on Monday morning, and supped with Sir Robert Cecil at his house in the Strand, London, on Tuesday evening. Supposing him to have taken two hours to ride from Shannon Castle to the mouth of Cork harbour, and to have occupied thirty hours in the passage to Bristol, and to have reached London by 10 o'clock at night, this leaves twelve hours for the land journey, 112 miles, or not quite nine miles and three furlongs per hour.

[4] Robert Carey, afterwards Earl of Monmouth, desirous to secure an interest with James I. by being the first messenger of his succession to the English crown, took horse from London between 9 and 10 o'clock in the morning, Thursday, March 24, 1603, and that night rode to Doncaster, 158 miles. Supposing him to have been thirteen hours on horseback, this will give a little more than twelve miles and one furlong per hour. On Friday he reached Widdrington, 137 miles; but did not get to Edinburgh (106 miles) till late at night on Saturday, because he had a severe fall by the way.

beth's death; of Mr. Calvert's exploit, a few years later;[1] and still more of Cooper Thornhill's famous ride[2] from Stilton to London, called by Granger the most extraordinary instance in history.[3]

In 1615, Ralph Lord Eure, Lord President of the Marches, visited Shrewsbury, and was received in a very distinguished manner. The bill of the bailiffs' expences on that occasion amounts to £87. 5s.

Paid for warders to attend Mr. Bailiffs att the quarell betwene Sir Robert Vernon and Sir Francis Prynce, 2s. 6d.

Feb. 2, 1615, paid by me Richard Harries, common serjeant, to diverse watchmen and wardors to attend to keepe the king's peace when it was rumored in towne that Sir F. P. and Sir R. V. were to feight.

Sir Robert Vernon of Hodnet, knight, was born in 1577, succeeded his father in 1591, and narrowly escaped being very seriously implicated in the strange insurrection of his cousin german, the Earl of Essex. Sir Francis Prynce was ten years his junior, a gay young gentleman of very expensive habits. Of their quarrel, which excited so much alarm in the civil authorities, we have found no other notice.

1616. Given to the King's Maties. Trompetors, and to the prince's players, 42s.

Repayd unto Mr. Francis Barkley, which he paid to the corporation, and was taken from him by the barons of the exchequire, 15s.

Charge of the corporation bestowed on the L. Garrett, the   day of May, 1617, £19. 6s.

Thomas Gerard, Lord Gerard of Gerards Bromley, had just been appointed President of the council in the Marches of Wales. That council no longer repaired, as formerly, to our town, for a lengthened residence; but each successive lord president appears to have made one solemn visit to Shrewsbury, the most considerable place under his jurisdiction, at the commencement of his presidency.

Paid Symyco and his man for serchinge for coles in the townes grownde, 9s. 8d.

Jan. 1619-20. Paid to a purcevant which brought a bundell of p'cla' concerning the prohibitinge of planting of tobacco in England, 3s. 4d.

From this time not a year elapses without frequent mention of bundles of proclamations. These instruments had occasionally been issued by every

---

[1] Bernard Calvert went from Southwark to Calais and back again between 3 o'clock in the morning and 8 in the evening, on July 17, 1620. Deducting 6 hours for the passage, leaves 11 for the journey by land, 140 miles, or something more than 12 miles and 5 furlongs per hour.

[2] Mr. Thornhill rode, April 29, 1745, from Stilton to London, back again to Stilton, and again back to London, in 12 hours and a quarter, 213 miles: this is more than 17 miles an hour!

[3] Biographical History, ii. 281. Vigneul-Marville gives the following as remarkable instances of dispatch:—A captain who went in three weeks from Constantinople to Fontainbleau; a courier who went in three days and nights from Paris to Madrid with the news of the massacre of St. Bartholomew; another, who went from Paris to Poland in twelve days; and he adds, that an abbé was the first courier who made the journey from Paris to Rome in eight days.—t. i. p. 544.

sovereign since Henry VIII.' and were then considered even on a footing with acts of the legislature. But the number of them greatly increased under the government of James I. His inconsiderate profusion reduced him to necessities which his parliaments were not always willing to supply, and which, therefore, his ministers were obliged to assist by new methods: and his remarkable want of judgement rendering him insensible of the rising spirit of the commons, their discontents gradually rose to that height which ended in the ruin of his son. From this time proclamations became a regular tax upon the corporation.

1619. March 10. Paid for two bundells of proclamations, one for light gould, and thother for ould hoggesheads, 6s. 8d.

1620. Aug. 15. Two messengers bringing two bundles of proclamations, one concerning tobacco-pipes: and another concerning tenants' rents.

1621. Paid to several messengers for bringing one bundle of proclamations concerning *greevances*, one other bundle concerning *lavish speech*, another prohibiting the eating of flesh.

1620-1. Mar. 20. Paid for three bundles of proclamations for the apprehending of Sir Gyles Monpessons, and other causes.

This knight was one of three persons who had obtained several oppressive patents from the crown. It was a scheme to enrich Sir Edward Villiers, brother of the reigning favourite, at the expence of the subject. The house of commons fastened upon it as soon as they met; the patentee made his escape, and fled abroad.

We have afterwards (Mar. 11, 1622) proclamations concerning the *redresse of greevaunces*; (Oct. 19) concerning *archery*; (1625) for *gentlemen and others to repayre to their own habitations at Christmas*; (March 4, 1633) concerning *the pike and longe bowe*; (1637) concerning *a pattente for carriage of letters*.

1621. Laid out in stocking up of the gorst in Kingsland, making the same into faggottes, and ridding and making cleane the growndes, £5. 4s. 6d.

1622. Paid for suing forth two severall *Quietus Est* for dischardging this towne and liberties from Tenths and Fifteenths, and for divers other extraordinary buisnes expended about that buisnes, and about answering a *Quo Warranto*, £14. 9s. 10d.

Paid to severall persons for search of a suspected seminary, one Clough, 4s.

A *seminary* was an English Roman Catholick educated at one of the English colleges established abroad after the final establishment of the Reformation under Qu. Elizabeth, which persons were dispatched into this country to propagate their religion. Mr. Clough was probably a member of the ancient family of his name long seated at Minsterley in this county.—See our vol. ii. p. 476.

1626. Oct. 2. Given to a poore distressed gent. and his wief, being inhabitants in Ire-

---

[1] A few occur in the reign of Edward IV. and perhaps earlier.

land, whoe had there howse and lands taken from them to builde a forte, as appereth by a testimoniall under the hands of the Councell of Ireland, 18d.

1629. Given unto Mr. Edward Vaughan for contriving the forte, £5.

We have no account where this fort was. There was one during the ensuing civil wars at the end of Frankwell, near Cadogan's cross,' but whether this was the same, and why it should be put into a state of defence now, when the country was in a state of repose, we are not able to say.

Sept. 17. Cakes and wine bestowed upon Mr. Talbott, who is nexte heyre to the Lord Talbott, 7s. 10d.

George Talbot, earl of Shrewsbury at this time, had no son, so that there could then be no person properly stiled Lord Talbot: but his next heir was his nephew John Talbot, Esq. of Longford, and he was probably the person intended.

Sept. 29. Paid Mr. Thomas Owen for serving as a burges of the parlamente for this towne and libertyes the laste sessions of the parlamente, for his chardge in travelling and there attendinge during the last session, according to the agreement of the commons, £13. 6s. 8d.

That session continued two months. We have seen above that in 1603 a town-clerk's journey to London and back, staying there 22 days, and certain undefined expences, amounted to £7. The same journey with a stay of 50 days, cost £6. in 1615, whence we may infer that the remuneration to a member of parliament was nearly doubled.

1630. Michaelmas. Spent on Sir Marmaduke Lloyd and other gentlemen of worship coming to the town, £1. 3s. 6d.
1633. Spent upon Sir Marmaduke Lloyd, on the election day, 10s.
1635. Wine and sugar to Sir Marmaduke Lloyd, 6s.

We cannot identify this knight, who appears to have made such frequent visits to Shrewsbury. He was probably of the Trenewydd family. Edward Lloyd, Esq. of that place, the great Shropshire antiquary, was son of *Marmaduke* Lloyd, Esq. of Trenewydd.

1632. Sept. 10. Spent upon the Countess of Arundell, 16s. 7d., also in sweet-meats, £1. 12s. 6d.

She was the Lady Alathea Talbot, who has been mentioned above, daughter and coheir of Gilbert earl of Shrewsbury. In 1635, she and her husband both came here: for there are charges—

Ringing when the earl of Arundell and his Countesse came to town, 4s. Provision for him, £11. 16s. 6d.
1631. March 31. Spent on the Lord Powes and Sir James Palmer, 4s. 4d.

' See above, p. 454.

William Herbert, Lord Powis, so created 1629. His daughter Catharine married to her second husband, Sir James Palmer.

1633. Bestowed on the Lord Newburgh, one of his ma^{ties}. privy council, £2. 13s. 8d.

Sir Edward Barret, bart. was created baron of Newburgh, in Fifeshire, in 1628.

1634. Oct. 2. Journey to the Earl of Bridgewater, Lord President of the Marches, to know when his Lordship would be in Shrewsbury.

This was the Lord President for whom Milton wrote the Masque of Comus, presented before him in Ludlow Castle this very year.

The next year produced the revival of the imposition of ship-money, for relief from which the subsequent petitions were preferred.

Term. Hillar. a° xi Caroli Regis, 1635.

Pro ballivis & burgensibus ville Salop, concernen' soluc̄o̅em monete pro edificac̄o̅e navis, £3.

For writing severall petic'ons to my lord of Arundell, two to my lord president, and three which were amended, to the lords of the privey counsell, at 16d. each, 8s.

1635. Sept. 29. Charge bestowed on Sir Nathaniel Brente, the Archbishop's visitor-general, when he visited in the town, £3. 2s. 8d.

Laud, anxious to repress the irregularities which had so long subsisted in the church of England, resolved, in 1634, upon a metropolitical visitation of the whole province of Canterbury, which was carried into effect in that and in the following year; and having, says his biographer, "some distrust of Brent, his vicar-general, he prepared one of his confidents" (perhaps Heylyn himself) "to be a joint commissioner with him. But afterwards, being more assured of Brent than before he was, he resolved to trust him with himself, [i. e. *by himself*,] and not to fetter him with any such constant overseer."[1] Sir Nathaniel, however, was far from steady to the cause of episcopacy; and "when he saw the presbyterians begin to be dominant, he sided with them, and became a frequent witness against Laud at his trial."[2]

1636. Nov. 22. Spent on my Lord Castell Illandes four pottles claret, 5s. 4d. Two ditto sacke, 4s. Two dozen fine cakes, 4s.

This was the celebrated Lord Herbert of Chirbury, who had been created an Irish peer by the title of Baron Castle Island, in the county of Kerry, in 1625; and by this title he appears to have continued to be designated, though he had been raised to the English peerage by his more known title, in 1629.

It has been already mentioned, p. 406, that a *quo warranto* was issued against the corporation in the reign of Charles I. The following extracts contain some particulars of the transaction. They occur in the time of Thomas Niccolls, esq. and Simon Weston, gent. bailiffs, i. e. 1636-7.

[1] Heylyn's Life of Laud, p. 285.   [2] Wood, Athenæ. in v.

Dispended concerning the answering of the Quo Warranto against the town, and in defending of the towne's right concerning the curate's place of St. Chadde's, in parte of a greater some, the same being yet unknown, in regard the solicitor's bills cannot bee had, £45.

Paid to the clerk of the privy councell for preferring the petition, for his fee, 40s.

For the letter from the privy councell, 10s.

To him that kept the councell-chamber dore, 1s.

Spent in travail to Hampton-cort & to Windsor, & staying ther from Friday morning till Wensday night, 16s.

For my paynes for attending there from Friday morninge till Munday night, for because I durst not goe to London, what you please.

The whole expences of suing out the new charter were £521. 19s. 2d.; and the Privy Council made an order in 1638, that it should be paid by an assessment on the burgesses and inhabitants of the town and liberties, and likewise on the foreign burgesses. The rolls of this assessment are still remaining, with the mayor's warrant to the collectors, dated Nov. 26, 1638, charging and commanding them in his Majesty's name to attach any persons that should be obstinate or refractory, and bring them before him, (the mayor,) "to doe and receave that which by the said order I am required." This was anticipating, perhaps not very judiciously, opposition to the demand; and in fact, though the money was almost generally paid, yet a few individuals refused compliance, and petitioned the privy council for redress. The chief of the defaulters were, Mr. Richard Hunte, Mr. Thomas Wingfield, Mr. George Hunte, Mr. Owen George, Mr. John Proude, and Mr. Adam Webbe. The final adjustment of the affair appears to have been left to Sir Thomas Milward, chief justice of Chester, and in that capacity a member of the council of Wales;[1] who, by letter of July 2d, 1639, directs Mr. Jones, the first mayor, to give notice to the persons interested, to attend him at his chamber in Ludlow Castle. The mayor, in reply, informs him that he had done so; but upon calling before him the six persons above mentioned, and upon perusal of the accompt, " there was not soe much difference but that I hope we shall divide it amongst ourselves, and not further trouble your lordship therein."

This hope, however, was not realized. The proposal that those who had already paid their own assessments, should bear, in addition, a part of the sums demanded from the "refractory," excited, we may presume, many murmurs, which assumed a bolder aspect as the difficulties of the government increased; and the success of rebellion in Scotland proved that the sovereign might be resisted with impunity, and even with reward. This we collect from the following letter, written by Mr. Jones's successor in office to the lords of the privy council.

[1] He is stiled of Eaton-Dovedale in co. Derby, and compounded for his loyalty in the sum of £360. Robert Milward his son was an assistant judge in the council of Wales.—Ottley MSS.

Righte Honorable,

I receaved an order made by your Lordshipps at the Inner Starr Chamber the 20th of November 1639, concerninge the raysinge of a cesmente formerly made by order from your Lordshipps, for the money imployed for the chardges of sueinge forth the newe charter of the said towne; whereby I am required, that I, the presente maior, should call before me Richard Hunte, gent. Thomas Wingefielde & Thomas Knighte, gents, late of & John Loe *and all others that shall refuse or have refused to pay the rates assessed upon them for the same busines, or shall or have refused to give security to appere before your lordshipps, as by the said former order was directed*,[1] and to require them to paye the rates assessed upon them; and in case they shall refuse or delaye soe to doe, that then I fayle not to certifie their said refusal or puttinge of [i. e. *off*]: whereupon your Lordshipps will send for them in custody of a messenger. Maye it please your Lordshipps, that I have called the aforesaid partyes before me; & all of them (save only John Loe, who paid me his cesmente within shorte time after I acquaynted him with your said Lordshipps order,) refuse to paye for the presente there said assessment, alledginge some frivilous excuses; and likewise the persons whose names are subscribed, delaye me with excuses and puttes-of. And I therefore humbly desire your Lordshipps to sende a messenger for them; being all able and sufficient men; and when these are ponished for there contemptes, all others will willingly paye there cesmentes; these beinge most the principall persons that oppose the paymente thereof. And so, with my humble dutye remembred to your Lordshipps, I humbly take leave, and reste

Att your Lordshipps comaunde,
Ro. BETTON Maior of Shrewsbury.

Salop, 30 Nov. 1639.

David Maddox, glover
Richard Prowde, baker
Edward Jones, ironmonger
William Lloyd, mercer[2]
Jonathan Gideon Rowley, draper
George Hunte, gent.
Richard Bagott, draper
Samuell Ireland, *draper*, gent.

Whether our Salopian Hampdens would have withstood the terrifick names of the *Star Chamber* and a *King's messenger*, cannot be known; for the King found himself at this very time under the necessity of convening a Parliament, and the privy council had something else to do than prosecute

---

[1] The words in Italics are interlined. [2] The words in Italics are erased.

a contest with a few inhabitants of a country town. The leading members of the corporation, too, would deem it prudent to desist from illegal and unpopular measures, which might expose them to the censures of a House of Commons. It is certain that all the money that had been collected was returned to the contributors; and the corporation took the whole charge upon itself.

Dr. Isaac Barrow, bishop of St. Asaph, uncle to the great divine of both his names, died here 24 June, 1680.

In August 1684, we are informed that the dukes of Ormond and Beaufort were entertained by the town. What brought the first of these noblemen here we have not heard; but the last of them visited Shrewsbury in his official capacity as Lord President of the Marches of Wales. He had held this distinguished office in an earlier part of the reign of Charles II.; and appears to have been reappointed in this year;[1] on which occasion he made a tour through his jurisdiction.

The duke was a person of great magnificence, being the same of whose princely way of living, ("above any other, except crowned heads," that Mr. Roger North "had notice of in Europe,") that writer gives so entertaining an account, in his amusing Life of Lord Guildford. Of the duke's reception at Shrewsbury we have no account, further than that he arrived here on Saturday August 2, was presented with twenty dozen of wine and twenty chargers of sweetmeats; after dinner viewed the Schools and Castle, and went that night to Ludlow. But a manuscript entitled "Notitia Cambro-Britannica, Voyage of North and South Wales, being remarks and observations in attending His Grace in his Progress and General Visitation there 1684 by T. D. gent." i. e. Thomas Dineley of Gray's Inn, records the order wherein he made his entry into Ludlow on the 17th of the preceding July; and no doubt the same was preserved wherever he went. We shall, therefore set it down in this place.

The Quarter-Master, or Harbinger for the Progress.
Four Sumpture Men in livery,
leading their baggage, covered with fair sumpture-cloaths of fine blew cloth, diversified and embroidered with the coat-armour of His Grace.
Three Assistants of the Stable in livery,
leading horses to supply accidents to the coach-horses on the road.
His Grace's Gentleman of the Horses, ... Lowe, Esq.
Six Pages in rich liverys, two in a brest.

---

[1] Hence the Peerages are to be corrected, which attribute his second appointment to James II.

Seven Grooms in His Grace's livery,
each with a led horse richly caparison'd, with saddles and housings richly embroidered and embossed with gold and silver. The device a portcullis with this motto in an escrowl, ALTERA SECURITAS.

His Grace's four trumpeters in rich coats,
their badges, His Grace's cypher in gold under a ducal coronet, both on their backs and breasts. Each had a silver trumpet, with gold and silver strings and tassels, and crimson-flower'd damask banners, embroidered with the coat-armour of His Grace; viz. the Sovereign Ensigns of France and England quarterly, within a bordure gobonated, Pearl and Saphire, within a garter. The motto in compartment.

Henry Chivers, Esq.
Lieutenant-Colonel of the Militia Foot in the County of Wilts,[1] richly equipped.

Of His Grace's Family,
Two Gentlemen at large.

| The Yoman of the wine-cellar, | The Groom of the chamber, |
| Tho. Parsons, gent. | Tho. Kemis, gent. |

in a brest.

Mr. Smith, musician.	Mr. Nichols, harper.
Mr. Aldred.	The Marescall, or Farrier of the Progress.
Mr. Wamwin, clerk of the kitchen.	Mr. Spiller.

in a brest.

Captain Spalding.	The Rev^d. His Grace's chaplain.
The Steward of the House.	The Steward outward.
Henry Crow, Esq. Secretary.	...Harecourt, Esq. His Grace's Solicitor.

Captain Lloyd and William Wolsley, Esq. steward of the Castle of Ludlow, Muster-Master of the County of Gloucester, and Governor of Chepstow Castle.

The Serjeant at Arms, Mr. Winwood,
with the white rod.

The Tipstaff, pursuivants, and other officers of the Court of Ludlow.

HIS GRACE THE LORD PRESIDENT OF WALES.

The Earl of Worcester, Sir John Talbot, the Sheriff of Salop [Richard Lyster, Esq. of Rowton], and a great number of Gentlemen of Quality in the rear.

---

[1] Mr. Dineley relates that on the way between Beaumaris and Lord Willoughby's house at Gwidder, Col. Chivers "rode three-quarters speed over Pen-main-mawr. A wise action!"

Then followed His Grace's chariot and two other coaches and six, in the first of which was Her Grace the Dutchess of Beaufort and the Countess of Worcester, &c.

The progress ended August 21, when his Grace left Troy and returned to Badminton.

1708. The Brown school begun. In 1779 removed into the Abbey Foregate. Having fallen into great neglect, it was renovated on the Madras system, and greatly enlarged in 1807, chiefly by the exertions of the Rev. W. G. Rowland.

1718. A great meeting of the Quakers here, from all parts of England; they had the Wool-hall four days to speak in.

1719. The lower walk, and two cross walks of the Quarry planted. Expence £65. 13s. Mr. Wright, a celebrated nursery-man, from whom a variety of the codling takes its name, was the person employed.

1719. Rowshill leased to Mr. John Thornhill for 99 years. He levelled it, and sowed it with rye-grass and clover.

1722. A regiment of foot commanded by Brigadier Stanwix, encamped on Kingsland during the summer.

1723. Sept. 4. Robert and William Bolas were executed for the murder of William Matthews and Walter Whitcomb at Beslow, June 19. They were hung in chains on the south side of the London road, a little beyond the 7th mile-stone, where the writer of this remembers the gibbet in 1775.

1726. Lamps were put up in several parts of the town at the expence of the several parishes.

1727. April 10. "Whereas the several gilds and innkeepers have withdrawn their contributions towards entertaining the judges, Agreed, that, for the future, the Corporation expend no more money on that account."

The judges of assize were refused the usual compliments by the Mayor. Upon which account the next assizes were held at Bridgenorth. This had long been a point much contested between the Judges and the Corporation; and the dispute was not settled as late as 1738, when the assizes were held at Bridgenorth; but it is believed that this was the last time.

In April was another meeting of Quakers from all parts of England.

1739. The *great frost* began on Christmas eve, and continued till March, thirteen weeks. The river Severn was froze up, and a tent was erected thereon, a sheep roasted, a printing-press set to work, &c.—There is an engraved view of the town taken as it appeared at that time.

1749. August 1. The hospital and school in Frankwell, founded by Mr. James Millington, draper, who died in 1737, were entered upon by the hospitalers and scholars.

1756. Thirty-seven colliers were brought to gaol for rioting and committing outrages in the county; it being a time of great scarcity. Four died in gaol: ten were condemned, whereof two were executed, and the rest pardoned.[1]

1759. A regiment of foot was raised and rendezvoused here; they were called the Royal Volunteers. Colonel Crawford had the command. On December 21st, the colours were received by the regiment, being carried

---

[1] Some circumstances attending this affair reflect so much credit upon the courage and humanity of the under-sheriff, that they deserve to be recorded in a note.

The trial took place at the Spring Assizes 1757; St. John Charlton, esq. of Appley Castle being high sheriff, and Mr. Leeke of the Vineyard his deputy. Ten of the rioters were left for execution; but the judge sent his report by express to the Attorney-General, with an intimation of the day fixed for the execution, and the individuals, four in number, who, as he deemed it expedient, should suffer the sentence of the law; which report had been transmitted to the office of Mr. Pitt, then Secretary of State: where it lay untouched, and was never laid before the King. The day of execution arrived, without any reprieve or respite; and Mr. Leeke was advised, and even pressed by several of the principal gentlemen in his neighbourhood, whom he consulted in this emergency, to leave all the prisoners to their fate. But he was so much shocked at the thought of executing so large a number, and was so much convinced that this could not be the intention of the judge, that he ventured to postpone the execution, and sent off an express to London, on the return of which he had the satisfaction of finding that his conduct was most highly approved of, and, still more, the consciousness that he had saved eight lives. The following is part of a letter written to him on the occasion by Lord Chief Justice Willes, then one of the Commissioners of the Great Seal.

Sir,

Till I saw your letter yesterday I was under the greatest uneasiness; for I took it for granted that all the ten rioters had been executed on Saturday last, as that was the day appointed for their execution; and upon my return from the Home Circuit on Thursday last, I found that by a shameful neglect in one of the Secretary of State's offices, (*I do not mean Lord Holdernesse's,*) no reprieve had been sent down; and as it was then too late to send one down, I saw no reason to hope that their execution would be deferred to a longer time. But though, to be sure, you have acted contrary to your duty, you have acted a wise, prudent, and most humane part; and you have not only my thanks, but the thanks of some of the greatest men of the kingdom, for the part you have acted on this occasion. . . . I once more thank you for what you have done, and am, &c.

We add part of a letter from Mr. Leeke's agent in town to him:

"My Lord Commissioner Willes was so afflicted . . . . that it really made him ill; and he did not, for two days, go into the king's closet, so much he feared the effect it might have upon the king's mind, if the affair was communicated to his Majesty while it was under that state of uncertainty. . . . . Thank God, your prudent and well-judged respite has prevented all the uneasiness and mischiefs that might have happened; and I have the pleasure to assure you, that no step was ever taken that has given more satisfaction, or gained more

in procession to St. Chad's church, where a sermon was preached by the Rev. Rowland Chambre, M. A. from Ephes. vi. 10.

1765. The Foundling Hospital built. Shut up 1774. Employed during the American war as a prison for Dutch prisoners. Converted into a Poor-house, under the name of The House of Industry, 1784.

Sept. 1766. Vails were abolished in Shropshire by a resolution passed at the Infirmary meeting. The grand jury at the Summer assizes had passed a similar resolution just before. It needs hardly be said that this was a fee expected by a gentleman's servants from every guest that dined at their master's table; a custom now preserved only at the official dinners given by the judges of assize upon the circuit.

1769. The Stone bridge, now generally called the English bridge, began to be rebuilt. It was finished in 1774. The cost of the bridge was £10,794.; but the total expence (including £1082. for the act of parliament and law charges) was £15,710; of which £11,494. was raised by a subscription, to which the late Lord Clive and Sir John Astley contributed £1500. each; Sir W. W. Wynn, £700.; John Newport, Esq. and Charles Baldwyn, Esq. of Aqualate, £600. each; Thomas Hill, Esq. of Tern, £500., and the Earl of Powis, £400.

1770. November 18. A great flood.[1]

1772. Dec. 6. The Shrewsbury Chronicle set up. The Salopian Journal did not follow till January 1794.

1774. April 1. Good Friday. A great fire in the Abbey Foregate. It broke out between two and three o'clock P. M. and continued raging for near five hours: in which time forty-seven houses, sixteen barns, fifteen stables, four shops, and several stacks of hay were consumed; besides five houses much injured. The sum of £794. 18s. 9d. was raised by subscription for

applause than this of yours has done. My Lord Commissioner Willes this day waited on the King with your letter, and has directed me to acquaint you, by his Majesty's order, that his Majesty entirely approves what you have done; and so does his lordship and all the judges who are in town, to whom it has been communicated."

Ancient Rome would have decreed her crown, OB CIVEIS SERVATOS, to an act of such *civil courage*.

[1] It exceeded by two inches and a quarter the flood of 1672, which had been deemed worthy of being recorded on a brass plate in a house in Frankwell.

This - is - to - let - you - know,
Y⁺ Seuern - up - to - mee - did - flow.
Dec. 21. anno 1672.

the relief of the sufferers, towards which the Drapers Company contributed £50. Of this £326. 8s. was paid to the objects of the charity; and £426. 7s. 4d. returned to the subscribers, being 10s. 9d. in the pound.

Aug. 26. General Paoli, so illustrious for his brave defence of Corsica against the French, came to this town, and staid two days; visiting, during that time, several of the first families here.

1779. Nov. 16. A great fire at Mr. Gronna's malthouse, at the bottom of Murivance.

1782. Baron Hotham laid a fine of £2000 upon the county, at the Summer assize, till they should build a new shire-hall. The new hall was used for the first time March 17, 1786.

1783. Aug. 23. The Shrewsbury Chronicle contains an extraordinary account of an immense globe of fire which appeared in the atmosphere about nine o'clock at night; seeming in magnitude about twenty times larger than the apparent face of the moon, with a tail like a comet, and moving with great velocity from S. W. to N. E., and apparently about one hundred yards above the tops of the houses.

1784. In this year a removal was effected of the signs which used to project from the houses into the streets.
Aug. 2d. The cent-anniversary of Sir Uvedale Corbett's club was kept at the Talbot; Robert Corbett, Esq. of Longnor, in the chair. It had been instituted in 1684, by the baronet whose name it bore, for the maintenance of whig principles in the county, and had been held once a quarter ever since; but it did not long survive this celebration of its hundredth year.

1787. County gaol begun upon: contract, £16,640. Finished 1793.

1792. New Welsh Bridge begun. Finished 1795. Expence £8000.

1795. Feb. 11. The Severn overflowed its banks to a greater height at Shrewsbury than was ever known. It exceeded the great flood of November 18, 1770, six inches and a half.

1800. Sept. 29. The school founded by Mr. John Allatt, who died in 1796, was opened.

1802. Sept. 12. A sturgeon 8 feet 6 inches long, 3 feet 4 in girth, and weighing 192 lb., caught in the wear below the Castle.

1806. The military *depôt* near St. Giles's built.

1811. May. The western side of the island, from Somersetshire, through the counties of Gloucester, Worcester, and Hereford, as far as Shropshire, was visited by most extraordinary storms of thunder, lightning, and rain. The greatest portion of its fury in this county exploded on the north-western declivities of the Stiperstones mountain, where the rivulets which feed the Rea or Meole brook take their rise. It cannot be doubted that a water-spout burst a little to the south of the White-grit mine, between seven and eight o'clock in the evening of Monday the 27th of the month; in consequence of which the streams which run by Minsterley and Pontesford poured such a prodigious quantity of water into Meole brook, that when it entered the Severn under Coleham bridge, it actually forced the current of the river backward towards its source, and realized an image on which poets are fond of dwelling as the characteristick of impossibility.—

> Quis neget arduis
> Pronos relabi posse rivos
> Montibus, & Tiberim reverti.

The devastation committed on the banks of those streams through which the torrent rushed, are more easily conceived than described. Houses, bridges, mills, trees, hedges, cattle, all fell a prey to its fury; and not fewer than sixteen or seventeen persons were said to have perished at Minsterley and Pontesford. A subscription was immediately commenced to supply the loss sustained by near two hundred families of cottagers, and the sum of £1862. 10s. 8d. was collected in a few weeks: of which £1322. 15s. 6d. was disbursed to the sufferers, and twenty-five per cent. returned to the subscribers. The liberality of the contribution was enhanced by the consideration that two other charitable subscriptions were going on at the same time: one for the British detained as prisoners by Bonaparte, and the other for the distress occasioned in Portugal by the invasion of the French.

1812. The Lancasterian school built.

1814. Column in honour of Lord Hill begun December 27. Expence, including the new road and lodge, £5973. Last stone laid June 18, 1816, being the anniversary of the battle of Waterloo.

1818. The new Butter Cross built.

1821. July 19. The Coronation of George IV. celebrated with great solemnity in Shrewsbury. The corporation, trades, and charity-schools, walked in procession from the Quarry to St. Mary's church, and the children were afterwards feasted in various parts of the town.

1825. St. Mary's alms-houses rebuilt.

The northern entrance into the town by the Castle Gates considerably lowered, and widened.

Thus have we endeavoured to trace the fortunes of our native town, from its first rude settlement by the fugitive Britons, through a long succession of generations; sometimes revelling in a barbarian licentiousness; at others crouching under tyrannick rule;—now torn by inward dissensions; and now guided by an orderly government,—till it has, at length, matured into that auspicious state; wherein the Empire, triumphant from a war which threatened the liberties of the world, and blessed with opulence and plenty, an extending commerce and manufactures universally flourishing, reposes with a security, to all appearance, solid; and Shrewsbury partakes of the welfare of the whole. Whether future historians shall hail the continuance of this prosperity, or mourn its reverse, will depend upon the uses to which we, and our successors, apply it: whether it excite within us gratitude to the GREAT GIVER, and attachment to the Constitution by which it is maintained, or tempt us into oblivion of our most sacred duties, at the call of restless and factious spirits, whose element is discord, and to whom alteration is improvement.

END OF THE FIRST VOLUME.

Printed by S. and R. Bentley, Dorset Street, Fleet Street, London.

TUDOR WYKEHAM GATE, MERTON COLLEGE

WITH PART OF THE BRIDGE

London Published by Harding & C.º Finsbury January 1823

Shrewsbury Tradesmen's Tokens.

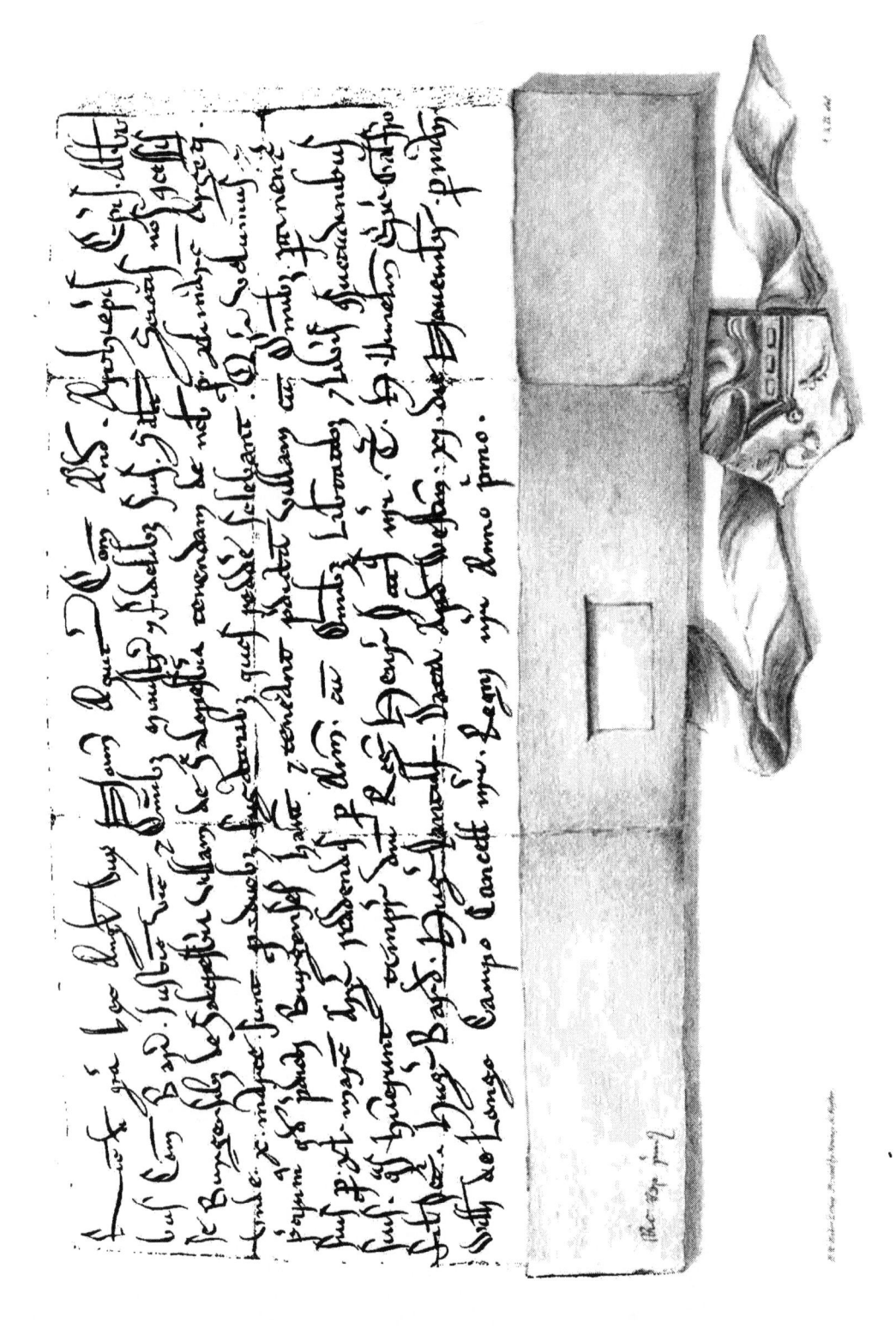

The earliest charter now extant, granted to the Burgesses of Shrewsbury. Anno 1 Rich. I.

London Pub.d July 1, 1825, by Harding, Mavor and Lepard.

Lightning Source UK Ltd.
Milton Keynes UK
UKHW02f0827260918
329483UK00008B/1071/P